War in Italy

1943–1945

War in Italy

1943–1945

A BRUTAL STORY

Richard Lamb

St. Martin's Press
New York

Library of Congress Cataloging-in-Publication Data

Lamb, Richard.
War in Italy, 1943–1945 : a brutal story / Richard Lamb.
        p.   cm.
"A Thomas Dunne book."
ISBN 0-312-11093-6
1. World War, 1939–1945—Campaigns—Italy.   2. Italy—History—
German occupation, 1943–1945.   I. Title.
D763.I8L35   1994
940.54′215—dc20   94-1116   CIP

First published in Great Britain by John Murray (Publishers) Ltd.

10 9 8 7 6 5 4 3 2

Contents

Illustrations

The author and publisher would like to thank the following for permission to reproduce photographs:
Topham, 1; Imperial War Museum, London, 5, 6, 12, 13, 14, 18, 19, 20, 21, 24, 25

Acknowledgements

I thank the staff of the Public Record Office, the Foreign Office Library, the Chatham House Library, the London Library, the Royal United Services Institute Library, the Imperial War Museum Library, the Library of the Italian Cultural Institute, the Wiltshire County Library and the Librarian of the United Oxford and Cambridge Club for their courtesy and help. I am most grateful to Biblioteca Civita, Trieste, the Istituto Regionale per la Storia di Liberazione del Friuli e Venezia Giulia, the Istituto delle Resistenze in Valle d'Aosta, and the officers and soldiers of the Commissione per lo Studio della Resistenza dei Militari Italiani all'Estero (alle dirette dipendenze del Ministro della Difesa), Via Sforza, Rome. I thank the British School in Rome for their hospitality and help.

I am greatly indebted to Denis Mack Smith for his generosity in lending many Italian books not available in this country, for his valuable help and advice and for reading the manuscript.

Transcripts of Crown copyright material from the Public Record Office, the Imperial War Museum and the captured Mussolini documents in the Foreign Office Library appear by kind permission of the Controller of Her Majesty's Stationery Office.

Many of the archives quoted in this book are hitherto unknown, and may cause accepted views to be revised.

When the British landed in Italy, I was one of the few Italian-speaking officers in the 8th Army, and I passed the whole campaign with the Royalist Italian Army on our side. Once hostilities ceased, I talked to many officers who had served with the Republican Army as well as with civilians employed by the Government of Salò. I felt considerable sympathy with them. The regular Republican officers were a typical cross-section of the officer corps of the pre-Armistice Italian army, similar to my friends in the Royalist Army, although there were exceptions. If I am dogmatic about opinion inside the Salò Republic, it is because I write from impressions gathered at first hand forty-seven years ago.

I thank all those who discussed the state of the Italian nation with me then, particularly the late General Alberto Scattini, the late General Achille de Biase, the late General Andrea Cucino, the late Colonel

Antonio Duran, Mario Cigersa, the late Carlo Cosenza, and the late Riccardo Posani.

I am most indebted to Mrs John McCaffery for her late husband's unpublished diary 'No Pipes or Drums' and for permission to quote from it; and also to the late General Achille de Biase for his privately published *35 Regg. Artiglieria G.C. Friuli*.

I give special thanks to Lord Jellicoe, for confirming that he actually did eat the letter from General 'Jumbo' Wilson to Admiral Campioni, Governor of Rhodes, on 10 September 1943 while he was sheltering under a rock after parachuting down on Rhodes during a battle between the Germans and the Italians. When I read this in the archives, I thought it was a joke. I have been unable to discover whether the SOE report that partisans crept up to German horse and mule lines and poured No. 9 shot down their ears to send them mad and to confuse the German vets is a joke. It is odd that such an unBritish way of waging war should be recorded without apology.

I thank John Murray and The Bodley Head for permission to quote from the works of Iris Origo and Primo Levi.

Grant McIntyre of John Murray has given me great encouragement, and I record my thanks to him; also to my wife, and for secretarial help to Joan Moore and John Mark.

I am grateful to the following for their time and generous help: Elena Aga-Rossi, Domenico Bernabei, Maria Burgos, Pier Arrigo Carnier, David Caesarini, the late John Colville, Gervase Cowell, David Dilks, Jim Davies, William Deakin, Monsignor Walter Drum, David Elwood, Gordon Etherington Smith, Ned Eyre, Dominic Flessati, Michael R. D. Foot, Ian Fraser, Lord Gladwyn, the Revd Robert Graham, SJ, Professor Giulio Guderzo, the late Field Marshal Harding, Fey von Hassell, Federico d'Henriques, Fior d'Henriques, Theo Hetherington, Kim Isolani, George Jellicoe, Keith Kilby, Ken Kirby, Brian MacDermot, Thomas Macpherson, the late John McCaffery, Junior, D'Arcy Mander, Martin Morland, Eric Moss, General Ilio Muraca, Professor Claudio Pavone, Detalmo Pirzio-Biroli, Professor Teodoro Sala, the late Max Salvadori, Professor Alberto Santoni, Maria Gabriella di Savoia, Enrico Serra, Christopher Seton Watson, Roger Sherfield, Jonathan Steinberg, General Alfredo Terrone, Professor Antonio Varsori, Ernest Wilcockson, Christopher Woods, and Allen Young.

This book is dedicated to the officers,
NCOs and men of the Royal Italian Army
with whom the author fought to liberate
Italy from the Nazis (1943–1945)

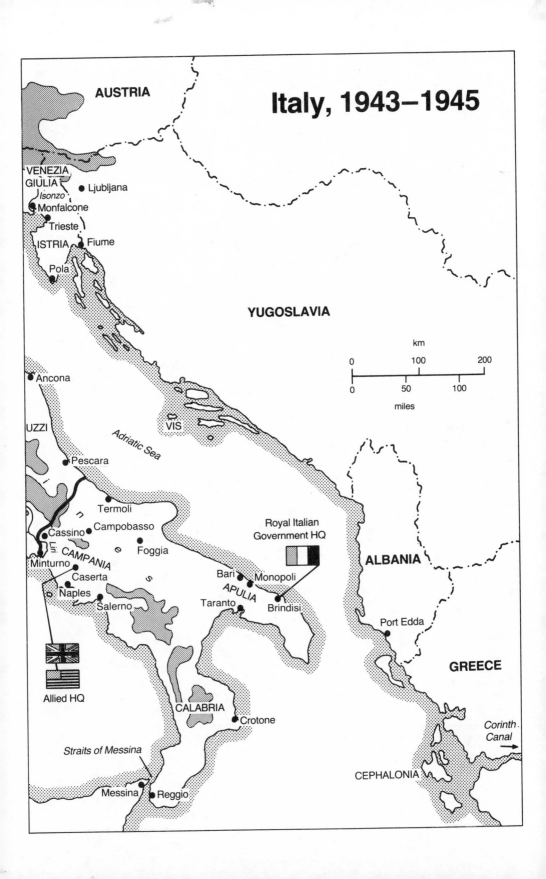

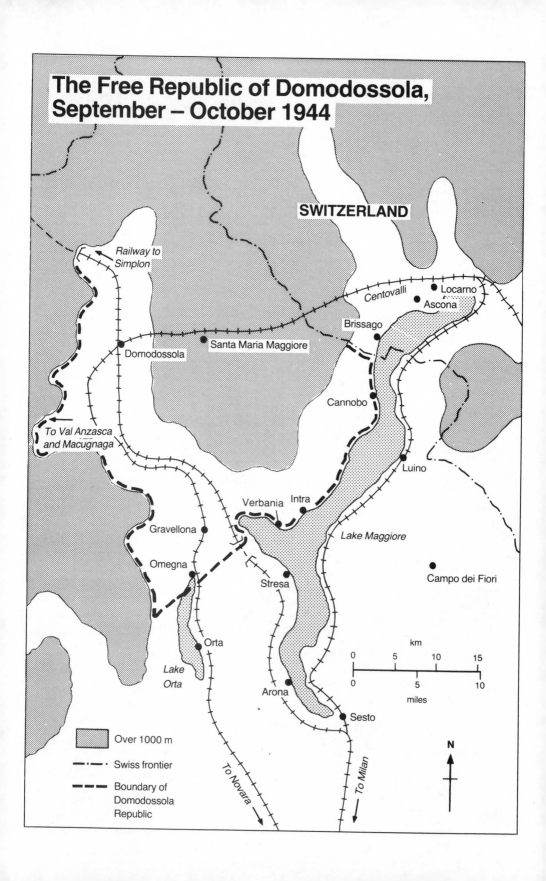

The Free Republic of Domodossola, September – October 1944

SWITZERLAND

Railway to Simplon

Centovalli

Locarno

Ascona

Brissago

Santa Maria Maggiore

Domodossola

Cannobo

To Val Anzasca and Macugnaga

Luino

Verbania Intra

Gravellona

Lake Maggiore

Omegna

Campo dei Fiori

Stresa

Orta

Lake Orta

Arona

Sesto

km

0   5   10   15

0   5   10

miles

To Novara

To Milan

N

Over 1000 m

Swiss frontier

Boundary of Domodossola Republic

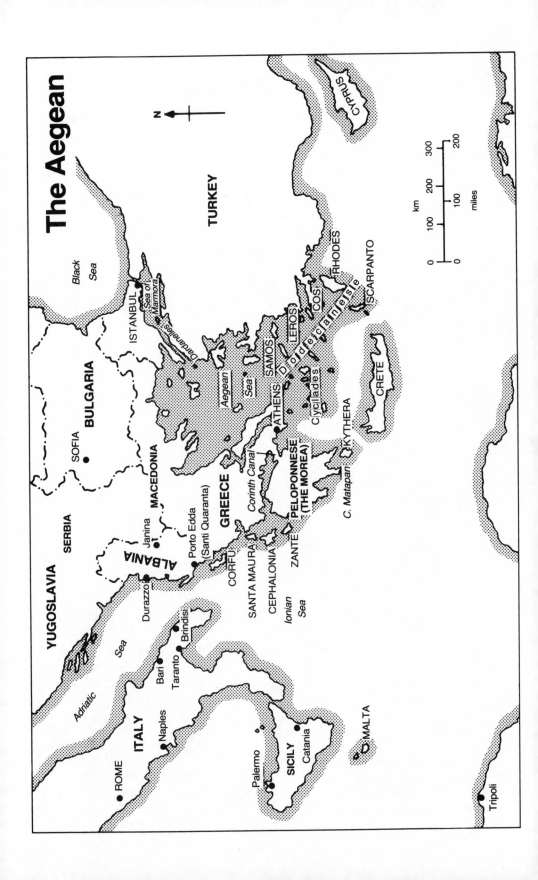

The Aegean

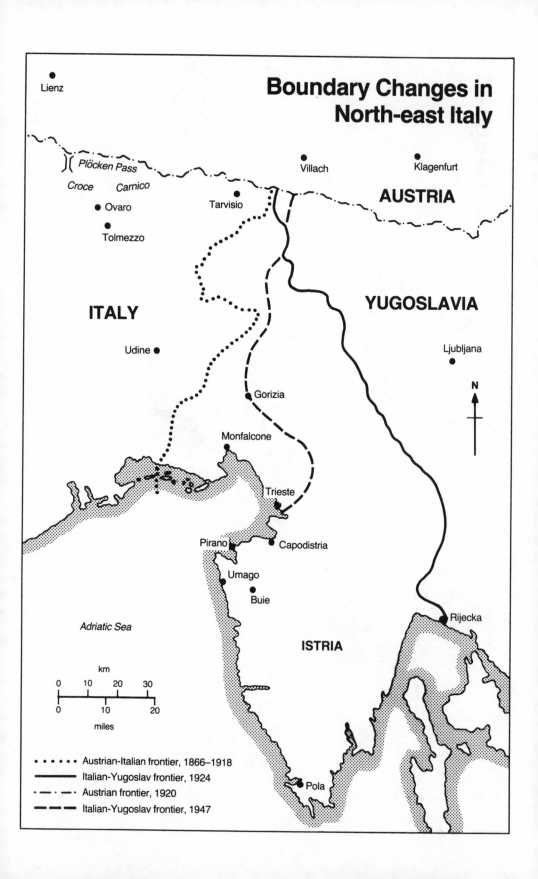

Boundary Changes in North-east Italy

Lienz

Plöcken Pass

Croce   Carnico

Ovaro

Tarvisio

Villach

Klagenfurt

AUSTRIA

Tolmezzo

ITALY

YUGOSLAVIA

Udine

Ljubljana

N

Gorizia

Monfalcone

Trieste

Pirano   Capodistria

Umago

Buie

Adriatic Sea

Rijecka

ISTRIA

km

0   10   20   30

0   10   20

miles

Pola

· · · · · Austrian-Italian frontier, 1866–1918

——— Italian-Yugoslav frontier, 1924

—·—·— Austrian frontier, 1920

— — — Italian-Yugoslav frontier, 1947

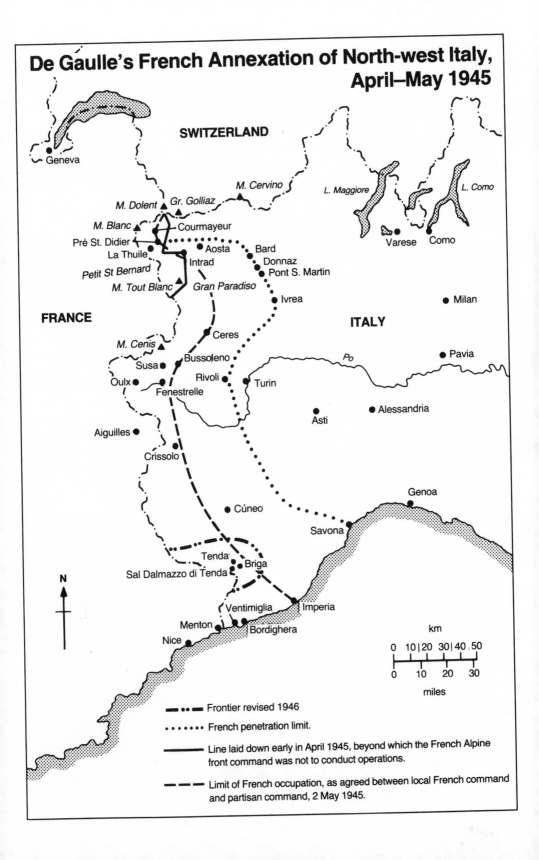

De Gaulle's French Annexation of North-west Italy, April–May 1945

SWITZERLAND

Geneva

M. Cervino

L. Maggiore

L. Como

M. Dolent ▲ *Gr. Golliaz* ▲

M. Blanc ▲ — Courmayeur

Varese

Como

Pré St. Didier ◄

La Thuile ● — Intrad — ● Aosta   Bard

Donnaz

Pont S. Martin

Petit St Bernard ●

M. Tout Blanc ▲   *Gran Paradiso*

Ivrea

Milan ●

FRANCE

ITALY

M. Cenis ▲

Susa ●

Ceres ◆

Bussoleno ●

Rivoli ●

Turin ●

Po

Pavia ●

Oulx ●

Fenestrelle ●

Alessandria ●

Asti ●

Aiguilles ●

Crissolo ●

Cúneo ●

Genoa ●

Savona ●

N
↑

Tenda ●   ● Briga

Sal Dalmazzo di Tenda ●

Ventimiglia ●   Imperia ●

Menton ●   ● Bordighera

Nice ●

km

0 10|20 30|40 |50

0   10   20   30

miles

–··– Frontier revised 1946

······ French penetration limit.

—— Line laid down early in April 1945, beyond which the French Alpine
front command was not to conduct operations.

– – Limit of French occupation, as agreed between local French command
and partisan command, 2 May 1945.

Introduction

HERE IS THE tragic story of modern Italy in her saddest hour. In 1940 Mussolini and the King plunged Italy into war with France and Britain, believing that a few days' fighting would earn her a victor's seat at the Conference table. What a contrast with Orlando's Government in 1918, when Italy went to Paris as a victorious power and showed moderation in pressing her demands against the losers!

After three disastrous years of war the Italians overthrew Mussolini, hoping for a separate Armistice with the Allies and freedom from the Germans. These hopes were illusory. All went wrong again. From September 1943 until the end of April 1945 Italy suffered the disaster of being occupied by two conquering armies at war with each other, and the peninsula became a battleground.

Unfortunately Anthony Eden, the British Foreign Secretary, nourished a hatred for Italy dating from 1935, when Mussolini humiliated him in Rome by rejecting out of hand British proposals for concessions to Italy at the expense of Abyssinia. Churchill in 1940 and 1941 was keen on 'soft' peace terms for an anti-Fascist government, to encourage resistance to Mussolini. When he and Roosevelt agreed at Casablanca in January 1943 on the 'unconditional surrender' formula for Germany and Japan, neither wanted to apply it to Italy. But Eden railroaded the War Cabinet into insisting on the inclusion of Italy, with a defiant message that Italy must be threatened: 'Knowledge of rough stuff coming should have desired effect on Italian morale.'

The demand for unconditional surrender sapped the morale of the anti-Fascists. When calls for peace negotiations came from them, Eden so misjudged their strength that on one occasion Churchill had to tell him, 'Do not miss the bus'; and when Mussolini was toppled on 25 July 1943, no plans had been made to land Allied troops in Italy before the Germans were strong enough to repel them.

During Badoglio's forty-five days of rule in Rome there were a series of lost opportunities. The most poignant was the rejection by General Carboni (commander of the strong mechanized forces defending Rome), with the vacillating Badoglio's approval, of Eisenhower's offer to land 82

1

US Airborne Division on the airfields around Rome. Convincing evidence that this operation ('Giant Two') would have been a success can be found in Italian and German sources, as well as American. If Rome had been taken in the first wave of the Allied onslaught on Italy, the German army would have had to withdraw to the north; and if Italy, at the moment the news of the Armistice hit the world, could have been seen fighting side by side with US troops to defend Rome and drive the Germans out of Italy, her prestige would have been high and her subsequent treatment by the Allies more generous. As it was, Badoglio and the King gave up the fight and fled ignominiously to Brindisi, so that the Italian army, without any form of leadership, disintegrated all over the homeland, and the units who stayed intact were bundled off as prisoners to Germany.

It is difficult to explain why the Italian army on the peninsula and abroad disintegrated on 9 September, while the navy and air force obeyed orders and escaped to Allied bases. An Italian Ministry of Defence team is currently investigating exactly what happened to the army overseas, and has uncovered considerable fresh evidence. Hitler ordered that all Italian troops fighting against the Germans were to be treated as *francs-tireurs* and shot as they surrendered, in order to minimize Italian military co-operation with the Allies; his generals obeyed these criminal orders. Generals Lanz and von Weichs bear the main responsibility for the horrifying massacres of surrendering Italian soldiers in Yugoslavia, Greece, Albania and the Aegean; they must be rated among the worst Nazi war criminals, but their Nuremberg trials have been overlooked by historians.

Mussolini was fully informed of the details of the massacres of the surrendering Italian soldiers. To his eternal shame he made no protest to Hitler. Mussolini too must have felt wholesale massacres were the best way to prevent Italian forces fighting with the Allies against Germany.

Churchill had set his heart on opening the route to the Dardanelles when Italy surrendered. He wanted not only to redeem his First World War mistakes, but also to avoid the inevitable blood bath of a cross-Channel invasion by linking up with the Russians to end the war earlier by conquering Germany from the East. A combination of the cowardice of Admiral Campioni in Rhodes, where the Italians greatly outnumbered the Germans, and the non-cooperation of the Americans, whose eyes and hopes were firmly fixed on landing in France, frustrated the British Prime Minister's design.

One wrings one's hands at the missed opportunity in Rhodes: General Wilson had sufficient troops in the Middle East to capture it, but with

Eisenhower opposed and Churchill in Quebec at the crucial moment, he did not act. Had Churchill been in London, he would have made sure that Wilson captured Rhodes despite the opposition of the Americans, and the route to the Dardanelles would have been open. The 1943 Aegean fighting is the least-known part of the military history of the Second World War, and the failure to take Rhodes a key feature of it.

Fifty years on, how harshly should historians judge Mussolini's conduct during the six hundred days of the Salò Republic? No words are too strong to condemn Mussolini for declaring war on France and Britain in 1940 (though it was with the King's approval), or for sending the Italian Air Force to bomb London, or for the despatch of Italian armies to fight in Russia, where they suffered a worse fate than their compatriots in Napoleon's 1812 campaign. His order in 1944 that all partisans captured carrying arms were to be shot out of hand was also callous and inexcusable.

By the earlier part of 1943 Mussolini was realistic enough to understand that the Axis had irrevocably lost the war; to save Italy (and Europe) from further unnecessary bloodshed, he made strenuous but little-known efforts, in combination with Hungary, for a separate peace. Sir William Deakin has made this clear in his book *The Brutal Friendship*. In the summer of 1943 the Duce began overtures to the British. He would have done better to try the Americans. He knew he had failed the Italian nation and searched desperately to find a way out for Italy, in sharp contrast to Hitler, who was willing to allow Germany to be destroyed if he lost. As he grew older, Mussolini, a cold-blooded thug in his early days of power, became more of a mountebank than a tyrant. Surprisingly, in spite of his earlier crimes he had earned the warm approval of British statesmen like Austen Chamberlain and Winston Churchill. Apart from the bloody and ill-famed Corfu incident in 1923, until the Ethiopian war in 1935 Mussolini had attempted to align his foreign policy with Britain's.

When he was rescued from captivity by the Germans in September 1943, Mussolini did not want to rule again, or to revive Fascism. He wanted to retire into private life. Hitler held out to him the bait that because of their long 'friendship' his presence at the head of a State in Northern Italy would result in better treatment for Italy; the Duce knew that the German generals, because Italy had betrayed Germany, wanted to treat her like Poland and the occupied countries.

Mussolini yielded to Hitler's insistence and agreed to head a new Fascist Government with headquarters at Salò on Lake Garda. As soon as he arrived at Salò he found that Hitler on 10 September had ruled that the Pre-Alps (Voralpenland) and the Adriatic coast (Adriatic Küstenland) had been removed from Italy. Two Gauleiters, Hofer and Rainer, had been given full powers to administer *carte blanche* these regions without reference to Mussolini. The annexed area contained eight 'provinces' – Friuli, Gorizia, Trieste, Quarnero, Ljubljana, Bolzano, Trento and Belluno. Some of the area had been Italian since 1866, part since 1920 and part since the fall of Yugoslavia in 1941. The whole had originally been part of the Habsburg Empire. If Mussolini had known this in advance, he might well have refused to form a Government. His despair was complete when in 1944 Hitler sent the White Russians, in the shape of Cossacks and Caucasians, into the Friuli with the ostensible aim of making this beautiful part of Italy their new homeland.

This book documents the treatment of Italy by the Nazis as the German generals sought revenge for Italian betrayal. This aspect of the war is little known. Mussolini's Fascist Government at Salò was a poor affair, but three of his ministers – Pisenti, Mellini and Mazzolini – were honourable. They are witnesses to the Duce's state of mind as he found himself unable to protect his fellow-countrymen from Nazi vengeance. His words, 'I have drained the poisoned chalice to the dregs', are evidence of his final despair.

Even Cadorna and Lombardi, the dedicated anti-Fascist leaders, have recorded that at their meeting with the Duce at Cardinal Schuster's palace in Milan, a few hours before Mussolini's death, they felt some sympathy for the fallen dictator.

Wading through all the written records of the Salò Republic has given the author a vivid picture of Mussolini's frenzied but abortive efforts to defend his people from Nazi tyranny, arousing some sympathy for Mussolini as he realized his inability to resist the hated Germans, and for his guilt over his terrible responsibility for plunging his fellow-countrymen into war. Mussolini made complaint after complaint to Hitler but in the end ceased, because he knew they would be ignored.

At the Verona trials in December 1944 Mussolini insisted that his son-in-law Ciano and other former Fascist colleagues should be sentenced to death. He may have been forced into this by Hitler, but these mock trials and the execution of two Italian Admirals in charge of land forces who had fought feebly against the Germans after the Armistice are a blot on Mussolini's final days.

The Nazi persecution of Italian Jews was shocking; fortunately, neither Mussolini nor his Salò Ministers were anti-Semitic, with the exception of the poisonous Preziosi. Many Fascist officials, and the Italian people generally, protected the Jews from what would otherwise have been wholesale slaughter. Indeed, Mussolini, his Minister for Home Affairs, Buffarini Guidi, and many of the Fascist administration tried to halt the deportations. However, no one should underestimate the grave harm done to Italian Jews by the anti-Semitic laws of 1938 and 1943.

In the north, which is the principal scenario of this book, the Germans imposed a regime of terror; arbitrary arrests were common, with widespread executions of innocent people. However, living conditions were tolerable: there was enough food and inflation was kept down, while work was available in the industrial zones.

In the southern part occupied by the Allies there was starvation, because the British and Americans could not spare enough shipping to feed the Italian population adequately, and production of homegrown food was limited. Inflation, aggravated by the Allies having fixed the value of the lira at too low a level, inflicted grave hardship. However, the population was free and political views could be expressed, although much irritation was caused by restrictions on political activity and travel.

In a poignant chapter in his book *Il Regno del Sud* (Kingdom of the South) Agostino degli Espinosa has described how in the early days of the occupation Americans and British requisitioned homes and frequently looted household goods, while the cafés and restaurants in Bari which had been requisitioned for the sole use of the Allied troops were surrounded by starving children waiting to rush in to take any leftovers from the plates. The bulk of the population only escaped starvation by buying Allied food rations on the black market. In Naples it was estimated that one-third of the food landed from ships was stolen and put on the black market. In addition, there was much drunkenness among the Allied troops, and prostitution rose to enormous proportions as mothers and sisters found it was the only way they could procure Allied rations to feed their starving families. Gradually the sufferings of the first months diminished; banks and shops functioned; schools were reopened, as were the Universities of Naples and Bari.

The problem of refugees in the south cut off from their homes in German-occupied Italy was almost insoluble. They had to live without work, or on wages at a starvation level. Indeed, many former partisans liberated by the Allies crossed back over the front line to continue the fight with full stomachs. Not only was food cheap in the north, but in the towns subsidized restaurants were opened to provide nourishing meals cheaply. These were conspicuously lacking in the south. Not unnaturally, the Americans and British became unpopular; one telling comment was that when towns and villages were first liberated the Allies were hailed with enthusiasm, but their popularity soon evaporated. 'The nearer you were to the front, the more popular were the Allies.'

The most important figure in the story of German-occupied Italy is Kesselring. As commander of the German army in Italy he had supreme authority. He acted like a brute. After the war, Field Marshal Alexander pleaded with Churchill to intervene to save Kesselring from the death penalty, on the grounds that he had been an 'honourable opponent'. Alexander knew nothing about Kesselring's authorization of the deportation of Italian Jews, the Ardeatine cave massacre, or the many atrocities against Italian civilians in revenge for partisan activities.

The transcripts of the trials of Kesselring and the other German generals, little used by historians, add up to an appalling indictment. Evidence given at the trial of SS General Simon, who was responsible for the worst atrocities against civilians in the partisan areas, is revolting. The trials of the German officers accused of war crimes are the best sources from which to authenticate the many atrocities which came to light after the war. On several occasions SS Colonel Kappler gave evidence in cold, matter-of-fact language, showing how he organized the pogrom of Roman Jews and the Ardeatine cave massacre of Roman civilians, calmly encouraging his men to kill hundreds in cold blood.

Pope Pius XII's role was minor, although it has attracted much controversy. His protection of Roman Jews (by ordering all convents and monasteries in Vatican territory to open their doors to them) was admirable. More contentious is his failure to protest to Hitler over the Jewish pogrom in Rome in November 1943, and the Ardeatine cave massacre of March 1944. Anxious to preserve a good relationship with the German authorities while Rome was occupied, he was persuaded by the Nazi Ambassador von Weizsäcker to remain silent. On the other hand, the way in which he used the Papal Nuncio in Germany, Orsenigo, to succour the 600,000 Italian soldiers kept in shocking conditions in labour camps in Germany cannot be too highly praised; the Vatican did much more than Mussolini's Ambassador in Berlin, Anfuso, to help these suffering Italians. However, although he hoped to play a major role, Pius XII could do nothing to help over peace negotiations.

In late 1943 the King and Badoglio were anxious to put an Italian army into the line to fight the Germans, mainly because the terms of the proposed Armistice specified that post-war treatment of Italy would depend on how much armed help she gave in her own liberation. Too much attention has been focused on the exploits of the partisans, and too little on the solid achievements of the Royalist army, who played an increasingly important part in the campaign as the Allies ran short of troops. Gallantly the officers in Badoglio's army overcame the shame of their defeat and co-operated loyally with the Allies, suffering heavy casualities in almost continuous hard fighting from December 1943 until the end. Rightly, their performance in battle earned the confidence of the Allied generals.

It is ironic that the Allies should have enrolled one section of the Italian army, while the Germans – admittedly with less success – put another section into the field. Graziani alleged that Italian officers, with their strong sense of honour, had a feeling of shame at having betrayed their German allies and felt they must continue to fight with them; this cannot be rejected altogether, but the author doubts whether it was an important factor. A mildly comic note was that German instructors and 'minders' who were training the Fascist army encountered exactly the same problems as their British counterparts with the Royal army. The complaints about German instructors and 'minders' made to Mussolini are identical with those sent to the Rome Government from divisions being trained by the Allies.

It is hardly known that the Fascist Republican army, including Borghese with his Decima Mas marines, who showed strong loyalty to Borghese personally and to Fascism, considered betraying the Germans: they made overtures to the Allies with a view to changing sides when Tito's Communist army advanced into Istria: at that time the Republican army was strong in north-east Italy. The Allies rejected these advances out of hand and may have missed an opportunity.

No one should classify all those Italians who after September 8 joined the Fascist armed forces or co-operated with the Germans as 'bad' Italians, or all anti-Fascists as 'good'. After 21 years of Fascism the younger adult generation knew no other type of government, and had been indoctrinated with hatred of the Allies and loyalty towards Germany. However, as the months passed brutalities and massacres by the Germans alienated almost all Italians, and through their own fault the Germans were in the end waging war amid an entirely hostile population.

The traditional friendship between Italy and Britain, dating back to the Risorgimento, had been badly dented by the British reaction to Mussolini's invasion of Abyssinia in 1935, yet the wonderful reception given to escaping British prisoners-of-war by the Italian people is evidence that a love of Britain was still strong in the hearts of the Italian people. A great number of British, Dominion and American POWs were given hospitality in Italian homes without payment, while their hosts risked their lives by harbouring them; our debt has not been adequately acknowledged – certainly not in terms of financial reimbursement.

Controversy surrounds the role of the partisans in German-occupied Italy. The SOE and OSS missions found ready hospitality, but unlike the POWs they were able to pay lavishly for everything. The partisans' chief value lay in the high number of enemy troops whom they tied up in counter-guerrilla activities. The Allies wanted the partisans to concentrate on sabotage and prepare to attack the Germans as they retired.

Unfortunately, both Alexander and Badoglio gave Kesselring some excuse for his reprisals by broadcasting that the partisans should shoot the Germans in the back.

The partisan movement was marred by continual squabbles between the Communists (Garibaldi) and the non-Communists (Green Flames), leading to internecine fighting and murders. In addition, irresponsible partisan leaders insisted on attacking German posts instead of confining themselves to sabotage and this led to savage reprisals against ordinary residents, which made the partisans unpopular with the civilian population. Glaring examples were two partisan attacks in Carnia in north-east Italy, on the last day of the war, which were strongly opposed by the civilian population. These were followed by brutal massacres of civilians – one by the Germans, the other by the Russian Cossack army fighting on the Nazi side.

Clashes between the Garibaldi and other partisans were especially frequent on the Yugoslav frontier after the Garibaldi fell under Tito's influence and proclaimed that part of Italy must become Yugoslav after the war. The Foreign Office became alarmed that the Committee of Liberation organizing the Resistance in Milan might become an alternative to the Rome Government; Eden minuted, 'We do not want a de Gaulle situation in Italy.' This violent Communist propaganda by the Garibaldi made Britain lukewarn towards the partisans, and during the last months of the war, although maximum supplies of food and clothing were dropped, arms supplies by SOE were limited. However, the OSS, the US equivalent of SOE, sent all the arms they could, indiscriminately to the Garibaldi and the others.

Both the British and the Americans feared that when the Germans withdrew civil war would break out in the north of Italy, with the Communists trying to seize power. Fortunately, thanks to the presence of the Communist leader, Togliatti, in the Rome Government, and to responsible Communist leaders on the CLN Committees in the occupied territory, this did not occur, although excesses and unlawful killings of many thousands did take place before Allied Military Government could operate.

Moves for a separate peace for the German army in Italy were made by Kesselring and the Nazi leaders as early as October 1944, but their actual surrender did not occur until after Hitler's death on 1 May 1945, and only five days before the general surrender of the whole German army. Long-drawn-out negotiations were handled in Berne by Allen Dulles, the US representative, and with hindsight it seems that an opportunity to end the war in Italy earlier may have been lost. However, Hitler's insistence that the Gothic Line should be held throughout the winter of 1944–5 and Alexander's proclamation to the Italian partisans to stand down cooled the Germans' ardour for surrender: it was clear there would be no Allied victory before the spring of 1945. SS General Wolff was the principal protagonist on the German side. He had played a prominent role in the Ardeatine massacre in Rome in 1944 and realized in the autumn of that year that Hitler had irretrievably lost the war. He was acutely conscious that he might be tried as a war criminal, and was anxious to work his passage with the Allies. He was a glib illusionist with his head in the skies.

Unfortunately Kesselring, who while he was in Italy toyed with the idea of a separate Armistice, was removed by Hitler to Germany in March 1945 to command not only the armies in Italy, but also the Western Front. Once within Hitler's reach Kesselring wavered, and his last-minute refusal to endorse the Armistice negotiated in Caserta by General Vietinghoff's emissaries is a final instance of his infamous conduct.

Mussolini's eleventh-hour efforts through Vatican channels to reach agreement with the Allies were unknown to the Germans, just as Wolff's efforts to surrender were hidden from Mussolini. Mussolini's last initiative was childish, and treated as such by the Vatican.

Italy's frontier problems came to a head when hostilities ceased on 2 May 1945. De Gaulle occupied the Valle d'Aosta and the north-west seaboard of Italy with French troops, in an undignified effort to claim this territory for France. He clung to his purpose and only withdrew when President Truman threatened to stop the issue of all rations and supplies to the entire French army.

Churchill and Roosevelt agreed that there should be no revision of Italy's north-east frontier with Yugoslavia until the post-war Peace Conference. Tito, with the support of Stalin, ignored this and occupied Pola, Fiume, Istria, Trieste and much of the Friuli, declaring it to be Yugoslav territory by right of conquest. The Yugoslavs behaved more brutally even than the Nazis, confiscating much property, deporting and executing countless harmless Italians. Citizens of Trieste still recall with horror the forty days of Tito's occupation.

Churchill and Truman ordered the Allied generals to prevent Yugoslav brutality, but Alexander, Harding and Freyberg were supine, despite prodding from Churchill. The official historian C. R. Harris has mangled the horrible tale of the Yugoslav occupation of north-east Italy, ignoring irrefutable evidence of their inhumanity.

Despite the whole-hearted collaboration of the Royal armed forces in the War of Liberation, Italy was treated as an enemy power in the negotiations for the post-war Peace Treaty. So harsh were the terms that the Italian Government baulked at signing. The most emotive issue was a limitation on the size of the fleet, which had rendered sterling service to the Allied cause; a substantial number of ships was to be surrendered to France, the USSR, Greece and Yugoslavia. The Italian Ambassador in London warned that the Italian Navy's 'self-respect and dignity' made acceptance impossible because it involved submission to nations which had played no part in the defeat of Italy, and that they would rather scuttle than hand over the ships. All Italian overseas possessions were taken away, but as a sop to Italian national pride she was awarded a ten-year Trusteeship of Somalia. Fortunately Trieste was returned to Italy in 1954 when the proposal to establish a Free Territory of Trieste under the United Nations, on the Danzig model, came to nothing. The new frontier which awarded a substantial area of pre-war Italy to Yugoslavia had some ethnic justification, but Italian communities on the Yugoslav side of the frontier suffered a cruel fate.

The Preamble to the Peace Treaty was particularly wounding to the Italians because it recorded Italy's aggression in 1940 and forced Italy to state that she would prevent the return of Fascism. So strong was feeling in Italy against the Treaty that many well-known figures who had played an important part in the War of Liberation refused to record their experiences in co-operating with the Allies, while memoir after memoir was published recording the exploits of the partisans.

Fortunately the Treaty was short-lived. In December 1951, less than four years later, ten of the twenty-one signatories recognized that the Preamble 'had been replaced by the spirit of the UN Charter', and that the clauses with respect to Fascism were 'superfluous'. The 'moral stigma' of the Treaty was removed, and the military clauses lapsed.

CHAPTER 1

Italy Changes Sides

WHEN THE ITALIAN Field Marshal Messe and the German General von Arnim surrendered their armies to the Allies at Tunis on 7 May 1943, most Italians felt they had lost the war. Although Italian troops had fought hard in Tunisia the nation was sick of war, and the Italian army put up little resistance when the Allies landed in Sicily on 10 July, although four German divisions on the island held up the Anglo-American advance. At the key naval base of Augusta the Admiral blew up the coastal defence batteries without a shot being fired, abandoned his post, and dispersed his men.

The one desire of the Italian nation was to get out of the war as soon as possible; Mussolini and Fascism were now hated, despite their popularity at the time of the Abyssinian War in 1935 and 1936 and, to a lesser degree, when Italy declared war on France and Britain in 1940. The Duce was held to have betrayed Italy, because he bore almost sole responsibility for taking Italy into the war.

All opposition parties had been suppressed by the Fascists in their 21 years of rule, but politicians of the former era still operated clandestinely and were plotting, ineffectually, to overthrow Mussolini. Italy was a police state; only the King was capable of ousting him. King Victor Emmanuel III was an intelligent but reticent man; twenty years of collusion with Fascism had dented the royal prestige, but under the Constitution of 1848 very considerable powers remained with the crown. After the Tunis defeat, the King was determined to topple Mussolini and make peace with the Allies. He put his faith in Field Marshal Badoglio and plotted with Ivan Bonomi, a prime minister in pre-Fascist days, to replace Mussolini with a new government nominated by the crown. Grandi, a leading Fascist and former Foreign Minister and Italian Ambassador in London, strengthened the King's resolve by agreeing to move a motion at the meeting of the Fascist Grand Council in July asking the Duce to hand back some of his powers to the King. This, Victor Emmanuel believed, would give him the justification he needed to dismiss Mussolini. Grandi's motion was passed by nineteen votes to seven but Mussolini was unconcerned, believing himself impregnable. The next day, 25 July,

Victor Emmanuel with uncharacteristic firmness and decision ordered the arrest of Mussolini and made Badoglio head of a new non-Fascist Government.

Britain and America were taken completely by surprise. Soundings had been made by Badoglio and his associates in Berne through the British Secret Service, and Badoglio had suggested that he should send out a well known anti-Fascist, General Pesenti, to try to raise an anti-Fascist army from Italian POWs. The British Foreign Secretary, Anthony Eden, cold-shouldered both these overtures and five others from monarchists and other anti-Fascists, so that no effort was made to concert Allied military plans with the likely overthrow of Mussolini. The Italian emissaries were told that nothing but unconditional surrender would be accepted from an alternative non-Fascist Italian Government wanting a separate peace. The 'unconditional surrender' formula had been determined upon at the Anglo-American Conference at Casablanca in January 1943. In 1940 and 1941 Churchill (at first with Halifax as Foreign Secretary) had been willing to offer 'soft' peace terms to a non-Fascist alternative Italian Government, with Cyrenaica remaining an Italian colony; he even searched for an Italian de Gaulle to recruit a non-Fascist army and administer the freed Italian colonies. Churchill did not want the 1943 formula applied to Italy, but Eden insisted. Thus, in 1943, with Italy down and out, Britain took the hardest possible line. 'Absolute silence' was the Foreign Office response in the summer of 1943 to dissident Italians, even though the date of the planned invasion of Sicily was approaching fast.[1]

As a result of the Allied failure to discuss plans for a coup with the anti-Fascists, the opportunity for an unopposed Allied landing in Italy was thrown away. On 25 July the Germans had only one incompletely equipped division in central Italy (plus some elements of paratroopers) and two divisions in southern Italy. Four German divisions were engaged in the fighting in Sicily; if Allied and Italian naval and land forces had co-operated, the German army in Sicily would have been trapped and unable to cross the Straits of Messina.

Apart from the forces engaged in Sicily, the Allies had six complete divisions in North Africa and Egypt and several independent brigades available, including the US 82 Airborne Division. They were short of landing craft, but these would not be essential for an unopposed landing and there were plenty of merchant ships. Harry C. Butcher, Eisenhower's ADC, even noted in his diary at this period that they were being offered 'more merchant ships than they could use'.[2]

Hitler was as surprised as the Allies. 'Badoglio has taken over – the blackest of our enemies,' he declared, and was desperately worried that Allied forces in collusion with Badoglio would arrive in Italy by air and sea, unopposed. This the Allies could have done.

Hitler's first instinct was to order the single German division in central Italy to occupy Rome (two hours away) and arrest the new Government. He said: 'The Fascist party is only stunned at present. We must act at once or the Anglo-Saxons will steal a march on us by occupying the airfields.' He was counting on help from the Fascists, which would not have been forthcoming, and on the availability of Mussolini, who was in prison on the island of Ponza. Admiral Dönitz, head of the German navy, dissuaded Hitler; 'The Rome operation', he said, —

> would certainly be opposed by the Italian armed forces and by the majority of the population. This would lead to a complete disruption of communications ... without the co-operation of the Italians the evacuation of our troops from the islands [Sicily, Corsica, Sardinia] is entirely out of the question.

In his book *The Brutal Friendship* Sir William Deakin emphasizes that the Dönitz minute is proof that if Hitler had attempted the Rome operation, his troops in Sicily would almost certainly have been lost.[3] Other historians assume Hitler could have occupied Rome if he had wanted to do so.

Badoglio issued a statement that 'the war [in alliance with Germany] would continue' under his Government. In the House of Commons Churchill said:

> The only consequence of the Italian Government staying under the German yoke will be that in the next few months Italy will be seared and scarred and blackened from one end to the other ... we should let the Italians, to use a homely phrase, 'stew in their own juice' for a bit and hot up the fire to the utmost.

Churchill's and Badoglio's statements decided Hitler not to make an immediate strike against Rome, but instead to send as many German divisions as possible into northern and central Italy, believing this would both protect his route to Sicily and help to prevent Italy changing sides. Both the Allies and the Germans were in doubt about Badoglio's intentions; it seemed possible that Italy would continue the war as a German ally. Accordingly, the Allies continued to bomb Italian cities, although there was considerable controversy in British and American circles about the wisdom of this.

Unfortunately, in choosing Badoglio to head his Government Victor Emmanuel had put his trust in a man of straw. At 72, Badoglio was past his best. He had no previous experience of politics, and although he was pro-monarchy and anti-German, he lacked resolution and was disinclined to take firm action.

Badoglio had led the Italian army to victory in Abyssinia in 1936 but had been sacked by Mussolini in 1940 when the Italian campaign against Greece became a fiasco. Since 1940 he had deteriorated fast, drinking a pint of champagne every day and passing his time either sleeping or playing bridge. He was devastated by the death of his wife and of one of his sons.

The King had hoped to find in Badoglio a man of action who would give strong leadership in the nation's crisis. He could not have been more wrong. As Head of Government Badoglio was supine, expecting his Ministers to take the initiative. He himself did nothing. For 21 years Mussolini, as Dictator, had decided everything himself: ministers, generals and civil servants expected a similar lead from Badoglio. None came. His forty-five days of rule in Rome were wasted. However, a demand by the Germans to the Italian War Office that British POWs captured by the Germans and now in camps in Italy should be handed over and sent to Germany was peremptorily refused by the Italian Foreign Minister.[4]

German divisions immediately poured over the Brenner Pass, without authorization from the Italian General Staff. Many German soldiers had 'Viva il Duce' written on their helmets, and German military currency was issued as if Italy was an occupied country. By 30 August there were seven fully-equipped German divisions in Italy, and all chance that she might escape from the war without fighting the German army had disappeared. For this Badoglio's inertia was responsible.

Field Marshal Kesselring, Commander-in-Chief of the German army in Italy, spoke to Badoglio immediately after the dismissal of Mussolini, and said he wanted to discuss what extra German troops would be stationed on Italian soil. Although it was vital that no more should come, Badoglio replied that this was nothing to do with him, and concerned only the War Office – a fatal dereliction of responsibility. Kesselring took this as *carte blanche* to send as many troops as possible across the Brenner and to occupy the blockhouses guarding the Pass. General Ambrosio, the Italian C.-in-C., complained to Kesselring about this on 31 July but Kesselring ignored the Italian's objections and Ambrosio did not try to get Badoglio to intervene. It was imperative for Italy's future that the Brenner Pass should have been closed to German troops the day Mussolini was overthrown, but Badoglio never even considered such action.

The King expected that, immediately on assuming office, Badoglio would begin negotiations with the Allies for Italy's peaceful exit from the war. Badoglio, who was continually in a panic that the Germans might arrest and execute him, acted slowly.

Fortunately Raffaele Guariglia, the new Foreign Secretary and a professional diplomat, was more energetic. After the King had expressed strong disapproval to Badoglio of his failure to make contact with the Allies, Italian missions were sent to Tangiers on 3 August and to Lisbon on 18 August to sound out the Allies and inform them that the Italians were ready to change sides; also that they feared the Germans would occupy Rome at any moment; they requested an Allied landing in southern France to take the pressure off Italy. When these messages arrived in London, Churchill was at sea *en route* for Quebec; Roosevelt was on holiday; and Eden was in the country. In Churchill's absence Eden persuaded the Cabinet to tell the Italians there could be no negotiation: only unconditional surrender would be accepted. The Allies seemed no readier than the Italians to prevent Hitler's armies occupying Italy.

To speed up negotiations, the Foreign Office sent an able young bilingual radio operator, Lieutenant Mallaby, to be a link by which the Badoglio Government could communicate with Eisenhower, the Allied Commander-in-Chief in the Mediterranean, and negotiate an Armistice. There was consternation when the Foreign Office learnt that he had landed by parachute in the waters of Lake Como and been arrested on 14 August. The Foreign Office sent a coded signal on 25 August to D'Arcy Osborne, British Minister to the Vatican, asking him to find out through the Vatican what had happened to Mallaby (who was now required for official negotiations), and if necessary to offer an important Italian POW in exchange. Osborne approached Cardinal Maglione, the Vatican Secretary of State; Maglione immediately got in touch with the Italian Foreign Office, who informed him that Mallaby was 'all right' and was being brought to Rome urgently. This shows how co-operative the Vatican were, and how anxious at least the Italian Foreign Minister, Guariglia, was to speed up the negotiations for an Armistice. When Mallaby arrived in Rome he used his codes and W/T link to connect the Italian Government with Eisenhower's Headquarters in Sicily to negotiate the terms of the Armistice.[5]

The Italian overture in Tangiers on 3 August had prompted Mallaby's despatch, and he was one of the very few who were briefed about an Italian approach to the Allies: the Foreign Office were horrified lest he should fall into German hands and let the cat out of the bag.

The King and Guariglia despaired of Badoglio's inertia. On Guariglia's initiative, General Castellano and a Foreign Office official, Montanari, a nephew of Badoglio's who spoke perfect English, were sent to Lisbon. On 18 August, in great secrecy, Castellano conferred with Eisenhower's Chief-of-Staff, General Bedell Smith, in the flat of the British Ambassador to Portugal. Bedell Smith knew it was urgent for the Allies to come to terms, because Eisenhower had fixed 9 September for the invasion of southern Italy with a landing at Salerno.

Castellano disclosed that he had no authority to negotiate an Armistice; he had come only to find out what help the Allies could give to the Badoglio Government in turning the Germans out of Italy. However, Castellano was able to give valuable information about German troop dispositions in Italy, and agreed to go back to Rome to find out whether the Badoglio Government would agree to unconditional surrender, and what help they could give when the Allies landed in Italy. Eisenhower was desperate to sign an Armistice so that Italian forces should not oppose the Salerno landings.

After discussions in Rome in which Badoglio displayed little interest, Guariglia authorized Castellano, after more valuable time had been lost, to fly to Cassibile in Sicily and inform Eisenhower that the Italian Government would accept 'unconditional surrender' provided the Armistice was announced after a landing 'in sufficient strength'.[6]

A short surrender document was signed in Sicily on 3 September by Castellano, who had been given full powers to agree terms. But Eisenhower was bluffing: his landing at Salerno was to consist of only five divisions, whereas the Italians had (unrealistically) asked for fifteen. The Americans, of course, could not possibly reveal the secret of the strength of the invasion force to a former enemy at this stage. However, Eisenhower generously promised that he would send the US 82 Airborne Division to land on airfields near Rome, and that after landing it would concert operations in accordance with the plan of the Italian army. The precise nuance of the phrasing was lost on Castellano, who understood no English; he thought it meant that 82 Division would operate under Italian command, and in his book *Come Fermai* claimed, incorrectly, that he had obtained an agreement for the American Division to be placed 'at the orders of General Carboni' commanding the Corps defending Rome.[7]

The American archives record the relationship:

> The airborne troops upon arrival will co-operate with the Italians in defence of Rome and COMPLY with the recommendations of the Italian High Command without relinquishing their liberty of action or undertaking or making any disposition considered unsound.

This undertaking is evidence of the confidence which Castellano had inspired. The landing was known as 'Giant Two'.

The Allies had fixed the Armistice date as 8 September, but it was kept secret from the Italians. It was agreed with Castellano that the airborne landings on Rome were to follow within a few hours of the announcement of the Armistice, with sea-borne landings at the mouth of the Tiber twenty-four hours later.

On 7 September General Maxwell Taylor, second-in-command of 82

Airborne Division, and Colonel Gardiner arrived in Rome to co-ordinate plans with the Italians for the air landings. To their horror they found no preparations had been made by the Italian General Staff, although Castellano had sent a detailed battle plan specifying that the Italians were to place horizontal searchlight beams on the airfields facing west, and amber lights around the airfield perimeters, to guide in the American aircraft. In addition the Italians were to provide 350 lorries, much equipment, and soldiers to dig trenches.

The plan had been read by Badoglio, but he had not ordered any action to be taken; so rotten was the Italian War Office after years of Mussolini's dictatorial rule that the plan had not been translated into Italian and circulated to the commanders who would have to take part in the battle. No orders at all to prepare for the landing had been issued. This must have been due as much to lack of will as to inefficiency. The last thing Badoglio, his ministers and generals wanted was to fight the Germans. Until the final moment of disaster they were mesmerized by the absurd hope that the Allies would rescue them from the German menace by landing in immense strength.

General Taylor felt that, as no preparations were being made, the 82 Airborne operation was too hazardous. He and Colonel Gardiner demanded to see Badoglio, who stated (falsely and without foundation) that the agreed date for the Armistice was 12 September, and therefore the air landings must be postponed. Mallaby relayed an urgent message from Taylor, and a furious Eisenhower called off the airborne landings but would not alter the date of the Armistice. Thus the Italians lost a heaven-sent opportunity to emerge from the war fighting side by side with US troops against the Germans.

There are several fanciful accounts of Taylor's and Gardiner's experiences in Rome on 7 September. Fortunately, their signed official report lies in the USAAF Headquarters archives.[8]

They disembarked at Gaeta at 7.50 p.m. from an Italian corvette which had rendezvoused with a British torpedo boat at the island of Ustica. They were taken by car up the Appian Way, where they noticed German troops were few and the defences unimpressive. In the outskirts of the capital they transferred to a closed Red Cross ambulance to go to the Palazzo Caprera opposite the War Office. There they were met by War Office officials, but found no conferences arranged for that evening. The Americans insisted on interviews, and General Carboni eventually appeared at 9.30 p.m. According to Taylor and Gardiner's written report, Carboni told them:

> Since the fall of Mussolini the Germans had been bringing in men and supplies through the Brenner Pass and also through Resia and Tarvisio with the result that their forces near Rome had greatly increased.

There were now 12,000 Germans principally parachutists in the valley of the Tiber who have heavy equipment including 100 pieces of artillery principally 88 mm. The Panzer Grenadier Division had been raised to an effective strength of 24,000 men with 50 light and 150 heavy tanks.

In the meantime the Germans had ceased to supply the Italians with gas [petrol] and ammunition so that their divisions were virtually immobilized and had only enough ammunition for a few hours of combat.

Carboni's assertion about petrol and ammunition was false: the Italian divisions had their full supply of ammunition and a large petrol depot at Mezzocamino on the Tiber, and further ammunition could be drawn from dumps within the divisional areas. Carboni continued:

If the Italians declare an armistice the Germans will occupy Rome and the Italians can do little to prevent it. The simultaneous arrival of US airborne troops would only provoke the Germans to more drastic action. Furthermore the Italians would be unable to secure the airfields, cover the assembly and provide the necessary logistical aid to the airborne troops. If . . . an Allied sea-borne landing is impossible north of Rome then the only hope of saving the capital is to avoid overt action against the Germans and await the effects of the Allied landings in the south.

To their horror, the Americans found the Italians had made no plan to defend the chosen air landing grounds of Cerveteri and Furbara, for which Castellano had sent detailed plans to the Italian War Office on 4 September.

Taylor and Gardiner reported that they reached Badoglio's private residence after midnight; the whole household was awake because of an air raid warning, and

General Carboni was received at once, while the American officers waited in the antechamber. After about fifteen minutes they were admitted and greeted cordially by the Marshal. Throughout the ensuing interview he made frequent expressions of his friendship for the Allies and his desire to enter into active co-operation.

Taylor asked whether Marshal Badoglio was in accord with General Carboni in considering an immediate Armistice and the reception of the airborne troops impossible of execution. The Marshal replied that he agreed with Carboni and repeated the same arguments. General Taylor asked if he realized how deeply his Government was committed by the agreements entered into by the Castellano mission. He replied that the situation had changed and that General Castellano had not known all the facts. The only result of an immediate Armistice would be a German-supported Fascist Government in Rome. He was asked if he feared the possible occupation of Rome by the Germans more than the renewed attacks of the Allied air forces which would certainly come if he rejected the Armistice. He answered with considerable emotion that he hoped the Allies would not attack their friends, who were only awaiting the right moment to join forces. If any bombing was to be done, let it be on the northern rail centres serving the German troops.

In reply to questions as to how he expected the Allied Chiefs to react to these changes, he expressed the hope that General Taylor would return and explain the situation. The latter declined to accept any responsibility for Italian interpretation of the situation, but offered to act as messenger.[9]

The next morning, 8 September, the day of the invasion, this telegram was sent to Eisenhower by Badoglio on Mallaby's radio set:

> Due to changes in the situation brought about by the disposition and strength of the German forces in the Rome area, it is no longer possible to accept an immediate Armistice as this could provoke the occupation of the capital and the violent assumption of the government by the Germans. Operation GIANT TWO is no longer possible because of lack of forces to guarantee the airfields. General Taylor is available to return to Sicily to present the views of the government and awaits orders.

The Americans also sent urgent signals through Mallaby that the airborne landing must be called off. By 6 p.m. some of the 82 Airborne Division were already in the air above the aerodrome of Licata in Sicily *en route* for Rome, and frantic signals had to be sent to recall them.

It had been agreed at Cassibile that the Armistice would be announced to the world simultaneously by Eisenhower and Badoglio between six and seven p.m. on the evening of 8 September. The first landings of the 82 Airborne troops would then take place on the aerodromes near Rome a few hours later, while before dawn on 9 September Allied troops would land at Salerno, south of Naples and 140 miles south of Rome, with other troops landing soon afterwards at the mouth of the Tiber. The role of the Italian army around Rome was to block all the routes to airfields designated for the landings, for four days.

It was tragic for Italy that the Rome airborne landing was called off at the eleventh hour. There can be little doubt that it would have been successful if the Italian War Office had co-operated with enthusiasm. Bedell Smith declared afterwards that he was convinced, as were the officers of his planning staff, that

> had there been in command of the Italian Divisions around Rome an officer of courage, firmness and determination and convinced of success, the plan could have been carried out.

The same view was expressed after the war by General Westphal, Kesselring's Chief of Staff.[10]

Badoglio was terrified of announcing the Armistice on 8 September, with no Allied troops to help to defend Rome; he was frightened of the Germans, and over-conscious of the possibility of his own capture and execution.

However, the King insisted that Italy should keep her word, as given at Cassibile, and simultaneously with the Allies Badoglio announced the Armistice on the evening of 8 September. Disastrously, his radio message failed to exhort Italian troops specifically to fight the Germans – he only ordered Italians not to fight the Anglo-Americans, and to resist 'attacks from wherever they come'.

The Allies landed at Salerno during the night of 8/9 September and were immediately counter-attacked by strong German divisions, suffering heavy losses. Italian submarines, however, who could have wreaked havoc with the invasion shipping, obeyed last-minute orders not to intervene. Had the Rome airborne landing been successful Kesselring would have been forced to withdraw his troops from Salerno, and the Allies could then have taken Rome intact. What is more, the dramatic news that strong Italian armour was fighting effectively with the Americans at the moment the Armistice was announced would have raised Italian prestige enormously with the Allies; it would have been a potent factor in securing a more favourable peace treaty, and undermined the morale of Italian pro-Fascists and pro-Germans.

As it was, Italian divisions were left alone to defend Rome against the Germans. Numerically the Italians were stronger. The motorized corps under General Carboni consisted of four divisions, two of them armoured, and on the evening of the 8th troop trains were bringing the infantry divisions Lupi and Re to the Rome area. Three other low-quality divisions near the coast were unlikely to be effective against the Germans.

Ariete, stationed north-west of Rome, was Mussolini's best armoured division, commanded by the courageous General Cadorna who afterwards won fame with the partisans in northern Italy. The second incarnation of an armoured division lost in North Africa, Ariete was equipped with the most modern tanks and armoured cars. The tanks had powerful 75 mm guns, and the division had just received new self-propelled 105 mm guns, the most modern in the Italian army. They were a match for the German armour.

Cadorna was opposed around Lake Bracciano, north of Rome, by the German 3rd Panzer Division. During the night and morning of 8/9 September Ariete had the better of the fighting with the Germans.

In the early hours of 9 September the War Office received news that some low-quality troops on the coast had surrendered to the Germans. General Roatta, the deputy Commander-in-Chief, panicked and reported that Rome was 'surrounded'. This was incorrect, but the news was too much for the nervy Badoglio, who told the King that the Government must flee to the east while at least one road remained open. At 5 a.m. the King and Queen and Crown Prince Umberto left with Ambrosio, de Courten the head of the Navy, and a few Ministers in a motor convoy making for Pescara on the Adriatic coast. Ariete and the other divisions defending Rome were ordered to disengage, and to occupy Tivoli to protect the royal flight. Badoglio claimed afterwards that he had ordered them east for an eventual link-up with advancing British troops. This was untrue: Badoglio wanted them at Tivoli only to protect his escape route.

The departure of Badoglio and the Government on 9 September left a vacuum in Rome. Telephone calls to the War Office from military headquarters all over Italy asking whether or not the Italian troops should fight the Germans were answered by junior staff officers who said 'We cannot help you. There is no one here.' Everywhere the Germans brutally attacked the troops of their former ally. Most of those taken by surprise surrendered, except in Yugoslavia, Corsica, Sardinia, Rhodes and the other Aegean islands. In Italy itself the Italian army in effect ceased to exist. Many Italian soldiers were shot, or sent to Germany in cattle wagons; most took the announcement of the Armistice as a signal to go to their homes as quickly as possible, by bicycle, train or on foot.

The royal convoy reached Pescara, embarked on a corvette, and the next day (10 September) landed at Brindisi in south-east Italy, not far from Montgomery's advancing 8th Army. There they tried to pick up the reins of government, but there was little they could do: in the intervening forty-eight hours, four-fifths of Italy had been occupied by German troops and most army headquarters had ceased to function.

The German High Command reported (accurately) to Hitler that by 14 September they had completely disarmed 56 Italian divisions and partially disarmed 29 others, with the capture of 700,000 soldiers and an immense amount of war *matériel*.

On 18 September Ambrosio told the Allies that 'Apart from Sardinia, Corsica and the Dodecanese, all the rest of the Italian army is surrounded by Germans and finished.' The AFHQ comment was, 'They can be written off.'[11]

The German swoop on the Italian troops was helped by a signal sent out by the War Office in Rome at just after midnight on the 9th to all headquarters, instructing them 'not to take the initiative in attacking the Germans'. Incredible as it may seem in view of the German attacks, it was not until 11 September that the War Office in Brindisi sent out orders to treat the Germans as enemies. When at midnight on the 8th Roatta had asked Ambrosio to order this, Ambrosio curtly refused. Probably he (and others) were looking for an escape line if they fell into the hands of the Germans; he was certainly dismayed by the news just received that the Allied landings were south, not north, of Naples. There is no evidence that Ambrosio or any of the Italian War Office envisaged a complete failure of the Allied invasion; they still grossly over-estimated the strength of the landing forces.

By 8 p.m. on 8 September, German officers had arrived at almost all the Italian headquarters in Italy, demanding either co-operation or surrender of arms, and a reply within one hour. Failing agreement, the Germans would open fire. The Germans occupied many key points and took possession of most outlying headquarters. Telephone lines were cut to isolate Italian commanders and, especially where German and Italian troops were intermixed, misleading propaganda was put out. However, there were instances of heroic resistance, and substantial casualties on both sides.

These German threats and attacks (Operation 'Axis') on Italian troops had been carefully planned in detail in advance, and took the Italians completely by surprise. Hence the Germans had an easy, if surprising, victory.[12]

On 9 September the Italian Motorized Corps fought stoutly against the Germans outside Rome. Ariete disengaged successfully (a difficult manoeuvre in battle) and retreated as ordered towards Tivoli. On 10 September Ariete moved forward again to the western approach to Rome, where 10,000 civilians armed with rifles supplied by the underground Socialist parties had rushed to Porta San Paolo to defend the city. It was reminiscent of the spontaneous rush to fight which had occurred in Rome on 3 June 1849 when Garibaldi dramatically threw back the French army from the walls of Rome. The armoured cars of Ariete were a great help to the guerrillas, but bitter, inconclusive fighting continued until evening, with heavy casualties on both sides. With no Government in Rome, chaos reigned. The veteran Field Marshal Caviglia assumed *ad hoc* control. Rome was out of reach of Allied fighters, but the Luftwaffe could bomb the city at will: Kesselring sent a brutal ultimatum to Caviglia – regardless of how many civilians were killed, he would immediately subject Rome to indiscriminate carpet bombing unless the fighting stopped. This persuaded Caviglia that he must ask for an armistice, and a truce was declared at 5 p.m.; Rome was denominated an 'open city', although no one knew what that meant. In order to stop the fighting, German aeroplanes had to drop leaflets explaining that it was all over.

Ariete retired to Tivoli in good order where the next day, under the terms of the truce, General Cadorna handed over to the Germans row after row of tanks fresh from the Fiat works and the latest armoured cars from Lancia. These were presented to the Germans for use against the Allies at the precise moment when they should have been in action defending beaches and aerodromes for massive American landings. The Italian corps fared so well in the fighting on 9 and 10 September that there can be no doubt they would have been capable of defending the Rome airfields during the four days needed for the full strength of 82 Airborne to arrive.[13]

CHAPTER 2

Mussolini Returns

IN THE CONFUSION of their unplanned departure from Rome in the early hours of 9 September, Badoglio and his ministers forgot the clause of the armistice agreed with Eisenhower which specifically stated that Mussolini should be handed over to the Allies. He was being held in a winter sports hotel on the Gran Sasso 120 kilometres from Rome in the Abruzzi, and it would have been simple to bring him under guard to join the royal convoy at Pescara. But no orders about him were given. By 12 September the Germans were in complete control of central Italy, and Mussolini was safe from the Allies. The Germans could have brought him by road to Rome, but Hitler wanted to dramatize the release. He ordered a flamboyant SS officer, Otto Skorzeny, to land with gliders on the Gran Sasso and bring Mussolini back in a small aeroplane to Rome. This was accomplished and given great publicity.

By allowing Mussolini to escape, Badoglio gave the Nazis a chance to create an alternative Fascist Government, and Hitler aimed to make maximum use of the discredited ex-Duce.

When, escorted by Skorzeny, Mussolini arrived at the Pratica di Mare airport near Rome, he told the Germans he wanted either to stay in Rome, or to join his wife and younger children at his country house, Rocca delle Caminate, near Forli. Hitler would not allow this; Mussolini was whisked off to Vienna.

He had no wish to return to public life, or to head a new Fascist State. During his captivity he had become philosophical, and intensely interested in his future place in the history of Europe; he had begun writing his memoirs. Hitler telephoned the Duce as he was trying to rest in a Vienna hotel, but Mussolini said he was too tired to discuss politics. The next day, 13 September, Mussolini was flown to Munich to be reunited with his wife Rachele and his family; reluctantly he began to prepare himself for future activity by studying the main events since 25 July, about which he had not been briefed. Ciano and Mussolini's daughter Edda were in Munich, but he met neither them nor any of the handful of former Fascist leaders assembled there by the Germans.

The next day Hitler summoned Mussolini north, to the Wolf's Lair at Rastenburg. On the long flight Mussolini tried hard to catch up with world and Italian affairs from notes and newspaper cuttings stuffed in his pockets. Finally, late in the afternoon of 13 September Mussolini and Hitler met. Hitler had decided that he would instal Mussolini as head of a new Fascist State in Italy, and greeted him warmly.

The other Nazi leaders, and the generals commanding in Italy – Rommel and Kesselring – wanted to treat Italy as an occupied country. It was thought that placing the Italians under German orders would make the country a more efficient base for the German army. Rahn, the German Ambassador to Italy, tried to persuade Hitler to abandon Mussolini and let Fascism rot. Anfuso, Mussolini's Ambassador to Germany, noted in his diary on 1 October that, according to Goebbels' Ministry of Propaganda, there was annoyance in the German army over the release of Mussolini, as otherwise Italy could have been treated as an occupied country.[1] But Hitler, moved by nostalgia for the former bonds between Fascism and Nazism, was more sympathetic to Mussolini.

Colonel Eggenreiner, Liaison Officer between the Wehrmacht and the Italian army, said after the war that following the events of 8 September German public opinion was 'exceptionally bitter' towards Italy because the alliance with Germany had been violated, a repeat of the treachery of the First World War. His view was that had it not been for the 'good discipline' of the army, German soldiers in Italy would have committed outrages against the civilian population in their anger and resentment. Anti-Italian feeling was certainly reflected in the atrocities against surrendering Italian soldiers, as will be seen. Eggenreiner thought the release of Mussolini on 12 September served to tone down German resentment, saying he had 'feared' that, but for the presence of Mussolini, Hitler himself would have taken reprisals far beyond anything the German army would have approved; he also stated pompously that he and Field Marshal von Rundstedt held a responsibility to see that the Italian army in German-occupied Italy was given 'decent or correct treatment'. In this they failed.[2]

At their first meeting Mussolini expressed to Hitler his reluctance to form a new Government. Immediately afterwards he held a conference with a 'rump' of his former Fascist colleagues, who had been brought to Rastenberg by Hitler; these included Pavolini, a leading Fascist who had been sacked by Mussolini from the Cabinet in February 1943, and Mussolini's early Fascist ally, Farinacci, the former Secretary of the Fascist Party. Pavolini urged Mussolini to head a new Government, but the Duce was indecisive: 'I cannot take a decision. I have not enough facts on which to form a judgement. I will see what I can do tomorrow.'

He had more talks with his former collaborators that evening, and some of his old enthusiasm returned. By the next morning he had agreed to Hitler's plan that he should head a Fascist Government in a new Republic.[3]

After 25 July Mussolini's former Fascist Party and Government had disappeared, largely unregretted by the Italian nation. At the last meeting of the Fascist Grand Council on 24 July Mussolini had said he was the 'most hated' person in Italy; his prestige, both with Italians and in German eyes, was low at the time of his 'rescue' by the Germans.

Mussolini was aware that without an army his new government would be impotent. The German General Staff were opposed. They knew that the Italian Officer Corps was strongly Royalist and might betray them again; at his first conference with Mussolini Hitler refused to commit himself over another Italian army.

Mussolini urged Hitler to make a separate peace with Russia. Ribbentrop backed Mussolini but Hitler, after drawing for Ribbentrop's benefit a possible demarcation line on a map, the next day refused to do any more.[4]

The new government Mussolini headed was a mere puppet, subservient to the Nazis and without real power. His ministers were a poor lot, with the exception of his choice for Foreign Affairs, Count Serafini Mazzolini, and his Minister of Justice, Pier Pisenti. Buffarini Guidi, the Minister for Home Affairs, had already been discredited for involvement in well-known frauds.

The previous administration dissolved on 25 July had governed through a mixture of Fascist officials and permanent civil servants. The main apparatus of this Fascist system had now disappeared. Pavolini, appointed Secretary of the Party, ordered all civil servants dismissed by the Badoglio Government to resume their functions. Many refused. Rahn, the German Ambassador to Italy, arrived at Hitler's headquarters and again argued strongly, but in vain, against reviving Fascism, saying it had no support and would only encourage anti-Fascist activity. Rahn could not persuade Hitler to alter his plans; he was sent back to Rome with Pavolini to rally collaborators for the new Fascism. But Rahn had persuaded Hitler, much to Mussolini's annoyance, that under no circumstances should the Duce be allowed back to Rome to set up his Government. Mussolini was left at Hirschberg Castle in southern Bavaria, under strict surveillance; he had no telephone contact with the outside world except through a German line which connected first with the exchange at Hitler's headquarters. Anfuso, a respected Italian diplomat who was Ambassador in Budapest, joined Mussolini and was accredited to Berlin; he was the only reputable diplomat who rallied to the new Fascism. On 18 September Mussolini broadcast to the Italian people on Radio Munich; he announced the creation of a new Fascist state for German-occupied Italy, and said Italy would take up arms again 'alongside Germany', and take 'revenge' on the traitors of 25 July. He also announced that the Fascist militia would be reconstituted, under Renato Ricci.

Pavolini re-opened the Fascist headquarters in Rome at the Palazzo Wedekind. He found most of the former prominent Fascist politicians had disappeared; they refused to come forward again. No impressive figures were prepared to join the new Government, and the number of recruits for Ricci's Fascist militia was derisory. At the German Embassy on 23 September Pavolini produced for Rahn a pathetic draft list of Ministers; it seemed Rahn had been proved correct, and that it would prove impossible to recreate a Fascist Government which could command any respect.

The only minister in Mussolini's Cabinet on whom the British Foreign Office reported favourably was Mazzolini, the Foreign Minister. In South America he had been

> honest, hard working, friendly and understandingly disposed towards the masses of Italian emigrants among whom he soon became very popular ... in 1937 he was transferred to Cairo. Although still loyal formally to the regime whose petty regulations like the 'Voi' and the use of uniform during working hours he strictly enforced, Mazzolini being an honest man was at this time showing to his subordinates signs of doubt in the soundness of the Duce's policies ... Mazzolini hoped until the last moment for a diversion which would keep Italy out of the war.... (later) In Rome Mazzolini did not like the atmosphere of intrigue and corruption veiled by a propaganda more bombastic than ever.

The Foreign Office thought it 'significant' that so many of the best-known former Fascists were missing, and had secret information that 'men who had held important and lucrative positions for years were now living in hiding from the neo-Fascists'.[5]

Mussolini was determined to buttress his position by raising a new, loyal army, believing this the only way to earn respect from the Germans; he also hoped it would give him some standing at a peace conference, should the war end in stalemate. Unfortunately, most Italian generals were strongly monarchist, and few of any reputation would lend their names to the shaky structure of neo-Fascism.

After the war, Dr Rahn told Sir William Deakin that in desperation he had personally approached Graziani, the Italian Field Marshal famous for his victories in the Abyssinian War and for his achievements as Governor of Libya. Graziani's reputation had been tarnished by his failure to repel Wavell's advance in the desert in 1941, and he was subsequently retired. He had offered Mussolini his services only hours before the Duce's arrest on 25 July, but a few days later made it clear that he was willing to serve under the King with Badoglio in power.[6] As a well-known general with past victories to his credit, his image could be used as a counterweight to Badoglio's.

Snubbed by Kesselring, who refused to see him after 8 September, Graziani was on the point of leaving Rome for good on 23 September when Barracu, a new junior Fascist Minister, arrived at his house. According to Graziani's evidence at his 1948 trial he had decided definitely to have nothing further to do with Mussolini, but Barracu persuaded him to go to the German Embassy, saying that if he did not, it would be 'cowardice'. At the German Embassy Graziani talked to Buffarini Guidi, who claimed that only Graziani's presence in the Government could stop Hitler pursuing a 'scorched-earth' policy in Italy. Then Graziani was introduced to Rahn and General Wolff; the Nazis told him Italy was 'war booty', and would be treated like Poland unless a strong neo-Fascist government was formed.

Graziani claimed that at first he would not accept, because he felt bound by his oath of loyalty to the King; but Rahn argued that his adhesion would spare Italy much suffering. Graziani claimed he did not want to join one side or the other – although he had a deadly hatred of the English, who had brought 'slavery and ruin' to Italy, and would never fight alongside them; but when the Germans outlined the alternatives for Italy, he yielded and agreed to become Minister of War, in order to try to save from disaster 'his native land which had been abandoned by the King'.[7] Rahn had told Graziani 'he could not answer for the consequences' if he refused.

At his trial, Graziani thus described his dilemma when he was confronted by Rahn on 23 September, and made an impassioned plea in self-defence; this was greeted by the public in the court-house with considerable applause, and cries of 'Viva Graziani'. Many Italians sincerely believe that by becoming Mussolini's Minister of War (and later Commander of the Fascist armed forces) Graziani was able to alleviate much of the harsh treatment intended by Germany for occupied Italy, and that without him and Mussolini Italy would have suffered even more. In the light of German atrocities and the horror of civil war it is doubtful, as will be seen later, whether this argument is sustainable. However, both the Duce and Graziani protested on numerous occasions to the Germans about outrages against the Italian population, and it is possible that had they not been in the Government, Italy might have been treated far worse.

According to Eggenreiner, Hitler did not share Rahn's joy about Graziani joining the Salò Government, and only agreed to it as a *fait accompli*. He felt Graziani would not be malleable enough. Eggenreiner added that at the time Graziani had said to him, 'What would happen to

Italy if I was not in the Government?' He stated he was given the impression that Graziani's chief motive in accepting the post was to preserve Italy from the dire consequences of having betrayed Germany.

A few minutes after Graziani agreed, Rahn issued a statement on the radio listing the Ministers of the new government, including Graziani. Mussolini was enormously relieved by Graziani's acceptance.

Rahn then summoned General Calvi di Bergolo to tell him he was dismissed and his Piave Division, which under the terms of the 10 September armistice between the Rome garrison and the Germans was to have kept order in Rome, dissolved. The new Fascist Government was banished to the north, and Rome became a war zone under the direct command of Kesselring.[8]

Mussolini's failure to persuade Hitler to allow the new Government to have its seat in Rome spelt the end of any real hope for the revival of Fascism; Italians had difficulty in taking seriously a government banished from the capital.

On 27 September Mussolini held the first meeting of his new cabinet at his country house at Rocca. He had to inform them that Hitler had annexed eight provinces and placed them under direct German rule; he also had to state that the Germans had ordered that his Government should operate from Salò on Lake Garda, near the German army's main headquarters. The Villa Feltrinelli was allocated to Mussolini; he went there on 5 October.

Graziani had an affectionate reunion with the Duce, although they had been on bad terms since his sacking after his failure in the desert. Mussolini told his ghost-like cabinet that he would concentrate on raising a new Fascist army, so that he would again have a powerful voice in German counsels.

Hitler added to Mussolini's ignominy by appointing a senior German officer, Colonel Jandl, with a 'small staff' of Italian-speaking German officers, to be Mussolini's 'minder'. Nominally he was Liaison Officer, but he watched over every action and decision of the Duce's. Jandl wrote to Hitler:

> My team is part of the immediate entourage of the Duce both in theory and in practice . . . we have established ourselves in a house next to the Duce's villa at Gargano. One of my officers, Lieutenant Dickeroff, lives in the Duce's house. This means that I know everything going on in the villa including who his visitors are and the ideas being discussed by the Duce's entourage. Thus I can let the German headquarters interested know anything that matters to them.[9]

After Hitler's friendliness and sympathy in Germany, Mussolini could hardly believe the news that a huge chunk of Italy from the Brenner Pass and extending to all Dalmatia had been put under direct German rule. He appealed to Hitler by letter from Salò on 10 October. He had great hopes that, because of his proclaimed friendship, Hitler would give way. Hopefully, but fruitlessly, he sent a copy of his letter to the Japanese Ambassador at Salò.

The great majority of the population are still stunned by the events from 25 July to 9 September, and swing from a desire for revenge to a state of resignation.

If we are to bring the life of the nation back to normal my Government must have the necessary independence to rule, i.e., give orders to the civil authorities depending on it. Unless we can do this the Government has no prestige, and is discredited and in consequence is bound to end ignominiously.

This would be against our common interest; it would have grave consequences and be a boon to the traitor Badoglio.

Führer! These are the factors which prevent the desired reorganization of life in Italy:

a) German headquarters send out a continual water-spout of orders about civil affairs. Often their order contradicts one by my Government. Italian civil servants are ignored, and the people given the impression that the Fascist Government has no authority except over matters entirely outside the military sphere. I could provide you with a mass of documentation, but it is not necessary. In the provinces of Emilia, Piacenza, Parma and Reggio German military authorities have sent out a demand that all civil regulations must have a German translation. In rural areas this is impractical. Let me tell you, Führer, that a single authority would remove this inconvenience.

b) It is my duty to tell you that nomination of a German High Commission for Innsbruck, Bolzano, Trento and Belluno has given a disastrous impression in every part of Italy. Removing the judicial powers from the High Court in Venice as ordered by the Commissioner has led to many injustices; this will be exploited by enemy propaganda, which is particularly active at the moment. The only one to profit will be the traitor Badoglio.

The Republican Government which I have the honour to head has a single aim – to enable Italy to take up again her role as soon as possible as a combatant. However, to achieve this it is essential that the German military authorities limit their activity strictly to the military field and in all other spheres allow Italian civil authority to function. Naturally these will collaborate with the German authorities whenever such collaboration is requested.

If my request is not complied with, both Italian and world opinion will look on my Government as incapable of functioning and the Government will fall, discredited and worse, in ridicule.

I am sure, Führer, that you will appreciate the importance of these arguments which I have set out and the grave problems which confront me. Their solution is not only in Italian interests, but in German interests as well.[10]

Hitler ignored this pathetic letter and a subsequent one, leaving Rahn to try to mollify Mussolini in conversation. It became clear to Mussolini that Hitler no longer looked on him as being of importance, and that his role was one solely of propaganda for the Reich.

A particular irritation for Mussolini was that the frontier of the province taken over by the Germans was only a few miles from Salò. They set up blockhouses, where all traffic was halted, sometimes with long delays. The nearest was Limone on the lakeside, where a special pass was needed to cross. At the time, the fighting front was 800 kilometres away.

Hitler's next decision, that Dalmatia (carved out of Yugoslavia and given to Italy in the spring of 1941) should revert to the puppet Fascist state of Croatia under the criminal ruler Pavelić, was a bitter pill for Mussolini. This beautiful and fertile littoral plain had been a prized possession of the Republic of Venice until Napoleonic days; its cession to Free Croatia – a puppet Ustase state set up by the Axis after the conquest of Yugoslavia in 1941, on territory which until then had been under the thumb of Italy – was part of the vendetta pursued by Hitler against Italy after 25 July.

Mussolini telegraphed to Hitler, imploring him 'to save 100 per cent Italian Zara from Croat occupation', after hearing that the Germans there had refused to recognize the new Italian Fascist prefect when the Croat part of the population protested against his nomination, although large crowds had gathered to express their desire to remain Italian. At nearby Spalato, the Croats had taken over and refused to provide Italian nationals with ration cards. For the third time Hitler ignored Mussolini's appeal.[11]

With no reply from Hitler to his two letters of entreaty and his cabled appeal about Dalmatia, the iron entered the Duce's soul. On 9 November he said to his private secretary Dolfin, 'How can Hitler expect me to co-operate when he annexes Trieste and Venezia? Each day we get more insults from the Germans. I have formed the impression that they regret allowing me to form a Government.' On 12 November he said to Dolfin:

It is absurd for those people [the Germans] to pretend to call us Allies. I would rather they took off their masks and said that we are an occupied territory and a subject people like all the others. That would put an end to the farce, and simplify our problems. None of you can stand aside while our fatherland gradually becomes enslaved.

On one occasion, hearing of a successful attack by the Bersaglieri (riflemen) fighting on the Allied side, Mussolini exclaimed, 'What gallant troops the Bersaglieri always are', giving vent to his true feelings about the Germans.

Mussolini raged to his colleagues about Hitler's refusal to respond to his letters, describing Rahn as 'bitter and acid' in talks. By Christmas Mussolini no longer wanted an Axis victory, although he knew that without one his star was set for ever.[12]

His German 'minders' reported Mussolini's every thought and conversation. Obviously the Führer profoundly distrusted his former ally. The young Italian-speaking German officer who lived in the Duce's house, Lieutenant Dickeroff, was only twenty-two, blond and good-looking, and possessed of some charm, despite being a convinced Nazi. He was easy-going and over-fond of cognac; he got on well with Mussolini, making friends and playing with the Duce's younger children.

Dickeroff reported on every visitor's conversation with the Duce to a Captain Hoppe on Jandl's staff; Jandl and Hoppe lived in a house a few hundred yards away. Each morning Hoppe and Dickeroff briefed Mussolini on the news from the various fronts, presenting it with a German slant which Mussolini ignored; he was under no illusions about Dickeroff's role.

The telephone system in the Villa Feltrinelli and the various Government offices functioned badly. The exchange was manned by Germans, who would often not put calls through. To call Rome took several hours – sometimes a whole day. The lines were so bad, being part of the German military system, that it was necessary to shout; this particularly annoyed Mussolini, who in private always liked to talk quietly.

Letters arrived by the sackful for the Duce, the majority from mothers of soldiers interned in Germany. Mussolini was greatly moved by them and usually replied personally – 'He is a good soldier who has done his duty' – promising to intervene; unfortunately, he was completely impotent in this sphere. The Germans called these internees *Badogliotruppen* and considered them unsatisfactory human material, 'useless for war and untrustworthy'.[13]

When Dolfin suggested that a meeting with Hitler might produce some satisfaction over the annexed provinces, Mussolini replied:

A meeting would solve nothing. Hitler has more important things to think of than our affairs. Immediately after my return to Italy I sent him by the personal hand of Graziani an extremely clear letter [10 October, letter quoted above] about the Commissioners in Bolzano and Trieste, I followed this up with a second letter which was even more 'precise', and then an impassioned telegram imploring him to intervene to save Zara which was threatened by Croat occupation. I have had no reply, only spurious promises from Rahn. I have no idea where it will all end. They have annexed Bohemia and

Sudetenland and now with their military occupation will do the same with Bolzano and Venezia Giulia. All they need is to win the war. Their attitude must lead to Italy refusing any military co-operation while we await our destiny. The Veneto, our most loyal region, will be the first to go. So recent are memories of Habsburg rule [Trieste had been Austrian until 1918] that at the moment people are not terrified of the Germans. But the German behaviour today is just a foretaste of what will come.

Every day, Mussolini went on, Rahn tried to beguile him with lies which contradicted the facts concerning the German seizure of part of Italy.[14]

Mussolini (as Denis Mack Smith has pointed out) had in the past always relied on press statements as his main tool of government, quickly establishing control over a network of newspapers to disseminate Fascist propaganda. But the machinery of government was almost completely lacking when Mussolini took up residence at Villa Feltrinelli in Salò on 5 October. Only a few civil servants had arrived – more were sent up from Rome by the Germans in December. Fascist prefects resumed what control they could of their areas, and reluctantly obeyed the Germans whose orders, as the Duce had pointed out to the Führer, frequently conflicted with those issued by Mussolini's ministers.

Most civil servants in the ministries in Rome had little love for Mussolini and, with the threat of Rome becoming a battle-ground, were determined not to leave their homes and families. On 10 October 1943 Barracu sent a personal message to the Duce to the effect that nearly all the Rome civil servants were involved in a 'subtle' plot to obstruct and make impossible the transfer of the ministries to the north; according to him, they refused to complete files for removal and would, when the order came to move, pretend to be ill. He claimed that at least fifty per cent of civil servants were in this plot. He wanted to check up on anyone who produced a medical certificate, and to send spies to interview them in their houses while a complete check of the necessary documents for the efficient transfer of functions was carried out by persons with 'impeccable Fascist credentials'. Barracu's attempt to supervise the ministries came to little when he himself was ordered north. Nearly all the civil servants disobeyed the order to go to Salò; they quietly returned to work when the Allies eventually occupied Rome, but were then frustrated by the British insistence that the Government should stay at Salerno.[15]

On 27 November Barracu complained bitterly to Rahn over the pillaging by three SS officers of food and clothing stores near Brescia; these belonged to charities set up by Mussolini for the needs of children and families who had lost their homes in north Africa, and had with difficulty been transferred from near Rome to the north. When the prefect of the province sent an official to stop the looting, he was threatened with a revolver by the SS officers. Barracu told Rahn he would resign from the Government if such behaviour continued, and asked for the SS officials to be punished. Like other Fascist Ministers, he found that complaints like this to Rahn fell on deaf ears. He did not resign.[16]

The only purposeful project of the neo-Fascist government was the creation of a new army. Graziani had arrived at Rocca delle Caminate on 3 October with an outline plan for a small specialized force of volunteers. Mussolini accepted it; on the same day he wrote to Hitler that Graziani would visit the Führer. 'All is quiet behind the front and every possible collaboration is offered to the German High Command while we prepare the new Republican Army.'[17]

CHAPTER 3

Italian Jews under the Nazis

ROMANS SOON DISCOVERED after Marshal Caviglia's armistice that Rome was an 'occupied' city, and any pretence to the contrary was a sham. At 1 p.m. on 11 September, the first full day of German control, Rome Radio announced: 'It is forbidden to carry arms . . . anyone killing a German soldier will be shot . . . the truce remains in force.' 'Truce' or not, that night a harsh proclamation signed by Field Marshal Kesselring appeared on the hoardings:

> Rome is under my command and is war territory subject to martial law. Those organizing strikes or sabotage as well as snipers will be shot immediately . . . Private correspondence is suspended. All telephone conversations should be as brief as possible. They will be strictly monitored . . . Italian civil authorities and organizations are responsible to me for the maintenance of public order. They will prevent all acts of sabotage and of passive resistance to German measures.

That night Rome Radio reported Hitler's announcement that 'the treachery of the Italians would not pass unpunished, and the measures against them would be very hard.'[1]

In 1555 Pope Paul IV had built a wall around the Jewish ghetto on the east bank of the Tiber. The gates were closed every night for 315 years, until the end of Papal rule with the unification of Italy in 1870 under King Victor Emmanuel II. Then the walls of the ghetto were torn down; the Jews were free, and accepted by their countrymen. Many prospered, but a great number of working-class and middle-class Jews remained in the former Rome ghetto, and in squalid streets on both sides of the Tiber, where a democratically elected Jewish Council of Fifteen organized community services for them.

After 1870 Jews became prominent in Italian public life, accepted by their fellow citizens with a tolerance scarcely equalled in any other country. They were to the fore in civic, professional and cultural life. Seven of Garibaldi's Thousand who invaded Sicily in 1860 were Jews.

Fifty Italian Jews were Generals in the First World War, and a thousand Jews won medals, including the youngest and oldest to receive the top award, the national gold medal. There was a Jewish Prime Minister in 1910, and by 1920 nineteen Jewish senators. In 1922 many Jews in public life embraced Fascism with fervour; some rich Jews in Turin were noted for their Fascism, and there were several Jews among prominent Fascist leaders. Their ardour for the Duce even survived his aping of Hitler in passing the anti-Semitic laws of 1938, although these laws inflicted grievous harm on Italian Jewry. Many professional men found they could not stay in practice; many businessmen had to sell their concerns. Younger people found their chosen careers barred; students found courses for higher education closed. As always in Italy the wealthy, the influential and the cunning were able to evade the laws, and there was tremendous variation in the severity with which they were enforced. Once the laws were operative Mussolini took no interest in their enforcement, cold-bloodedly ignoring the misery which followed from his flamboyant adoption of the Nazi line. But the numerous cases in which they did not operate should lead no one to underestimate the plight of Italian Jewry after the 1938 laws.

During the war Jews who fell into the hands of the German army were consigned almost without exception to concentration camps and extermination; this did not happen to Jews who fell into the hands of the Italian army before the armistice of September 1943. Italian officers saved the Jews because they felt it was 'unworthy and immoral' to send them to death camps, and to prevent this they often risked their own lives at the hands of the Germans. A few German officers may have protested, but none took the same active steps to save the Jews as the Italians.

In France until 11 November 1942, when the Allies landed in North Africa and the Axis took over Vichy France, the Vichy Government and the French police co-operated willingly with the Nazis over deporting Jews, and out of 75,000 French Jews ultimately deported over 42,000 had gone by then – many from unoccupied France.[2]

When the Germans occupied southern France in November 1942 Italy was given a large zone of occupation running from Toulon up the Rhône valley to the Swiss frontier near Geneva.

The SS expected to continue their work of deportation in the Italian zone. They soon met formidable obstacles. The French prefect of the Alpes Maritimes complied with SS orders to put all Jews in his zone into concentration camps set up by the Germans; but the Italian High Command forbade this within their area. Ciano, the Foreign Minister, ruled that treatment of Jews was 'purely an Italian affair in their zone of occupation' and the prefect's order 'must be suspended'.

An account in *The Times* of 21 January 1943, based on accurate information, reported that in the Italian zone the Italians had cancelled the Vichy order that all Jews must wear the humiliating Star of David. General Ambrosio, in charge of the Italian occupying forces, ordered that laws against Jews were reserved to the Italian military authority, and that 'the Vichy Government must revoke arrests and internment already carried out'.

Jews soon began to migrate from the German zone into the Italian zone; the SS in France reported to Himmler that the Italians were treating the Jews so well that unless this ceased, wholesale migration into their zone could not be prevented.

When Ribbentrop came to Rome to see the Duce at the end of February 1943, Mussolini admitted that the Italian army 'lacked the proper feeling on the Jewish question'. Pietromarchi, the Italian diplomat who was present, reported that the Duce cut Ribbentrop off 'sharply' when Jews were discussed. In any event, Mussolini took no firm action in support of the SS, and Ambrosio's kindly policy towards the Jews in the Italian-occupied zone of France prevailed until the September 1943 armistice. As a token gesture, the Italians told the Germans they intended to make a coastal strip of 50 kilometres 'Jew-free' and to transport Jews to the interior, but there is no evidence of any serious attempt to accomplish this.[3]

In Greece and Yugoslavia the Italian army did as much to save Jews from the Germans as in France. When the Yugoslav army surrendered in April 1941 Hitler allowed Italy to annex the Dalmatian coast and islands; an independent Croat State was set up, nominally under Italian control and the rule of the Duke of Spoleto (a close relation of the King of Italy), but actually dominated by the Croatian terrorist, Pavelić. Serbia and its capital Belgrade were under the rule of a German puppet Government.

In Croatia Pavelić created a brutal police force on SS lines, known as the Ustase. They massacred half a million Serbs living in Croatia, and persecuted and killed Jews and gypsies indiscriminately. Thousands of Jews fled to Italian territory in Dalmatia, seeking Italian protection. This was granted.

The Italian army also occupied certain zones in Serbia, under German rule. Here too the Jews applied for protection to the Royal Italian Army, and here again it was granted. In August 1942 Hitler asked Mussolini to hand over all Jews in the Italian army zone. Mussolini agreed formally, but a handful of Italian diplomats and generals said 'No'.[4]

On 21 August 1942 Otto von Bismarck, Minister at the German Embassy in Rome, called on Lanza d'Ajeta at the Italian Foreign Office and asked the Italian Government to order their military authorities in Yugoslavia to 'actuate those measures devised by the Germans and Croats for a transfer in mass of the Jews of Croatia to the east'. Von Bismark admitted to d'Ajeta that this would lead to their 'elimination'. Mussolini wrote 'No objection' on von Bismarck's official request, but did nothing to ensure that it was complied with by his subordinates. The diplomat Pietromarchi recorded that von Bismarck had asked for the Jews to be surrendered so that they could be 'destroyed', but had been refused.[5]

Ribbentrop was furious. He described the Governor of Dalmatia, Giuseppe Bastianini (later Italian Foreign Minister), as 'an honorary Jew' and demanded action by the Italians. The Italians made a pretence of complying. They rounded up Jews who had fled into their military zone, but instead of handing them over to the Germans for extermination, put them into an Italian camp at Kraljevica (Porto Re) on the Dalmatian coast, where there were already many Jewish refugees. When General Roatta, commanding the Italian troops in Yugoslavia, visited the camp on 28 November 1942, five Jewish bankers and industrialists thanked him officially; according to one survivor, Roatta said that if he had submarines available he would transport them to Italy 'where they would be really safe'.

By the summer of 1942 the number of Jews resident in Dubrovnik, in Italian-controlled Dalmatia, had gone up from 200 before the war to over 1,000, because of the influx of refugees from Croatia and the German-occupied part of Yugoslavia, and in Mostar from 50 to 200. General Ambrosio assured these Jews 'they would not be molested'. Governor Bastianini had reported to Rome in the middle of May 1942 that the migration of Jews into Italian-occupied territory had reached alarming proportions, and must cease. Ciano suggested Jews coming from Croatia should be sent to concentration camps in a part of Croatia 'occupied by us'. General Roatta, the military commander, refused because 'we have guaranteed them a certain amount of protection', and the Croats would send them to death camps.[6]

On a visit to Rome on 13 September 1942, Roatta discussed the Croat Jews with Pietromarchi. Roatta said: 'It is out of the question [to hand them over to the Germans]. They have placed themselves under our protection. The Croats have asked us to hand them back. I naturally opposed it with a flat refusal ... Now there is an order from the Duce.' Mussolini was unwell and found it difficult to supervise all departments; his 'no objection' minute was ignored. The Italian army continued to protect the Croat Jews until the September 1943 armistice.

The Germans complained bitterly that Mussolini would not give direct orders to Roatta to hand over the Jews. Himmler came to Rome to urge Mussolini to take action; the Duce sent an order that the Jews in Dalmatia were to be divided into Italian Jews and Croat Jews, the Croat Jews to be handed over to the Croats. General Picche, who would have had to carry out this order, minuted on 14 November: 'The decision to consign the Jews would be the equivalent of condemning them to death and has provoked very unfavourable comments ... among the troops ... and among the rest of the population ... at this moment an act of clemency would in the opinion of most people be very opportune.'

When Roatta came to Rome on 17 November the Duce agreed that *all* Jews could remain in the Italian concentration camp at Kraljevica, thus rescinding his previous minute to agree to deportations as requested by von Bismarck.

The Axis occupation of Greece in 1941 placed Athens in the Italian area of occupation. The Jewish population of the city rose by 5,000 as refugees from the Germans sought safety with the Italians. However, after the September 1943 armistice the Italians could do nothing to help the Jews in Athens.

During the summer of 1943 the Italian army and police held around 2,700 Jews in Yugoslavia 'for protective reasons', and permitted thousands of Greek Jews to live normal lives under Italian protection. Mussolini tacitly permitted this, behind Hitler's back and much to German annoyance.[7]

Even after the 1938 laws were passed, the Turin Jewish Council publicly reaffirmed their faith in Mussolini (albeit with some dissension). Their President, General Guido Liuzzi, told a meeting Mussolini had reassured him that 'no harsher measures would be passed'. A rich banker, Ettore Ovazza, argued that anti-Fascist and Zionist Jews had been responsible for the current wave of anti-Semitism. Some Florentine Jews also reaffirmed their loyalty to Fascism and attacked Zionism in an isolated instance. Mussolini created a distinction between Fascist and anti-Fascist Jews, so that certain Fascist Jews became *discriminati*, with privileges. He may have intended this to indicate that there was a gulf between him and Hitler over the Jews.[8]

In Turin the banker Ovazza, who had been shown personal friendship by the Duce, had published a Jewish Fascist newspaper, *La Nostra Bandiera*, which was so virulently anti-Zionist that Mussolini asked for its editorial line to be 'toned down'. Ovazza maintained a pro-Fascist stance until the armistice of September 1943; the German take-over of northern Italy and the presence of Nazi troops caused him to flee with his family to the Hotel Lyskann at Gressoney in the Valle d'Aosta, taking much of his fortune in notes with him. Gressoney was near the Swiss border and he hoped to slip over if threatened with arrest. His son was assassinated by the guides who had promised to take him to Switzerland, when they found he was carrying a fortune in bank notes. On the evening of 9 October, SS officers came to the hotel, forced Ovazza to pay the SS overnight bill, and the next morning took him and his wife and daughter to Intra on Lake Maggiore, shot them and burnt their bodies in a stove in their barracks.[9]

At Salò Mussolini was usually apathetic, and there is no evidence that he took any initiative over persecuting Jews. But Hitler's will was now supreme in occupied Italy, and he had no intention of allowing the mild Fascist anti-Semitic laws to continue; he was determined to send as many Italian Jews as possible to his death camps.[10]

On 11 September 1943 there was grave foreboding within the ghetto, where the bulk of Rome's 12,000 Jews lived. Pius XII had not protested vigorously against the slaughter of Jews in Germany and other countries occupied by the Nazis. He had, however, aided Italian Jews, chiefly by helping them to emigrate. With Kesselring's proclamation the Pope realized Roman Jews were at risk, and as soon as he received assurances from the Nazis that the occupation forces would respect the extra-territorial status of the Vatican and all Vatican-owned buildings in Rome, he personally told his clergy to open monasteries and convents to all Jews in need of refuge, without discrimination.

The Nazis soon went into action against the helpless Jews of Italy. During the second week of occupation Himmler telegraphed to SS Major Herbert Kappler, head of the Gestapo in Rome:

> Recent events in Italy make it necessary that a final solution is found to the Jewish problem in the territories occupied by the armed forces of the Reich. The Reichsführer [Himmler] requests Obersturmbahnführer Kappler to put into operation immediately all necessary preliminary measures to ensure that operations [against the Jews] can be carried out quickly and secretly within the city of Rome. Further orders will follow.

Hotels near the Swiss border filled with rich Jews from Turin and Milan, their luggage stuffed with currency and jewels and false identity papers. Himmler ordered the SS to carry out a round-up of Jews in the hotels and luxury villas around Lake Maggiore; forty-nine Jews were put to death out of hand by the SS; many bodies were found floating in the lake.

Kappler claimed he did not want to carry out deportations. At his trial he stated that he believed there was 'no Jewish problem in Italy', and thought that 'unlike the Geman Jews, the Italian Jews had not grown rich off the backs of the people'. He knew that in Rome they were mostly poor and orderly, and did not believe they had any connection with the mythical 'international Jewish conspiracy' so feared by the Nazis.

Kappler was a rabid Nazi and Jew-hater. However, his knowledge of Italy was good: he believed that Fascism was dead; he did not want Mussolini restored; and, as he saw it, deporting the well-behaved Jews of Rome would add considerably to his difficulties in keeping the city calm. Kappler's views were ignored by Himmler and Hitler. On 24 September Himmler dispatched a Top Secret order to Kappler calling for all Rome Jews to be rounded up and sent to the east for 'liquidation', regardless of age, sex or nationality. Kappler was instructed to mount a 'surprise' action lest many Jews should go into hiding.

General Rainer Stahel, the military commandant of Rome, was not a rabid Nazi (later he was to be sacked by Hitler for being too friendly towards the Romans and the Vatican). Stahel immediately contacted Mölhausen, the German Consul in Rome, asking him to try to obstruct the deportation order. With the German Ambassador, Rahn, living at Mussolini's base in Salò, Mölhausen was the senior resident diplomat in Rome.

Mölhausen, Stahel and Kappler held a conference with Kesselring. Kesselring himself was not anti-Semitic: there is evidence that he had helped to save Jews in Tunisia. The only consideration which weighed with him was how many troops would be needed for the anti-Jewish action. Kappler said that in addition to his own Gestapo personnel he would need one motorized battalion. 'That settles it,' said Kesselring. 'I will not approve it. I need all my available forces to defend Rome. It would be far better to employ the Jews on constructing defence works.'[11]

On his own initiative Kappler conceived a plan to raise funds from the Roman Jews in return for a promise of good treatment. He thought this would be a sop to Himmler and Hitler, and might avoid the pogrom which he and Kesselring did not want. Accordingly he threatened Foà, the leader of the Rome Jewish community, that 200 Jews would be deported unless he was given a ransom of 50 kilograms of gold: this was blood money. The Rome Jews, helped by many Catholics and with a generous offer from the Pope to make up the balance if necessary, raised the 50 kilograms and took it to the German Embassy with an Italian police escort. Kappler received it, promising that, in return, no Jews of Rome would be molested. His staff officers behaved abominably, disputing the weights, and refusing to give any receipt. However, the Italian police escort were witnesses.

The relief among the Jewish leaders in Rome was short-lived. The next morning SS men and Gestapo came to the main synagogue, and two German academics who were experts on Jewish history began to catalogue the manuscripts and codices, as a preliminary to the sequestration of this unique historical library. Most of the library was removed, together with two million lire from the synagogue safe. Kappler's men also took a complete list of Roman Jewish families. Alarm signals rang through the Roman Jewish community; some (but not all) left their homes and hid.

Ignoring Kappler's objections, Himmler ordered the immediate extermination of the Roman Jews. On Himmler's instructions Eichmann, the mainspring of the holocaust, sent the thirty-year-old SS Captain Theodor Dannecker, who had previously led teams for the deportation of Jews from Paris and Sofia, to Rome with an 'execution team' of 44 SS. Dannecker arrived on 6 October and showed Kappler his order to arrest the 8,000 Jews living in Rome. Kappler at first demurred, but then handed over to Dannecker the list of names and addresses purloined from the synagogue a few days previously.

After Dannecker's call, Kappler conferred with Stahel and Mölhausen on how to prevent the atrocity. Mölhausen sent a personal telegram to Ribbentrop, the Nazi Foreign Minister, to the effect that Kappler had been ordered to deport 'for liquidation' all the 8,000 Roman Jews, but that General Stahel would only authorize it on express orders from Ribbentrop. Kesselring, when informed, also objected to the deportations, and the next day Mölhausen again telegraphed personally to Ribbentrop stating that Kesselring wanted the deportations postponed and would prefer to employ the Jews in fortification work around Rome.

Hitler would not hear of any postponement; Ribbentrop sent a telegram to Mölhausen ordering him not to interfere, reminding him that all questions concerning Jews were the exclusive concern of the SS, 'in which the Foreign Office must not interfere'.

Mölhausen informed Weizsäcker at the Vatican of the proposed deportations. Weizsäcker told the Pope. Pius XII immediately personally ordered the heads of all the numerous extra-territorial enclaves to open their sanctuaries to any non-Aryans in need of refuge. According to Michael Tagliacozzo, the acknowledged leading authority on the episode, 477 were sheltered within the Vatican and another 4,238 in the monasteries and convents of Rome. Thus the Pope saved a great number of Jewish lives.[12]

The 16th October 1943, a Jewish sabbath, was a black day in the history of Rome. At 5.30 a.m. Dannecker's SS thugs went into action, brutally seizing 1,259 Jews or suspected non-Aryans in the ghetto and surrounding quarters, regardless of age, sex or ill-health. Of the Jews on the list which Kappler had obligingly supplied to Dannecker, all those still at home were seized. They were brought in trucks to the Collegio Militare, near the Vatican, where they were left without proper clothes or food.

The next day the Vatican Secretariat was informed by one of their members, Don Igino Quadraroli, of the miserable conditions of the Jews imprisoned in the Collegio Militare, and also that there were many baptized Christians among those held there. Pius XII wrote to Stahel emphasizing that there were many practising Christians among the detainees. This produced the release of the baptized Christians but made no difference to the plans to deport the others. Two days later all the Jews left in the Collegio Militare were shipped in cattle trucks by rail to Auschwitz, where the majority were sent to the gas chamber; a few of the strongest young men were made to work, in coal mines or in Warsaw. Out of 1,041 Romans taken on the train, only fifteen survived to return after the war to Rome to relate their experiences.

The deportation train passed through Padua; the Bishop of Padua informed the Vatican that the occupants were in a pitiable condition, and asked the Pope to take urgent action. The Vatican was later informed that when the train passed through Vienna station the prisoners were begging for water.[13]

News of the arrests spread quickly through Rome and Albrecht von Kessel, number two to Weizsäcker, contacted the German Embassy in Rome and asked Mölhausen to take the matter up urgently with Ribbentrop in Berlin. Mölhausen refused to act without the official intervention of the Pope. Von Kessel then went to see Father Pancrazio Pfeiffer, a German abbot who was the Pope's liaison officer with the Germans in Rome, but Pfeiffer could not persuade Pius XII to follow up his letter to Stahel with an official protest to Hitler. Cardinal Maglione, Vatican Secretary of State, told Weizsäcker that 'The Holy See would not want to be forced to utter formal words of disapproval'; whereupon the German Ambassador replied that he admired the attitude of the Holy See in maintaining 'a perfect balance' (between Germany and the Allies), and asked Maglione to do nothing which might provoke an attack on the Holy See. Weizsäcker added that the orders to arrest the Jews had come from the 'top', and that he did not want to treat the conversation as 'official'. Finally, Maglione implored Weizsäcker to do something for the 'wretched Jews', saying he left it to Weizsäcker's judgement what was best.

Among the Jews arrested was a lawyer, Foligno, who worked for the Vatican. From a Jewish family, he had been a Catholic from birth and had an Aryan wife and children. As the result of the request from Maglione through Weizsäcker, Foligno was released and took refuge in the Vatican.[14]

At that time, Pius XII and his advisers had some grounds to fear that protesting to Hitler would result in the violation of the extra-territorial rights of the monasteries and convents and the consequent capture of many Jews and anti-Fascists hiding in them. Protests by the Dutch clergy had only produced more barbaric treatment of Jews and anti-Nazis in Holland. However, the threat of a German attack on the Vatican City had receded because the Nazis were short of troops in Italy at the time.

On 31 October Maglione completely misled D'Arcy Osborne, the British Minister, by informing him that as a result of the Pope's protests many Jews had been released after the raid on the ghetto; as we have seen, the Pope had only succeeded in achieving the release of baptized Catholics. On 2 November, Osborne told the Pope that his Holiness underestimated his own moral authority, deriving from the 'reluctant' respect in which he was held by the Nazis on account of the large Catholic population in Germany. At this meeting the Pope told Osborne that he would never leave Rome, for his own protection or for any other reason, unless he was forcibly removed; and that he had no grounds for complaint against General von Stahel or the German police, who had hitherto respected the neutrality of the Vatican.

Osborne emphasized to the Pope that the idea of Rome as an 'open city' was a farce because it was wide open to the Germans, who were stripping it of all supplies and transport, arresting Italian youths, officers and even *carabinieri*, and using their usual merciless methods of persecution against the Jews. Osborne's argument that the Pope underestimated his own standing in Germany had little effect on Pius XII.[15]

Father Pfeiffer advised the Vatican against complaining to Stahel again, on the grounds that this German general was already strongly opposed to the arrests (actually, Stahel had provided Dannecker with three companies of SS troops for the round-up). Instead, the Pope asked the German Bishop Hudal, head of the German College (an ardent nationalist who, to his shame, had in 1937 given qualified approval to the Nuremberg anti-Jewish measures), to write to Stahel:

> ... I earnestly request that you order the immediate suspension of these arrests both in Rome and in its vicinity. Otherwise I fear the Pope will take a public stand against this action, which would undoubtedly be used by the anti-German propagandists as a weapon against us.[16]

Stahel merely passed the letter on to Ribbentrop; the next day, Weizsäcker informed Ribbentrop that Hudal's letter represented the Vatican reaction correctly. Weizsacker added:

> The Curia is particularly upset [*betroffen*] because the arrests took place as it were under the Pope's own windows. The reaction could be muzzled to a certain extent if the Jews were used for labour service here ... People say that when similar incidents took place in French cities, the Bishops took a strong stand.
>
> The Pope, as Bishop of Rome, cannot be more reticent than them. People are also drawing a parallel between the stronger character of Pius XI and that of the present Pope. Enemy propaganda abroad will certainly use this event to disturb the friendly relations between the Curia and ourselves.[17]

Ribbentrop ignored Weizsäcker's letter, but encouraged by Weizsäcker Pius XII ordered the extra-territorial monasteries and convents in Rome to open their doors even wider to Jews seeking asylum, and allowed a number to take refuge within the Vatican City itself. Weizsäcker warned the Pope that any Papal protest 'would only result in the deportations being more severe. I know how our people react in these matters.' Pius XII eschewed formal protest to Hitler, but his open-door policy saved the lives of a great number of Roman Jews.[18]

Cardinal Maglione told Weizsäcker that during this 'terrible war' the Holy See always deemed it prudent not to give the German people the impression that the Vatican was in any way 'anti-German'. This was the Pope's consistent attitude throughout the nine terrible months of the German occupation of Rome, which continued until June 1944. For this Pius XII has been accused of lack of courage. Most of these attacks are unjustified, but his predecessor, Pius XI, would have taken a more vigorous stand. When Hitler came to Rome in 1938, Pius XI had closed the Vatican Museum (which Hitler wanted to visit), departed to his villa in the country, and declared that in Rome the Nazi pagan cross should not hang beside the Christian. Unlike Pius XI, Pius XII was a diplomat, not an outspoken fighter for his cause.

It cannot be proved that Hitler would have tempered his atrocities if Pius XII had been more outspoken. The Pope did exercise a tremendous influence on the people, and a stronger stand by him might have caused Italian Fascists to hesitate before handing over Jews and helping the Nazis in other atrocities. However, no matter how vigorously the Pope had protested either about the deportation of the Roman Jews or, later, about the Ardeatine massacre, it is most improbable that Hitler would have countermandered his orders for either atrocity. It is more likely that a Papal *démarche* would have triggered off a violation of the sanctuary status of the Vatican and the extra-territorial convents and monasteries, and even caused Hitler to occupy the Vatican physically despite Kesselring's reluctance to waste troops inside Rome. It might also have resulted in the Nazis inflicting greater hardship on Catholics in occupied Europe.

Pope Pius XII has been charged with being 'anti-Jewish'. This is unsustainable, in view of the asylum he provided for the Roman Jews during the Nazi occupation of the city. Pius XII was a diplomat who believed that to keep silent was the lesser of two evils: *ad maiora mala vitanda* (to avoid greater evils). Whether he was right or wrong is for history to judge, but the widespread accusations of indifference to suffering or of 'unchristian cowardice' are based on slender evidence.

Von Kessel put the case well, writing that he and Weizsäcker warned the Vatican, the Curia and the Pope himself against rash utterances. To offer any opinion on a question of martyrdom would have been entirely out of place for us Germans, whose Head of State was a criminal ... would it not have been better from the point of view of human dignity, of Christendom and the Catholic church, if Pius XII had assumed the martyr's crown even without achieving any practical results ... I was convinced then and am still convinced today that he almost broke down under the conflicts of conscience. No one could relieve him of the responsibility ... but who can now maintain ... that he found the wrong answer when he avoided martyrdom.[19]

Hitler's immediate reaction to the overthrow of Mussolini in the coup of 25 July had been to plan a counter-coup by which the King and the members of the Badoglio Government would be captured, and Mussolini and the Fascists reinstalled; he actually issued an order that the troops were to go 'right into the Vatican'. Although he was eventually dissuaded by his advisers, Hitler continued to toy with the idea. Pius XII was informed – correctly – that Hitler had planned to send 3,000 SS to Rome to occupy the Vatican and deport the Pope. An unconfirmed story relates a plan by Count Galeazzi for the Pope to travel to San Felice Circeo, between Naples and Rome, and thence by ship to Spain; Sister Pascalina Lenhert, the Pope's secretary, is said to have gone to San Felice to make the necessary arrangements. At San Felice there was a villa on a cliff above the sea, accessible only with great difficulty over a narrow rocky path above a precipice. The plan was that the Pope should hide in the villa; within forty-eight hours a boat would take him to Spain, where the dictator General Franco had offered to shield him from the Nazis. It is claimed that the devoted Sister Pascalina went to reconnoitre the villa, damaging her foot in a slip over the rocks in the process. However, it is unlikely that the Pope even toyed with the idea of flight. When it came to the crunch, he categorically refused to follow the example of Pius IX, who fled to Gaeta in Bourbon territory to escape from the Liberals in Rome in 1848.

Pius XII declared:

> Rumours of Nazi intentions to kidnap me are not flights of fancy but must be taken seriously. However, I will never leave Rome nor the Vatican unless I am chained and taken away by force.

There is incontrovertible evidence that Hitler, determined to occupy the Vatican, was only deterred with difficulty.[20] Hitler summoned General Wolff, the SS Commander in Italy, to the Wolf's Lair on 13 September 1943; Wolff was told to make urgent plans to occupy the Vatican, kidnap the Pope and remove him to Liechtenstein, and put in safe-keeping all the archives and treasures of the Vatican. The Führer asked Wolff how long it would take him to prepare such an operation. Wolff said he would have to find Latin and Greek scholars to examine the archives, and would need a month for this. Much annoyed, Hitler agreed to the delay, saying he would have preferred to attack the Vatican immediately. Wolff argued that in the chaotic situation in Italy, the only firm authority was the Church; he had established good relations with the ecclesiastics, and without their co-operation he had too few SS and police units in Italy to keep order. Wolff promised Hitler that if the plan to attack the Vatican was put in cold storage, he could guarantee to keep Italy calm by lenient treatment, and the Italians in the part occupied by the Germans would become allies again. Reluctantly Hitler agreed to postpone kidnapping Pius XII. Wolff then sent a message to the Pope that he and the Curia were in no immediate danger.[21]

Although he always refused to risk an out-and-out confrontation, Pius XII's record of opposition to Hitler throughout the war is impressive. When Ribbentrop came to Rome in March 1940, the Pope demanded the right to send a Papal Nuncio to occupied Poland. Ribbentrop replied 'Impossible' because Poland was under military rule. Pius XII then attacked him about German persecution of the Church in Poland; Ribbentrop replied that the Church must not meddle in politics. When Cardinal Maglione gave Ribbentrop a list of German atrocities the latter insolently replied with a list of alleged atrocities committed against Germans by the Poles.

When Hitler invaded the Low Countries in May 1940, Pius XII refused to condemn the Germans as aggressors, although he expressed sympathy with the victims of the war. In 1940, at a time when there were doubts about how much of the British Expeditionary Force it would be possible to evacuate through Dunkirk, there was a discussion in the British Cabinet over the cession to Italy of Djibuti, Gibraltar and a stake in the Suez Canal – concessions for which Pius XII continued to press until 10 June 1940 when, to his horror, Mussolini declared war on France and Britain.

The reaction of the Catholic Church in Italy to the declaration of war in 1940 recalled their behaviour during the Abyssinian War. Several bishops issued pastoral letters expressing their patriotism, and these helped to make Mussolini popular. The Italians expected a short war, followed by a peace conference from which they would gain territorial acquisitions at the expense of France and Britain.

After the fall of France, Hitler made a speech in the Reichstag offering Britain peace. Pius XII supported Hitler's move, hoping to play an important role in the peace-making; but Churchill would have none of it.

When Germany attacked the Soviet Union in June 1941, Catholics in Italy became keener on the war, evidently seeing it as a crusade against Bolshevism; indeed, Mussolini hoped the Pope would declare it a religious crusade, thus boosting Italian morale. Pius XII refused categorically. He uttered not one word of encouragement for the war against Russia, saying no more than he had at the time of the German invasion of the Low Countries; but some Italian clerics blessed the Italian soldiers who were defending freedom against 'Red Barbarism'.

Stalin cleverly pretended that he wanted to collaborate with the Pope and to improve the lot of the Catholic and Orthodox Churches in Russia. He set up a Department of Church affairs in Moscow, and reopened some Catholic churches. Some Anglican clergymen who went to Moscow were impressed by Stalin's propaganda; but Cardinal Heenan, then a Monsignor, wrote after his visit that the large congregations in Moscow churches had been 'rigged'.

The Vatican was unimpressed, noting that in twenty years of Soviet rule 24,000 churches had been destroyed or converted into cinemas, etc., while thousands of priests had been murdered. President Roosevelt, wanting to send aid to Russia, was shocked by a poll of American Catholic clergy which revealed that 90 per cent were opposed to US aid to Russia. Myron Taylor was sent to Rome by the President in September 1941 to try to persuade Pius XII to support the Russians in the fight against the Nazis. The Vatican reply was a hope that, as a result of the war waged in Russia, Communism would be defeated, Nazism weakened, and both subsequently destroyed. Clearly, the Pope hoped Hitler would first destroy the Russian armies and then himself be destroyed by the Allies. But the result was a modification of the attacks by fire-eating American bishops.[22]

In 1942 Pius XII, increasingly worried by the starvation and the appalling conditions in German-occupied Poland, tried in vain to organize Red Cross aid. Hitler would allow no Nuncio in Poland and, despite the Pope's protests, ruled that Orsenigo, the Nuncio in Berlin, had no competence in occupied countries. In the spring of 1942 Pius XII received Father Pirro Scavizzi, the chaplain on an Italian hospital train which had passed through Poland on its way to the Russian front. The Pope had given Scavizzi considerable sums in cash to distribute to the Polish population, and Scavizzi had learnt much from Polish priests about the internal situation. After giving the Pope a detailed account of the appalling conditions in Poland, he implored Pius XII to excommunicate Hitler and his coterie. The Pope was much moved; on his knees and holding up his arms, he declared his agony at what he had learnt; he was very near to excommunicating Nazism and denouncing to the civilized world the bestiality of the extermination of the Jews, but was aware of threats of ghastly reprisals, not only against himself, but on the whole population of the occupied territories; after many tears and prayers he had come to the conclusion that his protest would have done no good but would have evoked the fiercest reprisals against the Jews and other defenceless people. 'Perhaps my protest would produce praise for me in the civilized world, but it would subject the poor Jews to a persecution even more implacable than they were already enduring.'

This decision to stay silent and not make a formal protest provides the main ground for the massive criticism levelled at Pius XII.

Catholic Poles in London reported that in the absence of a public protest from the Pope there were serious accusations against the Holy See of pro-German bias, and despair among Catholics in Poland. Pius XII replied that a public protest would only aggravate the suffering, citing what happened when the Dutch Bishops issued a pastoral protesting at Nazi outrages in Holland: Hitler had ordered the arrest of 40,000 Dutchmen and their deportation to concentration camps. He actually drafted a protest but then burnt it, telling his secretary that the Dutch Bishops had caused 40,000 deaths but his protest would cost 200,000. When his secretary advised him to keep the draft as a record, the Pope replied, 'Better not', because the Nazis might penetrate 'here' one day.

The Catholic Bishops inside occupied Poland also counselled prudence. The Pope sent a Father Paganuzzi to Poland (on another Italian army hospital train) with a personal letter to the Archbishop of Cracow (Sapieha) and a large quantity of leaflets printed in the Vatican explaining that although the Holy See was doing all it could for the Polish population, their efforts were brought to nothing by the Nazis. The Archbishop immediately burnt the leaflets, for fear of German reprisals, and wrote back to the Pope that although he was desolated not to be able to distribute them and publish the Pope's letter, to do so would only produce fresh reprisals: the penalty for publishing anything not authorized by the Germans was death. Other letters to the same effect were received at the Vatican.[23]

On 30 April 1943 Pius XII wrote a significant letter to Bishop Preysing in Berlin: 'As far as episcopal declarations are concerned, we leave to local Bishops the responsibility of deciding what to publish from our communication; the danger of reprisals, as well as, perhaps, of other measures, counsels reserve.'[24]

For better or worse, fear of reprisals governed Pius XII's actions during the German occupation of Rome from September 1943 to June 1944.

The persecution of the Roman Jews did not end with the 16 October pogrom. The Fascist *Questore* (Chief of Police) in Rome, Caruso, co-operated enthusiastically with Kappler's minions; by the time of the liberation of Rome by the Allies on 4 June 1944, Caruso had handed over to the Nazis another 1,084 Roman Jews for transportation, in addition to delivering seventy-eight Jews to make up the numbers to 335 for the Ardeatine cave massacre of 28 March 1944. Disregarding the 'sanctuary agreement' between the Germans and the Vatican, Caruso seized six Jews in St Paul's in February 1944, two of whom were Swiss. This produced a sharp protest from Pius XII to the Germans in Rome (he could not complain to Mussolini, because the Vatican did not recognize the Salò Republic). Mussolini duly rebuked Caruso after protests from the Vatican had been received via Spain. However, there is no doubt that Caruso was incited by the Germans to make the St Paul arrests.[25]

Hitler was determined to try to exterminate all Jews in the Fascist-occupied part of Italy. Mussolini had, perforce, to obey his German partner. At the end of November 1943, the Salò Government agreed unenthusiastically to anti-Jewish laws which were far more ferocious than those of 1938. On 1 December all the newspapers and radio stations of the Republic carried the following statement, issued to the press by Buffarini Guidi:

> All Jews living on the national territory are to be arrested no matter what nationality they are. All their goods are to be sequestrated by the State for the benefit of the poor. Those Jews who are of mixed birth will be placed under special surveillance.

Buffarini Guidi deliberately delayed publication of the statement for twenty-four hours after the news had leaked out in order to give as many Jews as possible the chance to flee or go into hiding.[26]

The new Italian laws stipulated that all Jews were to be placed in concentration camps which would be 'specially fitted out' for them (*attrezati*). The main 'specially fitted out' concentration camp at Fossoli near Modena was an arable field with irrigation ditches surrounded by barbed wire and concrete towers for the guards, with only a canal for sewage, and for some weeks hardly any tables or seats. At Trieste the Germans installed their own concentration camp in the rice factory at San Sabba. Several Italian historians claim there was a gas chamber there for the execution of Jews. This is incorrect. When the Allies arrived in Trieste on 2 May 1944, some Jews were found in the camp alive and reasonably well. The Trieste camp was a staging-post for Jews, mainly from Dalmatia and the islands off it, in transit to Dachau after the September 1943 armistice. The large furnace for drying rice had been used to burn the bodies of some partisans whose corpses were brought to San Sabba by lorry.

Thousands of Italian Jews were placed in these and other small camps, from where almost all travelled in cattle trucks to their death at Auschwitz.[27]

In simple and moving language, the Italian writer Primo Levi has related his own experience on a death train from Fossoli to Auschwitz. Because of the racial laws he left his home in Turin and tried, unsuccessfully, to help to set up a group of partisans in the mountains. He was captured in December 1943 by the Fascist militia, and during interrogation admitted he was an Italian Jew. He was immediately sent to Fossoli, which he described as a vast concentration camp for all the categories of Italian people not approved of by the new-born Fascist Republic. Soon, over 600 Italian Jews were held there. On 20 February a detachment of German SS arrived. They 'upbraided' the Italians for deficiencies in the kitchen and the lack of wood for heating, and even said an infirmary should be opened. It was typical of the SS to bother about the efficiency of the camp when they were about to commit an atrocity against the inmates. The next morning they ordered all Jews in the camp to be ready for departure on the following day, with the threat that ten would be shot for every one missing from the roll-call. Levi writes:

> With the absurd precision to which we later had to accustom ourselves, the Germans held the roll-call. At the end the officer asked 'Wieviel Stück?' The corporal saluted smartly and replied that there were six hundred and fifty 'pieces' and all was in order. They then loaded us on to the buses and took us to the station of Carpi where the train was waiting with our escort for the journey. Here we received the first blows: and they were so surprising and senseless that we felt neither physical nor mental pain. Only deep amazement that any man can hit another without being angry.
>
> There were twelve goods wagons for six hundred and fifty men; in mine we were only forty-five, but it was a small wagon. Here then, before our very eyes, under our very feet, was one of those notorious transport trains, those which never return, and of which, shuddering and incredulous, we had so often heard, exactly as we had been told they were – goods wagons closed from the outside, with men, women and children pressed together without pity, like cheap merchandise, for a journey towards nothingness, a journey towards the bottom. This time the wagons are for us.
>
> It was the discomfort, the blows, the cold, the thirst that kept our spirits up in the void of bottomless despair during the journey and after. It was not the will to live, nor conscious resignation, for few men are capable of such resolution, and we were only an ordinary sample of humans.
>
> The doors had been closed at once, but the train did not move until evening. We had learnt of our destination with relief. Auschwitz was a name without significance for us at that time, but it at least implied some place on this earth.
>
> The train travelled slowly with long, unnerving halts. Through the slit we saw the tall pale cliffs of the Adige Valley and the names of the last Italian

cities disappear behind us. We passed the Brenner at midday of the second day and everyone stood up, but no one said a word, and I looked around and wondered how many, among that poor human dust, would be struck by fate. Among the forty-five people in my wagon only four saw their homes again; and it was by far the most fortunate wagon.

We suffered from thirst and cold; at every stop we clamoured for water, or even a handful of snow, but we were rarely heard; the soldiers of the escort drove off anybody who tried to approach. Two young mothers, nursing their children, groaned night and day, begging for water. Our nervous tension made the hunger, exhaustion and lack of sleep seem less of a torment. But the hours of darkness were nightmares without end. Then someone would light a candle, and its mournful flicker would reveal an obscure movement, a human mass, extended across the floor, confused and continuous, sluggish and aching, rising here and there in sudden convulsions and immediately collapsing again in exhaustion.

Through the slit, known and unknown names of Austrian cities, Salzburg, Vienna, then Czech, finally Polish names. On the evening of the fourth day the cold became intense: the train ran through interminable black pine forests, climbing slowly. The snow was high. During the halts, no one tried any longer to communicate with the outside world; we felt ourselves by now 'on the other side'. There was a long halt in open country. The train started up extremely slowly and the convoy stopped for the last time, in the dead of night, in the middle of the dark, silent plain.

On both sides of the track rows of red and white lights stretched as far as the eye could see; but there were none of those mingled noises which indicate inhabited places even from afar. By the wretched light of the last candle, with the rhythm of the wheels, with every human sound silenced, we waited for what was to happen.

The climax came suddenly. The door opened with a crash, and the dark echoed with outlandish orders in that curt, barbaric barking of Germans in command with which they give vent to a millennial anger. A vast platform appeared before us, brightly lit, a little beyond it, a row of lorries. Then everything went silent again. Someone translated; we had to climb down with our luggage and deposit it alongside the train. In a moment the platform was swarming with shadows. But we were afraid to break that silence; everyone busied himself with his luggage, searched for someone else, called timidly, in whispers.

A dozen SS men stood around, legs akimbo, with an air of indifference. At a certain moment they moved among us, and in a low tone of voice, with faces of stone, began to interrogate us rapidly, one by one, in bad Italian. How old? Healthy or ill? And on the basis of the reply they pointed in two different directions.[28]

A few 'healthy' young men, including Primo Levi, were taken in lorries to the 'work' part of Auschwitz. Levi and a tiny fraction of the 'healthy' who survived disgusting brutalities, hardship and starvation at the hands of the Nazis at Auschwitz, returned to Italy after the war to reveal the loathsome story. The remainder, separated by the blows of the guards, were hurried off and pushed into the gas chambers.

Buffarini Guidi, at the Ministry of the Interior, knew exactly what was happening. He was described in a British Foreign Office briefing on the Salò Government as 'not being unduly severe with anti-Fascists'. Buffarini was appalled at the inhuman treatment meted out by the Nazis to his fellow countrymen, and in vain implored Mussolini to intervene. The Duce knew he was powerless; his inability to aid Italian Jews and prevent the insensate slaughter added to his melancholy and frustration, because it proved he ruled the Salò Republic in name only. The Jewish pogrom increased his apathy. Still, it must be remembered that in November 1938 Mussolini had expressed warm approval to Hitler of Kristallnacht, the hideous outrage against the Berlin Jews. Then, Mussolini had been at his peak of admiration for Hitler personally and for Nazi foreign policy; by November 1943 he had travelled a long way in the opposite direction.[29]

On 4 January 1944 the Salò Government at German insistence passed a further law sequestrating all the wealth and assets of Jews. However, on 20 January Buffarini Guidi protested to the Germans against the 'illegal' deportation of Italian Jews, and asked the Italian commandants of concentration camps not to hand over Jewish internees to the SS, and on 19 March he asked heads of provinces not to deprive Jews of all their means of living. Mussolini also instructed Anfuso in Berlin that the Embassy must intervene on behalf of deported Italian Jews. The Nazis were intransigent and these efforts were abortive.[30]

Eichmann sent his extermination experts, Frederick Bosshammer and Theodor Dannecker, to Milan to carry out the arrests. Mussolini and Buffarini claimed that under Italian law all Jewish members of mixed families and those over 70 were exempt. This was hotly disputed by Bosshammer, who provided the staff and guards for the camps. Numerous claims for release of Jews married to Aryans were made by the Fascist prefects to the Germans but few were granted. Bosshammer complained to Mussolini that the Salò laws were not rigid enough, and demanded that the definition of a Jew should be the same as in Germany and include even baptized Christians.

In January 1944 Hitler forced Mussolini to make the poisonous Giovanni Preziosi Minister for Jewish affairs at Salò. He had been violently anti-Semitic since before the First World War, and had spent many years in Nazi circles in Germany where he was well known to Hitler. A fellow member of Mussolini's Salò Cabinet has described Preziosi as 'a single-minded racist and mad hater of Jews with a complete obsession about the need to exterminate all Jews in Italy.'[31]

Preziosi was a defrocked priest who had been a well-known Naples journalist. His only merit in Mussolini's eyes was his personal influence with Hitler. Although at one time he had subsidized an anti-Semitic periodical of Preziosi's, Mussolini described him as 'repulsive, a real figure of a defrocked priest'. Preziosi's behaviour towards the Italian Jews amply justifies Mussolini's description. Preziosi and Buffarini Guidi hated one another and were always at daggers drawn.[32]

Preziosi wrote to Hitler with hysterical accusations that other members of Mussolini's Cabinet were pro-Jewish; with Bosshammer's help, he extended the pogrom to cover the aged and the sick, even combing out monasteries, hospitals and lunatic asylums for Jews, so that geriatrics and the insane arrived at the concentration camps.

When Preziosi was told of his appointment to the Salò Cabinet as Inspector for Race, he wrote to Mussolini from Munich:

> How can we pretend that we have a solid front with Germany when within our ranks there is anyone who has a drop – even a single drop of Jewish blood? History tells us that whoever has one drop of Jewish blood in his veins is part of the race. In Italy we look on half-Jews as non-Jews and good Italians. The most dangerous Jews are the one-quarter aryanized ones who shelter behind our inadequate racial laws.

He went on that nothing would 'do' except the complete extermination of all Italian Jews, and that anyone with a drop of Jewish blood must be rooted out of public life – from the army, the judiciary and all municipal and state office. He also fulminated against Freemasonry, and told Mussolini that throughout the 22 years of Fascist rule, Masons and Jews had combined to throw 'mud' at Fascism.[33]

This ridiculous letter from an obvious maniac and fanatic would have left Mussolini unmoved but for the fact that Preziosi had the ear of Hitler, and unless Mussolini pandered to him would denigrate all the members of the Salò Government and make it seem even less worthwhile in Hitler's eyes.

In May 1944 Preziosi submitted to Mussolini a memorandum proposing new laws against the Jews on the lines of the Nuremberg laws of 1935; his aim was 'to eliminate from Italian public life all Jewish blood'. The historian Professor Stephen Roberts has correctly described the Nuremberg laws as creating 'a class of helots in Germany', and as 'prostitution of a legal system in the service of an insane racial prejudice'. Once the Nazis had passed the Nuremberg laws, a German Jew had no civil rights; he was not a citizen; he could not vote or attend a political meeting; he had no liberty of speech; he could not become a civil servant or judge, a writer or publisher, and was barred from nearly every occupation for the educated. Mussolini, while paying lip-service to Hitler's anti-Semitism, at no time wanted such intolerance in Italy.

Buffarini Guidi minuted to Mussolini: 'Such laws would be an aberration. Preziosi wants to create Jews so that he can enjoy persecuting them.' Mussolini agreed with Buffarini Guidi and ignored Preziosi, so that no further anti-Jewish laws were passed at Salò until 16 April 1945, by which time the impotent Italian Social Republic hardly existed.[34]

Fortunately, in Mussolini's Republic the sympathy of the population lay with the Jews, and the majority of civil servants and local government officers were opposed to persecution. However, Italy was an occupied country; and although Dannecker was short of soldiers, he was nevertheless able to force the subservient Fascist police to carry out the arrests, although they often tried not to co-operate.

Bernard Berenson, the art historian, noted in his diary in November 1943 that masses of Jews were in hiding and that the Fascist prefect of Florence, 'the moment he was installed, warned Jews to leave their homes and go into hiding'. In December Berenson noted, 'The prefect is beside himself and threatens to resign if the executions are insisted on.'[35]

Thanks to the tolerance of the Fascist police and frontier guards, several hundred Jews escaped over the frontier into Switzerland, while many more joined the partisan resistance movement in the hills. The Nazis offered rewards for the disclosure of the hiding places of Jews, and a few Italians, activated by either greed or racism, denounced their Jewish fellow citizens. Notorious in Rome was a Jewess, Celeste di Porto, known as Black Panther, who betrayed to the Nazis the whereabouts of 50 Roman Jews, including 26 who later died in the Ardeatine massacre.[36]

The President of the Jewish community in Venice, Giuseppe Jona, was visited by an emissary of Bosshammer who demanded a list of all the 2,000 Jews living there. Jona asked him to return the next day, and during the night warned his fellow Jews to go into hiding. He then destroyed all the lists and committed suicide.

Iris Origo wrote in her diary on 28 November about the 'Jew hunt' in Florence. 'Last night they searched even the convents, hunting out and capturing the poor wretches who had taken refuge there including even a two-month baby deserted by its panic-stricken mother. A new law has now declared all Jews to be enemy aliens.' She also noted that there had been two corpses on the death train from Rome when it arrived at Padua.[37]

When at the end of November 1943 Mussolini, in obedience to Hitler's wishes, had initiated further laws against the Jews, Bosshammer told his superiors in Berlin that 'the final solution' of the Italian Jewish problem was 'within easy reach'. Eight months later he reported to Berlin that the liquidation of Italian Jewry was not 'a practical proposition' because of the lack of co-operation from Italian Fascists. Mussolini frequently protested to the Germans against the sequestration of Jewish property, and in the Government only Preziosi wholeheartedly endorsed Nazi policy.

The leading authority on the German persecution of Italian Jews, Meir Michaelis, believes four-fifths of Italian Jews alive in Italy and Rhodes on 8 September 1943 (including foreigners) survived, despite the frenzied efforts of Dannecker, Bosshammer and Preziosi; he calculates that, out of 32,000 Italian Jews and 12,500 foreigners, 7,682 perished. There were 8,369 deportees, of whom only 979 returned home, including one baby born at Belsen. Some 415 Jews survived imprisonment in Italy, including 95 who escaped – some on their way to the death camps.[38]

If Mussolini had allowed the Nazis to have their way, a high proportion of Italian Jews would have perished. One redeeming feature of the Salò Republic was this attempt to thwart the Nazi effort to exterminate Italian Jews. However, it was the Italian people themselves who saved the majority of Italian Jews from death at the hands of the Nazis, risking their own lives to help them hide and flee.

CHAPTER 4

Kesselring's Atrocities

ON 23 JANUARY 1944 when the Allies landed at Anzio, on the coast thirty-three miles south of Rome, they sent radio calls to the partisans asking them to sabotage German lines of communication and 'to strike against him everywhere'. The Germans forced the landing troops back into the beachhead, so hastily-laid partisan plans for widespread attacks were put into cold storage. However, the leaders of the old political parties, who had met and formed the Junta at Bari in January 1944, were impatient for action by Italian patriots, and in March they called on freedom volunteers to fight until 'all of Italy is liberated'. Right-wing members of the Badoglio Government did not approve, claiming it was wiser to 'express one's anti-Fascism by carrying out intelligence for the Allies and fighting the Nazis with a clandestine press'. Around Rome, anti-Fascists responded to the Junta appeal by making attacks on petrol and ammunition dumps and shooting isolated groups of German soldiers.

Pope Pius XII was strongly opposed to the belligerent tactics of the Junta. He wanted Rome to be 'an open city' and after the German occupation Weizsäcker, the Nazi Ambassador to the Holy See, had encouraged this idea, telling his Holiness (with Ribbentrop's approval) that 'the sovereignty and territorial integrity of the Vatican will be respected and . . . furthermore the Germans undertake to conduct themselves in such a way as to protect Vatican City from the fighting.'

The Allies refused to entertain the idea of Rome being an 'open city', for the reason that almost all the German military supplies to both the Anzio and Cassino fronts were passing through the capital by rail and road. The Pope turned a blind eye to the fact that Rome was the focal point of the German lines of supply.

The Nazis were enforcing a harsh regime on the citizens of Rome. A curfew was imposed, with the risk of the death penalty for those who disobeyed it; many able-bodied young men were rounded up and sent to work inside Germany. The Pope did not oppose these police measures; instead, he tried to comfort his flock with soup kitchens and food supplies.

In March 1944, 'open city' was a meaningless German propaganda phrase. The British and Americans would not give 'open city' status to Rome while German rail and road convoys passed through it, and ignored the Pope's angry protests when bombs aimed at German convoys killed civilians. The Swiss correspondent of the *New York Times* reported that 'all through the hours of darkness an unending stream of tanks, motorized artillery and lorries loaded with munitions passed through Rome, and the Americans were continuously machine-gunning the roads north and south of the capital.'[1]

Partisans in Rome planned an attack on German soldiers inside the city. Each day a company of the 3rd battalion SS Police Regiment under General Wolff paraded flamboyantly through the centre of Rome, in flagrant breach of the Germans' 'open city' proclamation. The partisans knew the role of this regiment was to provide manpower for repressive police measures against the Romans; they had the reputation of being 'notoriously cruel', and were described by a Swiss observer as behaving in Italy as in Russia.

The Rome partisan commander, Carlo Salinari, had a watch kept on this daily German parade and organized a heavy bomb attack on the German soldiers as they marched up Via Rasella in the centre of the city on 23 March 1944. Courageous patriots let off bombs in the Via Rasella which killed 32 German SS soldiers and wounded many others. All the conspirators escaped.

Hitler ordered fifty Italians to be killed for each dead German; only with difficulty was he persuaded to reduce this to ten for one. His orders were brutally carried out with the murder of 335 Romans in the Ardeatine caves on the southern periphery of Rome hours after the bomb attack. Italians will never forgive the perpetrators of this nightmare atrocity. Field Marshal Kesselring was in overall command in the theatre; when Jodl, Hitler's Chief of Staff, told him of the Führer's decision, Kesselring agreed that he must 'achieve a deterrent effect', and issued an order to the Commander of 14th Army, General von Mackensen, to 'Kill ten Italians for every German. Carry out immediately.' These orders were handed down to Herbert Kappler, head of the Gestapo in Rome, by General Mältzer, the German Commandant of Rome – a drunkard.[2]

A story has been fabricated that Eugen Dollmann, an interpreter and an intimate of Hitler, who was Himmler's personal representative in Rome, asked the Pope to intervene in an attempt to prevent the massacre; it is said that at 6 p.m. on 23 March Dollmann talked to Pancrazio Pfeiffer, Abbot of the Salvatorian monastery and the Pope's unofficial liaison officer with the Germans. Dollmann claimed that he urgently pressed Pfeiffer to persuade the Pope to intervene, hoping to avoid an immediate and bloody revenge in the belief that, if only the massacre could be delayed, second thoughts might prevail at Hitler's headquarters. Late in life, after he had published his memoirs, Dolmann claimed that he had suggested to Pfeiffer an alternative plan, by which all the families of the Germans killed in Via Rasella would be flown to Rome to join in a solemn funeral procession across the city while the bells of all four hundred Roman churches tolled. The only penalty would be that the city of Rome would pay compensation to the families of the Via Rasella victims. Pfeiffer, according to Dollmann, agreed to put the plan to the Pope, while Dollmann himself suggested it to Wolff and Himmler for onward transmission to Hitler. Dollmann declared that the Pope refused to act on this suggestion.

In his book *Death in Rome* Robert Katz, an American historian of German Jewish descent, accepts the Dollmann story as true, and makes out a case that Pius XII maintained an absolute silence, both over the Ardeatine massacre and over the deportation of the Jews. Katz was sued for defamation by Pius XII's niece, and an Italian court gave him a suspended sentence of thirteen months' imprisonment.[3]*

Kappler had told Kesselring that he could find 320 hostages who had already been condemned to death, but when he examined his records he found there were only three, although several hundreds more were under arrest on suspicion of anti-German activities. Working all night, Kappler could produce only 270 names of Italians under German arrest, and he had to ask the Italian Fascist Police Chief, Caruso, for another 50. Buffarini Guidi, Mussolini's Minister of the Interior, was in Rome and authorized Caruso to comply. In his post-war trial, Kappler related all these details with scrupulous accuracy.

By midday on 24 March, a list of 320 prisoners had been drawn up, for execution the same day. Staff officers in Mältzer's headquarters refused to take responsibility for carrying out the atrocity, and Kappler was forced to use his own Gestapo. He had twelve officers and sixty-one men available. The Gestapo officers organized a mass execution in the large Ardeatine caves, which it was planned would be sealed off afterwards by German engineers. Another German soldier died of wounds received in the Via Rasella bombing, and on his own responsibility Kappler coolly added ten innocent Jews to the death list without consulting Kesselring.

On 24 March, lorry after lorry brought Italians from the Regina Coeli prison to the Ardeatine caves. At the trials of his colleagues Mältzer and von Mackensen, Kappler gave evidence that with hands tied behind their

---

*To his indignation, Katz even subpoenaed the Jesuit Vatican historian Robert Graham as a defence witness.

backs the victims were ordered to walk in and kneel. Then they were killed by revolver shots through the neck. There were so many corpses that the last arrivals were forced to clamber over the pile of dead. Kappler gave evidence that after the massacre he told his men to get drunk on brandy because they were so shocked by what they had done, and that he shot many Italians with his own hand to encourage the others to do the same. Hearing the cries of other victims before their own death added to the cruelty of the massacre. In an affidavit for Kesselring's trial, Kappler described in matter-of-fact language how 'in a companionable way' he led a German private by the arm into the cave 'where together they executed Italians' – a strange example of German companionship.[4] The matter-of-fact language makes the horror even more nauseating. It is clear the victims were given no opportunity to see a priest or make other arrangements:

At about 1400 hours the first transports began to move and I, and a number of my men, went to the cave. As each truck arrived at the cave the persons concerned, always five at a time and each accompanied by an SS man, were led to the end of the cave. All persons had their hands tied behind their backs. At the end of the cave five were made to kneel down together, and at the given order they were shot in the back of the head by the accompanying SS men at short range. The next five were shot by officers, and I was one of these officers. After the execution of each five, the five SS men went to the exit and in the meantime, another five SS men brought in the next five victims. After I had fired my shot I went out and controlled the following: Priebke's checking of the lists; the preparations for the engineers to blow up the cave; and the measures for cordoning the area. I then drove back to my headquarters and returned to the cave at about 1800 hours.

I found on arrival that Hauptsturmführer Wotjan had not yet fired a shot. I spoke to him in a comradely manner and went into the cave with him to fire another shot at his side and at the same time as he.

I had not yet received Caruso's list and sent Obersturmführer Tunath to his office, so that he could assist Caruso in speeding up the transport of the persons listed by Caruso himself.

The execution was over at about 2030 hours. I left the cave before the end of the execution at about 1900 hours.

... The measures as such I thought justified at the time and still do so now according to the laws of war ... I have lately had doubts.[5]

At the post-war trial of Kesselring, Kappler also stated in his evidence that when Wolff arrived in Rome on the evening of 24 March 1944 he warned that the killing of 320 Italians was not 'enough': that he wanted, like Himmler, to blow up the slum quarters of Rome where the 'Comunisti' lived. Kesselring's staff were consulted and reported that the deportation to concentration camps of the populations of San Lorenzo,

Tiburtino and Testaccio would need two divisions of soldiers, who could not possibly be made available. However, Wolff told the Enquiry into the Beatification of Pius XII in April 1974 that he had always wanted to treat the Italians 'with a light hand' (*mano leggero*), and that he went to Rome on 24 March to try to stop harsh measures of reprisal. But as Wolff was operating directly under Himmler, who wanted even more drastic reprisals, Kappler's evidence seems plausible.

On 24 March, Pius XII seemed to be more concerned about the presence of armed Communists in Rome than about reprisals; he had convinced himself (falsely) that the Via Rasella bombs were the work of Communists. He wrote a short piece for the Vatican newspaper *Osservatore* asking for no 'ill-judged violence', because those who had to maintain public order would react 'with a series of painful reprisals which cannot be estimated.' Obviously he had no idea of the extent of the atrocity planned by the Nazis.

The Germans wanted to keep the site of the killings a secret, but at the same time to advertise the shootings as a deterrent to the partisans. A press statement was issued while the shootings were in progress on 24 March to the effect that on 23 March thirty-two Germans had been killed and others wounded by 'a vile ambush carried out by the *Comunisti-Badogliani* . . . The German command has therefore ordered that for every murdered German ten *Comunisti-Badogliani* criminals be shot. This order has already been executed.'

The Nazis knew there was widespread fear in Rome that the Communists would take over the city after the Germans left, so to couple Communists with Badoglio was cunning. The partisans issued their own communiqué, claiming that their actions were

> legitimate and real acts of war aimed exclusively at German and Fascist military objectives which contributed to saving the capital from aerial bombardments, destruction and casualties . . . The 320 Italians massacred by the Germans cry for revenge. It will be pitiless and terrible . . . Patriotic and partisan guerrilla actions in Rome will not cease until the city is totally evacuated by the Germans.

The Pope's reaction was disappointing. He was the Bishop of Rome and an unthinkable crime had been committed against his flock. The victims were not Communists, but ordinary citizens of Rome, and the Vatican knew this perfectly well. Pius XII himself appeared neutral – or almost on the Nazi side – writing in the *Osservatore Romano* on 26 March:

> Thirty-two victims on the one hand, and on the other three hundred and twenty persons sacrificed for the guilty parties who escaped arrest . . . we call upon the irresponsible elements to respect human life . . .

This almost insinuates that the partisans were the guilty ones, responsible for the deaths of the 320 Roman citizens. Of course, it was not until the morning of 25 March that Pius XII learnt the details of the massacre; not only was it too late to prevent it, but Weizsäcker was impressing on the Pope the ever-present danger that Hitler might violate the extraterritorial convents and monastries and capture the refugees in them.

Mussolini was horrified when he learnt of the Ardeatine massacre, and ordered the release of all political prisoners not accused of murder, to prevent them being seized by the Germans. The Fascist Prefect of Police, Botoli, responsible for carrying out the releases, ran into considerable trouble because the SS had infiltrated the Fascist police.[6]

Consul Filippo de Grenet, a young Italian diplomat, was one of those shot in the Ardeatine caves. He had been arrested and held in Regina Coeli prison on suspicion of co-operating with pro-Badoglio elements, but no charges had been made against him. He was a friend of Mazzolini, Mussolini's Foreign Minister, and Alberto Mellini, another diplomat at Salò. Mazzolini made a furious protest to Rahn about the massacre. According to Mellini, de Grenet's Foreign Office colleagues in Rome were so shocked that they refused to go to Salò. De Grenet's execution led Mazzolini to alert Mussolini, and hence to the Duce's order for the release of all political prisoners.[7]

Two Italians took an active part in the massacre. They were Pietro Caruso, the Fascist *Questore* of Rome, and Lieutenant Pietro Koch, who headed a vicious squad of Italian SS. As we have seen, at Kappler's request Caruso actually produced a list of 50 extra Roman civilians to be added to Kappler's.[8]

The Fascist *Giornale d'Italia* produced an article by its director stating that all those killed in the Ardeatine massacre had taken part in the Via Rasella attack, and that the shooting of hostages was justifiable by a 'strict and severe application of the laws of war'. *Il Messagero* called the Ardeatine atrocity 'reasonable German justice', and stated that the British and Americans were encouraging irresponsible elements to organize terrorism in the city. *La Fascista* wrote that '32 soldiers of the Reich who belonged to the police forces helping to keep Rome peaceful tragically lost their lives in the most ferocious attack'. The clandestine press told the Romans the truth: 'From the grave where the bodies of the unavenged martyrs lie, a solemn imperative cry goes out: "Fight for the Italy which they nobly have consecrated with their blood."'

It was impossible to keep the site of the atrocity secret. A peasant herding his pigs on the hill above the caves had seen the victims being forced into the caves and heard the shots; he informed his parish priest, Don Camarotta, who went to the entrance and prayed, giving 'conditional absolution'. With two other priests, Don Michele Valentini and

Don Ferdinando Georgi, Camarotta entered the caves on 27 March. They could not reach the bodies, but found a horrible stench of putrefaction. On the 30th, with the help of youths, the three priests found a hole and stumbled over the decaying corpses. They immediately notified Monsignor Respighi, a Vatican official. The next morning Respighi sent for Valentini and told him the Vicariate (the office of the Pope as Bishop of Rome) would be informed at once of what had been found at the Ardeatine caves. Respighi spoke to a high official in the Vatican and asked if the Holy See could make diplomatic representations so that the victims could have proper burial. The Pope did not respond.

Meanwhile, many Romans, guessing that members of their families under arrest who were now missing had been murdered, made pilgrimages to the caves and left wreaths of flowers. The Germans sent soldiers to block the hole, and orderd Don Georgi's arrest – about which the Vatican made no complaint.

After the war a small group of relatives of the victims, encouraged by neo-Fascists, filed a civil action against the leaders of the partisan forces responsible for the Via Rasella bombs. They got nowhere. The Supreme Court declared that Rome was never an 'open city' because of the large German concentrations there, and that the Via Rasella attack was 'an act of war' committed at a time when Rome was only a few miles from the battle front. The Court concluded that 'every attack against the Germans was a response to appeals from the legitimate Government . . . and thereby constituted an act of war.' Through their organization ANFIM (National Association of Italian Families of the Martyrs), most of the families of the Ardeatine victims maintained a close association with the leading Rome partisans.[9]

Von Mackensen and Mältzer were tried before a British military court martial in Rome in November 1946. Their principal defence witness was Kesselring; the prosecution's, strangely enough, was Kappler. The defence claimed that Kappler had completely misled von Mackensen and Mältzer by pretending he held enough prisoners under sentence of death to make up a list of 320. Both von Mackensen and Mältzer pleaded that Hitler's order for the reprisal was justified, and disclaimed all knowledge of how the executions were carried out. Defence Counsel contended that the reprisal was legal. They were found guilty and sentenced to be shot, but this was commuted to life imprisonment. Mältzer died in prison, but von Mackensen was released in 1952.[10]

In May 1948 Kappler and five of his staff were tried by Italians before the Rome Military Tribunal, charged with homicide and with provoking 'with premeditation' the deaths of 335 persons. The Tribunal sentenced Kappler to life imprisonment – the severest penalty possible under the laws of the new Italian Republic. His five co-defendants were acquitted. Kappler was asked whether he had appealed to the actual bombers to surrender. He replied, 'I had neither authority nor time to make such an appeal.' There is evidence that Hitler soon lost interest in the Via Rasella incident, which perhaps supports the claim that, if the Pope had intervened and secured a postponement, the barbarity might have been avoided. However, the Holy See described the events as 'the double massacre of the Via Rasella and of Le Fosse Ardeatine'. Today, controversy still rages in Italy as to whether the Via Rasella attack was, or was not, a potent blow against the German army of occupation. Kappler was never reprieved, but he was released because of ill-health in 1979, twelve months before his death.

The evidence showed that it was Kesselring who gave the order to the SS to execute ten Italians for every German killed in the Via Rasella. He stated in evidence that he had been under the impression that only Italians already sentenced to death would be killed; he admitted in cross-examination that he had made no enquiries to ascertain whether he had confirmed death sentences on as many as 320. It was implausible for him to claim that he believed 320 had been condemned to death, because he had previously reserved to himself the right to confirm all death sentences passed by military courts on Italian nationals. Kappler strongly denied that he had told Kesselring he had 320 prisoners condemned to death, because the actual number was only three.

At Kesselring's rear headquarters was his legal expert, General Richter Keller, a judge; Kesselring never consulted Keller about the Ardeatine executions, and ordered the formation under his command to carry out the massacre without enquiring about its legality in international law. The prosecutor at Kesselring's trial said that Kesselring was happy to let 'the black sheep of the German army [the SS] do his dirty work for him; it was the dirtiest bit of work.' It is impossible to disagree.

Kesselring, like Kappler, took no steps to enquire whether the perpetrators of the bomb attack had been arrested, so that they might be punished instead of the hostages. In such a case, Hitler might have countermanded his 'ten for one' order. Instead, Kesselring condoned Kappler's rough-and-ready methods of obtaining 320 Romans for execution without enquiring whether or not there was any hope of catching the partisans responsible. Kesselring admitted that he took no measures to ensure that his order was humanely carried out.

At the British court martial in Rome of Mältzer and von Mackensen, the defence claimed that these generals had tried to find the partisans responsible for the bombs and had issued a statement on Rome Radio asking the perpetrators to give themselves up so as to spare others from execution as a reprisal. This is untrue. No such appeal was made on the evening of the 24th. Rosario Bentivegna, the chief organizer of the Via Rasella bombing, said in 1982 when asked if he would have given himself up: 'With hindsight I say No . . . but then, in the heat of the moment, I do not know what I would have done. Perhaps with my comrades I would have organized some armed operation to stop the massacre. We would have come forward armed and determined to sell our skins as dearly as possible.' Antonello Tombadori, Bentivegna's chief collaborator, said in 1981 that he would have been in a dilemma if such an appeal had been made.[11]

The only way in which Kesselring and his fellow German commanders could have aborted Hitler's orders for the massacre would have been by capturing and punishing the partisans responsible for the attack. They made little effort to do so, and instead mollified Hitler by obediently carrying out his order for immediate reprisals.

Kesselring was charged before the British court martial, not only with the Ardeatine cave massacre, but also with 'inciting and commanding German troops to kill Italian civilians as reprisals in violation of the laws and usages of war'.

On 17 June, as partisan threats to the Germans escalated, Kesselring had issued a vicious order:

> The fight against the partisans must be carried on with all means at our disposal and with utmost severity [complete sentence underlined by Kesselring]. *I will protect any commander who exceeds our usual restraint in the choice and severity of the methods he adopts against partisans* [author's italics]. In this connection the principle holds good that a mistake in the choice of methods in executing one's orders is better than failure or neglect to act.

What Kesselring meant by 'our usual restraint' is vague. If killing ten innocent Italians in Rome for every German killed in March 1944 was 'usual German restraint', one's mind boggles at what Kesselring now envisaged.

On 1 July Kesselring issued further orders, calculated to worsen the atrocities: 'Every act of violence committed by partisans must be punished immediately . . . Wherever there is evidence of considerable numbers of partisan groups a proportion of the male population will be shot.' Under the heading 'Killing of hostages' Kesselring ordered: 'The population must be informed of this. Should troops be fired at from any village the village will be burnt down. Perpetrators or the ringleaders will be hanged in public.' Kesselring in effect gave *carte blanche* to German subordinate commanders to commit atrocities, and promised to protect them if they went too far. He is not the first commander of an occupying army to have done so.[12]

It must be admitted that the British gave a certain provocation to Kesselring. In broadcasts by the BBC to Italy on 19, 20 and 27 June 1944, Field Marshal Alexander asked the partisans to shoot German soldiers in the back. The broadcasts included the phrases 'kill all German soldiers who are left in the rear . . . Act in the same way as the patriots of Teramo.' (At Teramo, the patriots had killed a number of German soldiers who had been cut off from their companions.) On 27 June Alexander broadcast the order, 'Patriots of Siena, attack the enemy from the rear while we attack him from the front and from the air . . . let your activities be such as to make travelling by road in cars or motor-cycles death for the enemy.' Kesselring replied in a broadcast that he regretted the 'immense grief which would be caused to Italian families who are without blame, following our reprisals. However, as the responsible chief I can no longer hesitate to prevent by the most repressive means this utterly despicable and mediaeval method of fighting. I give warning that I shall use these means forthwith.' When this was reported to the Foreign Office in London, Archibald Ross minuted: 'It looks as if General Alexander was not quite careful enough in his choice of words, and the Germans have not unduly distorted his appeal.'[13]

Badoglio also got onto dangerous ground in a broadcast from Bari in which he ordered partisans to attack German Command Headquarters and small centres – 'Kill the Germans from behind in order to escape their retaliation and thus kill even more.' Kesselring's counsel quoted this in defence at his post-war trial.

By the end of July Kesselring's orders were:

1. Captured partisans [*francs-tireurs*] are not prisoners of war, and will be shot on the spot. [An attempt by the Red Cross to have Italian partisans classified as regular soldiers and not *francs-tireurs* came to nothing.]
2. Civilians will also be shot who:
   a) supply partisans with i) Food, ii) Shelter, iii) Military information [spying];
   b) carry arms (including hunting weapons), ammunition, explosives, or any other war *matériel*, or hide such, or who do not immediately report to German authorities weapons, ammunition, etc., concealed by others;
   c) commit hostile acts of any kind against the German Armed Forces (particularly tyre and communication wire sabotage);
   d) plunder.
3. i) Where partisan bands operate in large numbers, hostages (preferably relatives of partisans or able-bodied sympathizers) are to be taken first from the population of the district in which they appear. In the case of brutal attacks these men will be shot. This fact will be made known to the population when the hostages are arrested.

    ii) If soldiers and others are shot at from any locality, the village will be burnt to the ground. Culprits or leaders will be hanged in public. Orders for the burning of villages and individual buildings can be given only by officers down to and including battalion commanders. *If German soldiers fall victims to attacks by civilians, up to 10 able-bodied Italians will be shot for each German killed* [author's italics].

4. Battle against partisans must always be conducted with utmost vigour. A mistake in the choice of means is always better than omission or negligence. Only immediate vigorous action serves as warning, and nips large outbreaks in the bud.

5. All civilians captured in battles with partisans and in the course of the reprisals will be sent to collecting centres for transfer to the Reich as labourers.[14]

On August 9, the commander of 118 Grenadier Regiment at Ravenna interpreted Kesselring's order as: 'When the actual criminals could not be found, hostages were to be taken and an appropriate number shot ... if crimes of exceptional violence are committed, especially against German soldiers, an appropriate number of hostages will be hanged. In such cases the whole population of the place will be assembled to witness the execution. After the bodies have been left hanging for twelve hours the public will be ordered to bury them without ceremony and without the assistance of any priest.'[15]

With his 'ten civilians for one German', Kesselring was authorizing atrocities on the scale of the Ardeatine cave massacre. Following this licence to kill, atrocity after atrocity occurred in an effort to wipe out the partisan threat. These became so frequent and well-known that Mussolini intervened. In a letter to Rahn in the middle of August he emphasized that punitive operations were being carried out indiscriminately against the local population, and not against the partisans themselves. The Duce's letter gave details of atrocities carried out by Germans against Italian civilians, including one at Borgo Ticino (Novara) where after four German soldiers had been wounded by unknown people, thirteen Italian civilians were rounded up and shot; 'the village was then evacuated and part destroyed by explosive'. Mussolini gave eleven examples of similar brutality, including the atrocity at Torelino near Udine where after a fire fight between the German troops and partisans, 32 civilians who had no connection with the partisans were machine-gunned to death, including women and children. This type of German behaviour was made inevitable by Kesselring's inflammatory orders. At Kesselring's trial it was proved beyond doubt that 1,000 Italians, including women and children, had been killed without trial of any kind. Even this must be far below the true total.

On August 21 Kesselring issued orders to all his commanders, sending a copy to Rahn to show to the Duce:

... Some incidents have occurred within the last few weeks which caused the greatest harm to the dignity and discipline of the German armed forces ... the Duce has complained bitterly to Dr Rahn about the method of execution of various ops against partisans and punitive measures which lately have been conducted against the local population and not against the partisans proper. The result has been that the confidence in the German Armed Forces has been gravely undermined, gained us new enemies and assisted the enemy's propaganda. The principle must be that all measures are to be taken against the actual partisans and not the innocent civilian population. I appeal herewith to the sense of responsibility of the various leaders ... The partisans are to be proceeded against with all possible means; in the case of unjustified attacks on the civilian population I shall however bring to justice the responsible persons unrelentingly.

This was hypocrisy on Kesselring's part. He had no intention of punishing German commanders who committed excesses; the Prosecutor at his trial pointed out that no examples of 'where Italians had been killed improperly' were given, nor was there any evidence of disciplinary action being taken.[16]

During Kesselring's trial, his astute defence lawyers tried to shift the guilt for the major atrocities onto the Waffen SS, by alleging that they were independent of Kesselring. Their commander, General Max Simon, contradicted this allegation at his own trial:

I cannot understand Kesselring's remark at his trial that 'If he made enquiries about SS officers the iron curtain came down.' I got my orders for everything from Army Corps [i.e., Kesselring] and only on personal matters and jurisdiction did I get orders from the SS Supreme Command in Berlin or their main office in Munich.[17]

A teleprint from Keitel, passing on Hitler's order of 1 May 1944 to the effect that Kesselring was 'in supreme command' of operations against partisans, was produced at Kesselring's trial. Kesselring had demanded a specific order from Hitler that SS and police were subordinated to him for 'anti-partisan warfare', because Himmler had opposed giving him authority over the SS.

At his own trial, General Simon said that he understood Kesselring's order of 17 June to mean

... all means at our disposal. I interpreted 'I will protect any commanders' to mean the door was locked for such officers who in the event exceeded their responsibility. The old principle of a greater scale gave me a clue to the first two sentences quoted.[18]

The behaviour of the Waffen SS under General Simon was horrific. On

12 August at St Anna di Stazema in Lucchese, an SS Major Walter Reder was responsible for killing 360 civilians; then, crossing the Apennines, he caused a further 107 to be put to death at Valla and a further 53 hostages at San Terenzo. On 24 August, assisted by the Fascist Black Brigade, the SS burnt Vinca to the ground and assassinated 108 partisans. On 16 September they destroyed Bergola with great loss of life. Between 29 September and 1 October the same SS perpetrated their worst atrocity, at Marzabotto, a small picturesque town in the foothills of the Apennines in Emilia near Bologna, along the road to Pistoia and close to the Bologna–Florence railway.

Two regiments of the Adolf Hitler SS surrounded the part of the town beyond the River Reno. In the suburb of Casaglia a crowd took refuge in a church to pray for safety. The Germans burst in and killed the officiating priest and three old people who could not obey the orders to get out quickly enough. The remainder, 147 in number, were then killed with machine-guns in the cemetery. Twenty-eight families were completely wiped out. A hundred and seven, including twenty-four children, were killed in the Caprata suburb. At Casolari 282 were killed, including thirty-eight children and two nuns. At Carpiano nearby, forty-nine including twenty-four women and nineteen children were assassinated, and the Nazis killed a further 103 in the neighbourhood, scouring one house after another. The final total killed at Marzabotto was 1,830, including five priests.[19]

In evidence at his trial, Simon stated that he passed through Marzabotto every day on his way to the front and, as many of his men were being killed by snipers, decided on a massacre instead of taking the inhabitants to a reception centre for trial; he also said airborne troops and Blackshirt Fascists were involved at Marzabotto in addition to the SS. Under cross-examination he added that he gave Major Reder and Major Loos *carte blanche* to act as they thought fit.[20]

After the war, Reder was sentenced to death by an Italian tribunal at Bologna in 1951. This was commuted to life imprisonment. Years later, Reder petitioned the Mayor of Marzabotto for mercy; a vote was taken among the inhabitants – only four voted in favour of his release, and 282 against.[21]

The Fascist secretary of Marzabotto reported the massacre to Dino Fantozzi, the Fascist prefect in Bologna, who went to Gardone and protested personally to Mussolini. At first Mussolini claimed to know nothing about it; eventually, impressed by Fantozzi's genuine horror, he yielded to his entreaties and phoned Hitler, telling him: 'You cannot protest about the Katyn cave massacre [at Katyn the Germans had found the bodies of thousands of Polish soldiers massacred by the Russians] when in Italy Marzabotto has happened.' (Mussolini had sent two Italian law professors to join the German Committee of Enquiry into the massacre of Poles at Katyn, so he was well briefed on the subject.) Hitler ignored the Duce's protest; Mussolini never again complained directly to the Führer about German army atrocities against Italian civilians.[22]

On September 15 Mussolini sent a second strong letter of complaint to Rahn, citing well-documented atrocities against Italian civilians, including women and children; he made it clear that atrocities by Kesselring's troops had not ceased after Kesselring's order of August 2. On the contrary, many women and children as well as men had been killed, with hundreds of houses burnt.

> The result is that the number of partisans increases as does the enemy propaganda and the feelings of hate amongst the people so unjustly and cruelly hit. As a man and a Fascist I can no longer take the responsibility even indirectly for this massacre of women and children on top of the enemy bombardment.
>
> I hope, dear Ambassador, you will once again take up the cudgels, because Kesselring's orders apply to all.

Once again Kesselring pretended he would try to stop the atrocities so justifiably complained about by the Duce. He wrote to Rahn on 23 September, for onward transmission to Mussolini:

> Dear Ambassador,
> I have read the translation you sent us of the Duce's letter to you in which exception is taken to a number of incidents arising during reprisals by German Armed Forces. I fully share the feelings which you expressed to the Duce, that no odium attaches to German troops, when they react with severe measures in cases of treacherous attempts on the lives of German soldiers. War is a rough trade, especially the fight against cunning and treachery. I strongly condemn excesses such as are mentioned in the Duce's letter and shall have the guilty brought to book when their guilt can be established, in accordance with the orders I have already issued. Moreover I will again give the express order to the troops that all reprisals are to be directed against the bandits only and not against innocent sections of the civilian population. Insofar as the bandits are not shot or otherwise disposed of in the actual fighting, I shall in future attempt to put an end by means of Courts Martial convened immediately, on the spot, to cases which are rightly condemned and are bound to damage our reputation. Thank you for your good wishes which I heartily reciprocate. Heil Hitler, (signed) Kesselring.

This was giving a semblance of legality to the massacres.

Kesselring followed up this letter with an order on the next day:

The Duce has furnished me with fresh instances of the behaviour of members of the forces in Italy which are contrary to my orders of 21 August and which are revolting in the way they have been carried out and are driving even the best elements of the population and those willing to fight on our side into the enemy camp or the partisans. I am no longer ready to stand by and see such things take place ... I further order that in future courts martial are to be immediately set up on the spot – this should obviate the above-mentioned misdemeanours.

The prosecution pointed out that there is no word in this order of anyone being punished for atrocities in the past.

This order was intended merely as a sop to Mussolini, and was not taken seriously by Kesselring's subordinates. Immediately a poster with Kesselring's signature was displayed in Milan: 'For each German shot, ten Italians will be shot'; and Kesselring ordered all proceedings of the Standing Courts which authorized reprisals to be kept secret. This was a cover-up to conceal that these courts in fact hardly operated. Kesselring did transfer the brutal German commandant at Bologna, but the notorious SS Majors Reder and Loos were allowed to continue to commit atrocities, unrebuked, under General Simon.[23]

The defence at Kesselring's trial were unable to produce evidence that his 'courts' reduced the level of atrocities, or that they functioned extensively.[24] The prosecutor at Kesselring's trial said that Kesselring's order for trials before executions was issued only to preserve an 'outward appearance of legality', and that it was not intended that the courts should genuinely dispense justice. Kesselring himself wrote in one of his orders (on 12 January 1945) that military tribunals were only meant 'to give the outside appearance of a lawful condemnation being kept up'.[25]

At his own trial General Max Simon stated that he did not set up Standing Courts before ordering 'immediate and urgent reprisals', although when villagers suspected of co-operating with partisans were rounded up, they were taken to reception centres and sometimes tried by courts with judges. Simon estimated thirty to forty per cent of those tried were sentenced to be shot, the remainder being taken away for labour service in Germany; almost no one returned home after being sent for trial. Kesselring's order that court trials were to precede shootings and burnings was clearly never taken seriously by the Waffen SS under Simon.[26]

Early on 9 August 1944 partisans in Milan exploded a bomb in a German lorry loaded with straw parked unguarded in the Viale Abruzzi. According to the report sent the next day to Mussolini by the Fascist prefect of Milan, eight passers-by were killed and fifteen injured, all Italian, and one German soldier suffered minor injuries. (Other sources claim, incorrectly, that five German soldiers were killed.) Kesselring at first wanted to retaliate by executing fifty suspected anti-Fascists, but Cardinal Schuster persuaded him to be more lenient: the next morning, only fifteen hostages were ordered to be killed. (The executions took place at the petrol station in Piazzale Loretto where, a few months later, Mussolini's body and that of Clara Petacci were strung up after they had been killed by the partisans.)

This time, the Germans made the Italians do their dirty work for them. Pertini, a responsible civil servant, wrote to Mussolini on 12 August that, without reference to him, the Germans had ordered a platoon of the MUTI (Fascist soldiers used for police work) to execute fifteen inmates of the Milan prison who had been arrested by the German SS on suspicion of being Communists and terrorists:

At 5.30 a.m. the execution took place in Piazzale Loretto, without witnesses. The fifteen individuals were bundled out of a lorry and ordered to stand facing a wall of a house under construction. The victims, all dressed in overalls, had no idea they were to be shot; they thought they were being taken to work in Germany. As soon as they realized their last hour had come they tried to escape in all directions. The execution platoon, taken by surprise, fired bursts of shots, wounding or killing them all. However, one succeeded in escaping while seriously wounded and climbed to the first floor of a house before he fell down dead in a pool of blood. Not until 8 in the evening would the Germans allow the bodies to be moved to the mortuary, and a large crowd surrounded the corpses all day with the horror causing many women to faint.

The killings and the brutal method have made the Milanese much more hostile to the Germans although there is universal execration of the perpetrators of the 'vile' killing of passers-by in the Viale Abruzzi; the next day there were stoppages in protest in many factories.

There is considerable doubt whether any of those executed had any connection with the outrage, but the Germans have issued placards stating they hold other hostages who will be shot if there are more acts of terrorism and sabotage.

Mussolini wrote a vigorous letter of protest to Rahn, stating that this massacre and similar ones were 'contrary to the natural feelings of Italians and offended their mild national characteristics'; in an interview, he protested to Rahn that these German excesses were 'inflaming' the Italian civil war, doing no good to German troops while causing enormous damage to the country. Rahn was polite, but refused to take the complaint seriously.[27]

Although the prosecution at Kesselring's trial produced incontrovertible evidence of widespread killings of Italian civilians following Kesselring's 17 June order, the whole story was not available until after the trial was over. As memoirs by partisans began to be published, further hideous crimes by the German army under Kesselring gradually came to light.

On more than one occasion Kesselring told Hitler that Italy should be treated as an 'occupied country'. If it had not been for Mussolini's presence at Salò, Italians in the German-occupied part of Italy would have been treated as badly as the Poles, or worse. At the Nuremberg Trials Weiszäcker claimed that, 'If the history of the Italian campaign is ever written, Field Marshal Kesselring, next to Pope Pius XII, will be called the saviour of Italian culture.' There is a fragment of truth in this statement, in that Kesselring had made some effort to save Italy's heritage of ancient monuments, but as far as the lives of Italians were concerned, Kesselring behaved like a barbarian.

Few historians give credit to Mussolini for his efforts to prevent German atrocities against his fellow countrymen. It is true that he did not make outspoken denunciations of German behaviour to Hitler although, as has been seen, he once raised it in strong terms. Mussolini was realistic enough to know that his standing in the Axis partnership had sunk so low that shrill protests might have been counter-productive. Nor did he focus press publicity on the killings, realizing that this would only rally more Italians to anti-Fascism.

Not all the German generals involved in crimes against Italian civilians were convinced Nazis and admirers of Hitler. General Peter Kreseman, who commanded 26 Panzer Division, produced convincing evidence at his trial that he was anti-Nazi and had protected Jewish employees of his family firm before the war. Yet he was sentenced to ten years' imprisonment for killing one hundred civilians in the Fucchio Marshes on the River Arno near Florence on 23 August 1944. It was clearly not a military operation, but a 'murderous massacre'. Partisans had sniped almost daily at German soldiers and caused casualties. Troops under German officers and a Fascist Bersaglieri officer revenged these losses in order to 'frighten the partisans'. They blew up houses and shot whole families in cold blood; many of the victims had no connnection with the partisans. Two hundred and fifty German soldiers combed the marshes, and armoured cars machine-gunned civilians. Kreseman ordered everyone in the area to be shot; most of the victims were evacuees or refugees.

Kreseman was aware of the order that the authority of a court martial must be obtained before reprisals were undertaken; he ignored this although there was a judge available at Division Headquarters in the rear – he was only told about the massacre after it had occurred. Kreseman did not order ambulances to come for the wounded after the shootings, and the parish priest gave evidence that the bodies of mothers and small children were left lying dead in the road.

At his trial, Kreseman said he had never read the written orders about reprisals from Kesselring, but that he had been told orally by Kesselring's staff officers that 'severe and energetic measures should be taken against partisans in every case'. According to Kreseman, General Senger afterwards approved his action, but no report of what happened was sent to his Corps Headquarters (14 Panzer). Significantly, no prisoners at all were taken to be charged before a court, and Kreseman admitted that he made no sort of reproach to his men for the killing of women and children.[28]

At Bardine San Terenzo in August 1944 there was a considerable amount of partisan activity against German troops. The 16 Reichsführer Division was deployed to counteract this. On August 20 seventeen German SS were killed and their vehicle destroyed by fire, and a German colonel and a passenger were killed in a staff car nearby. SS Majors Reder and Loos sent troops to search various villages; they looted and burnt houses, and took 53 civilians to the burnt-out German vehicles. Some were tied to the vehicles, others to posts, and forty-nine were shot. Their bodies were not removed.

The parish priest testified that on 21 August 1944 at Bardine he saw

... on both sides of the road a number of bodies. The majority of these were tied by the neck to fencing posts; others were tied in similar manner to poles which support the wires. All had been shot. I counted 53 corpses. These men were not of Bardine or San Terenzo. They had been brought by the SS from Mozzana Castello.

I later saw, in Valla, 107 bodies of men, women and children. These were all persons of San Terenzo and all had been shot. Five were men, the remainder women and children.

In the vicinity of the German truck I found two notices written in Italian. These had been left by the Germans after the hostages had been killed. The signs read:

'This is the way all anti-Fascists and enemies of the Axis shall end.

This is the first revenge for the seventeen Germans killed at Bardine.'

For four days the reprisals continued, and a total of 369 persons in the area, mostly women and children, were massacred, and 454 houses totally destroyed. One member of the execution squad, a twenty-year-old SS conscript captured in October 1944 by French troops, stated that his platoon was ordered to shoot civilians, including women and children, indiscriminately, and to burn a whole village. When the church would not burn, the SS sergeant put burning straw into it: this disgusted the twenty-year-old, who was a Catholic. He went on that in one village thirty or forty women were put up against a wall and mown down by machine-gun fire.[29]

Private David Russell, a New Zealander, was captured after fighting with partisans who had attacked the German headquarters and killed German soldiers at Porto Canavese on 9 December 1943. Russell was an escaped POW. The Germans shot him and seventeen partisans on the spot, without trial. In April 1947 General Tensfeld was charged with the murder of David Russell and these partisans, and also with killing Italian hostages at Borgo Ticino near Novara; this was one of the massacres about which Mussolini complained. After a trial lasting five days Tensfeld was acquitted, although he admitted frankly he had been in Borgo Ticino on the day of the second atrocity.

General Tensfeld had been appointed SS and Police Führer and given the specific task of preventing the partisans infiltrating Turin when the General Strike was being called there in August 1944. Thirteen out of thirty villagers were selected to be shot at Borgo Ticino on 13 August 1944, and although the village paid a large fine, Tensfeld's subordinates insisted on going ahead with the executions and burning 50 houses and taking away much loot. A commander in the Decima Mas was in the village and protested, but he only succeeded in securing the release of two Blackshirts. The actual perpetrators of these two atrocities were not found after the war.[30]

There is doubt about the role of the Decima Mas in this atrocity. At his trial for war crimes after the war, before an Italian court, Valerio Borghese was charged with allowing the Decima Mas to take part in both the massacre at Borgo Ticino and the one at Porto Canavese; these charges were not proved. The evidence produced at the Tensfeld court martial, about the Decima Mas commander protesting, may have been untrue.[31]

Two British soldiers, Gunner Cornish and Private Jakeways, were murdered by the SS on 20 December 1944 at Borgo near Tranto in the Val Sugano. With their usual attention to detail the Germans ordered the grave-digger to dig two graves and the undertaker to prepare two coffins. The British were then taken to the cemetery with their hands tied, and shot from behind. Their bodies were left for the Italians to bury. They had been making for Switzerland but had joined with the partisans in a raid on a police station. The SS Commander was acquitted at a court martial, and those actually responsible were never tried. No attempt had been made to hold a Court, as per Kesselring's instructions.[32]

Particularly gruesome reading is the long trial by British court martial of SS General Simon, the commander with overall responsibility for this atrocity and all those committed by Reder and Loos. He was sentenced to death on six charges for war crimes which took place between 11 August and 30 September 1944. He was not tried until August 1947. Emmanuel Shinwell, Secretary of State for War, commuted the death sentence to life imprisonment. Simon was responsible for all Major Reder's massacres – not only Bardine, as has been seen above, but also Molina di Quosa, 11 August; St Anna and Val di Castello, 12 August; Apuan Alps, 23–27 August; Bergola Poscalina, 16 September; Stella Rosa Brigade, 24–30 September; Marzabotto, 29 September–1 October.

Many other similar instances are documented in the Simon trial in the British archives, the direct result of Kesselring's orders to take harsh measures against the partisans. The transcript and documents occupy five bulky files in the Public Record Office. The squeamish should not read them, or look at the horrendous photographs accompanying them. Simon was found guilty as being 'responsible' for the massacre of Marzabotto and all the other atrocities committed by the SS Majors Reder and Loos listed above between 11 August 1944 and 30 September 1944.

On 1 October 1944 at Bressanone, near Bolzano, three unknown escaped British POWs were butchered in a barn by German soldiers. They were unarmed; the German officer in charge was sentenced by a War Crimes Court to fifteen years' imprisonment. The bodies were riddled with bullets. The incident must have been reported to the German superior military authority who, fortified by Kesselring's instruction, ignored it.[33]

Orders issued by the SS and Police Leader West in January 1945 make it clear that the execution of innocent persons was continuing, but that the Germans were trying to cloak it with an appearance of legality. A new order on reprisals was issued on 8 February 1945 after discussions which had lasted since 9 December. It contained the instruction that 'for sentencing purposes it must be established at least formally that they were sentenced to death for assistance to partisan units, desertion, etc. The word "hostage" provokes politically negative feelings of sympathy amongst the population.'[34]

On 23 October 1944 Kesselring was involved in a motor accident in which his staff car collided with a heavy gun on tow. He received severe head and face injuries, and was hospitalized in Germany. He was back in command in Italy in early February 1945. By then the partisan threat to the German army had become even more serious. Kesselring thought his temporary replacement, Vietinghoff, had not been tough enough and, disregarding Mussolini, insisted on more severe reprisals.

He gave subordinate commanders authority, not only 'to arrest relatives of culprits', but also 'to destroy groups of houses or portions of towns when the inhabitants had supported the partisan bands' and to 'execute partisans or partisan helpers'. He again paid lip service to decisions 'being referred to a standing court' but laid down that even junior commanders had authority to take reprisals 'if there was danger in delay', without reference to their superiors or the Court. This gave German commanders *carte blanche* to execute prisoners and those helping them, regardless of sex or age, and to destroy as many houses as they liked.[35]

Captain C. M. Woods (former Foreign Office adviser on SOE documents) has written to the author that in the final days of the war he saw retreating German troops at Pedascala, north of Vicenza between Schio and Asiago, burn the whole village with its inhabitants in their houses; there could have been no time for a Standing Court to operate. Woods saw the burnt corpses, and has photographs. Even in defeat, the habit of brutality initiated by Kesselring in 1944 died hard.

Such anti-German feeling was publicly demonstrated in Rome at the Mältzer and von Mackensen trials that it was thought advisable to try Kesselring in Venice. His appearance in Rome might have caused a riot. Kesselring was condemned to death by the British court martial in May 1947; immediately both Alexander and Churchill intervened to have his death sentence commuted – not because of any inherent objection to the death penalty, but because they were not aware of the full extent of Kesselring's inhuman behaviour. Churchill asked the Prime Minister (Attlee) to arrange for a long enough interval between promulgation of the verdict and its execution for the matter to be raised in Parliament. Neither Attlee nor the Attorney General, Hartley Shawcross, was interested. Leslie Rowan, Attlee's Private Secretary, minuted to the Prime Minister that Bellenger, Secretary of State for War, was not inclined to intervene but that Attlee should be careful because 'Churchill was on to it', while Shawcross refused to give an opinion.

Churchill had received a letter from Field Marshal Alexander, who wrote: 'I am unhappy over Kesselring's death sentence. Personally as his old opponent on the battlefield I have no complaint against him. Kesselring and his soldiers fought against us hard and clean.' This was irrelevant; the charges on which Kesselring had been convicted did not relate to conventional warfare in Italy.

General Harding (later Field Marshal) was the confirming officer. The Judge Advocate General, Sir Foster Macgeach, advised Harding that he saw no reason to commute the death sentences either on Kesselring or on the other German generals concerned in the Ardeatine cave massacre, Mältzer and von Mackensen. However, Harding commuted all three sentences to life imprisonment.

One of Harding's grounds for commutation was flimsy, that Kesselring's orders of 17 June and 1 July 1944 were 'operative' for only 'a limited and comparatively short period'. He was on stronger ground in recording that it would be 'against his conscience' to confirm the sentences of death on Kesselring, Mältzer and von Mackensen, since Kappler would 'almost certainly' be given a lesser sentence. Kappler was about to be tried by an Italian court, and under the laws of the new Italian Republic there was no death penalty.

Harding also wrote, implausibly, that the evidence showed that if Kesselring had challenged Hitler's orders for immediate and dramatic reprisals after the Via Rasella bombs, 'he would have exposed himself to the charge of being unwilling to take prompt and adequate measures for the security of his troops when they were in a critical situation'.[36]

In 1950, Colonel A. P. Somerset of the Judge Advocate General's department, who carried out the interrogations of all the German generals in Italy after the Armistice, took up the cudgels for Kesselring, then languishing in a German gaol under sentence of life imprisonment. Somerset argued to the Foreign Office that the Kappler trial had established that Hitler, not Kesselring, was responsible for 300 of the deaths in the Ardeatine caves, and that Kappler was solely responsible for the remaining 50. Somerset was influenced by the fact which had come to light that Hitler, at the same time as he ordered the Ardeatine massacre, spent two hours arguing with Goering whether 76 escaping RAF officers should be shot, or only 50. Somerset also pointed out the 'priceless service' rendered by Kesselring to the American Historical Division during his imprisonment.

Somerset's plea is hard to understand, because he knew the full details of Kesselring's responsibility for the Ardeatine massacre. On 22 February 1946 Somerset had interrogated General Harster, the head of the SS police in Italy. Harster testified that on the day of the Via Rasella bombs Kappler had told him on the telephone that the 'army' – that is, Kesselring – had issued orders that hostages in the proportion of ten to one were to be shot, and that he (Kappler) had been detailed to select them. Kappler told Harster he would have to work throughout the night

> . . . selecting from the prisoners in his custody those who were suitable [i.e., those legally sentenced to death or convicted of crimes punishable by death]. By order of the army [Kesselring] he now had to select hostages in the proportion of 1:10 to the increased number of dead, and the number of people at his disposal and of those handed over by Wehrmacht departments and Italian police would not reach required figures; that as the army [Kesselring] insisted on the given number, he would under the circumstances have no alternative but to draw on a number of Jews in his custody.

This statement makes it clear that Kesselring cold-bloodedly assented to the murder of innocent Jews.[37]

Kesselring's memoirs, published in English, were described by Roscoe Drummond in the *New York Herald Tribune* in September 1955 as

> . . . the most pernicious, purposeful, massively misleading pro-war pro-Nazi-innocence propaganda . . . this guileful apologia of Nazi aggression and its subtle effort to persuade his own country, as did his predecessors in the thirties, that the German army really never lost the war. There is not an honourable word in it . . . the ruthless, immoral, iron-heel evil doctrine of Kesselring.

Kesselring has some interesting passages on the German occupation of Italy, although his book bristles with lies – including his claim that he prevented the deportation of Jews from Rome. He says that von Richthofen generously placed the German ground organization at the disposal of Mussolini's air force after the Republic of Salò was created, even though the Italians had little to offer, while Italian pilots were retrained on German aircraft under German instructors; although there was fellowship among the airmen, the Fascist air force was not 'fit for operations'.

Kesselring states that the conduct of operations against the guerrillas after May 1944 was allotted to him, and that the SS were under his 'absolute authority' in their 'operations against the partisans', while in the war zones and along the 'military coastal' areas the partisan war was in the hands of his army commanders. According to Kesselring, only in June 1944 did the partisan threat become 'serious'. He wrote, 'In Istria in the mountain part of Fiume, Trieste and Gorizia, the mass of the population was with them; they disorganized our supply route, through Villach into Italy and Yugoslavia.'

As Colonel Somerset noted in his plea on Kesselring's behalf in 1950, Kesselring during the interval between his arrest and his trial in June 1947 curried favour with the Americans (whose POW camp he was in) by assiduously and competently co-operating with the American Historial Division in writing the history of military operations during the Second World War. He defended in his book his orders of 17 June, 1 July, 15 August and 24 September for atrocities against the partisans. He also stated, incorrectly, that all the 'stories' of crimes reported to him by Mussolini turned out when investigated to be lies or exaggerations. Unfortunately for Kesselring, the evidence against him is cast-iron.[38]

There are few left who knew Kesselring. Sir Ian Fraser, who was Reuters' correspondent in Berlin between 1947 and 1956, has described him to the author as:

> . . . a man of medium height, rather sloppily dressed, with a pleasant easy manner. He was a typical Bavarian with a noticeable Bavarian accent and in every way the antithesis of a Prussian (or the Englishman's idea of a Prussian). He had a sense of humour.
>
> He was proud of having made for himself a career in both the Army and the Luftwaffe, and of having reached the top. He looked on himself as a political general. Rommel he described as 'a prima donna and the bane of his life' who required careful handling as he would always go to Hitler behind his (Kesselring's) back. Kesselring believed he had handled the Italians well and had fought a most successful rearguard action.
>
> He was proud of his efforts to save the cultural monuments of Italy. Kesselring related that the German Foreign Office used the principle of

Sippenhaft (kin arrest) to justify collective action against partisans, and they stole the principle from the history of Scotland with the massacre of Glencoe, which Nazis liked to recall. Kesselring's line was that there was a war on, the Italian partisans were in breach of international conventions, and their activities were extremely damaging to the German war effort, so that the reprisals he ordered were the type of reprisal that any military power would feel justified in authorizing in such circumstances.

According to Fraser, Kesselring himself never tried to shift the blame for the atrocities onto the Gestapo or the SS: this was a ploy by his able defence counsel, which could not be sustained in the face of the signal from Keitel dated 1 May 1944 which showed Hitler had ordered Kesselring to be head of all anti-partisan operations, in spite of strenuous objections from Himmler. Kesselring had demanded and obtained complete authority.[39]

CHAPTER 5

Verona, 1944

AT SALÒ, MUSSOLINI decided to give his new Republic a Socialist image. In this way he sought to win support from trade unionists and the left, who were anti-monarchist. It was the throw of a desperate man and achieved little, except to annoy the Germans, who were strongly opposed to any nationalization of Italian industry. Mussolini called a Fascist Congress at Verona on 14 November 1943 to counter-stamp his Socialist proposals. The Conference was a farce. An eighteen-point manifesto written by a crypto-Communist, Nicola Bombacci (an eccentric with long white hair, looking like a bogus prophet), was circulated to all delegates, who were told to endorse a new Socialist philosophy which ran counter to the 1922 Fascist creed. Rahn objected strongly to the draft, and Mussolini was forced to tone down some of his proposals for expropriating private industry, and also to cancel altogether a clause about the importance of ensuring 'Italian territorial integrity'. The Germans, having peremptorily annexed the eight provinces in north-east Italy, would not hear of this: Hitler had no intention of returning these lands to Italy, and indeed Goebbels wrote at this time that the Veneto ought also to be ceded to Germany.

According to the manifesto, a future Parliament would declare the monarchy abolished and create a Socialist Republic to be elected every five years. Private capitalism (despite German objections) was to disappear eventually.[1]

Mussolini gave his approval to the agenda for the Verona Congress, but did not honour it with his presence. He feared that his personal prestige would be dented by angry, critical speeches from the delegates. He sent a message that everything must be 'started anew', and that as soon as possible 'we must pass from inertia to being a fighting nation'. Cosmin, the Fascist prefect of Verona, who as will be seen had just perpetrated the cold-blooded murder of an escaped British officer POW and an Italian boy, supplied a corps of black-shirted ushers and attendants from the soldiers available, in an effort to lend the rag-bag assembly some dignity.[2]

In Mussolini's stead Alessandro Pavolini, his number two and the Fascist Party Secretary, presided. Even Pavolini was constantly interrupted, both by the old Fascists of the march on Rome of 1922, and by over-enthusiastic new recruits to the Party. The most significant debate was on how to deal with the 'traitors' of 25 July 1943 who had been responsible for the coup against Mussolini. Unanimously the Congress voted for a Special Court to try all those in Fascist hands, and condemn them to death.

The eighteen points were approved unanimously, but debates on the key questions of how the Fascist Party should operate in future, and on the creation of a new army, revealed much discord.[3] As Mussolini told Dolfin, his personal secretary:

> It has been a complete mix-up. Nothing but muddled chatter and no clear views. There were some strange symptoms, including expressions of views supporting Communism. Nobody out of all those who produced a hotch-potch of ideas said they wanted to fight. It is at the battle front that the fate of our Republic will be decided, and certainly not by political debate.

Buffarini Guidi told the Duce that the majority of the delegates 'were despised by the population, who looked upon them with disgust and real terror'.[4]

There was a dramatic moment when Pavolini rose, asked for silence, and revealed that the Fascist Commissioner in Ferrara, Igino Ghisellini, had been shot by partisans. In Fascist fashion the delegates shouted, 'Everyone to Ferrara. We will revenge him with our blood.' It was only with difficulty that Pavolini persuaded the Assembly to continue their debates, by promising that everything necessary would be done in true Fascist style. Brutal reprisals were then taken against anti-Fascists, not only at Ferrara but elsewhere in Lombardy, and this marked the beginning of the Italian civil war. Mussolini to his credit objected to the reprisals, saying they were 'bestial and pointless', but in this he was a prisoner of his own Party and was forced to agree to Pavolini's 'eye for an eye, tooth for a tooth' policy, although he rebuked Pavolini for overdoing it.

However, Mussolini showed no mercy in the case of his own son-in-law, Count Ciano. When they had met in Germany immediately after Mussolini's liberation they had a friendly talk. Ciano explained why he had voted for the hostile resolution at the last meeting of the Fascist Council, and Mussolini appeared to accept his version without rancour. Mussolini was also cordial with Ciano at a large family lunch party, although his wife Rachele berated her son-in-law for betraying the Duce. Now, faced with Hitler's demand for revenge upon the traitors, and with the remnants of the Fascist Party in full cry for blood, Mussolini set up a special court at Verona, knowing that it would result in Ciano being condemned to death.[5]

After the 25 July coup Ciano, fearing arrest by the Badoglio Government as Mussolini's son-in-law and close political associate, had persuaded
the Germans to organize for him a secret flit with his family to Munich.
It was a disastrous move; he should have gone to Spain, as did Grandi, the
mover of the fateful resolution at the Fascist Grand Council on 24 July.
Reassured by Mussolini's friendliness when they met again in Germany,
Ciano in November asked the Germans, through Anfuso, for permission
to go back to Italy, where his wife Edda already was. The Germans
agreed, but to Ciano's dismay as soon as he landed at Verona airport he
was arrested and placed in the Scalci prison. The Nazis had insisted that
Ciano be accompanied by an SS agent, Frau Beetz (Hildegard Burkhardt).
The Gestapo had attached her to Ciano's household in Munich, ostensibly
as an interpreter but really as a spy, charged with discovering the whereabouts of Ciano's secret diary and private papers, which it was thought
might prove damaging to both Mussolini and Hitler.

The Fascist Party wanted Ciano's trial to begin immediately. Unfortunately for them, Mussolini's original Minister of Justice, Antonino
Tringali-Casanova, died suddenly and his successor Pier Pisenti (whose
book is a valuable source on the Salò Republic) was opposed to political
revenge. Mussolini too dithered; finally, at a meeting of Fascist ministers
on 24 November, Pavolini successfully moved a motion to set up the
Special Tribunal.

The Duce now himself prepared the papers for the trial; he was put
out when Pisenti informed him that no proof existed of a conspiracy
among the members of the Grand Council. Pisenti, an able lawyer, told
Mussolini:

> Duce, I have analysed the documents, and the charge is not valid; there is not
> the slightest proof of conspiracy by those who signed the resolution by Grandi
> and the Royal House. Voting was carried out in the correct manner and it
> was you, Duce, who asked for a vote. I assure you, the charge of betrayal
> can in no way be substantiated in court.[6]

However, the Germans sent Mussolini a memorandum (or confession),
written by Field Marshal Cavallero in prison in Rome after his arrest
by the Badoglio Government in the hope of rehabilitating himself with
the Royalist Government. When the Germans occupied Rome on 12
September Cavallero was freed; he expected to become the head of
Mussolini's new army. But Badoglio – perhaps deliberately – had left the
Cavallero memorandum on his desk when he made his precipitate flight
from Rome on 9 September, and it fell into the hands of the Gestapo.
Cavallero's statement made it clear that there had been a conspiracy among
generals and politicians to depose Mussolini, in which Cavallero himself

had been involved up to the hilt. As soon as Cavallero realized his confession was in German hands, 'he committed suicide'. Mussolini knew Cavallero's written evidence would show Ciano 'guilty' of conspiracy, and he personally passed it to the President of the Special Tribunal.

The President was Aldo Vecchini, a Fascist lawyer sacked by Badoglio from his chairmanship of the Italian Bar. The other judges were strong Fascists with extremist records who included the leaders of the reprisal raids on Ferrara and Brescia. Ciano and his fellow accused – Marshal de Bono, Tullio Cianetti, Giovanni Marinelli, Giuseppe Pareschi and Luciano Gottardi – could expect no mercy. Like the Verona Conference, the trial was a farce. All the accused declared they had not intended their vote for the Grand Council motion to mean that they desired the downfall of Mussolini. The prosecutor emphasized the existence of a plot headed by Grandi, produced the Cavallero memorandum as evidence, and demanded the death penalty. Cianetti (who on the next morning, 26 July, had withdrawn his vote against Mussolini) was sentenced to thirty years' imprisonment; the others were sentenced to death.

There was a bizarre attempt to save Ciano, so melodramatic as to be worthy of Hollywood. His wife Edda was completely loyal, and his Gestapo minder Frau Beetz was in love with him. Edda's affection had survived years of knowing her husband to be a philanderer, and long periods of separation. She had spent several months during the winter of 1942/43 skiing in the mountains, never seeing her father or taking any interest in the Italian political crisis which threatened his and her husband's careers. Frau Beetz had spent many hours alone with Ciano in his prison cell, ostensibly trying to find out the whereabouts of his diary and documents, but at the same time succumbing to his charm and good looks. Ciano's last days were cheered by her devotion, and his vanity flattered.

When it became clear Ciano would be condemned to death, Edda wrote three letters – to Hitler, to her father, and to General Harster, the military commander in northern Italy. In all three she threatened that if her husband were not released within three days of the end of the trial and allowed to go to Switzerland, she would unleash 'a devastating campaign against the Axis' by revealing to the world the contents of Ciano's diary, letters and other documents, which were 'enormously damaging to Hitler and her father'. If Ciano were released, she promised they would both retire into private life. In her letter to Mussolini she added, 'I have waited until today for you to show me the slightest feeling of kindness and love. If Galeazzo is not in Switzerland in three days ... I shall make merciless use of all I know.'

Frau Beetz was also ready to go to great lengths to save Galeazzo, and she devised an ingenious plan. Two SS soldiers were to be dressed in Italian uniform, and with the consent of the prison staff they would seize Ciano;

he would be sent immediately by air to Hungary and then to Turkey. Once Edda knew Ciano was safe she would hand over to the Germans the diaries and documents. Himmler was informed, and agreed; Edda sent him specimen documents as a sign of 'good faith'. However, as soon as Hitler heard of the move he was furious and threatened drastic punishment to all concerned if it were carried out. Beetz said after the war that Himmler probably changed his mind too; she was always doubtful whether Himmler would have honoured his agreement to send Ciano to safety.[7]

Once the death sentence was announced, on 10 January, Cosmin and Pavolini wanted the condemned men executed as soon as possible for fear that Mussolini might change his mind and commute the sentences. They ordered an execution squad to be ready at dawn the following morning. But all the condemned now made an appeal to the Duce for clemency – Ciano most reluctantly, and only to help the others. Pavolini and Cosmin passed a busy night trying to get the appeal for clemency rejected, and the death sentence confirmed, by some high authority.

The public prosecutor, Vincenzo Cersosimo, suggested the right authority was General Umberto Piatti dal Pozzo, the local Army commander who had his headquarters in Padua. Pavolini and Cosmin went hot-foot to Padua. The General immediately produced his legal adviser and refused angrily to confirm the sentences, saying it was quite outside his competence as he was only concerned with recruiting. Frustrated, Cosmin and Pavolini moved on through the night to Brescia where they tackled the Minister for Justice, Pisenti. Pisenti told Pavolini that the appeals must go direct to Mussolini. Pavolini replied that it was entirely a matter for the Fascist Party, and the Duce must be left out of it. Pisenti was adamant. Furious, Pavolini went on to Maderno, near Mussolini's headquarters, to see the Minister of the Interior, Buffarini Guidi. Buffarini Guidi would have nothing to do with it, and told them to ferret out a general who would take responsibility. At Verona General Italo Vianini was the head of the National Guard, but Vianini refused point-blank to entertain the idea of confirming the death sentences. After two hours' argument which ended in deadlock, Renato Ricci, Mussolini's Commander of the Militia, telephoned to Vianini and said he had talked to Mussolini, who had ordered the shootings to go ahead. Vianini was still reluctant to sign the death warrants but Tamburini, the Chief of Police, wrote a memorandum stating that Ricci had telephoned ordering his subordinate, Vianini, to sign. Vianini then yielded.

At last Pavolini, at six in the morning, had authority to go ahead. At eight o'clock the executions took place, with horrible inefficiency; all the prisoners had to be finished off with pistol shots. The Fascist radio immediately announced the news, preceded by the Fascist anthem. Mussolini was angered by this, saying to his secretary, Dolfin, 'The

Italians love to show off always. They are either savages or buffoons.'

Mussolini, through Dolfin, had kept in touch with the Verona court-house by telephone, and was told of the death sentences at 5 p.m. He must have passed agonizing hours of indecision, because at 5 a.m. the next morning he had asked General Wolff whether or not he should intervene. Wolff said he could not give an official reply, but his private view was that Mussolini should not.

According to Dolfin, when the Duce first heard of the death sentences he said that Ciano was among those who had deliberately 'provoked the catastrophe' at the meeting of the Grand Council, but that Gottardi and de Bono probably 'did not understand what was going on'. However, Mussolini cold-heartedly made no move to reprieve Gottardi and de Bono, sacrificing them either to his overwhelming desire for revenge or to ingratiate himself with Hitler. Before the trial Mussolini had said, 'As far as I am concerned, Ciano is already dead.'[8]

The Verona trial shows Mussolini at his most cruel and inhumane, revealing a deadly hatred of all who obstructed him. To kill his own son-in-law despite the impassioned entreaties of his daughter was unforgivable.

The Verona executions did not satisfy Mussolini; probably he feared what Hitler would think of him if he was merciful. He pursued his ven-detta. Former Fascist officials who had co-operated with the Government during Badoglio's forty-five days were arrested and charged; initially, Mussolini thought they should all be executed. They included leading Fascists like Farinacci, Starace and Carlo Scorza, and a lower-echelon official, Alessandro Tarabini, who had allowed the Fascist Party in Milan to dissolve on 26 July. However, Mussolini relented; although these men were charged with capital offences, he intervened, and they were released.

Mussolini's naval commanders fared less happily. Admiral Inigo Cam-pioni, who as will be seen co-operated for several weeks with the British troops on Leros, was sentenced to death and executed. Admiral Luigi Mascherpa, who for only 24 hours fought the Germans on Rhodes, was also tried and executed. The charge against them was that they had obeyed what was 'manifestly a criminal order', from the War Office in Rome on 8 September, not to resist Anglo-American landings. The two Admirals were executed on 24 May 1944; this aroused great indignation among the regular officers of the Republican army, navy and air force.[9]

Admiral Gino Pavesi, who had surrendered the island of Pantellaria to the British almost without fighting, and Admiral Primo Leonardi, who had abandoned his post at the naval base at Augusta in Sicily, were also tried, and condemned to imprisonment. However, their senior service colleagues made sure that their prison conditions in an army fortress were as comfortable as any officers' mess.

CHAPTER 6

Mussolini's New Army, and the Fate of 600,000

As 1943 CAME TO an end Mussolini, frustrated by his impotence and the way in which the German military authorities overruled his Government's instructions, became more and more determined to create a new Republican Army. Without it he felt he could never regain political influence with the Germans.

Immediately on becoming Head of State again, Mussolini had appointed Renato Ricci to head and re-create the former Fascist militia, the Black Brigades. These had been army formations under the direct control of the Fascist Party, and quite separate from the Royal Army. Ricci and Pavolini wanted only the Fascist militia, and disliked the prospect of an army under Graziani and out of the control of the Fascist Party. They were both strongly opposed to Graziani, realizing correctly that if he were in charge of well-trained and well-armed regular Italian divisions, he could at any moment cock a snook at Mussolini and even change sides. Undoubtedly this was in Graziani's own mind as well, and he was also motivated by the belief that the stronger the Republican Army, the better the Italian bargaining position in any negotiations for an armistice with the Allies.

In the controversy between Ricci and Graziani, Mussolini firmly sided with Graziani, who on 9 October flew from Rome to Hitler's headquarters at Rastenburg (The Wolf's Lair) with instructions from Mussolini to ask Hitler for help in forming the new army. Keitel, Hitler's Chief of Staff, alarmed Graziani by telling him he wanted all Italy to be under military government. This intensified Graziani's resolution.

On 10 October, in a personal interview, Graziani made a formal request to Hitler for twelve divisions to be formed out of the 600,000 Italian soldiers who had surrendered and been shipped off to forced labour camps in Germany after 8 September. Hitler refused. He thought that as these Italian soldiers and officers had changed sides once and refused to take the Fascist oath, they would be unreliable, and disloyal to Germany. Hitler did, however, appreciate that Graziani was the only man of resolution and personality in Mussolini's Salò Government, and, after listening to his arguments against military government, eventually conceded that, while the areas immediately behind the battle front should be treated as 'occupied', the remainder, excluding the eight provinces which had been brought under direct German rule, might be governed from Salò by Mussolini's token government.

At his lowest ebb, in Germany in September 1943, Mussolini had told both Himmler and Hitler that he would agree to all rearmed Italian troops operating under German command. Yet at his first Cabinet meeting he led Ricci to believe that the Party would control all armed forces. When Graziani returned from Germany he fired Mussolini's imagination by the picture of a new Italian army which, according to Graziani, should be 'apolitical' and have nothing to do with the Fascist Party. Mussolini then even wanted to put Ricci's Black Brigades under Graziani. Graziani persuaded Mussolini that the Black Brigades were universally hated, and that the formation of an exclusively Fascist Army would unleash civil war.[1]

Rahn, the German Ambassador, sent Mussolini the formal minutes of the Graziani talks at Hitler's headquarters. Points included were:

All Italian resources must be mobilized to defend the deep flanks and long coasts and relieve the German forces engaged in battle on the main front.

Subordinate Italian units consisting of volunteers under German command are required for coastal artillery engineers and ground personnel for the air force.

Military internees are not to be considered for incorporation in such units . . .

The creation of larger Italian formations is envisaged at training establishments outside Italy [i.e., in Germany; author's italics].[2]

As Hitler had refused out of hand to allow the soldiers in the labour camps to be recruited for new Italian divisions, and had expressly forbidden Graziani to visit these camps to raise volunteers from the internees, Mussolini was faced with a problem in finding enough manpower for the army. Hitler had told Graziani he would consider finding equipment for four new Italian divisions and training them in Germany. Mussolini now decided upon a conscription order for those born in 1923, 1924 and 1925, in conjunction with determined propaganda efforts to find volunteers.

The German High Command, meanwhile, was strongly opposed to the creation of a new independent Italian Army. They told Hitler it would be a drain on their resources which would pay few dividends, and that nearly all the Italian officers were pro-monarchy and highly unreliable. 'The only Italian Army that will not be treacherous', Keitel said, 'is one that does not exist.'

Mussolini now chose General Emilio Canevari, a loyal Fascist and an intelligent writer on military subjects, to go to Berlin to try to negotiate a firm agreement for four new Italian divisions. Canevari was told to suggest that at least some officers and NCOs should be recruited from volunteers in the German labour camps, while confirming that the majority of the troops would be either conscripts or volunteers recruited in Italy. Although hampered by his own lack of German, Canevari at length won agreement from the German High Command in Berlin to the formation of four Italian divisions, and brought it back to Mussolini. At a Cabinet meeting on 28 October Mussolini declared it to be an 'excellent agreement', that he would find sufficient recruits from the call-up and volunteers, and that Ricci's militia would form part of Graziani's new army. Ricci was busy raising his Fascist Black Brigades to keep law and order, and Mussolini's statement produced a shouting match between Graziani and Ricci. No proper decision was ever reached, and for the rest of the war the Black Brigades operated sometimes under Ricci, sometimes under Graziani, and often under direct German command.[3]

Mussolini made another pathetic effort to persuade Hitler to allow him to recruit from the labour camps in Germany, cabling to Keitel, 'I would feel dishonoured if among so many internees [600,000] we could not find 50,000 men for the four divisions. For political reasons it would be impossible for me to send conscript recruits directly to Germany.' Keitel replied patronizingly that it must be the Führer's decision, but as far as he was concerned, 'I do not want any internees.'

On 11 November a formal Protocol was signed, after more discussions between Keitel and Canevari. This enacted that not more than four divisions should be equipped and armed by the Germans, and that 'Marshal Keitel had ruled that the personnel must come from recruits enrolled in Italy'. Mussolini made a last appeal to Hitler:

> Do allow these men [the internees] who want to volunteer to have the honour of fighting so that we can avoid the bitter humiliation that while the traitors are raising an army for the Anglo-Saxons the Italian Republic cannot do likewise.

Hitler relaxed, but only to the extent of allowing 12,000 volunteers from officers and NCOs to leave the camps, emphasizing that the remainder of the four divisions must come from Italy.[4]

By 13 December 44,000 conscripts from the call-up had presented themselves at the barracks. Propaganda for volunteers produced another 6,000. This indicated some residual enthusiasm for Mussolini and Fascism, but unemployment and the difficulties of buying food must also have been a potent factor influencing enrolment.

A 'shadow' northern Italian army was in fact already in existence, for Himmler's SS were enrolling as many Italian soldiers as possible in the Italian SS, where they took an oath of loyalty to Hitler and came under German orders. All senior officers were German, and it was stipulated that they should wear Italian uniform with German shoulder straps and collar badges. After his first talk with Mussolini on 24 September, Himmler had sent orders to the SS General Wolff in Italy that enrolment should begin, and much to the annoyance of Ricci, who had not been party to the Mussolini/Himmler agreement, more recruits volunteered for the SS than for his Black Militia Brigades. The Germans offered higher pay and better rations. However, Himmler gave strict orders that only ex-Fascists were to be enrolled, and that the Italian SS must remain independent of the Salò Government.

The Germans enrolled in their Italian SS 13,000 volunteers from the German labour camps, despite a warning from Canevari that their military value would be zero. More than half deserted as soon as they got back to Italy.[5]

After the 8 September armistice, some elements of the Italian army on the mainland had remained loyal to Mussolini. In addition to the Nembo Division in Sardinia, whose performance there is covered later, some units of the Folgore Division stationed in Calabria swore allegiance to the Third Reich, and went into the line against the Allies at Salerno. These units from the Folgore and Nembo Divisions amounted to about 4,000 men, while some 6,000 of the Decima Mas under the command of Valerio Borghese were ready to fight by the side of the Germans.

Borghese had commanded the two-man human torpedoes which put 73,000 tons of British shipping out of action in Mediterranean ports for the loss of only six men. His most effective operation was in Alexandria harbour on the night of 18 December 1941, when he damaged the British battleships *Queen Elizabeth* and *Valiant* so badly that they took many months to repair (this was the week after the *Repulse* and *Prince of Wales* had been lost in the Gulf of Siam).

On 8 September Borghese's Decima Mas marines were in barracks at the naval base of La Spezia. They had so high a reputation as fighters that the Germans did not dare to call on them to surrender. Eventually, on 14 September, a German officer came to negotiate with Borghese, who agreed to fight with the Germans against the Allies. Kesselring only wanted units, like the Decima Mas, Nembo and Folgore, who had demonstrated their loyalty to Germany. The remaining Italian soldiers they hoped to enrol in the Italian SS, to be commanded by German officers and treated as soldiers of fortune with other volunteers to the German cause, such as the German-speaking Swiss.

As a result of an appeal in October by Graziani, many dispersed Italian soldiers, mostly officers, had reported to barracks; they needed the pay. But the Germans wanted no truck with them in battle, and ordered that they be formed into large working parties for the army and the airfields. Graziani noted that many Italian soldiers were doing menial tasks, such as looking after the gardens of German officers. A bitter note of discord was the higher pay and better rations of the Italian SS, and the way in which the Germans siphoned off Italian clothing, blankets and boots to the SS, while other units went poorly clad and shod.

Soon there were about 200,000 Italian soldiers in Republican Italy serving directly under the Germans. Mussolini's forces were desperately short of arms, because the Germans had pillaged the Italian depots, even sending thousands of machine-guns to Romania. To Mussolini's fury, the Germans issued an order that all barracks and depots previously occupied by the Italian army were now 'German property'.

By Christmas 1943 it was clear that the Allies had become bogged down at Cassino in a battle of attrition and would not be able to make a rapid advance to capture Rome. Some revival of support for Fascism was noticeable. This was fanned by astute propaganda about the damage American air raids were doing to Italian towns. These raids had a negative value: they did little damage to German lines of communications, but alienated ordinary Italians. The Fascists put up large notices on the ruins of burnt-out houses and buildings: 'This is the work of your so-called liberators.' Civilian casualties were heavy in many towns, and included women and children.

Important discussions were held in Rome from 16 to 18 January 1944 between Kesselring, Rahn and Graziani – at the German Embassy, not at the Italian War Office. This was significant in itself: Rahn, as interpreter of Hitler's orders, was the effective ruler of Republican Italy. A luncheon party was held on the 18th, from which Kesselring excused himself on the ground that he was on a strict diet.

Rahn ruled firmly that it was useless to continue discussing the recruitment of further Italian soldiers, at present interned in Germany, for the new divisions, explaining that it would be too difficult to 'extract' the men from the different industries, factories, etc., in which they were 'employed'. The real reason, of course, was that Hitler had vetoed it. However, Kesselring gave a sop to Graziani by agreeing to allow one coastal defence battalion currently operating under Kesselring's orders to be withdrawn and made available for the new divisions.

Graziani reported to Mussolini that it 'was highly uncertain (*aleatorio*) and problematic' whether the four divisions would ever be formed, that Kesselring was most reluctant to allow large Italian units to go into the line, and that he wanted to use Italian troops only in small groups mixed in with German units.

Graziani argued strongly that Italian troops in large units would be more effective, his overriding argument being that this would improve Italian morale, especially if there was a large-scale counter-offensive; and that if Italian soldiers could be seen to be 'chasing the invader out of the homeland, it would arouse the whole nation'.

Kesselring insisted that Graziani should remove his headquarters from Rome, taking away as many officers as possible as they were 'little hot-beds of treachery'. Graziani repeated the request he had made to Hitler that he should be allowed to go to the labour camps in Germany and call for volunteers. Kesselring ruled firmly that Graziani must rely instead on conscripts from Italy. Graziani also complained that the Germans would not allow him to draw clothing and blankets from the Italian depots.

Kesselring would not commit himself to a counter-offensive south of Rome, but stated that the Führer had ordered him to hold firm and plan for a counter-offensive to be put into operation at the right moment.

Graziani produced figures which showed that there would be sufficient manpower available for four divisions even allowing for the heavy demands (40,000) of von Richthofen, the German air force commander, for soldiers to labour on the airfields, although he exaggerated the numbers of conscripts who would come forward. Kesselring agreed with Graziani that several thousand men should be transferred from Ricci's Black Brigades to the new divisions.

When Graziani complained that the Germans had no faith in the loyalty of the Italian troops, Kesselring apologized and said he was only empha-sizing that fighting on the front was 'very tough'. Graziani then launched into an impassioned defence of the Italian army, recalling that after Caporetto in 1917 there had been an 'age of gold' on the Piave in 1918, with boys of eighteen under his command fighting splendidly. He pro-mised that if he commanded four divisions now they would do equally well, insisting that, at the time of the 9 September armistice, it was not the troops but the leaders who had betrayed the country. He reiterated the argument that he must be allowed to recruit in the labour camps, adding that Ricci would never hand over any of his Black Brigade because of the mounting threat from the partisans, which was already causing Ricci to seek the aid of the army. Kesselring again apologized because the German General Hans Leyers had asked Graziani to send regular troops to aid Ricci, and maintained that, although he wanted to see the new divisions at the front as soon as possible, he could do nothing about recruiting in German camps except refer the matter to Keitel at Hitler's headquarters.

Graziani's biggest diplomatic success was to persuade Kesselring to agree that the Italian SS Huntziger Division (13,000 strong) should be released from German control and become part of the new divisions.[6]

The minutes of the January Conference in Rome must have been melancholy reading for Mussolini; when Graziani had written to him on 13 January that he thought the Germans could contain the Allied armies south of Rome, Mussolini had replied that he did not share Graziani's optimism: 'Even the man in the street knows how, even slowly, the Germans are retreating.' However, there were positive signs of support and even enthusiasm for a new Fascist Army.[7]

Many regular officers who had gone home after 8 September now reported to their regimental headquarters in northern Italy; their example encouraged NCOs and other ranks to do the same, and the numbers of available troops kept on increasing.

The regular officers of the Italian army in the Fascist-held part of Italy were in a difficult position in the winter of 1943–4. Many had served for twenty years under Fascism, including three years of war, and after the forty-five days of Badoglio's rule in Rome they had to make agonizing decisions. There were many instances of officers first joining the Republican army and then, when they realized the true situation, deserting to the partisans in the hills. Against this, after the war Borghese could truthfully claim that a number of ex-partisan officers had enrolled in the Decima Mas.

Should one blame the Italian regular officers who joined the Republican Army? It must be remembered that at first after the Armistice the Resistance hardly existed. Nor were the Allies generally looked on as liberators. In the large towns which had been heavily bombed before the armistice there was rancour at the destruction and loss of life in what were clearly non-military targets. Italy was still being heavily bombed and, for months after 8 September, hardly existed as a state. It was a territory in which millions were doing their best just to exist and provide for their families, without any proper government. Fascism was still just alive; the Allies and the Germans were equally feared. It is not surprising that many thousands should have volunteered for Mussolini's army and co-operated with the Nazis and Fascists in maintaining law and order, when the legal government of the King and Badoglio was sitting, impotent, in the small port of Brindisi in the extreme south-east of the peninsula.

One senior career officer who wanted to desert the partisans and join the Republican Army was General Piero Operti. On 8 September 1943 he was Quartermaster-General of the Italian 4th Army in the south of France on the east of the Rhône. When his headquarters was surrounded by Germans he fled, with several hundred millions of lire (worth several million pounds) in cash belonging to the Army, to Cherasco in the mountains near Cuneo. Here he joined up with the partisans and became head of their organization. However, he found the partisan bands dominated by Communists, and he quarrelled with them. Further discouraged by the arrest by Fascists of all his staff officers, Operti asked for an interview with Zerbino, the Fascist prefect of Turin, on 26 January 1944 in a small town near Cuneo. Zerbino informed Mussolini that in their talk Operti, although not a Fascist, deplored the actions of Badoglio, which 'had brought Italy to ruin'; he proposed a truce between the German and Fascist troops and his own partisans, apart from the Communist brigades, during which Republican troops operating under his orders would wipe out all the Communist bands in the province of Cuneo. Zerbino told Mussolini that Operti's suggestions ought to be 'studied' and 'taken seriously'. However, the Duce would have no truck with Operti, minuting to Zerbino a few days later, 'I repeat, you are to liquidate this so-called more or less patriotic rebellion. There is no place for Operti in the Republican Army.' Operti was accused after the war of having kept some of the 4th Army's cash for himself; there was a rumour that he had a private plane. From the book he subsequently published in his defence – in which he makes no mention of his interview with Zerbino – it would appear that he used the cash to give 1,000 lire a month to any family in the Turin area who looked after one POW. These subsidies were paid through three liaison officers, and ceased after their arrest in February 1944.[8]

In his personal files Mussolini preserved a stirring account of the loyalty of one naval lieutenant whose faith in Fascism and the Axis stayed strong after the armistice of 8 September. In January 1944 the Admiralty sent his moving tale to Mussolini. On 9 September Lieutenant Massa of the Naval Engineers was serving on the Italian submarine *Otaria*, at sea in the Adriatic. Although nearly all the officers wanted to stay loyal to Fascism the submarine, after first trying to reach Cattaro, sailed under British escort to Taranto. Here Lieutenant Massa was shocked by the way in which the British were using skilled Italian naval ratings for menial work, unloading supply ships in the docks. *Otaria* was then transferred to Naples with the dreary task of using her generators to supply extra electricity for the inadequate supply in the town. Now even more strongly anti-Ally and pro-Axis, Massa decided to defect to fight with the Fascists; after being arrested by the Canadians while trying to cross the line, he escaped and eventually stole a boat on the Adriatic in company with two warrant officers who were equally ardent for Fascism. They rowed all night and landed on a beach, only to find to their dismay that they were still behind the lines of the British 8th Army. Without food, they hid in olive groves and vineyards for three nights before they found another rowing boat, which by dint of hard pulling through another night took them to a beach behind the German lines. The Germans, delighted with their Fascist sympathies, gave them a warm welcome. This saga was a good boost to Mussolini's morale, and indicates that not all courageous and daring young Italians were anti-German and pro-Allies at this stage of the war.[9]

Mussolini also carefully retained among his papers a similar account of courage, and of loyalty to Fascism. Captain Rino Grassi was Admiral's Secretary on the cruiser *Eugenio di Savoia*. When his ship surrendered at Taranto, Grassi deserted and travelled via Naples to the front line north of Sessa Aurunca on the west coast. His account of his travels shows how roughly and discourteously the Allies were treating surrendered army and naval personnel. Eventually, with great courage, he swam the Garigliano with a companion of similar Fascist faith; his companion was shot but Grassi reached the German lines safely and immediately volunteered for the Republican Army. His tale of courage and resolution was balm to Mussolini.[10]

On 22 January 1944, four days after the Kesselring–Graziani conference, the Allies made a sea-borne landing at Anzio near Rome. At first it looked as if Rome must fall, but Kesselring stabilized the front and pinned the invading troops down within a small perimeter. Much to Churchill's annoyance the US general in command, John Lucas, failed to take advantage of the chance to slip into Rome and cut Kesselring's supply line. Kesselring was so short of infantry with the opening of this new front that he welcomed any troops Graziani could send to him. Part of the Decima Mas, the Nembo and the Folgore Divisions went into wet trenches in the marshes, acquitted themselves well and were praised by the Germans fighting alongside.

When the Barberigo battalion of the Decima Mas went into action on the Anzio perimeter near Folignano they suffered such heavy casualties in fierce fighting that they had to be withdrawn. However, the units from the Nembo and Folgore were more fortunate, and they stayed in the line until the Allies began their break-out at the end of May. Then they too suffered unsustainable casualties. There was a stirring incident when Major Mario Rizzati of the Nembo Division, over fifty but an inveterate fighter, was cut off between Castel Porziana and the road to Ostia by the advancing British. He tried to form a defended area to help the Germans to cross the Tiber, and when a British tank approached, stood his ground in the middle of the road before being killed. His second-in-command, Captain Sala, used captured British tanks to bring his platoon to the bank of the Tiber, which he crossed in German canoes; once over the river, the Germans provided him with transport to escape to Milan.[11]

Earlier in the fighting, Major Rizzati had been highly praised by the Germans for help given by his company at Salerno, and was known to Mussolini for his courage and example. Mussolini's perturbation may therefore be imagined when the Fascist censors forwarded to him a letter from Major Rizzati to a girl-friend in Trieste which contained the words, 'I fight for the honour of the Italian flag and our fatherland, and certainly not for the Government of Salò', following this up with abuse of Fascism and its leaders, and describing Mussolini as 'the repentant Magdalene'. Mussolini asked Jandl to bring Rizzati to Salò during his unit's rest period out of the line. Rizzati, accompanied by three brother officers, was interviewed in the Villa Feltrinelli by Dolfin, on behalf of the Duce, about the 'treasonable letter'. Rizzati refused to withdraw any of his criticisms, saying he had accurately described his own point of view, which was shared by his fellow officers and soldiers. He said:

> My battalion has fought for years [in Spain and North Africa]. More of us are dead than alive, and more will soon die. We live amidst sand and mud, deprived of everything. We put string into our boots instead of laces; we button our tunics with barbed wire and we fight because we do not want anyone to have the right to say all Italians are cowards and betrayers without honour. We recognize only Italy, and this belief is enough.

His brother officers told Dolfin they agreed one hundred per cent.

Mussolini was unfortunately too busy to see Rizzati, whom Dolfin persuaded to write a note for the Duce explaining his point of view. On reading this note, which was not conciliatory, Mussolini said, 'Although Rizzati is headstrong and impulsive, he is the type of Italian who writes the history of our nation', and told Dolfin to assure Rizzati that his unit would have everything they needed, and that he looked on him and his soldiers as the best type of Italian. Afterwards Mussolini wished he had talked to Rizzati, saying they had both 'suffered and tormented themselves' for Italy.[12]

This incident enables us to glimpse the dilemma which faced officers in the Italian army after 9 September; many, though no lovers of Fascism, had their loyalties torn; for them, there were two 'enemy' armies on Italian soil; their betrayal of German soldiers, who often had been friends, left them with a feeling of guilt.

The conduct of the Fascist troops at Anzio induced Kesselring to take a kindlier view of the fighting potential of the Italians. The cadres for the new divisions were taking shape and the Germans were allowing the Italians access to German stores.

At the end of January Graziani reported that the total available armed forces of the Republic were 203,500, half of which were 'at German disposal'. Of the four new divisions to be trained in Germany, he had 16,000 for the Monte Rosa (12,000 already in Germany, 4,000 ready to go); 14,000 for the San Marco; and for the third and fourth divisions,

4,000 so far. On 12 February Graziani was able to report more optimistically to the Duce on the prospects for a substantial and worthwhile Fascist army.[13] At Vercelli on 9 February 2,600 soldiers had taken an oath of loyalty to Mussolini, and Graziani had made an impassioned speech. Even allowing for Graziani's desire to impress Mussolini, his report is probably reasonably accurate. He wrote that after his speech there was spontaneous applause and warmth and the atmosphere among the soldiers and onlookers was full of 'real patriotism'. He reported that, in spite of many difficulties, the concentration of the first new division in preparation for departure to Germany was proceeding satisfactorily, and he was taking steps to speed it up, although General Leyers was uncooperative about releasing conscripts who had been taken as labourers from Italy to Germany. Fifty officers and 2,200 other ranks had been released from the labour camps in Germany and enrolled in the SS. Graziani went to see them at Biella and Vercelli in their barracks, where they were under the control of the Germans. He found them in a pitiable condition after their internment, but in spite of this they had taken a personal oath of loyalty to the Führer.

At Vercelli he found that Ricci's Black Brigades had set up a battalion of young soldiers from fifteen to eighteen years old, 300 strong; he was angry because they were being given three times more pay than his soldiers, and had been told they would be trained as officers for the new army. Graziani told the Duce he had no plans to train more officers, who were 'two a penny' at that time.

At Novara, Graziani enjoyed another successful ceremony, with 1,300 soldiers taking the oath before a crowd of civilians 'who gave enthusiastic, lively and spontaneous applause, although the local political situation is not good' – partisans from the hills had carried out raids near the town, nor were the police, according to Graziani, over-loyal to the regime.

At Alessandria on 10 February, Graziani was even more enthusiastic. He held a parade of 4,600 soldiers in front of a large crowd and reported it as 'a truly superb spectacle' because the soldiers were 'so well disciplined'. His speech was this time interrupted by loud bursts of applause, and when two battalions of Bersaglieri marched past in perfect order there were 'uncontrollable waves of emotion from the crowd' so that there was 'a feeling of *rinascita* (rebirth)'. His experiences at Vercelli, Novara and Alessandria led Graziani to ask Mussolini to try to appear in public much more, because the Italian people wanted to see their leaders and hear why Italy had to fight against the British. At Novi and La Spezia, Graziani was also happy with what he found; at La Spezia the Germans told him they had complete faith in Borghese.

Graziani summed up to Mussolini that his inspections confirmed the *rinascita* of the Italian army, and that Mussolini ought to feed 'this new love of their country which was beginning to warm the hearts of Italians who had been so cast down and struck off balance by the inauspicious (*infausto*) crisis of July–September'.[14]

After visiting the Maesarle battalion of the Decima Mas at La Spezia, Graziani sent the following rousing appeal to Kesselring to allow them to take part in the defence of Rome and join their companions around the Anzio bridgehead:

La Spezia, 11 February.

From Graziani to Kesselring:

The Duce and I are immensely keen that another Italian unit should share in the defence of Rome beside their brave German comrades who are writing at Nettuno a magnificent page of military glory. We have ready a magnificent battalion of volunteers enrolled under the banner of the Decima Mas, which has never been struck; it is composed of picked troops, mostly veterans of many battles, stirred by a pure faith and unlimited enthusiasm.

They cry out loudly that they want to shed their blood for Rome. You will understand how much their high morale would mean for the rest of the new armed forces of Italy which we are creating if this unit could under your infallible guidance take part in the battle. If so, the Duce and I would be truly proud. Naturally you can deploy them wherever you find opportune; our only condition is that you put them into battle as soon as possible to chase the enemy away from Rome.[15]

Kesselring now had some faith in the loyalty of the Italian SS troops, with their oath to Hitler and their German officers, and sent two Italian SS battalions into the line against the Anzio beachhead on 17 March 1944. They went into wet trenches in the marshes similar to those the Decima Mas had occupied in January, and were interspersed amid German units in groups one company strong.

German officers sent back, on the whole, almost glowing reports: Italian equipment was 'adequate', apart from some deficiencies in machine-guns, but the Italians were too prone to indiscriminate firing – 'shoot, shoot and shoot again', while the Italian mortars had an 'unusually good performance'. German liaison officers stated that:

Italian SS co-operation is extremely good. All our orders are conscientiously carried out. They are keen to learn from us and realize there are some weaknesses in their weapons compared with ours. All ranks are decidedly battle happy and courageous . . .

Conduct and discipline of the Italian soldiers is extremely good. They are well trained to bear bad conditions and their behaviour under enemy fire is impressive. All of them, soldiers, NCOs and officers, are animated by an honourable fervour, and they display a strong feeling of comradeship with our soldiers. This is shown particularly by their readiness to help our wounded.

Delighted by these reports, Mussolini had them translated and published in *Avanguardia*, a Fascist newsheet published in Milan. Some Italian historians have doubted whether the *Avanguardia* reports were genuine, but the original German documents are among the Duce's papers, with handwritten notes by him: the *Avanguardia* extracts are authentic, not mere Fascist propaganda.

The Germans provided excellent convalescent accommodation for the wounded Italian SS, in a luxurious private clinic on Lake Maggiore, Casa di cura Rovetta, while Italian SS officers were allocated a first-class hotel as rest accommodation.[16]

Kesselring was so impressed with the fighting qualities of the Fascist Italians at Anzio that he withdrew his reservations about equipping four Italian divisions, and on his advice Hitler ordered that the project was to go ahead with as much help as possible.

In December 1943 General Canevari in Berlin had tried in vain to persuade the Germans to allow him to go to the labour camps of the surrendered Italian soldiers to recruit enthusiastic Fascists for the new divisions; he complained bitterly to Mussolini that the German General Staff and Speer, the Nazi Minister of Works, preferred to see 'magnificent' Alpine troops repairing and cleaning the roads of Berlin rather than fighting for the Axis. As a result Mussolini had to climb down and send his conscript recruits straight into Germany for training to make up the numbers. Canevari also complained of the difficulty of equipping the new recruits with uniforms and arms, the Germans having commandeered the depots at Vercelli where most of the recruits were; and that the clergy, in confession, were refusing absolution to young men who intended to take an oath to Mussolini on their formal enrolment.

In addition, the Germans, especially the Todt labour organization, went through the lists of the conscripts and insisted that young men with special skills should join the labour organizations, because they were 'indispensable'; and the national railways took many intelligent boys to make up their shortage of personnel. A continuing difficulty was the inadequate rations allowed to Graziani's men by the Germans: Canevari emphasized that Italian soldiers must have the same rations as the Germans because anti-Fascist propaganda was successful in telling the recruits that they would be made to die 'of hunger and cold'.[17]

By the spring of 1944 Graziani's new divisions were being trained in good conditions at Grafenwöhr and Paderborn in Germany. Living in comfortable German army barracks with sympathetic Nazi instructors and good rations, clothing and the best of German arms, the morale of the young Italian soldiers grew strong. Graziani was enthusiastic over the reports he received of the San Marco Division at Grafenwöhr. This was the pick of the new army, formed out of some of Borghese's troops and volunteers, and owing much to Borghese's enthusiasm and charisma.

Meanwhile, at Salò Mussolini was becoming increasingly depressed by the way in which the Germans were treating northern Italy as an occupied country, and the manner in which Ambassador Rahn ignored his complaints and those of his ministers. Rahn was young for his post (44), but intelligent and a fervent Nazi. He had no knowledge or love of the Italians; he was 'a difficult character', subject to unexpected and inexplicable changes of mood. If Mussolini or any Italian civil servant did not immediately carry out Hitler's orders as imparted to them by Rahn, he considered it a personal insult. In place of a pleasant working relationship, there was always tension between Mussolini and the German Ambassador. Mussolini liked to discuss new problems in relation to his previous experience, bringing in the historical and philosophical background; Rahn ignored the knowledge Mussolini had gained from ruling Italy for twenty years, and considered him an obstacle to the efficient execution of German policy in Italy. He was always pragmatic, bored by the Duce's flights of fancy; there was no meeting of minds, and Rahn was a bad choice to collaborate with Mussolini.

So it was that when in April Graziani suggested the Duce should visit the San Marco Division, Mussolini eagerly grasped the opportunity to get away from Salò, into an Italian army environment. Hitler offered to meet the Duce at Klessheim, near Salzburg. Mussolini agreed reluctantly; he recorded at the time that such a meeting would be useless, because although Hitler always gave him special treatment as an old and 'privileged' friend, he would do nothing to help 'the martyred Italian people'.

The meeting at Klessheim, on 22 April 1944, was not a success. When Mussolini complained of the harsh treatment of Italy, Hitler made the excuse that it would be folly for him to send divisions to fight in Italy if his supply routes were not secure. This was cold comfort for Mussolini. Graziani had a violent disagreement with Keitel about the dismantling of Italian armament factories to send the machinery into Germany. Mussolini suggested to Hitler, unsuccessfully, that he ought to make peace overtures to the Russians. For a moment Hitler faltered, but the next day ordered Ribbentrop not to make any move. Hitler went on at length to Mussolini, both in private and in conference with their entourage, about his plans for new secret weapons – flying bombs and automic warheads – which he claimed made an Axis victory certain. Mussolini half believed him.[18]

It was a great relief to the Duce when he and his retinue reached the Divisional Headquarters of the San Marco at Grafenwöhr in Bavaria on 24 April. Mussolini presented each battalion with new Italian tricolour flags with Republican rather than Savoy markings, and inspired the troops with a fiery speech. His powers of oratory had not deserted him. He began by telling the soldiers they were guests in a friendly country who, after

hard years of war, had been transformed into an undefeatable nation with
an iron will and become one vast workshop and military barracks. He
went on:

> The shame of our betrayal will not be expunged unless we fight the invader
> who contaminates our soil. Beyond the Garigliano [the Allies were held at
> Cassino and on the river Garigliano] you will find not only the bivouacs of
> the hard-faced British but Americans, French, Poles, Indians, South Africans,
> Canadians, Australians, New Zealanders, Moroccans, Senegalese, Negroes
> and Bolsheviks. You are to have the privilege of fighting this witches'
> cauldron of bastard nations who respect nothing and nobody as they invade
> Italy . . . In these training grounds stand the foundations of the new
> Republican Army. You have the special privilege of being part of this great
> new edifice and you will have the outstanding honour of taking her into war.
>   Your fatherland counts on you, and I am sure that you will give her far
> beyond her hopes.
>   The day must come when the lion of Saint Mark, whose triumphs in the
> day of the Empire of Venice are famous, will carry on his wings new and even
> more splendid victories.

His speech was received with delirious applause and an enthusiasm which
amazed the German instructors, who had hitherto thought the Italian
soldiers apathetic. Mussolini was delighted. First he talked to them
through the window of the officers' mess and then he went outside to be
surrounded by the men, many of whom clasped and kissed his hands. As
he drove off in the dark there was 'frenetic enthusiasm'.

As his train passed Bolzano and other Italian towns on the return
journey to Lake Garda, crowds flocked to the stations to greet the Duce.
Mussolini had not been seen in public since before 25 July 1943. Now,
with all Italy under threat of becoming a battlefield between the Allies
and the Germans, the fear of Communists approaching from the east, and
US air raids destroying large parts of Italian towns, Mussolini seemed to
be a father-figure who might lead them out of war into peace. His temporary new popularity was not the outcome of any real love of Fascism,
but a response to the comfort of seeing the familiar face of someone who,
it was felt, could rescue Italy from a dreadful plight.[19]

The call-ups in the spring were unsatisfactory. Only 40 per cent of
those summoned enrolled and there were many desertions. The death
penalty and reprisals against families were threatened as a punishment for
non-compliance, but the evidence is that such harsh measures were not
implemented. By the end of July 1944 the Republican Army numbered
400,000 men. Graziani still had several battalions in Italy, while the Italian
SS had over 100,000, the Militia around the same figure, and the four

new divisions in Germany almost 80,000. Kesselring now began to consider bringing back to Italy the San Marco and Monte Rosa Divisions, to use them against the partisans. He suggested that Graziani should command a Ligurian Army consisting of Italians and two and a half German divisions.

However, the fall of Rome on 4 June 1944 had shaken Italian confidence in a German victory, although the Allies' cross-channel invasion into Normandy at the beginning of June had been contained by the Germans within a small bridgehead. The Germans were still fighting strongly south of the Apennines, and there was no real threat that the Allies would cross the River Po. Graziani and Kesselring agreed that another visit by Mussolini to the Italian divisions being trained in Germany was needed to improve morale.

Mussolini felt that the presence of the four Italian divisions on Italian soil was vital to keep the Republic in existence, because since the fall of Rome the partisan movement had become an increasing threat to his authority.

In the middle of June a long memorandum about the training in Germany had been sent to the Duce by Colonel Manfredini. This revealed that the Italians were having to endure many pinpricks from the Germans. All Italian soldiers on being enrolled in the new divisions had to swear an oath of loyalty to the Republican Government: 'I swear on my word of honour that as an officer or soldier of the Republican Army I will fight vigorously and bravely with the Germans and obey unconditionally and without hesitation all orders and show in this war that I am a brave soldier.'

In the second half of May the German Inspector of the Italian divisions, General Ott, addressed a conference of senior officers and told them that a second oath would now be required, to the person of the Duce, and they must indoctrinate the troops so that they would swear it. This was: 'I support the Fascist Republic Government and I declare myself ready to fight in the new army of the Duce under the German High Command against the common enemy of the Italian Republic and the great German Reich.' The Italians pointed out that the second oath of loyalty to the Duce was completely superfluous, but when it became clear that this was a direct order from Hitler, made without consulting either Graziani or Mussolini, the officers acquiesced with bad grace.

Even more to their annoyance, Ott told them that the German liaison officers who had been acting as instructors would stay permanently with the divisions even when they were fighting at the front. The senior officers flared up at this 'insult', saying they would not allow their men to be put under fire if they had German 'controllers' at their side. The instructors who were to become 'controllers' were almost all between 22 and 25, whereas the senior Italian officers were in their fifties, veterans of the First World War when many of them had been wounded and 'highly decorated'. Colonel Manfredini emphasized to Mussolini that he would find it 'easy' to imagine the effect on morale of the 'controllers' becoming 'instructor–commanders'.[20]

A document which illustrates the fury of the Italians at being put under German 'minders' or 'controllers' is a memorandum from Major Giuseppe Santoro, commanding the second battalion of the 5th Regiment in the San Marco, to his Divisional Commander:

> Our soldiers who hate the Germans are exclusively those who have been in German internment camps. One cannot deny the Germans do everything possible to make themselves unloved. One German colonel is a mad hater of Italians. The Germans treat our staff with contempt and my liaison officer ('controller') Ten Möller has admitted, and this is confirmed by his Commanding Officer Major Büttner, that he only pretends to seek my opinion before he gives orders. I am convinced that the Germans would like to see the Italian army disbanded, and it may be all part of a plot to sabotage Hitler, similar to the recent attempt on his life.
>
> I am ready to fight as a simple soldier, but I cannot command a battalion any longer and most certainly not in the front line when I must accept, although an Italian officer, a condition of complete inferiority to the Germans.[21]

As will be seen, the British had an identical problem when they equipped Royalist divisions with British equipment and provided instructors who were to become 'controllers' when the units were at the front.

Manfredini went on that among all ranks there was an impression that the divisions were at the 'complete mercy' of the German military authority; they felt sure the German High Command had strongly opposed their creation, only consenting because of a 'precise' order from Hitler based partly on political grounds and partly on the Führer's great affection for the Duce. They also thought the German staff officers had gone slow with their training, and that it was they who had insisted on the instructors remaining as 'controllers'.

In May the Germans had recalled their most modern sub-machine-guns and replaced them with old Italian Berettas, inferior and out of date. The troops had only half the weapons laid down in their establishment, and only one quarter of the horses. It was highly doubtful if the shortages would be made good before the divisions began to go back to Italy, as planned, in July.

Manfredini also highlighted the depressing effect on the troops of the loss of Rome and the German retreat, but said that if the Po valley was defended, the divisions would be eager to take part; however, if the industrial part of Italy were lost, 'we would definitely not see our divisions fighting for the fatherland'.[22]

The new divisions amounted to almost 60,000 men, of whom 14,000 came from the German labour camps for the prisoners of 9 September 1943, and around 46,000 from volunteers and conscripts, plus a few ex-partisans who volunteered after being captured.[23]

Mussolini decided to visit the training camps of all four Italian divisions; to see Hitler and have a showdown with him about the treatment of the internees; and to demand the immediate return to Italy of the four divisions. The itinerary was: 16 July, visit to Monte Rosa Division at Münsingen; 17 July, the Italia at Paderborn; 18 July, morning, San Marco at Grafenwöhr; afternoon, Littorio at Sennelager. Then the Duce was to go on to confer with the Führer at the Wolf's Lair.

This tour was Mussolini's Indian Summer. As he started off towards the frontier in a motor cavalcade which passed through several Italian towns, crowds gathered in the streets and gave him an enthusiastic reception. Fortunately there were no air raids. He boarded a special German train at Trento and early in the afternoon of 16 July was at Münsingen, in spite of a long delay at Munich because of air raids: black smoke hung over the city, and Mussolini was irritated when one of the Germans in his entourage told him it was only an anti-aircraft exercise.

Once again Mussolini's hypnotic powers aroused the enthusiasm of the young Italian conscripts; his impact was intensified by the romance, for the soldiers, of seeing his familiar face in alien German surroundings. The men gave a spontaneous, enthusiastic response to Mussolini's speech, as did the officers; after all, they had been brought up and enrolled in the army during the heyday of Fascism.

Mussolini was much put out at having to curtail his visit to the San Marco Division because of air raids; he had conceived a special affection for these troops. Nevertheless, he was able to mingle with the soldiers as he had in April, amid similar scenes of enthusiasm.

Paderborn and Sennelager are German training areas similar to Aldershot. At Sennelager, Mussolini watched the Littorio Division's manoeuvres, even running from one vantage point to another to see better. When he made his speech, many of the troops were in tears. Both Mussolini and Graziani were visibly moved and became temporarily euphoric. Graziani's peroration was, 'the Germans have given us back our legions'. Then he caught Rahn's eye and stopped: he was standing near a statue of Arminius, who in AD 9 had annihilated the Roman legions of Varus with the soldiers of the Teutonic tribes. After his speech Mussolini disappeared into a crowd of soldiers who flocked around him, intent on assuring him of their loyalty and ardour.

On 20 July, von Stauffenberg nearly killed the Führer with a bomb at the Wolf's Lair at midday; the attempted coup and rebellion failed when Hitler was only wounded, not killed as had been anticipated. That afternoon, with his arm in a sling, Hitler was able to greet Mussolini when his special train reached Rastenburg after an interminable delay. But he was far from being himself, while Mussolini was relaxed and buoyant, cheered with the warmth of his reception by his soldiers. When Mussolini was told of the bomb plot, he was elated, realizing that Germans were plotting against Hitler in the same way as the monarchists had betrayed him on 25 July 1943. He felt the score was now even. Mussolini told Graziani, 'We no longer have a monopoly of treachery.'

At the Wolf's Lair, while Hitler was showing Mussolini the damage to his conference room from the bomb, Keitel summoned Graziani into another room. Keitel said he needed three of the four Italian divisions for the Russian front, instead of sending them back to Italy. Graziani lost his temper and told the German that such a move would be the end of Mussolini's rule in Italy. They yelled and cursed; Vittorio Mussolini, the Duce's son, said he had never witnessed such a 'brawl'.

Meanwhile, Mussolini was having an easier passage with the Führer. Hitler's main idea was to get rid of the Duce as soon as possible so that he could concentrate on rooting out and revenging himself on the conspirators. For once, Mussolini felt superior. During a hurriedly-arranged tea party, Hitler agreed that all four divisions should go back to their homeland, and promised Mussolini that the military internees would have much better treatment and there would be no more deportations. Typically, Hitler later reneged on his pledge of better treatment for the internees, although he had mildly accepted a written memorandum which Mussolini handed to him outlining the proposals.

As he made his adieus to the Duce, Hitler whispered to Rahn, 'Be very careful', although a minute before he had told the Duce, 'You are possibly my only friend in the world'. Hitler feared, with justification, that Mussolini might betray him. This was the final meeting of the two dictators.[24]

Reports about the ill-treatment of the captured Italian soldiers in the labour camps had by now alerted Mussolini; the condition of the few thousand officers and men who had been released and allowed to return to Italy was shocking. Only a handful of POWs from Badoglio's army were given proper treatment as under the Geneva Convention.

The 600,000 Italian soldiers captured after 8 September had been shipped in cattle wagons to labour camps in Germany where they lived under appalling conditions, forced to work long hours in German factories and mines. The labour camps for Italian civilians (amounting to 200,000) who had volunteered for work in Germany under trade union organization before 25 July 1943, and for those rounded up and deported to Germany after 9 September 1943, were much better. Little complaint could be made of their conditions, given the shortage of food in Germany. Prior to 9 September 1943, Italian civilian workers in Germany had been treated well.

Mussolini was very conscious of the bad treatment meted out to the surrendered Italian soldiers, but every complaint to Rahn and to Hitler had been ignored. Fascist generals visited the camps continually under the aegis of an organization run in Berlin by Anfuso, the Italian Ambassador, and any prisoner who would opt for Fascism received better treatment. But only a small proportion of the 600,000 soldier-prisoners volunteered for Graziani's army.

As soon as he returned to Salò, Mussolini circulated copies of the memorandum he had given Hitler to the German authorities in Italy, with an appended note: 'The Führer has given special orders to transform Italian military internees into special civilian workers or to draft them into military units.' He was wishfully deluding himself. Their atrocious treatment was not changed.[25]

In Berlin, Anfuso was similarly deceived about Hitler's more sympathetic attitude to the Italian military internees. Early in August he issued a leaflet which raised their hopes but proved a complete illusion.

FOR THE FORMER INTERNEES
AN IMPORTANT MESSAGE FROM THE ITALIAN AMBASSADOR

Companions

As you know, on 21 July [*sic*] the Duce and the Führer came to an agreement about your future which realizes your hopes and those of all Italians who like you are forced to suffer from the consequences of the coup that consigned your country to the enemy. The Government of the Republic has always considered its first duty is to alleviate your suffering, and has succeeded in obtaining your liberty. From this moment you are no longer internees, but free citizens in an allied country where your duties will be purely civilian.

From 31 August the German authorities have agreed that your transformation into civilian workers will be an accomplished fact. Each one of you will benefit from an individual work contract with normal wages, enjoying all the social benefits guaranteed to civilian workers by German law. A better standard of life equivalent to that enjoyed by average German workers will be guaranteed to you by the German authorities.

The leaflet went on to say that this better treatment was due to 'passionate' efforts by the Duce, who would do everything in future to see that their lot became better and better.

It was a cruel deception on the part of the Germans. On 15 August, in a letter to the Duce enclosing the leaflet, Anfuso had to write that he was running into great difficulties. He wanted the Germans to allow a large proportion of the internees to be recruited to the Republican Army. The Germans refused. The Ministry of Labour said they would not release the internees unless an equivalent work force was sent from Italy to replace them, while the Wehrmacht refused to allow the 30,000 officers to become either free labourers or recruits to the Republican Army, because they were 'unreliable politically'. It was an inauspicious start.[26]

The Germans paid lip-service to the 20 July Hitler/Mussolini agreement in a bogus ceremony at a prison camp near Berlin where about 1,500 military internees were held. Count Mazzolini, Mussolini's Deputy Foreign Secretary, and Ambassador Anfuso were present at the removal of the gates and the cutting of the barbed wire. This was a cosmetic gesture which affected only a minute proportion of the 600,000. The appalling conditions in which the vast majority were existing remained unchanged.

On 12 September Anfuso confirmed this, writing to the Duce that the 'senseless inhumane treatment' of the military internees continued and there was no 'real' improvement in their living conditions. Indeed, he found that the German attitude towards the Italians had hardened, resulting in even worse treatment for the internees. If Mussolini still had any faith in Hitler's goodwill towards him, this letter must have removed it.[27]

In the autumn of 1943 the Salò Government had set up an office in Berlin to try to help both military internees and civilian workers in Germany. It was known as SAI (Servizio Assistenze Italiani) and carried out visits of inspection to the camps. Its reports were horrific.

On behalf of Mussolini, Anfuso had in June 1944 delivered to the German Government a protest couched in the strongest terms about the treatment of the 'internees'. This stated that there were continuous reports of brutal treatment, especially when their work output was deemed insufficient. This maltreatment had resulted in many deaths, and made the Italians so hostile to the Germans that 'a deep abyss was developing between the two countries'; many internees bore the scars of beatings. All the internees were looked on as traitors and enemies of Germany, and treated accordingly. 'The rules of international law are not respected in the camps – while workers from the east enjoy privileges and living conditions almost equal to the Germans themselves, the Italians are subject to ever worse treatment and ever lower rations.'

Anfuso demanded that the German Government should issue firm orders that Italian prisoners were to be treated as well as those of other nations, that their hours of work should be in accordance with the Geneva rules for prisoners-of-war, and that better rations must be distributed, especially for those doing heavy work. He pointed out that one camp considered too bad to house Russian prisoners-of-war had been used for Italian military, and that the Germans removed medicines from Red Cross parcels intended for the internees. He also asked for the repatriation of the sick and disabled in return for more fit workers coming from Italy.

Attached to the report was a detailed list of atrocities. In the Saarbrücken area there was a high percentage of deaths in camps, and executions were 'not rare', while the torn uniforms of the prisoners were a pitiable sight. At Görlitz, rations were quite insufficient for internees doing heavy work and relief parcels sent from Italy were tampered with, while Italian civilians living in the town were not allowed to send in extra rations. Sick men were made to work and beaten if they could not, so that some died on the factory floor. Several internees had to be hospitalized because of beatings, and their treatment was worse than that given to French and Germans in the same area. At the factory of Petersdorf, the hours of work were 72 per week, on quite insufficient rations. At Ludwigsfeld the hours were twelve per day, with an additional two hours of cleaning. One internee had been wounded in the shoulder by the bayonet of the interpreter and could not move his arm. The same soldier was beaten three weeks later because he could not work properly with his bad arm, and Anfuso's representative had seen horrible scars from this beating.

At Luckenwalde, the inmates had to do heavy work on starvation rations; out of 1,370 internees in one group, 232 were in hospital; in another group, 227 out of 1,061 were in hospital. Many were suffering from tuberculosis (often galloping), pneumonia or malaria, and there had been 73 deaths in the hospital in six months. Had it not been for the help given by the nearby French camp, their state would have been worse. In the mortuary, bodies lay unburied for weeks.

The general policy of the Germans was to punish internees with beatings rather than imprisonment, so that offenders could still be made to work. As a final comment on conditions, Anfuso's memorandum made it clear that because of lack of washing facilities the internees were nearly all tormented by bed bugs and lice.[28]

The Papal Nuncio in Berlin, Monsignor Cesare Orsenigo, wrote an objective and authoritative account in June 1945 of the suffering of the Italian 'internees'. Its accuracy cannot be challenged.

The internment of the military in Germany lasted from September 1943 until the capitulation of Germany – i.e., around twenty-one months [this is further evidence that Hitler did not change their status after his promise to Mussolini on 20 July 1944]; the great majority suffered painful personal deprivation and acute moral suffering so that a great many became ill and died. A few who professed themselves Fascists had decent treatment.

1 The first immediate horror for the internees was the way in which they were arrested. The soldiers were made prisoners not only in Italy but in all the other countries (Greece, Albania, France, etc.) where they were stationed. The reason was solely that they had obeyed orders from their sovereign on 8 September 1943. They were made responsible for a political decision with which had nothing to do. The tradition in Italy is for the military to keep themselves hermetically sealed from politics.

2 They were transported, many without kitbags, in summer uniforms, without food, closed in cattle wagons with no hygienic arrangements.

3 Thus shut up they travelled slowly to the north with unexplained stops and no food. Once at their destinations they were scattered; some in Serbia, others in Croatia, others in Alsace, many in Poland and the greater number in Germany.

4 Their barracks were a bitter disillusionment. They were interned (one might say thrown) on small pieces of ground surrounded by barbed wire and guarded by German soldiers who saw in every one of them a traitor to Germany. The so-called barracks were primitive in the extreme.

Orsenigo knew what he was writing about because he frequently visited the internees. He stated that many officers in the *Oflags* spent the day in complete idleness (which was even worse for many than forced labour in mines or factories), sitting on a few square yards of miserable ground under a perpetually grey sky in a cold northern climate, with nothing to eat but boiled cabbage and potatoes, under the eyes of a German soldier always ready to shoot or to punish. The dormitories were inadequate, according to Orsenigo, with three tiers of bunks, 250 men sleeping in dormitories designed for a hundred. Many had to sleep on pallets of straw on the ground; there was a lack of blankets, so they suffered intensely from the cold. Orsenigo commented that it was not surprising that bronchitis, pleurisy and TB became so rife that by December 1944 hospitals were overcrowded with the sick.

The plight of the internees was aggravated because the Germans would not allow the International Red Cross to visit and the internees had no 'protecting power', like other prisoners-of-war. The Germans told the Vatican that Mussolini's Fascist Government was the protecting power. According to Orsenigo, Mussolini's office (the SAI) set up to protect the internees was 'just a convenient instrument in the hands of the Germans to enable them to carry out all sorts of illegal acts and try to force the internees to become Fascists'. In the absence of a genuine protecting power, Pope Pius XII instructed Orsenigo to visit as many camps as possible. In 1944 he carried out twenty visits, many more than Anfuso, the Ambassador to Germany.

Orsenigo reported that in each of the twenty camps he visited in 1944 he found the same misery, the same pernicious shortages of food, blankets and clothing; the German commandants acknowledged his complaints courteously but said it was impossible to do anything, alleging a general scarcity of food, and that illness was due to the climate being unsuitable for Italians brought up in the sun.

Orsenigo was particularly concerned about the extent of TB among the young Italian soldiers; at that time the disease was almost incurable, although its progress could be halted by transfer to a warm climate. He felt that infection might be reduced by sending the worst cases home, and made sixty such demands for this to be done to the German authorities. Not until 14 March 1944 was the first train sent back to northern Italy carrying bad TB cases. Orsenigo commented:

> The train was not a success. At Verona the hospitals had not realized what demands would be made upon their resources. Many very sick soldiers had to be sent home to their families because of shortages of hospital beds. When their parents and neighbours saw their sons, they were horrified; a few months before they had left home in the pink of health and vitality and now they came home like skeletons and were dying. This produced 'dangerous resentment' among the Italian population. The German authorities in Italy soon became aware of this and advised their counterparts in Germany not to send any more trainloads.

Between March and October there were only two more trains. The Vatican and the Italian doctors pressed the SAI in Berlin for action, to be met with the excuse that lists were being prepared; in January 1945, with Mussolini's help, a few trains arrived.[29]

On 3 March 1945 the Italian Ambassador to the Holy See (representing the Royal Government) in Rome sent a note to inform Maglione that at the concentration camp of Siedlice (Warsaw) the Germans had shot 1,000 Italian officers. The news caused a furore in Italy and abroad.

Anfuso's copious letters to the Duce about the military internees reveal that he was more interested in recruiting for the Republican Army than in alleviating the pitiable conditions in which the captured soldiers were held. Mussolini, in contrast, personally organized quantities of food parcels. According to Ponce de Leon Mellini, his deputy Foreign Secretary, several hundred food trains went from Milan via Switzerland to the camps, but 'not all the material sent arrived at its destination'. Mussolini told Mellini that most of the interned soldiers had betrayed him, but 'it is my duty to help them, even if they are and will remain my enemies'.

The Pope also took a personal interest in succouring the internees; the Vatican bought large quantities of vitamins, other medicines and special invalid food in Switzerland, and sent clothing and nourishing food. Without the Mussolini and Vatican train-loads, many more Italians would have died in captivity.

In his notoriously unreliable memoirs, the prominent Fascist Bruno Scampanato alleged that 283 train-loads of food were sent from Italy by the government, of which 280 arrived safely. On the same page he claimed falsely that the Royal Legation in Berne managed to delay the hospital trains passing through Switzerland with the result that several very sick soldiers died on them.

As the Allies bombed Berlin, causing great destruction, Italian internees were forced to clear up the damage. These *Badogliotruppen*, as they were called, were treated with contempt, their shabby uniforms and general appearance aroused derision.

As the Russians advanced towards camps where the Italian internees were held, the Germans set the internees free and told them they could go back to Italy. This was impossible. The Germans provided no transport, and most of the soldiers were too weak to walk.

The chaplain of the military internees camp at Görlitz in Silesia reported to the Vatican on 7 March 1945:

> Our camp is also being evacuated. But how? Half of our men are in no state to face a walk of hundreds of kilometres with wood sandals, half-naked, with jackets and trousers unchanged for eighteen months, and bare-headed. Under these conditions it would be madness to set them on the road because they would only die *en route*. They will stay here, and I will stay with them.[30]

Eventually those who survived of the 600,000 straggled back to Italy after the German surrender in May 1945. The deportation and maltreatment of these soldiers captured in September 1943 was a hideous wrong perpetrated by Germany; not until all those deported and their children are dead can Italy forgive Germany for this crime.

CHAPTER 7

The New Army Disappoints

IN AUGUST 1944 Wolff asked Mussolini to form a new German-officered Italian SS Division, although he must have known this would impinge on the resources and manpower available for regular Republican Divisions. Mussolini was furious and on 14 August he wrote to Himmler (who was Wolff's superior):

> Recruiting in Italy is impossible. Many internees in Germany are loyal to the Republic and ready to fight. I propose you create an SS Division in Germany [from the internees].
>
> The sick and invalids recently returned from the internment camps in Germany are in a miserable condition; news of this has led Italians to decline to volunteer for labour in Germany.

However, Mussolini decided not to press Himmler for recruits from the soldiers interned in Germany, commenting: 'It would be harmful to bring home men whose attitudes could easily send them into the enemy camp.' Himmler never replied to the Duce.

Mussolini then wrote to Goebbels that there were far too many German officers and civilians in Italy employed in non-combatant roles, and asked him to reduce these 'officers to the absolute minimum since many of these officials have shown no sign of Fascist or National Socialist sympathies'.[1]

Like Himmler, Goebbels did not reply. They looked on any suggestions from Mussolini, the head of a puppet Government in an occupied country in the war zone, as 'cheek'. The letters are evidence of Mussolini's frustration at being unable to create a strong enough army to give him credibility in the eyes of the German generals. At the end of the month he told his Cabinet he intended to tell Rahn that 'either he should be allowed to govern, or he would resign'.[2]

Mussolini's spirits revived when he found that Hitler kept his word given on 20 July: the San Marco Division returned almost immediately, and the Monte Rosa in August. However, a nasty hiccup developed over the return of the other two divisions being trained in Germany, the Littorio and Italia.

At the end of September Mussolini received a shock when Keitel told the Italian liaison unit in Berlin that the Italia Division would be dissolved and the men used for anti-aircraft (Flak) units on the Russian front, and threatened that the Littorio Division would be used in the same way. Dismayed, Mussolini wrote to Hitler on 29 September:

Führer,
I am informed that two divisions will return to Italy but it is proposed to dissolve the Italia. I must tell you, Führer, that this would be a grave blow to the authority of the Fascist Government and I implore you to prevent it. Everything possible is being done, and will be done, to provide you with the men you need quickly. This is in the interests of Italy and our joint venture. I am sure, Führer, that you will give me once again a proof of your friendship and your solidarity with me, and sure of this I send you as always my most cordial greetings and best wishes.

Mussolini[3]

At the Wolf's Lair on 20 July Keitel had asked Graziani for 24,000 extra Italian soldiers for Flak units. By the end of September, 8,500 had already gone and another 2,000 were ready. General Morea, the head of the Italian mission in Berlin, wrote on 8 October to Keitel praising him in flowery terms and begging him not to disband the two Italian divisions being trained in Germany 'over whose head the sword of Damocles was poised' for the sake of the 'authority of the Duce'. He reminded Keitel that Mussolini had already sent an extra 80,000 men for the Todt labour organizations, and promised that the necessary extra men would soon be found.

Mussolini wrote pathetically to Goering the next day that everything humanly possible was being done by his Government to send the men and war *matériel* required by Germany, and that

the authority of my Government would suffer a dangerous setback if I lost one of the four divisions which the Führer had allowed to be trained in Germany in such a friendly and generous gesture to form the nucleus of a future Republican Army.

I plead with you once again, dear Marshal, to re-examine the question from the political angle, and try and keep in being the two divisions. Meanwhile, I will with all my energy gather the 6 or 10,000 men which you need and send them to the Reich as quickly as possible for the use of the German armed forces.

Mussolini's servile letters for once produced the required result, and on 14 October Morea telegraphed to the Duce that the Littorio would be returning to the homeland immediately, and that he was negotiating for the return of the Italia.[4]

The Italia Division was saved, but only temporarily, because while it completed its training in Germany the Germans continued to harass Mussolini by demanding more and more soldiers for their anti-aircraft units. After his frenzied efforts to stop the Italia being broken up, Mussolini's need to supply many thousands more soldiers to go to Germany (who he felt would be better deployed in keeping up the strength of his own cherished divisions) became a running sore. To add to his bitterness, he was acutely aware of the plight of those 600,000 Italian soldiers held by the Germans in forced labour camps, as detailed in Chapter 6.

On 9 November, Rahn gave a luncheon party on Lake Garda to mark the imminent return of Ambassador Anfuso to Germany. It was a tense affair. Barely able to hide their hostility, Pavolini, Buffarini Guidi and Anfuso sat down at table as Rahn's guests; immediately an acrimonious discussion began about Hitler's demand for 24,000 extra men to be sent to Germany, failing which the Führer would insist on splitting up the newly-trained Italia Division. Rahn threatened aggressively that, unless he was given guarantees within the next three days that another large contingent of Italians was ready to leave for Germany immediately and the remainder of the 24,000 within ten days, the dissolution of the Italia 'was inevitable'. Buffarini Guidi assured Rahn that 4,000 police would be sent to Germany right away. As a stalling tactic, the Italians promised to send a senior officer to visit every barracks as soon as possible to recruit all available soldiers for Germany. Rahn interposed that he would send Consul Molhausen to help. This the Italians did not approve, claiming it would be 'counter-productive' – the recruitment must be an all-out Italian effort. After this most unsatisfactory lunch the three Italians begged the Duce to go into action urgently to stop the break-up of the division and a 'more-or-less indiscriminate round-up' by the Germans.[5]

Thus prompted, Mussolini wrote to Goering again on 11 November:

I am told 50,000 Italians from the Balkans are in the Vienna area, used as soldiers and workers by the German headquarters in that zone. An equal number of Italians are coming from France and Belgium to west Germany. I beg you, my dear Marshal, to take out of these contingents part of the 12,000 men you need for your Flak units so as to ease my task in the spirit of friendship which you have always shown me.[6]

The archives show that Mussolini's figure of 50,000 Italians in the Vienna area was an understatement. Germany was determined to bleed

Republican Italy white of manpower. Fortunately the soldiers, police and labourers who went to Germany in the autumn of 1944 were treated much better than the unlucky 600,000 taken to Germany immediately after the September armistice a year earlier.

Goering did not respond to this humiliating appeal; but as train-loads of reluctant Italians arrived in Germany in part satisfaction of his insatiable demand for manpower, Hitler relented and gave orders for the return of the Littorio and Italia Divisions to Italy at the end of November 1944.

The San Marco was deployed along the Ligurian coast to defend Genoa, but the risk of an Allied invasion there was minimal, and the San Marco saw no action against the Allies. In December, the Littorio took over German positions in the high Alps on the French frontier west of Cuneo. The Allies had invaded southern France on 16 August, landing a strong Franco-British-American force on the Riviera, and immediately pushed north to Vichy and Lyon to link up with Eisenhower's armies invading Germany. The Allies had no intention of wasting troops on attacking Liguria; their plan was to pin down as many of Hitler's divisions as possible in Italy so that he could not withdraw any of them to defend Germany.

After the war, Graziani at his trial claimed that his Republican Divisions had prevented a 'Gaullist' invasion of north-west Italy. This is a myth without foundation, not shared by Mussolini, as will be seen. The Allies at first placed a thin web of outposts in the high Mediterranean Alps on the Franco-Italian frontier; when the snows came these were withdrawn. The frontier on the coast between Ventimiglia and Mentone was defended by German troops, with the San Marco Division well to the rear. The Littorio was scarcely involved in fighting against the Allies in the Mediterranean Alps although there were clashes at high altitudes.[7]

As soon as the new divisions returned to their home soil, large-scale desertions began. This was not surprising. Those soldiers with homes in the southern part of Italy occupied by the Allies had not seen their families since before 9 September 1943, and could not even exchange letters, let alone go home on leave. They knew that the Allies were moving inexorably up Italy; by hiding in towns or remote rural areas, they could emerge in Allied territory as the Germans withdrew and quietly go home. It would be wrong to attribute most of the desertions to anti-German or anti-Fascist feelings. The majority of the men were not politically aware. Italian soldiers are immensely loyal to their comrades and officers, but home ties come first. Poor rations and bad pay contributed. When Republican troops came into contact with the partisans, both officers and soldiers deserted in droves. Some were tempted by the prospect of a better life with the rebels; many were revolted by reports of atrocities by the Germans and the Black Brigades against civilians in the anti-partisan warfare.

There was a fierce propaganda war between the Resistance and the Fascists. Newspapers, leaflets and posters were printed in huge numbers by both sides, with one urging all soldiers to join the partisans to liberate their country, and the other asking them to defend their homeland against the brutal Anglo-Americans whose bombs were devastating Italian towns while Italians in Allied-occupied territory were being starved and maltreated.

According to Graziani, there were 5,000 desertions from the new divisions during the first weeks after their return, but Rahn claimed it was as high as 10,000. A report dated 17 December to Graziani from General Agosti, Divisional Commander of the Littorio, on the French frontier, is revealing:

By 12 December the whole of the Division arrived in its alloted quarters. When the first five convoys bivouacked on the Po they found to their surprise that a temporary local truce had been made with the partisans. This resulted in 300 deserting to them.

Subsequent convoys ran into air raids on the Brenner railway north of Trento, and the line became blocked. Instead of being discouraged, the soldiers with spirit and discipline helped to repair the railway and continued on foot for 100 km without any desertions, in spite of losing twelve dead and fifty-six wounded from more air raids.

Many units had to bivouac in areas full of rebels; several soldiers were contacted by their families who suggested they should desert. Eventually some soldiers found themselves near their homes and succumbed to the desire to fall into the arms of their dear ones. However the veterinary unit, the divisional workshop and two battalions of Alpini and the reserve battalion showed the highest sense of duty and affection for the Division.

Now the Division has taken over positions in the front line from German units, despite severe deficiencies in weapons and equipment. The double equipment, German and Italian, is a severe drawback. However, the troops are well enough equipped to fight the partisans.

To make up the deficiencies I have asked for several thousand 'Mitra' [submachine guns] which will help my soldiers to show what stuff they are made of. We are short of boots and wool socks. In spite of many shortages the morale of the troops is fine.

The Division is immobile. According to our war establishment we should have 127 cars, and we have only 64; instead of 241 lorries we have 70; instead of 241 motor cycles, only 15; and only 16 tractors instead of 84.

As for mules and horses, we have only 2,301 instead of our establishment of 8,136. We can do without the horses for operations in the high mountains, but more mules are absolutely essential.

I sincerely hope that when we come to fight alongside our German comrades in the final offensive we shall have the necessary new weapons, and also not be immobilized by lack of transport.[8]

In October Mussolini, alarmed by reports of the indiscipline of the San Marco Division at Savona, called for a report from the Prefect, Miraschelli:

The San Marco, 16,000 strong, arrived during July and the first days of August.

This immediately produced a sharp uplift in the morale of the population because it stopped the lies that Republican Divisions did not really exist; it gave an immediate feeling of relief to the population, especially in the hills, that they would be protected against the ever-increasing and impudent pressure of the partisans; it also removed the ever-present fear of an enemy landing on the Ligurian coast.

These factors made the majority of the population welcome the San Marco soldiers with kind sympathy and often with spontaneous affection. Alas, relations between the San Marco soldiers and the population are now the reverse of what was expected.

The directives of General Princivalle, however, gave the troops the impression that they would have to fight first with Italians and then with Anglo-Americans.

The soldiers had been forbidden to go with German girls in Germany and there were subversive elements in the ranks of the San Marco. There was a series of incidents because Italian girls who went with German soldiers were attacked and had their hair shorn by Italian soldiers. Reaction by the Germans threatened grave consequences.

Then came the looting – bicycles, radios, and sewing machines were the most popular but pianos, silver, furniture and every type of garment were also seized. Forty-three soldiers stole thirty-seven radios at Albenga. Hundreds of houses were requisitioned for lodgings and at Albenga alone the civilians have suffered damage amounting to several million lire. Officers do nothing to prevent the looting. A musical instrument shop in Savona was sacked, and a concert was given by a Regimental Band in a villa near the city two days later using the stolen instruments.

This shows what a painful delusion was the great joy with which true Italians hailed our soldiers. It is clear that there has been a disintegration of morale in the breasts of these units.

Since the end of their training in Germany the morale and solidarity of the Division has been lowered by friction between the conscripted recruits and those recalled to the colours for Italy and former internees in Germany.

Many internees volunteered to fight anew from true patriotism, but many others had mental reserves and were hostile to any feeling of 'rebirth' and thought this was the only way of getting back to Italy. This clash is very obvious among the officers.

To make the San Marco worthy of its glorious tradition and the spiritual tone that the new Republican Army needs, you must drive out all the dross and the waverers and the timid. Action must begin with the officers. Once led by officers ready to sacrifice themselves for our faith, the Division will be impervious to enemy propaganda, the voices of traitors or the temptation to enrich themselves by selling stolen property; they will become full of the right aims so that they will be a single Fascio.

That among the ranks of the San Marco there are good elements is proved because at this crisis, with so much cowardice and desertions by comrades, many soldiers daily volunteered to transfer to the Black Brigades in the hope of finding fewer subversive elements; they prefer to wear a black shirt to the grey-green. [Mussolini knew the attraction of the Black Brigades was the better pay and rations, and this argument cannot have impressed him.]

They must have more and better rations, more socks and boots, uniforms and ammunition; some troops ask the Fascist headquarters for cartridges, pistols and hand-grenades. The Germans are well aware of all this, and will not comment on the morale of the Division.

I am sure that, once all the difficulties which damage the morale of the troops and produce propaganda for the enemy are removed and discipline is stronger, you can rely on a type of spiritual recovery which alone can give you the certainty that the San Marco will respond nobly to its duty in action.

I keep in contact continually with the Divisional Commander, to ease his task.[9]

This sycophantic report, couched in the cloying language which Fascist civil servants used to satisfy the Duce's vanity, must have made it clear to Mussolini that the San Marco, the flower of his New Army, was an undisciplined rag-bag, corrupt and likely to betray him at any moment. It should have shattered any lingering hope that a resurgent army would restore his position within the Axis. Yet his hopes persisted despite equally depressing reports on the Monte Rosa and Littorio Divisions.

When the Monte Rosa first arrived at Piacenza in November, they made a good impression. They were well disciplined, and proud of their training in Germany. But as their contact with the civilians of this large town increased, their morale was lowered, and many succumbed to the arguments of anti-Fascists and partisans. There were large-scale desertions, and according to the report sent to Mussolini by one Fascist informer, many of the volunteers who had been in German labour camps had only volunteered in order to get back to Italy, where they planned to desert and join the partisans.[10]

A devastating report came to the Duce on 10 November, detailing mass desertions from the Vestone Battalion of the Monte Rosa. For a week from 26 October this unit, commanded by Major Paroldi, had been engaged in operations (*rastrellamento*) in the hills south of Genoa against partisans around Bobbiò Cereto. Paroldi was in touch with the partisan leaders, who offered him a senior command with the partisans; he agreed to desert and bring over as many of his battalion as possible.

On 2 November, orders came from Divisional Headquarters to move to Chiavari, on the coast; Paroldi refused to obey, and the next day he saw the partisan leaders again. He then persuaded all his battalion (except for three officers and fourteen men) to desert with him and join the partisans. The German cadre were made prisoners, the stores and money-chest sacked, and the battalion took command of the area which was under control of the partisans.

The next day, 4 November, the Commander of the 3rd Company at Scoffera held a meeting with his troops and gave his soldiers the choice of joining the partisans or going to Genoa with him. Eventually only four officers, ten NCOs and 110 men, together with five German instructors, arrived at Genoa out of a total strength of 800.

The fate of the rest of the German instructors – one officer and twenty NCOs and soldiers – was 'unknown'.

The Littorio Division followed the Monte Rosa to Piacenza and created a better impression, being considered by many in the town as 'magnificent soldiers'. But contacts with anti-Fascists soon lowered their morale too, and desertions began. The same Fascist informer told Mussolini that the new divisions should be stationed as far away as possible from large towns, so that it would be more difficult for the men to desert and hide.[11]

In October the Germans gave Graziani command of a new army group, Liguria, to defend the Ligurian coast and the French frontier; Liguria consisted of the Italian divisions, plus three German divisions. Graziani at first promised the Italian divisions they would fight only the Allies, and not the partisans who were their fellow countrymen. However, the partisans were so active that he could not keep his word.

The archives of the Salò Republic show how those bright hopes for the divisions at the time of Mussolini's visits in the summer proved to be a day-dream. As they crossed the Brenner Pass on their homeward journey spirits were high, but once in Italy their morale deteriorated disastrously.

On 4 October Mussolini wrote to Kesselring, demanding that his new divisions should be used in combat against the Allies:

Where are the Italian divisions which returned from Germany at the end of July? What are they doing? Why are they not used? Why are the enemy armies using the peoples of five continents to attack Italy while the Italians, the best Italians, are not allowed to contribute to her defence? . . . inaction rapidly leads to the demoralization of troops. When the divisions returned to Italy they had real courage and determination. Now they are scattered along the Ligurian Apennines as a defence against a sea-borne attack which the British have no intention of carrying out after their conquest of the main Apennines and France. This has produced desertions and defections to the partisans, who now number a good 94,000 and are well armed in units, some as large as divisions.[12]

The Duce reiterated this request three weeks later, saying it was essential 'for political reasons' that his new Division should defend the Po Valley.

Kesselring yielded to the Duce's entreaty, and deployed the Monte Rosa on a quiet part of the west end of the Gothic Line between Pontremoli and Lucca in mid-October. Mussolini continually urged Kesselring to use the four Italian divisions combined with German ones in a large-scale counter-attack to drive the Allies out of Florence and beyond the Arno. The German generals were lukewarm, telling the Duce that though they might reach the banks of the Arno, a further advance would be difficult because of the overwhelming superiority of the Allied air force.

In November Mussolini wrote to Hitler that the Axis must resume the offensive, but he ruled out 'the eastern and western Danube fronts' and recommended 'an Italo-German massed force of eighty to a hundred thousand men to attack in Italy in the winter, when the enemy's superiority in armoured vehicles and planes cannot be exploited to the full . . . this would turn the situation upside down and constitute the first longed-for day of sunshine.'[13]

This was childish and impractical but, possibly because of the Duce's letter to Hitler, Kesselring allowed Mussolini, not the grand counter-offensive he desired, but a mini-offensive in which the Monte Rosa were to take part with the Germans, in the wild and remote but romantic Serchio valley which drops into the Arno near Lucca, west of Florence.

In the autumn attack on the Gothic Line the Americans had captured the town of Barga, 100 kilometres from Florence and 37 from Lucca; then the whole offensive petered out, and Barga stayed in the front line. The Americans thought the valley of the Serchio was sure to stay quiet during the winter, and accordingly entrusted its winter defence to the US 92 Division, whose infantry consisted of Negro battalions and the Brazilian Regiment. Brazil had entered the war against Germany in 1942 and sent an expeditionary force to Italy. The Americans knew that the fighting qualities of the black US infantrymen and the Brazilians were below average, but never dreamed that the Germans would attack in that sector. On the night of Christmas Day, troops of the Monte Rosa Division supported by 16 SS Panzer Grenadiers broke through the US front line and captured Barga. The US 92 Division retreated hurriedly in disorder, and on Boxing Day 1944 the combined Nazi and Fascist forces occupied both banks of the Serchio just north of Lucca. There was dismay in Florence. Some Italian mothers forbade their daughters to go to the *thés dansants* with Allied officers in the best hotel, fearing a new Fascist–Nazi occupation.[14]

Perhaps fortunately for the Allies, the Germans had never intended this to be the all-out attack which Mussolini and Graziani wanted, but only a reconnaissance in force. The crack British 8th Indian Division went into the line to replace the 92nd and immediately counter-attacked. Graziani's Italian troops were no match for fierce, battle-hardened Gurkhas, and Barga was recaptured. A Gurkha officer back on leave in Florence after the action declared to the author, 'On our first patrol we captured two Brazilians, one German, two Italians and three Negroes.'

However, Mussolini was so heartened by the news of the partial success of his troops that in January 1945 he went to visit the Italia Division in the mountains between Pontremoli and Aula. Although the weather on Lake Garda was springlike, the Cisa Pass over the Apennines was deep in snow. Mussolini trudged cheerfully through the snow while his entourage, including his German doctor Zachariae, had to push the cars through one drift after another in a freezing wind. Aula was derelict and abandoned but Mussolini, ignoring the snowstorms, pushed on to Pontremoli, where he slept soundly on a camp bed under two horse blankets, happy to be with his Italian soldiers.[15]

Grave complaints about the lack of equipment and weapons for the Italia Division had been sent to the Duce in November. Graziani told him he had to buy clothes on the black market, and there were serious weapon deficiencies, especially in sub-machine-guns. Mussolini had instructed Graziani to inform Kesselring that he would never visit the Italia until they were properly equipped by the Germans and an effective fighting force – 'I will visit a division, not a club of gymnasts.' He added that unless the Germans improved the anti-aircraft defences within three months, no one – not even pedestrians – would be able to use the Italian roads or railway lines.[16] However, the Duce was so elated by the news of the successful attack on Barga and reports of the good showing of the Monte Rosa that he relented. The Divisional Commanders of the Monte Rosa and Italia continued to make fierce complaints to Mussolini, who sent ever more emphatic protests to Kesselring about the lack of equipment and clothing; he also protested that the Todt organization was luring away his fighting soldiers by offers of better rations and pay, while the Germans were doing nothing to feed the Italian civilians in the battle area, who were consequently in a dire state. His complaints achieved little.[17]

So perturbed was Mussolini by the deficiencies in clothing of the Italia that on his return to Garda he bypassed both the Italian and German High Commands and ordered the immediate requisitioning of lorries and drivers, and on 2 February personally sent 2,000 pairs (assorted sizes) of boots with laces and 30,000 pairs of winter socks to Divisional Head-quarters. He gave orders that this small convoy was to travel only at night, to avoid the risk of being caught in air raids on the bridge at Cremona over the Po; ensured that the German officers at Salò issued a valid German pass to the officer commanding; and demanded immediate reports of its departure and arrival. There can be few instances in the history of military warfare of a Head of State involving himself so closely in supply details, but Mussolini knew well the low priority the Germans were giving to the needs of his Divisions.[18]

In the middle of February 1945, reports from General Carloni com-manding the Monte Rosa can have brought only cold comfort to Mussolini. Although Carloni wrote enthusiastically about the success of the December attack on Barga, much was amiss with the Monte Rosa Division, and even more with the Italia, who were now also in the line.

Carloni confirmed that the December attack had overrun all the enemy's prepared positions and captured useful observation posts, which made it much easier to defend the Serchio valley, and this success had done wonders for the morale of his troops. The Germans now trusted him so well that they had put 216 Regt Granatieri under his command on the left bank of the Serchio. Carloni claimed his division had repelled all the counter-attacks in January, so that the units of the Italia Divi-sion who were relieving his would find they had an easy sector to defend. However, when he met the Italia he had a shock: 'They were com-pletely without transport, seriously short of weapons, uniforms torn from being worn too long, boots in a shocking state, while they were often without rations because there was no transport to bring them up. The Bersaglieri had marched through the snow on the Cisa Pass in a pitiable condition.'

Carloni made it clear to General Fürstein, commanding XXI German Corps, that the Italia would not be fit to hold the line for another fifteen days. This made Fürstein angry; he refused to listen and on 28 January sent Carloni a written order that the Italia must immediately relieve the Monte Rosa, who were to be moved to the Western Alps.

Carloni's forebodings about the Italia proved correct. As soon as they were attacked, two officers, five NCOs, and sixty other ranks of 2 Bersaglieri abandoned their posts and ran away, leaving German and Monte Rosa units to recapture their positions. The 2 Bersaglieri were then put into reserve, so that 'the untrustworthy elements could be eradicated', and one officer and three Bersaglieri were court-martialled and shot for trying to surrender to the enemy.

In a further report, Carloni stated that he had managed to improvise a column of donkeys, which made it easier to supply the Italia; but desertions had become serious, with 80 during the week ending 4 February, some defecting to the enemy in groups. The majority of these had families in the south. Carloni had two more Bersaglieri shot for attempted desertion, and sacked one company commander.

On 5 February, American and British troops had attacked, together with Italian partisans wearing Alpini hats, and neither the Monte Rosa nor the Italia put up much resistance, although a counter-attack by the Germans soon recaptured the lost positions. Because of more desertions, 'disloyal' elements of the Bersaglieri were withdrawn; this much improved the fighting performance of the Italia and they supported the Germans well once the line was stabilized.

When General Manardi commanding the Italia arrived, he found that desertions amounted to 1,000 from the Bersaglieri and 60 (mostly gun crews) from one battery of artillery. Optimistically, Carloni reported that they expected the Bersaglieri remaining after the purge to stay loyal.[19]

Mussolini must by this time have realized that his new divisions could never play an important role in a major German offensive, as he had suggested to Kesselring in October; they were not a patch on the Italian divisions which had defended Tunisia in 1943, eighteen months before, which Field Marshal Montgomery had reported as 'fighting harder than ever', or on the Ariete Division which Rommel described as putting up 'a magnificent fight' after Montgomery had achieved his break-through of the Alamein line; the fighting quality of the new Royal Italian Army with the Allies more nearly approached the standards of North Africa in 1942.[20]

Kesselring removed the Italia and Monte Rosa from the line and ordered them to change over to an anti-partisan role in March 1945, because the 150,000 men of Ricci's Black Brigades could not contain the partisan threat. Thus by the end of March 1945, to Mussolini's chagrin, all his divisions were engaged in civil war against the partisans, except for some mild fighting between French patrols and the Littorio in the Mediterranean Alps.

On the Riviera, General Aldo Princivalle quarrelled with the German generals responsible for defending the French frontier, and was replaced as Commander of the San Marco by General Amilcare Farina, who was more acceptable to the Germans because of his long record of devoted military service to Mussolini. He had commanded a battalion in Spain, and been much decorated. Salò propaganda did its best to create a father-figure out of Farina, but he was forced to shoot a number of his soldiers in a

frantic effort to put a stop to desertions. After the war, Graziani claimed
that the San Marco and the other divisions had been received with 'unfor-
gettable enthusiasm by the mass of the civil population'; the evidence
points to the contrary.[21]

Jealous Blackshirt observers noted that at Desenzano a small crowd
barracked the Alpini who had arrived from Germany, and that the
Monte Rosa were received 'coldly' at Stradella, while at Genoa when
they paraded through the town there were disturbances, with anti-Fascists
inciting them to desert. Padre Eusebio, a cleric Fascist agitator, wrote to
Mussolini about the traitorous officers in the San Marco, and the Duce
wrote to Farina, 'You have got some officers who deserve to be boiled
in oil.' Other reports stated that there was hostility between the officers
who had been in German labour camps and consequently hated the Nazis,
and the officers who had been recruited within Fascist Italy who were
more enthusiastic for the Germans. Delays in paying the troops contributed to the general lowering of morale.[22]

According to Farina, by mid-September there had been 1,400 desertions from the San Marco and over 1,000 from the Monte Rosa. General
Ott, who had worked hard to train the Italians in Germany, was furious,
and complained that neither Farina nor Carloni were tough enough with
deserters. As a result, Divisional Courts of Justice were set up, and more
recaptured deserters were sentenced to death. But shootings and the threat
of many years in prison did little to stop the desertions, particularly of
those soldiers who had been given leave. At least 50 soldiers from the San
Marco were shot – mainly to satisfy the Germans.

General Lemson, the Commander of the German XIV Corps, commented on 15 February that the Italian police refused to seek out the
deserters because they were confident that the Anglo-Americans would
soon take over their territory; he wanted severe measures taken against
the families of deserters. The Fascist civil authorities did practically
nothing; there were only a few token arrests (the Italian historian Panza
has been able to document only four arrests of parents, despite wide
research) and imprisonments of fathers of deserters, and no shootings.[23]

General Farina had repeatedly assured his men in the autumn that
they would never be asked to fight their own countrymen and would
only defend Italian soil. However, at Altara and Carcare near Savona in
March he had no choice, because considerable numbers of San Marco
troops deserted to join the partisans in the mountains on the French
frontier, while partisans frequently attacked the San Marco to capture
rations and arms. The cemetery at Altara became known as the 'White
Crosses' because here were buried, with the same ceremony and by the
same priest, partisans, San Marco soldiers killed by the partisans, and
Allied airmen.

In a raid in mid-March the partisans killed thirteen San Marco soldiers. Farina in retaliation captured thirteen partisans who should, on Mussolini's explicit orders, have been shot. They all came from villages near Altara; the thirteen mothers came in a body to Farina's headquarters to plead for the lives of their sons. By now the Allies had crossed the Rhine and were advancing fast into Germany from the west, while the Russians were approaching Berlin. Farina must have seen the writing on the wall which spelt the imminent doom of the Axis and Fascism; he spared the lives of the thirteen partisans, sending this letter to their mothers:

30 March 1945

To Signora .... *Mother of*
Prisoner ....

Remember. They betrayed and killed men of the San Marco not only once but several times. And now you ask me to free your son who is a hostage. OK, I free him, and send him back to you.

You remind me it is Easter. But let me remind you that with this letter I must send others (which I showed to you) to the other mothers; and they will receive them on Easter Day. 'Your son has been killed by traitors.' I repeat by traitors.

As a mother welcoming home her own son alive and well, I ask you to ponder. We cry Italy, Italy, Italy! but when you came with the twelve other mothers I showed you the corpses of thirteen of my men.

Now that you are happy with your son at home you can cry Italy, Italy, Italy! What can you and the other happy mothers holding the hands of their sons say to the mothers of my dead soldiers, except 'Death, death, death'?[24]

This moving letter conveys the intolerable tensions which civil war was inflicting on the Italian people. Fortunately, before the final surrender, as will be seen, the Allies had declared that the Fascist army would be treated as POWs like the Germans, and on 1 May Graziani formally surrendered his army with the honours of war. A horrible chapter in the history of Italy was closed; an amnesty was granted to the officers and many were re-employed, although Borghese and Graziani were tried as war criminals by Italian courts.

CHAPTER 8

Aegean Tragedy and Atrocities

ON 9 SEPTEMBER 1943 the Italian garrison in the Aegean islands out-numbered the Germans, especially in their own possessions, although the Germans had many more tanks and aircraft. Unfortunately, during the forty-five days after Mussolini's overthrow the Italian War Office did nothing to alert or prepare their garrisons for conflict with the Germans. The Italian generals and senior officers in these outposts away from the mainstream of the war had in many instances become friendly with their German counterparts, and with their highly-developed military sense of honour found it distasteful to betray their former allies. However, the Italian officers were also intensely loyal to the monarch and respected the oath they had taken to him. They were nominally Fascists because other-wise advancement in the Italian army was almost impossible, but they had little real love for Mussolini or Fascism.

Unfortunately, the British and Americans made no move to contact the Italians in the Aegean islands, even though Enigma decrypts showed that the German Headquarters were aware of the near-certainty of the armistice (but not the date), and had ordered their garrisons to be prepared to disarm the Italians on receipt of a code word.

As has been seen, an Italian delegate had made the first move for Italy to change sides on 4 August; from then until the armistice was signed on 3 September, the British and Americans haggled over the details of the surrender terms, although the Italians wanted to make military co-operation a priority. Churchill, Eden and the Americans were adamant that the armistice terms must include 'unconditional surrender' – a term not calculated to stimulate the Italians to change sides and fight the Ger-mans. Alexander, Harold Macmillan and Eisenhower in North Africa were driven frantic by the leisurely progress made by their Governments. In August Macmillan, the British Resident Minister in the Mediterranean, cabled urgently to London that Eisenhower should in an emergency be allowed to sign a document which would take Italy out of the war 'over-night'. If this had been done, the disaster which befell the Italian forces in the Aegean might have been avoided. To complicate matters further, when the armistice was actually signed on 3 September Churchill, Eden and Roosevelt were in Canada for a summit conference, and issued no urgent orders for Anglo-American-Italian co-operation. Incredible as it seems with hindsight, no plans whatsoever were drawn up before the armistice by the British and Americans for military co-operation with the powerful Italian forces in the Aegean.

This is even more surprising when it is recalled that Churchill was desperately anxious to exploit the Italian surrender by pushing the Germans out of Rhodes and the Dodecanese islands so that the sea route to the Dardanelles might be opened up. He was longing to erase his First World War failure at Gallipoli; the Americans did not share his enthusiasm for this strategy. If Churchill had given orders for plans for military co-operation to be prepared in advance, and if certain Italian commanders had shown more courage and loyalty to their king, good use could have been made of the Italian garrisons on the islands, and Churchill's aim of a sea connection with the Russians through the Dardanelles might have been realized. General 'Jumbo' Wilson, General Officer Commanding in Cairo, let Churchill down; he was unintelligent, lacking in initiative and political sense.

Rhodes was the key to the Dardanelles, and on instructions from Churchill in August General Wilson had worked out a plan ('Accolade') to assault Rhodes on 1 September; 8th Indian Division and other picked troops in Egypt were trained for the operation. On 27 July, two days after Mussolini's fall, Churchill minuted, 'I hope that the planners are all keyed up with plans for taking Rhodes on the assumption that the Italians ask for an armistice'; and ten days later he minuted again:

> Here is a business of great consequence, to be thrust forward by every means. Should the Italian troops in Crete and Rhodes resist the Germans and a deadlock ensue, we must help the Italians at the earliest moment, engaging thereby also the support of the populations . . . This is no time for conventional establishments, but rather for using whatever fighting elements there are. Can anything be done to find at least a modicum of assault shipping without compromising the main operation against Italy? . . . Provided they are to be helped by friends on shore, a different situation arises. Surely caiques, and ships' boats can be used between ship and shore?
>
> I hope the Staffs will be able to stimulate action, which may gain immense prizes at little cost, though not at little risk.

Although Churchill's strategy was one hundred per cent right, no such action was taken by Wilson. Had the British been able to give immediate sea-borne help to the Italians in the islands they could have kept the Germans at bay; there were in the Middle East ample British troops to reinforce the Italians and overcome the German Aegean garrisons, should the first shock assaults on the Italians be defeated. Unfortunately,

Eisenhower had overall command in the Mediterranean; he and his government rejected Churchill's view about the importance of the Eastern Aegean. All the resources for sea-borne landings were under Eisenhower's control, and Churchill could not give him orders. Eisenhower refused to allot to Wilson the shipping resources needed for an opposed landing on Rhodes and other islands, and sent what was surplus to the requirements for a landing on the mainland of Italy to the Far East, or to England for the cross-channel invasion in 1944. Churchill objected in vain, telling the Americans that 'it would be a profound mistake, since Italy was in measurable distance of a collapse'.[1]

However, the Americans insisted and the British plan for the invasion of Rhodes on 1 September had to be cancelled. Had 'Accolade' still been ready on 8 September, the Italians would have held Rhodes for the Allies. The history of the fighting in the Aegean between the Germans and the Italians is little known, but the following account makes it plain that if the British in the Middle East had been prepared and in touch with the Italians before the armistice, the outcome would have been very different.

British hopes that the Germans would be thrown out of the Aegean were jeopardized by orders from the Italian War Office following the signing of the armistice on 3 September. Memorandum OP 44, which was not activated in time (as will be seen), laid down that Italian troops were to act against the Germans only if attacked; even worse was Memorandum N 2 of 6 September, addressed to all Corps Commanders in the Balkans and the Aegean. This ordered them to say 'frankly to the Germans that if they [the Germans] did not commit acts of violence, Italian troops would not make common cause with the rebels [Greek and Yugoslav partisans] nor with the Anglo-American troops if they made landings'.

By ordering 'no common cause' with the Anglo-Americans, Memorandum N 2 breached the terms of the armistice signed by Castellano on 4 September; this weakened the Allied Generals' faith in Italian intentions to fight seriously against the Germans, and had unfortunate consequences, as will be seen.

At 9.30 p.m. on 8 September, after a talk with the Germans, the Italian Commander in Athens of the 11th Army, Vecchiarelli, sent out a radio message in clear to all his subordinate commanders. There are varying versions of this message, but the one intercepted by Allied Forces Headquarters in Algiers must be authentic:

The Italian troops of the 11th Army will adopt the following line of conduct. If the Germans do not offer armed violence, Italians will not use their arms against them, nor will they make common cause with the rebels or with any Anglo-American forces who may land. They will, however, meet force with force. Every man will remain at his post and his present task. Exemplary discipline will be enforced by every possible means. The above will be communicated to the corresponding German HQ.[2]

This intercepted signal, in conjunction with Badoglio's delay over announcing the armistice a few hours before, created a bad impression of Italian military intentions at Eisenhower's headquarters. The Italian War Office broadcast from Rome at fifteen minutes past midnight on the night of 8–9 September Order 24202, to the effect that requests by Germans to move troops within the Italian areas of occupation were not to be in any instance 'considered a hostile act', and the Italian commanders were authorized to tell their German counterparts their own movements and intentions. As a result of this order, the Germans were able to occupy many key positions, from which they destroyed the Italian army. Order 24202 also instructed the Italians to 'negotiate with the Germans' to gain time.[3]

This was extraordinary because prior to its initiation the Italian War Office had confirmation from several sources that many German commanders had already threatened Italian headquarters with 'either disarm or surrender'. At Ambrosio's trial after the war, a military court ruled that Order 24202 'contradicted OP 44'.

As has already been noted, when the War Office was preparing to flee from Rome two hours later, Ambrosio and Badoglio refused a request from Roatta to send out a signal to all headquarters to activate Memorandum OP 44. This failure to activate OP 44 was disastrous. Obviously Ambrosio and Badoglio, terrified of the Germans, hoped in this way to prevent German attacks on the Italian army and on themselves. They had no idea of the revenge which was in Hitler's mind.

Before the War Office left Rome at 5 a.m. on 9 September, Roatta did, by telephone, order 'force to be met with force'. Yet not until the War Office arrived at Brindisi on 10 September did Ambrosio authorize a radio signal in clear to 'treat Germans as enemies and fight them with all force available'. By this time, many of the Yugoslav, Greek, Albanian and some of the Aegean garrisons had succumbed, together with the greater part of the Italian troops in Italy.

General Lanz in Athens had tricked Vecchiarelli into believing a promise that the Germans would not attack the Italians, provided that Italian units garrisoned the coast defences in Greece for fourteen days. After this, the Germans would make sure all the Italian troops in the Aegean were repatriated, provided they left behind their weapons, guns and ammunition, to ensure that none of this material should fall into Anglo-American hands on their return to Italy. The Germans had no intention of honouring this pledge, but on 9 September the duped Vecchiarelli sent out a disastrous order to his commanders to begin negotiations to cede their arms to the Germans. Vecchiarelli had no authority from the Italian War Office to issue this order.[4]

The Greek island of Cephalonia* is only 200 miles from the Italian coast at the mouth of the Gulf of Corinth. On 8 September the Italian Acqui Division who were the garrison on the island greatly outnumbered the Germans, but the island is so close to the mainland of Greece that the Germans were in a position to send massive reinforcements quickly while the nearby aerodromes on the mainland gave Germany air superiority. On Cephalonia the Germans committed a crime against humanity by massacring all the large Italian garrison when they surrendered after hard fighting. Only the military chaplains were spared, and if it were not for them it would be impossible to piece together the horrific story.

On 9 September, the first day after the Armistice, the German and Italian units remained in their positions amid a cold silence, although some German soldiers had joined in when the Italian soldiers rejoiced at the news of the armistice which they thought was the end of the war for them. At eight in the evening General Gandin commanding the Acqui Division received the order from his Italian superior General Vecchiarelli in Athens that his troops were to 'cede' all their weapons including artillery to the Germans, and would in due course be sent back to Italy by sea.

Gandin was amazed by this order because it contradicted the order sent by the Italian War Office from Rome during the preceding night to treat the Germans as 'enemies'. He cabled to Athens that he rejected it because it contradicted the spirit and facts of the Anglo-American armistice (also it was partly indecipherable). In vain Gandin tried to contact the Italian War Office (which was *en route* to Brindisi from Rome), and Italian headquarters on the other Greek islands. A number of his more senior officers felt that it was 'dishonourable' to fight against the Germans, until the day before their allies. However, Captain Renzo Apollonio (who was strongly anti-Fascist and anti-German) and others warned Gandin that if the order was given to lay down arms, the bulk of the troops would refuse to obey. Apollonio was in touch with a band of Greek guerrillas and Greek officers, who offered the collaboration of a Greek battalion.

---

*Cephalonia is the largest of the Ionian islands, consisting of bare limestone mountains slashed by fertile valleys with luxuriant vegetation. It was badly damaged by an earthquake in 1953. Cephalonia and the island of Sami fifteen miles to the east are the Kingdom of Ithaca in *The Odyssey*.

On the morning of 11 September the Germans put Gandin on the horns of a dilemma with an ultimatum: by seven in the evening he must make up his mind. He held a conference of senior officers, and consulted the chaplains. Both advised surrender. Gandin agreed with them, personally; but meanwhile he had at last succeeded in setting up radio communication with the Italian War Office in its new headquarters in Brindisi; and there had been skirmishes, initiated by the Germans, in which the Italians had suffered casualties. Gandin complained bitterly to the German officer who was negotiating the surrender, Colonel Barge, and as a delaying tactic asked for the negotiations to be carried on in future by a German of at least the rank of General. Then came news that Colonel Lusignani, in command on the neighbouring island of Corfu, had overcome German attacks and had the island under his complete control. Lusignani also reported that, on other islands, the Germans were disregarding their promise to repatriate Italian soldiers, sending them instead to internment camps in Germany. Stragglers who arrived in Cephalonia from the nearby island of Santa Maura confirmed this news.

On the morning of 13 September two motorized lighters full of armed German troops tried to enter the port of Argostoli. On the orders of Captain Apollonio, without consultation with Gandin, the Italian artillery opened fire and sunk one lighter; the other put up the white flag. The artillery, inspired by Apollonio, also opened fire on German positions on the island. Gandin ordered this artillery fire to cease while he reopened negotiations with the Germans. Then a German *parliamentario* (a bearer of a flag of truce) arrived by sea with a senior Italian air force officer who had gone over to the Fascists; they asked Gandin to leave his division on the island until it could be sent back to Italy, while Gandin himself was asked to take over the job of Chief of Staff with the new Republican Army.* Gandin sent messages to all his units that negotiations were in progress with the Germans and a settlement was likely in which the whole division could retain its weapons.

The next morning, 14 September, General Lanz commanding the German XXII Mountain Corps arrived by boat; he sent an angry telephone message to Gandin that firing at the German lighters was 'an act of hostility', and by the hand of Colonel Barge a signed order that the Acqui were to lay down their arms immediately. By now, after tortuous changes of mind, Gandin had decided to throw in his lot with Badoglio and the king. His staff told him that soundings taken among the troops revealed them to be almost a hundred per cent in favour of fighting the

---

*Mussolini, in Vienna, had been persuaded by the Germans to offer Gandin the command of the Fascist Army, before Graziani was approached.

Germans. And, finally, a written order had arrived by sea from the War Office in Brindisi that the Acqui were to fight the Germans. According to the Italian official history, 'By now an irresistible hatred of the Germans was growing ever stronger among the soldiers and their impatience had reached a point where it could not be curbed.' Three Italian officers who tried to organize a surrender were shot by their troops.

During the morning of 14 September Gandin ordered his division to occupy positions from which they could launch an attack on the Germans, and told the Germans that hostilities would begin 'at 9 a.m. on the 15th' unless he received 'a favourable offer'. At that moment came the ominous news from the island of Zante that General Paderni had laid down his arms and his 400 soldiers had been sent as 'internees' to Germany.

During the morning of the 15th, German Stukas from the mainland made frequent bombing raids; they also machine-gunned the Italian positions and dropped propaganda leaflets threatening that any Italians taken prisoner while fighting would never see Italy again.

In their initial attacks the Acqui captured 400 prisoners and the guns of a self-propelled battery, but the Stukas were causing serious casualties. German sea-borne reinforcements landed in the dark, and bitter fighting continued until the 19th, with the Germans gradually becoming superior in numbers and the Stukas devastating the Italian positions. Gandin asked Brindisi to send air and sea help to prevent the German landings, which were now taking place in daylight. The Italian War Office replied that this was 'impossible'.[5]

Here lies a mystery. On 9 September, over 300 Italian war planes with pilots loyal to the Badoglio regime had landed on the aerodromes of Lecce and Brindisi behind the 8th Army lines. The pilots wanted to go into action immediately against the Germans. One Italian air force officer said afterwards to the author: 'We asked for petrol and ammunition. Instead, we were told to fly our aircraft to Tunis, out of range of the hard-pressed Italian troops on Cephalonia.' Meanwhile, Gandin had sent a motor-boat belonging to the Red Cross to Brindisi with details of the situation, requesting immediate help by sea and air, and more ammunition: after three days of fighting his dumps were nearly exhausted, whereas plenty of German supplies were coming in by sea.[6]

No Italian ships intervened. Under the terms of the armistice they had mostly gone to Malta, far from the war zone. If some Italian destroyers had instead been sent to Augusta in Sicily, they could have intervened in Cephalonia. Allied warships were also available, but none were sent. However, on 19, 20 and 21 September the Allies allowed Italian fighter planes to make sorties to Cephalonia from Lecce. There were too few of them to have a real effect on the battle, but they shot down one Messerschmitt and machine-gunned German positions.

One Italian air force officer told the author at the time that the Allied Command were too frightened that the pilots would transfer their allegiance to the Germans to allow strong Italian air intervention over Cephalonia, and the Italian War Office suggestion of an Italian naval force under Admiral Bonetti was turned down for the same reason. Only on the 24th, a few hours after both islands had surrendered, did the Allies consent to seven Italian destroyers going to Cephalonia and Corfu.[7]

On 20 September, reinforced German troops made a decisive attack supported by relays of Stuka bombers. Gandin's troops fought until their ammunition was nearly exhausted, and at 11 a.m. on 22 September they put up the white flag. Just as they surrendered a signal came from the Italian War Office that all available Italian war planes would attack the Germans on Cephalonia while squadrons of US fighters and bombers would attack the aerodromes on the mainland from which the Stukas were flying. Ambrosio concluded his signal with praise for the valour of the Acqui. Had the Allies authorized such an operation a week earlier, the outcome might have been different.[8]

The XXII Mountain Corps had received a special Führer order to massacre all the Italian soldiers who had fought on Cephalonia. As the German soldiers entered the positions of the surrendering Italians, they mowed them down with machine-guns. General Lanz gave orders that all officers belonging to the Acqui except Fascists, those of German birth, doctors and chaplains, were to be killed. The Acqui troops not shot in cold blood on their positions were marched down to San Teodoro. There they were incarcerated in the 'Cassetta Rosa' town hall, next to a convent. The first to be shot was Gandin, followed by all his staff officers.

The German orders specified that the Acqui troops were to be shot just outside the town by detachments of eight German soldiers, each under an officer. Staff officers were to be killed singly; others in groups of two or three. Inside the town hall the chaplains administered the last rites, and one, Father Romualdo Formato, has written movingly of three officers who linked arms as they walked out to be executed, saying 'We have been companions in life. Let us go together to paradise.'

According to the official Italian history, the soil of the island became a carpet of corpses. The Germans specified that the bodies must lie where they would not be seen by other German soldiers or civilians, and were not to be buried. Instead they were to be 'ballasted', put on rafts and sunk in the sea. The Germans compelled twenty Italian sailors to do this, and when they had finished they too were shot, to make sure they could not give evidence of this crime to the civilized world.

An official report from Lanz to Army Group E stated that 5,000 of the Acqui Division who surrendered had been treated in accordance with the Führer's orders – that is, shot dead. Father Romualdo Formato's published account details how 4,750 officers and men were shot dead, either at their posts under the white flag on the field of battle, or in San Teodoro.[9]

Out of 12,000 Italian troops on Cephalonia on 8 September, 1,250 fell in combat and almost 5,000 were put to death by the Germans after the surrender; these included sailors and nearly 100 medical orderlies with Red Cross armlets. About 4,000 who had surrendered their arms without fighting were imprisoned in a barracks on the island; they received only starvation rations and were subjected to severe hardships. In October they were embarked on three ships destined for Greece, all three of which hit mines and sank as soon as they left port. The Italian prisoners shut up in the holds had no chance; the few who jumped into the sea were machine-gunned by the Germans to prevent them escaping. The sea became a mass of corpses. About a thousand Italian soldiers who had managed to escape from the Germans after the surrender joined up under Captain Apollonio with the Greek guerrillas, and when the British captured the island in November 1944, 1,200 Italian soldiers (some of whom had escaped from other islands), who had fought with the Greek partisans against the Germans, were repatriated with Captain Apollonio to Bari on British and Italian ships. In Bari, they all volunteered to fight with the Italian Army of Liberation under the Royal flag.[10]

A 22-page account of the appalling events on Cephalonia was sent to Mussolini at Salò (the document is marked 'Seen by the Duce'). It was written by a Foreign Office official named Segenti who stayed on the island through the fighting; he described the atrocities in lurid detail. To Mussolini's eternal shame, he made no protests to the Germans after reading the document on 14 January 1944. Segenti was repatriated by the Germans via Berlin to Rome. His report made it clear that the Germans had no intention of treating the units who had fought against them as prisoners-of-war, and that after 'forced marches, whole units were machine-gunned, together with all the Divisional staff'. According to him, only forty officers out of the 500 in the Acqui Division escaped execution, although a few more might have joined the guerrillas or disguised themselves as ordinary soldiers in the internment camps.[11]

It is a disgusting tale. The Cephalonia massacre was worse than Katyn, General Lanz's crime was worse than those of his fellow generals Jodl, Keitel and Kesselring, all of whom were sentenced to death and hanged. Lanz was sentenced by the Military Tribunal at Nuremberg to 12 years' imprisonment, described by the official Italian war historian as 'a mild sentence'. In 1954 an Italian attempt to have Lanz arraigned before an Italian court came to nothing, the judge ruling that the evidence was insufficient.

The reason for Lanz's light sentence was that the Nuremberg court, deceived by false evidence, did not believe the Cephalonia massacre ever took place. Lanz lied in his evidence to the court, stating that he had refused to obey the Führer's order to shoot all the Italian soldiers because he had been revolted by it. He claimed the report to Army Group E (quoted above) that 5,000 soldiers had been executed was a blind to deceive his superiors into believing he had obeyed the Führer. He stated that only a few of Gandin's officers had been shot with their commander, after their guilt had been established by a court martial, and that they were those mainly responsible for organizing the resistance. He claimed that fewer than a dozen staff officers had been shot, and that the remainder of the Acqui Division had been transported first to Patras and then to Piraeus. Sworn affidavits from Germans who had been with Lanz in September 1943 were produced to corroborate his prevarications; they were from Germans, apparently of extreme respectability and leading impeccable post-war lives – including General von Butlar of Hitler's personal staff, who had been involved in the orders for the Rome massacre in the Ardeatine caves. They all swore the massacre had not taken place.

Reading the evidence of Lanz and his defence witnesses reminds one vividly of the old adage that the bigger the lie the more likely it is to be believed. It also pinpoints how dangerous it is for historians to rely on evidence produced at the Nuremberg Trials in reaching conclusions.

The judges accepted that Lanz had prevented the massacre and that it never took place. As a result Lanz received a lighter sentence than General Rendulić, who had been responsible for executing several hundred Italian officers after bogus court martials in Split and Yugoslavia. Rendulić was sentenced to 20 years' imprisonment, although his actions in no way approached the enormity of Lanz's massacre of the Acqui Division on Cephalonia.

It remains a mystery why no Italian evidence was produced at this Nuremberg Trial. The trial began in June 1947 and sentences were passed on 19 February 1948. The terms of the Italian Peace Treaty had aroused extreme indignation, and it is possible that the Italian Government refused to co-operate. The International Military Tribunal at Nuremberg, which originally consisted of the British, the Americans and the Russians, had been by now superseded by a purely American Court. Details of the Cephalonia massacre were already well known in Italy as a result of books and newspaper articles by the chaplains and medical officers who had been spared, and by survivors who had escaped to the hills to join the Greek partisans.

Lanz's defence counsel made great play of the prosecution's failure to produce any Italian evidence, and claimed that Gandin had no orders from the War Office in Brindisi to fight, so he and his Division were therefore either 'mutineers or *francs-tireurs*' who had no right to be treated as POWs. It was also stated that a request from Gandin, after what was alleged to be his court martial, to speak on the telephone to General Jodl (whom he knew) was refused. It is extremely unlikely that anything approaching a court martial took place, and the defence produced no evidence of it. There was a clash between the defence counsels for Lanz and Field Marshal von Weichs, Supreme Commander SE Europe, when it was claimed on behalf of Lanz that he was later considered 'unreliable' because of his failure to carry out the Führer's order for the Cephalonia massacre; von Weichs's counsel felt this was shifting guilt on to the Field Marshal. Von Weichs was taken ill during the trial, and the case against him was dropped.[12]

All the War Crimes Trials before the International Military Tribunal at Nuremberg were unsatisfactory. When the British ran short of money and tired of the proceedings, the USA – the only nation whch could afford to do so – embarked on a further series of trials (including that of Lanz), which they were entitled to do under Control Council Law No. 10, the authority for the original Nuremberg Trials. Prosecution standards were even lower than in the earlier cases. Weizsäcker, for example, was arraigned before this Tribunal and sentenced to seven years, even though it was made clear that he was anti-Nazi, and had risked his life to stop the war; his entreaties to the Pope not to intervene over the pogrom against Roman Jews or the Ardeatine cave massacre, which were questionable, were not even raised by the prosecution.

As on Cephalonia, the Italian garrison on Corfu considerably outnumbered the German troops, and likewise on the evening of 8 September there was rejoicing by the Italian soldiers and Greek civilians over the likely end of the war. The Germans stayed aloof.

The next morning the Italian Commander, Colonel Lusignani, gave orders that all naval ships not needed for the defence of the island should return to Italy with as much surplus war *matériel* as possible. Like Gandin, Lusignani received the order from General Vecchiarelli to hand all his arms over to the Germans. Lusignani refused out of hand, and instead deployed his troops to fight the Germans; he also freed all Greek political prisoners. He held a conference of officers, who stated that their troops' morale was good, and they would fight wholeheartedly. On the morning of 10 September Colonel Klotz, who commanded the Germans on the island, and Colonel Spengelin saw Lusignani and asked him to lay down his arms. They met an abrupt refusal. At 1 p.m. on 11 September a motor-boat with a white flag reached the island carrying a German emissary; the German suggested that the island should remain in Italian possession while the German units stayed quietly in their quarters. Later in the afternoon another German emissary arrived by boat, demanding the surrender of the island and the handing-over of arms. When Lusignani again refused, the Germans said they would stand by the afternoon's preliminary offer. Meanwhile, more Italian troops arrived by sea from Port Edda in Albania.

On 13 September, German Stukas bombed the Italian positions; the Italians attacked German units while their anti-aircraft guns opened fire on the Stukas. Four German aeroplanes which tried to land on the aerodrome were shot down. In mid-morning the same German emissary appeared again by sea, this time accompanied by Colonel Carlo Rossi, a staff officer from General de Bona's XXVI Corps Headquarters in Greece, with an order to Lusignani to lay down his arms. However, Rossi whispered to Lusignani: 'The Colonel has only signed this order under threat of death. I advise you to fight because you are on an island.' Lusignani curtly refused the German invitation, and within an hour a convoy of German boats and barges attempted to land on the island. They were repulsed, with heavy losses.

That night 3,500 more Italian troops arrived from Port Edda, bringing the Italian garrison of Corfu up to 8,000. But the reinforcements were not of high calibre, and in their hurry to embark they had left behind their artillery shells and small-arms ammunition. Most of the soldiers escaping from Albania had only one object – to get back to Italy as soon as possible.* A ship was sent back to Port Edda, picked up 600 rounds of field gun shells (75 mm), and returned safely with them. Lusignani now sent radio messages to the Italian War office in Brindisi requesting air and naval support. This was refused on the grounds that the Allied military authorities would not allow Italian pilots to fly combat sorties.

With the help of Greek guerrillas Lusignani overran all the German posts and sent 400 German POWs back to Italy. This proof of success induced the British High Command to allow the Italians to send naval and air help to the island, and on 18 September Italian fighters flew over Corfu and Italian torpedo boats arrived from Brindisi carrying rations and medical supplies. They returned with 1,760 Italian infantry who were not expected to be of much use in combat. German batteries on the mainland of Greece pounded Corfu while the Italians replied.[13]

At dawn on 20 September two British parachutists appeared from the sky. They were Major Oliver Churchill and his radio operator; they brought messages of congratulation to Lusignani from General Sir Henry ('Jumbo') Wilson, Commander-in-Chief Middle East, and General

---

*When the Italians sent ships to Port Edda to bring soldiers back direct to Italy, General Mason-Macfarlane complained to Badoglio that he had used three valuable merchant ships which should have taken reinforcements to Corfu.

Eisenhower, C-in-C Allied Forces Headquarters Algiers, and a promise that all aid requested by radio would be sent. Unfortunately, the radio to Allied headquarters refused to function, and no aid was sent. Major Churchill promised a British general would soon arrive to co-ordinate British help. He did not arrive. The same day, the Italian air force bombarded attempted landings by the Germans. However, without considerable outside naval and air help, Corfu was doomed. Stukas dominated the sky, and during the night of the 24th a sizeable German force landed with tanks. There was bitter fighting in which about 500 Italians were killed, and the Italian batteries were captured. An Italian torpedo boat which intervened was sunk by Stukas.

Lusignani's situation deteriorated as shoals of fresh German troops disembarked. His ammunition began to run out, and in despair he sent one message after another on 23 and 24 September to Brindisi, requesting air and naval help and tanks. Nothing resulted. One cable read: 'I have certain knowledge that the enemy either today or tonight will make major new landings. I repeat, naval action against the landing beaches is indispensable.' On 23 September Lusignani reported that he would even then be able to stabilize his position if he were given air support. On 20 September, the date of Major Churchill's arrival in Corfu, General Wilson had asked General Eisenhower to send forces to take over Corfu, and General Mason-Macfarlane and a British mission made plans to go to the island to liaise with Lusignani.[14]

However, not until 24 September did the Allied Command plan a major operation of support for Corfu. It was too late. On the night of the 25th substantial German reinforcements had landed, and despite fierce resistance the Italian strong points and the aerodrome were overrun. At 5 p.m. on the 25th, Lusignani and his personal staff were captured. They were shot out of hand by the Germans. By midnight the port was in German hands, and all the senior Italian officers in command there were also shot.

The few Italian fighter aircraft which flew over the island from Lecce were impotent against the massive numbers of Stukas. By the 26th at midday all Italian resistance had ceased. Forty-one Italian officers were shot by the Germans as they surrendered on the field of battle, but atrocities did not reach the same proportions as on Cephalonia. According to the official Italian history, this was thanks to the 'absence' of Major von Hirschfeld, who had been chiefly responsible for the Cephalonia massacre. There was no massacre of surrendering other ranks, but during the night of 29 September the surviving officers were interrogated, and many were shot through the head with pistols or put in sacks and thrown into the sea. Several corpses with their hands tied behind their backs were thrown up by the sea onto the beaches. The official German order to shoot Italian officers on Corfu was almost identical to the one issued for Cephalonia, except that Colonel Remold was given authority to 'spare' anyone he chose.

The remainder of the Italian troops were sent to Germany to be interned. On the night of 10 October, several thousand captured Italian soldiers were embarked on ships *en route* for Germany. Allied aircraft bombed them, and as one sank and the Italians tried to swim to the shore, the Germans machine-gunned them as they had off Cephalonia.[15]

Winston Churchill was gravely disappointed to be told by General Wilson, on the day of the Italian armistice, that any enterprises other than 'a walk-in' against Crete or Rhodes, or small-scale raids, were 'impossible' unless Eisenhower provided more resources. Wilson told Churchill that a full-scale attack on Rhodes (the 'Accolade' operation), with one infantry division, two armoured regiments and a parachute battalion, would require six weeks of preparation; the 8th Indian Division, which had been trained for the operation, had been taken by Eisenhower for Italy. However, Wilson reported that small-scale help 'would be given to the Italians within a few days'.[16]

When the armistice was announced, Admiral Inigo Campioni was Supreme Commander of all the Italian forces in the Aegean, and also Governor of the Dodecanese Islands. His headquarters were in the town of Rhodes. Italian forces on the island of Rhodes amounted to 37,000, but their weapons were out-of-date and they had no armour. The German troops on the island numbered only 6,000, but they had tanks, self-propelled guns and all the latest weapons. The Italians were deployed chiefly along the coast as a defence against landings; the Germans, who were highly mobile, were concentrated inland.

Far away from the real war, the Italian troops had become slack and soft; there was a lack of ships for transport of supplies, and the Italians concentrated on feeding themselves from the resources of the island. The Germans, on the other hand, alerted as soon as Mussolini fell, were ready to attack their former allies. Substantial German armoured reinforcements arrived in August; Field Marshal von Weichs, who in August had been appointed to command all south-east Europe, paid an unexpected visit to the German troops on the island without giving previous notice to the Italians.

The Italian military and naval headquarters were within the town of Rhodes, the main port on the north-east tip of the island. No warning of any kind was received by Campioni from Italy before the news of the armistice burst on 8 September. At 8 p.m. the German Commander, General Kleeman, had an interview with General Forgiero, Campioni's deputy. After various courtesies, Forgiero requested Kleeman to order his troops to stay quietly within their own quarters while he ordered the Italians to do the same. Kleeman said he had no authority to agree, and the talk ended. Meanwhile the German plan 'Asse' was put into operation, German units moved to threaten the airport, and all units were put on battle alert. At 8 a.m. on 9 September Kleeman saw Forgiero again. The German insisted that his troops must have freedom of movement on the island to repulse an Allied invasion, that Italian aeroplanes must not use the airport, and that there must be no communication with the British. Forgiero refused.

At midnight on the 9th Kleeman asked Forgiero for an interview with Campioni; while he was in bed, Forgiero was shocked to hear that the Germans had captured the airport of Marizza and made the Italian air personnel there prisoners. Kleeman promised Forgiero he would withdraw his troops, but would leave them 'encircling' the airport in case British planes landed. In the Castle of Rhodes, Campioni and Kleeman talked. Deceitfully, Kleeman promised to give orders that the Germans would not attack the airport of Gaddura provided the Italians allowed his troops full liberty of movement. While the talks were in progress Kleeman was handed by a special messenger a secret order to disarm the Italians by force as soon as possible. On his way back to his headquarters in the centre of the island, Kleeman and his aides found that the Italians had set up a considerable number of road-blocks which would make it impossible for German units to circulate: at one, they had to abandon their car, cross on foot, and search for another German car on the other side.

General Scaroina, who commanded the 13,000-strong Italian Regina Division in the centre of the island, had been told by Kleeman on 9 September that no attacks would be made on him. But on the morning of the 10th his headquarters were suddenly surrounded by German tanks and armoured cars. There was a back way out which Scaroina tried to use, but as he went through the garden he was arrested by German soldiers who had killed his guards and were hiding in the bushes.

Soon fighting was in progress all over the island between the Italian troops under General Forgiero and the Germans. Italian artillery caused severe casualties to the Germans, but massive Stuka attacks took a heavy toll of the Italians. However, in one sector the Italians took 200 German prisoners and a German battery of 88 guns. Scaroina was told by the perfidious Kleeman that unless the Italians surrendered immediately, he and his staff and 3,000 Italian soldiers captured would be shot, and the island subjected to indiscriminate bombing. As the main airfield of Marizza was now in German hands, Scaroina feared an inhuman slaughter would result.

During the night of 9 September three British parachutists landed near

the town of Rhodes and told Campioni that the British would land an
infantry brigade and a strong force of tanks on 15 September. Campioni
told them he could hold out for several days and keep possession of the
port of Rhodes, but that he had already lost the airfields. Campioni
begged the British to send at least a token force immediately. The British
Colonel Kenyon, arriving by sea from Cos, promised to try to hurry up
British reinforcements.

Towards midnight on the 10th Scaroina did what the Germans wanted
of him; he gave them a letter addressed to Campioni advising surrender.
Early next morning a German staff officer set out with an interpreter
for Rhodes. The Italians insisted on blindfolding the Germans; with difficulty they passed the road-blocks because of the fighting, and Italian
soldiers shouted abuse at the Germans. The German interpreter noted
that Campioni seemed on the point of yielding immediately he read
Scaroina's letter. At 3.30 Campioni agreed to the German terms, and
fighting ended.

In the surrender document signed by Campioni, the Admiral was to
remain civil Governor of the island, while Kleeman was to become military commander. This was a German trick. Campioni soon found any
orders he gave were ignored by the Germans, and resigned after a week.
The Germans then shipped him back to Germany and on to Italy, where
Mussolini had him executed for obeying the orders of the legitimate
Royalist Government and fighting the Germans for a few hours.

Although the surrender document stated that the Italian ships in the
port of Rhodes would not sail away, nearly all of them escaped by night,
carrying with them a good number of Italian soldiers who wanted to
continue the fight against the Germans, and put in to Cos, Leros or
Castelrosso. Other Italians took to the hills and woods to fight with
Greek guerrillas, and a sizeable number escaped in small boats to Cos or
Leros or to the mainland of Turkey.

As they had on the other islands, the Germans gave the surrendering
Italians on Rhodes the choice of swearing an oath to Hitler and becoming part of the German army, volunteering to work for the Germans, or
being sent to internment camps in Germany. By far the larger part of the
Rhodes garrison stayed faithful to their legal Government and accepted
deportation. Fifty Italian soldiers were shot as traitors by the Germans
after so-called trials, and 40 without trial.

According to the official Italian history, 1,600 Italian soldiers escaped
after the surrender; 1,900 swore the oath to Hitler and became part of the
German army; while 4,330 from all the islands volunteered for labour.
The oath hastily improvised at Hitler's headquarters included the sentence: 'In the name of God I swear unconditional obedience to the head
of the German armed forces, Adolf Hitler, in the fight for my Italian

fatherland against their enemies, and I will be ready as a brave soldier to put at risk at any moment my life because of this oath.' This was hardly calculated to appeal to Italians. It was emphasized to the Italians that if they did not swear this oath they would not be regarded as prisoners-of-war under the Geneva Convention, but as 'internees', with infinitely harsher treatment.[17]

It is a sensitive point for Italian military historians that Campioni and Scaroina were so lily-livered when Italian troops on Rhodes vastly out-numbered the Germans, and threw in the sponge when the battle was far from lost. The official Italian historian recorded ruefully, 'It was an unexpected and inexplicable surrender and cease-fire while Italian counter-attacks were being got ready for the next day.' General Wilson reported to Churchill:

> We got a mission there ... and the Italian Commander Campioni seemed ready to co-operate 48 hours later. However, he threw in his hand and made a pact with the German commander in the island although there are 35,000 Italians to 7,000 Germans. It was a great pity that we were ordered to send to India the ships which we had asked to be allowed to hold for an assault-loaded brigade. If we could have pushed this brigade into Rhodes on the day after the armistice was signed I think we could have seized and held the island.

It was restrained of Wilson to describe as 'a great pity' the despatch of landing-craft to India; Churchill had stronger words for this US decision. Campioni, despite his premature surrender, was decorated post-humously by the post-war Italian Government. This must have been to draw attention to his infamous execution on Mussolini's orders, as his behaviour on 11 September was cowardly.[18]

Major Dolby, an Italian-speaking SOE parachutist whose real name was Count Drobski, tells an interesting tale. On 8 September, he, Major Lord Jellicoe and a W/T operator were urgently kitted out to drop on Rhodes with General Wilson's written message for Campioni that British help was coming. There was already a secret radio station on Rhodes transmitting messages to Cairo.

As the armistice was announced on the evening of the 8th, the party took off from Cairo West aerodrome; the weather was clear over the Turkish mainland, but thick cloud made it impossible for them to jump over Rhodes, where their target landing point was near the golf course to the south of the town. The next night was clear and the three jumped, landing near the target point. Dolby broke a leg and became separated from the others; he could only crawl into a ditch once he had released himself from his parachute. He found himself in the middle of a gun battle, and at first feared he was within the German lines. Then to his intense relief he heard excited Italian voices; he called out in Italian, and soldiers came to him. They were friendly. As soon as an officer arrived he explained he was the bearer of an important message from General Wilson to the Governor. The officer reacted well, produced cigarettes and brandy, put Dolby on a stretcher and took him in an armoured car to his regimental headquarters. There the commanding officer was a Fascist, almost hysterical because of the German attacks. He refused to send Dolby into Rhodes that night, but as soon as his back was turned the younger officer obligingly drove Dolby to the Castle in Rhodes in a motor-cycle combination, his broken leg stretched out. Before he left the battle area Dolby instructed the Italian soldiers to call out 'Jellicoe, Dolby says you are OK', in English; teaching them to say this, according to Dolby, was the most difficult part of the whole mission.

The Castle at Rhodes is a massive stronghold defended by a triple circle of walls. During the period of Italian occupation, between 1912 and 1943, it was completely rebuilt and could have been defended like a Maginot Line fortress if Campioni had been willing to risk waiting for British help to arrive.

Dolby was immediately received by Campioni in his office in one of the magnificent state rooms of the Castle. Campioni appeared pleased to see Dolby, and was cheerful and even optimistic, saying the Germans were trying to contact him and he thought they would come to some friendly arrangement by which each side would keep their sphere of influence on the island. Campioni stated that some of the Germans were not fighting well, and there had been two cases of over thirty Germans surrendering in a group.

Dolby formed an unfavourable view of Campioni's and his staff officers' military capabilities, although he liked them and they were charming and friendly to him. He lay on a stretcher on the floor talking to the Governor while younger Italian officers plied him with brandy and food.

Eventually Jellicoe and his wireless operator turned up at the Castle. They knew neither German nor Italian, and when they heard Italian voices at first mistook them for German. They had heard the shouts of 'Jellicoe, Dolby says you are OK', but feared it was a German trick. Wilson had given Jellicoe a flowery letter to Campioni, welcoming him as an ally and promising help within a few days. Jellicoe, for fear the Germans might capture this letter, had eaten it while sheltering under a rock.

Dolby told Jellicoe that he had sized up Campioni and the Governor was unlikely to make a strong fight against the Germans unless British troops arrived at once. Accordingly they sent a wireless message to Cairo asking for the immediate despatch of at least a token force of 200 parachutists who they knew were available. Their view was that this would bolster the morale of the Italians and 'force the hand of the Governor'. No immediate reply came from Cairo, which worried the British because they knew how urgent action was if the island was to be saved.

Even with the brandy Dolby became so tired that he asked for a bed for the night; the next morning he was taken to the Italian hospital where the surgeon said he could not put the leg in plaster because it was too swollen, but he put it in splints.

That morning a message come from Wilson that he would send a strong force to hold Rhodes on the 15th but that the ships would not be assault-loaded and Campioni must at all costs keep the harbour of Rhodes in his own hands. Campioni wanted to keep the presence of the British mission a secret because he was frightened that knowledge of their presence would increase the German determination to capture the port and town of Rhodes.

Jellicoe refused to stay in hiding in the Castle. Campioni refused to see the British Brigadier Turnbull, saying (alas, with foresight) that he had endangered his life by seeing Jellicoe and Dolby; but he obligingly lent an Italian seaplane (both aerodromes being in German hands) and Dolby returned to Cairo to hospital.* Here the portly Director of Plans, General Hayman, came to see him just as the news of the Italian surrender on Rhodes came, and heard the details of how the Prime Minister's favourite project had miscarried because of his headquarters' failure to prepare an assault force in time.[19]

The Italians are much to blame for the loss of Rhodes, especially when one considers their great numerical superiority, but it is strange that Churchill did not insist on a plan being made to land a British force there on the night of the Italian armistice being signed. This must have been due to his absence in Quebec. Operation 'Accolade' had been cancelled but between the 3rd and 8th Wilson could have organized a scratch substitute operation so that with Campioni's co-operation a sizeable British task force of tanks and infantry could have disembarked in Rhodes harbour on the night of 8 September.

The Americans' dislike of operations in the Aegean was a serious problem. A typical signal from Eisenhower to Wilson was: 'There is a limit on resources for Aegean in view of absolute necessity of concentrating all available forces on maximum build up in Italy.' However, GHQ MEF knew the capture of Rhodes was Churchill's cherished objective and they should have planned in advance an operation to reinforce the Italian garrison immediately after the signing of the Italian Armistice.[20]

---

*In a letter to the author Earl Jellicoe praises Campioni for his co-operation in sending him and his wireless operator to Castelrosso by torpedo boat and providing the sea-plane to send Dolby back to Cairo.

As the Allied armies advanced slowly through southern Italy, Churchill pressurized the Americans to allow the landing craft and ships employed at Salerno on 8 September to be used in the recapture of Rhodes. He was intent on opening the route through the Dardanelles to Russia, and could not bear the advantages of Italy's abandonment of Germany to be lost.

Churchill wrote to Roosevelt that if Rhodes was not recaptured, Cos would be lost, which would be 'a complete abandonment by us of any foothold in the Aegean which will become a frozen area with most unfortunate psychological and political reactions in that part of the world instead of great advantages'.

Unfortunately, with Campioni's surrender of Rhodes German aircraft were able to dominate the skies, and the Aegean became 'a frozen area' for the Allies. Eisenhower adamantly refused to release the necessary ships for a major effort to retake the islands.

Churchill sent Wilson a war cry, 'Kick spur and practice', and told him that the islands of Cos, Leros and Samos must be held. These three islands had been in Italian hands since the 1912 war between Turkey and Italy, and fortunately had only Italian garrisons and no German troops. The Italian garrisons were loyal to the Crown, and Wilson reinforced them with British troops. Cos was close to Rhodes and had a good aerodome. Spurred by Churchill, Wilson now fixed 23 October as D-Day for the capture of Rhodes with a task-force including an armoured brigade. The Germans were determined to pre-empt this by capturing Cos; at dawn on 3 October a strong German force landed on the island after devastating air bombardments from nearby Rhodes.

There was a mix-up between the British and the Italian defenders; a British convoy carrying reinforcements was due at the same time and the Italian coast batteries, who might have inflicted severe damage on the German ships, did not open fire in time, thinking the ships were British, while most of the Italian defending troops on the coast stayed too long in the air raid shelters. Simultaneously with the landing from the sea, German parachutists dropped from the sky, while the British and Italian positions were subjected to continuous heavy attack from German bombers and fighter aircraft. Allied aircraft could not intervene effectively because the Cos aerodrome was unusable and the aerodromes in Libya and Cyprus were over 200 miles away; by dark on 4 October, Cos had fallen to the Germans. As soon as he heard of the German landings early on 4 October, Churchill took the unusual course for a Head of State of sending a personal message to the British officers on the island; he knew of the German atrocities against surrendering Italian soldiers on the other islands, and wrote:

1. Pope Pius XII among the people of Rome after the bombing of the city on 19 July 1943

2. Mussolini is greeted by Hitler and Ribbentrop, 10 September 1943, after his escape from the Gran Sasso

3. Crown Prince Umberto with loyal supporters of the monarchy *en route* from Rome to Brindisi, September 1943

4. General Taylor meets Badoglio for the second time at Brindisi, October 1943

5. Enthusiastic young Italian soldiers in an American military bus head for the front line to fight Germans, 10 December 1943

6. Italian soldiers with their mules give help to the Allied armies in the mountains, Winter 1943-4

7. Graziani and Borghese displaying their German Iron Crosses, near the Anzio bridgehead, April 1944

8. Mussolini kisses the Republican banner before presenting it to the San Marco Division, July 1944

9. Bersaglieri parade for Mussolini in Germany, July 1944

10. A rapturous welcome for Mussolini from troops of his new Divisions in Germany, July 1944

11. Mussolini greeted by Nazis at a German training camp, with Barracu, the Fascist Minister, Summer 1944

12. Partisans round up Fascists in Rome after the city's liberation, June 1944

13. Italian villagers mourning their dead after a massacre by Germans near Arezzo, July 1944

14. A typical young parachutist of the Nembo Division fighting with the Corpo di Liberazione, July 1944

15. Dromedaries from the steppes of the Ukraine drawing a gun belonging to the Cossack army in Friuli, Christmas 1944

16. Two Cossack brothers at Osoppo, typical of the White Russian army, Christmas 1944

17. The author with officers of the Friuli Division amid the cheering citizens of Bologna when the city was liberated, April 1945

18. Partisans at Bologna after its capture by the Friuli Division, April 1945. The picture is clearly posed

19. Crown Prince Umberto with the Friuli Division in the line on the Senio, March 1945

20. Graziani despondent after surrendering to the Americans on 28 April 1945

21. Lieutenant-Colonel Viktor von Schweinitz signing the surrender at Caserta on 29 April 1945 on behalf of General von Vietinghoff. Behind him, in civilian clothes, is General Wolff's representative, SS Major Max Wenner

22. April 1945: SS Colonel Idolo Globocnik and Gauleiter Friedrich Rainer. Rainer kept Trieste quiet; Globocnik persecuted Jews

23. Cossacks and Germans retreating up the But Valley, 2 May 1945

24. A Tito-organized demonstration in Trieste in favour of annexation by Yugoslavia, 12 May 1945

25. The anti-Fascist General Bellomo after being condemned to death by a British court martial, August 1945

Personal from the Prime Minister to Lt. Colonel Kirby or O. C. Cos. We rely on you to defend this island to the utmost limit. Every measure is being taken to help you. Tell your men the eyes of the world are upon them. Tell the Italians that a terrible fate will befall them if they fall into the hands of the Hun. They will be shot in large numbers, including especially the officers, and the rest taken not as prisoners of war, but as labour slaves to Germany. If they strike hard for freedom and for the United Nations, they will be sent home to Italy at the first opportunity.[21]

Churchill was right about the terrible fate awaiting the Italian defenders. After the white flag was hoisted on Cos British soldiers were treated as prisoners-of-war, but Italians as traitors to their allies, and *francs-tireurs*. Eighty-seven Italian officers were shot by the Germans when they surrendered.

A number of Italian and British managed to escape in small boats to Leros and to the mainland of Turkey, from where the Turks obligingly allowed them to travel to Palestine; others hid in the mountains.

Churchill, furious about the loss of Cos, which jeopardized the recapture of Rhodes, wrote to Wilson:

1   I do not understand why you have not reported the measures you are taking to rescue and support the garrison of Cos which is fighting in the hills. No explanation has been furnished us why a sea-borne attack by seven transports escorted by only three destroyers encountered no opposition and was not effectively attacked when unloading or when returning either from the air or from the sea.

2   What are you going to do now to resist the attack on Leros and Samos to which you refer as likely? Strong reinforcements in cruisers and destroyers have now been sent you. With such forces at your disposal, do you consider another sea-borne attack on these islands possible, observing the enemy have only three destroyers? How is it that none of our submarines was able to attack the seven transports all the hours they were lying off Cos? Why did the Hunts [destroyers] not attack?

3   You report that the troops on Cos had no artillery and no mortars. They had been in occupation for nearly ten days and you should explain the condition of their equipment. Is it possible that the Durham Light Infantry Battalion did not even have its unit equipment in mortars?

The loss of these islands and the garrisons you have put into them will constitute a most vexatious miscarriage, for which the fullest explanations will be required.

This castigation from Churchill persuaded Wilson, against his better judgement, to try to hold three important Italian islands near the Turkish coast – Leros, Samos and Castelrosso. Fortunately the Turkish Government was co-operative, allowing British warships to sail through their territorial waters; Turkish ships also carried supplies to Leros.

On 10 September a small detachment of the Special Boat Squadron from Alexandria entered Castelrosso harbour at dawn and found no Germans there. The Italian commander, Captain Rossi, was described by the commander of the British detachment as 'greatly depressed but co-operative, with the morale of his men low so that a similar force of Germans would have had no difficulty in gaining control of the island'. The civilian population was elated by the arrival of the British.

On 13 September the same detachment entered Cos harbour and were warmly welcomed by the local inhabitants. British parachutists dropped on the Antimachia aerodrome and the Italian units co-operated in organizing its defences. The Italian commander, Colonel Leggio, had a garrison of 4,000 who were widely dispersed, and he emphasized that he needed immediate reinforcements. Once Beaufighters and Spitfires landed on the aerodrome, Leggio became confident.

On 16 September the SBS detachment entered Vathi harbour on the island of Samos. Here they found the Italian commander, General Soldarelli, equally co-operative but greatly worried because part of his garrison consisted of 1,500 Fascist militia who were threatening to march on the town and take control by a *coup d'état*. When the Fascist commander saw British troops and planes, he became mild and ready to co-operate. Only 210 out of his 1,500 Blackshirts stayed loyal to Mussolini, and these were sent with a 'selected escort of Greek guerrillas who would stand no nonsense' by fast caique to Turkey. The Turkish Government obligingly allowed these Fascist POWs to be routed onwards to Palestine. Strict orders were issued to the censors in Cairo and Algiers that there must be no mention of Fascist Italians fighting with the Germans disclosed to the press.[22]

Commander Mascherpa commanded the Italian troops on Leros; as soon as Campioni surrendered on Rhodes, Badoglio promoted Mascherpa to Admiral. This helped to abort bogus messages from Campioni in Rhodes put out by the Germans ordering the Italians on the other islands not to fight any more.

There were 8,000 Italian soldiers and sailors on Leros. Major Lord Jellicoe arrived by sea on 12 September and on behalf of General Wilson promised full co-operation by the British. By 20 September there were over 2,000 British troops on the island and General Frank Britterous was put in command of them and the Italians. He was Irish and Roman Catholic; he quickly made friends with his Italian colleagues, but was found wanting by his superiors. General Wilson told Churchill he considered Britterous too weak with the Italians – Wilson did not believe it paid to be too friendly with former enemies – and a bad organizer. His staff training had been in peace conditions with the Indian Army twenty years before; he immersed himself too much in detail instead of making an adequate overall plan. He quickly chalked up a gaffe by issuing a proclamation that Leros was 'occupied' by the British – he had forgotten it was Italian territory. General Wilson ordered Britterous to issue another statement that the British had come to 'co-operate with' the Italian garrison.

By 17 October there were three British infantry battalions on the island, with a Brigade Headquarters. General Britterous was replaced by Brigadier Tilney on 6 November, and plans were made for a vigorous defence. Meanwhile the Germans concentrated their Stukas on continual devasting raids on Leros. Wilson was dissatisfied with the Italian troops there. He informed Churchill that although the Italians stayed loyal to the armistice terms, they were co-operating only half-heartedly, and statements by Badoglio were not enough; Mascherpa seldom left his air raid shelter, and had 'no grip on the situation'. In addition, according to Wilson, some of Mascherpa's staff officers were unreliable, and it was essential that another commander be sent, one with 'more spunk'. The Italian War Office ordered Mascherpa to place himself completely under British command, and also sent picked officers to replace some of his staff.

At Eisenhower's insistence, on 4 November Ambrosio in Brindisi dismissed Mascherpa and appointed another Admiral to succeed him at once – 'a more energetic commander who will consider himself under the British Military Governor of Leros'. Before Mascherpa's successor could reach Leros, the island had surrendered.[23]

As Wilson had predicted, without nearby air bases Leros was indefensible. Allied negotiations with the Turks to use aerodromes on the Turkish mainland broke down, and the Germans had complete command of the air. Four thousand German troops supported by Stukas began landings on 11 November. This time there was no surprise. The Germans carried out a continuous bombardment of British and Italian gun positions and successfully dropped several hundred parachutists. On 16 November Brigadier Tilney decided to surrender, and Mascherpa concurred. Tilney imposed one condition, which was that a British hospital ship should be allowed to take away the wounded.

A report sent by General Hall from Leros said that the Italians 'alone had heavy weapons on Leros'; although their guns were sited to cover the beaches where the Germans landed, there is 'no evidence that they fired a shot or that the Italians offered any serious resistance to the enemy'. This was not borne out by a long report from Brigadier Tilney, and Earl Jellicoe in a letter to the author said he saw Italian shells landing on the beaches as the Germans came ashore.[24]

Giuseppe Teatini gives in *Diario dall' Egeo* a fascinating account of his experiences as a young officer in Rhodes and Leros. He was a true Commando-type who escaped from Rhodes; on arrival in Cairo, he was deemed to be the courageous sort of Italian needed to improve morale on Leros. According to his evidence, Tilney and Hall completely under-estimated the fight put up by the Italians, and their statement that Italian batteries did not fire on the disembarking German troops is untrue.

On 5 November Mascherpa had been asked to attend a conference in Cairo to discuss the defence of Leros with General Wilson. He refused to go. British staff officers reported that Mascherpa's attitude was that *he* was in command; and that his staff refused to obey the British, and even refused to disclose 'essential information'.

As many as half the Italian forces on Leros were the remnant of mer-chant ships' crews, who were not even armed. The British reported that during the last few days before the invasion, when they saw how many British troops were on the island, Italian morale improved markedly and they complied readily with all British requests. It is probable that neither British nor Italian guns fired upon the invading craft until they had beached, because there was no way of informing the artillery observation posts whether the invaders were friend or foe.[25]

The British lost 600 dead and many wounded on Leros. About 250 British escaped to Turkey. The three British infantry battalions, who had arrived in good fighting trim, were made POWs. The German casualties amounted to 520 dead and wounded. Against this, the Italians suffered only fifteen dead and eighteen wounded – evidence that they fought only half-heartedly.

Once again the Germans shot Italian officers, either in the field or after the surrender. The Italian official history gives the number as twelve army officers and four naval officers. However, by 18 November the Nazis could no longer allege that Italian troops were *francs-tireurs*, because Italy had made a formal declaration of war on Germany.

Pro-Nazi historians claim that the September executions of surrender-ing Italians were legal because, since Italy and Germany were not at war, they had the status of *francs-tireurs*. Eisenhower, conscious that Hitler was using this excuse, and anxious to remove it, asked Badoglio at Malta on 29 September, on the occasion of the signing of the formal Italian surrender, to make a formal declaration of war on Germany. Badoglio, who must have been aware of the summary executions of large numbers of his fellow countrymen, refused, saying it was the prerogative of the king. However, on 13 October a formal declaration of war was trans-mitted to the Germans through the Italian Ambassador in Spain. Thus, when Cos surrendered, all legal excuse for summary executions had dis-appeared. Yet the Germans continued to shoot surrendering Italians on Leros, and in Greece and Yugoslavia. It was cold-blooded slaughter, all part of Hitler's calculated plans to minimize Italian military co-operation with the Allies.

With the loss of Leros, the British decided not to try to defend the other, smaller islands.

There is in the Italian Foreign Office files a transcript of the talk at Malta between Eisenhower and Badoglio. When Eisenhower emphasized that Italy must immediately declare war on Germany in order to put an end to the German excuse that they were legally justified in massacring Italian soldiers after surrender, Badoglio did not appear to understand the remark. When Ambrosio agreed that the Germans looked on the Italian army as *francs-tireurs*, Badoglio then stated that a more important reason for not declaring war was that too little of Italy was under the control of the Royal Government, and that the king himself did not want to declare war. This indicates how unaware the ageing Italian Prime Minister was of the atrocities being committed by the Germans against his fellow citizens, and it is a reflection on both him and the king that Eisenhower should have had to make this plain to Badoglio.[26]

An intercepted Enigma signal from the Germans on Cos, decoded at Bletchley, stated that 97 Italian officers had been shot on capture. This impressed Churchill, who noted in a squiggle that this evidence was 'conclusive but cannot be referred to', and largely thanks to his insistence, the US and UK Governments warned Germany on 10 November through the Swiss Government that they would hold personally responsible for his actions 'any German who treats otherwise than in accordance with the laws of war members of any of the countries fighting at the side of Great Britain and the United States against Germany, including members of the Italian armed forces.'

Hitler did not allow this warning to filter down to his troops in the Aegean. Almost the last signal received from Mascherpa stated that Italian officers captured on Leros were being shot by the Germans. Churchill cabled to Wilson, 'Did the Huns murder the Leros lot of officers, as on Cos?'[27]

Mascherpa was sent back to Italy by the Germans, and like Campioni was put to death by Mussolini after a bogus trial, then honoured posthumously by the post-war Italian Government. Leros, like the remainder of the Cycladian islands, was so close to the coast of Turkey that many Italians escaped to the mainland, where the British and Italian military attachés in Ankara negotiated their passage to Palestine. Four thousand soldiers of the Cuneo Division arriving there were anxious to fight again against the Germans, but to their grave disappointment were only used by the British as labour battalions.[28]

On Crete on 8 September there were about 21,700 Italian troops. Again they vastly outnumbered the Germans, but again there were no offers of help from Cairo. The Italian Commander, General Carta, although he said he was in favour of resistance to the Germans, fled to the hills to avoid capture, and on 24 September left the island in a British naval craft for Cairo. Once Carta had fled from his headquarters the Italians accepted a German ultimatum, and laid down their arms on 11 September. Vecchiarelli's order was largely responsible.

Tragically, more than 7,000 Italian soldiers drowned as they were being transported by the Germans from Crete to the mainland of Greece *en route* for internment in Germany. British bombers sank two large ships close to the shore in Suda Bay; as a few Italians tried to swim to safety, they were machine-gunned by the Germans. Extraordinarily, after this incident Mussolini sent a message to the German garrison commander, General Brauer, thanking him for his kindness to Italian soldiers. Evidently, all the Italians who had fought against the Germans after 8 September were beneath Mussolini's consideration.

When he arrived in Cairo, Carta was sent by the British to Brindisi, where he had great difficulty in giving adequate explanations to the Italian High Command of why he had left his post.[29]

In mainland Greece on 8 September Italy had over 170,000 troops, outnumbering the Germans. The Italians were strung out along the coast in small units; their role was to maintain order, fight the partisans and defend the coast.

The smaller German force was concentrated in large groups, with plenty of armour and transport so that they were highly mobile. Against the Germans the ill-equipped Italians, without armour and short of mechanical transport, stood no chance of victory. In addition, the Germans had complete control of the air; the few Italian war planes on Greek aerodromes were recalled to southern Italy on the evening of 8 September.

The Germans had drawn up plans well in advance to capture the Italian strong points if there was a surrender to the Allies. As has been seen, General Vecchiarelli, the Army Commander, knew his troops had no chance of success; to further his one aim of persuading the Germans to allow them to return to their homeland, he disregarded the orders from the Italian War Office. Instead, as already noted, he ordered that his troops should not initiate hostilities against the Germans, and should not make common cause either with the partisans or with the Anglo-Americans. At 9 p.m. on the 8th the German General von Glydenfeldt demanded that Vecchiarelli should either hand all Italian arms over to the Germans, or agree to fight alongside them. Vecchiarelli refused, and insisted that the Germans allow his army to return home as soon as possible. Glydenfeldt told him that the German intention was to allow the Italians to return home, and that talks should be resumed with a more senior German general. Meanwhile, the Germans cut all telephone lines to the Italian headquarters and attacked various Italian units. At 11 p.m. on the 8th General Lanz saw Vecchiarelli and reached an agreement whereby the Italians would stay in charge of coastal defence for fourteen days, after which they might go home with all their armaments.

At 4 a.m. on 9 September Vecchiarelli was informed that General Lohr, Supreme Commander in the Mediterranean, had ratted on the Lanz agreement: although the Italians would eventually be allowed to go home they must lay down all their arms immediately. Vecchiarelli declared after the war that, while he considered this to be contrary to the honour of the Italian Army, resistance might result in useless shedding of blood; he therefore ordered his troops to surrender their arms and prepare for embarkation.[30]

As soon as convoys of Italian soldiers reached Athens, expecting to take ship for Italy, they were directed by the Germans to the railway station and sent off in cattle trucks to concentration camps as internees, not POWs. Then the Germans ransacked the Italian depots, hospitals and car parks, with the air of conquerors. Vecchiarelli's faith in German promises was betrayed within 48 hours.

An Italian diplomat in Athens who stayed loyal to Mussolini reported:

I will not comment on the strange attitude taken by General Vecchiarelli, which is quite out of tune with Italian military tradition, when he was faced with a dilemma by the Germans.

As Italians we deplore the shameful handing-over of arms when the numerical superiority of our soldiers should have resulted in most favourable treatment; our whole army is liquidated, with its arms and supplies sequestrated and one part transported to Poland as prisoners, the rest either taking refuge with the partisans in the mountains (who do not give them the hoped-for welcome) or throwing away their uniforms and trying to shelter with Greek civilians.

The worst impression, particularly damaging to morale, has been given by the abandonment of our *matériel*, which in the streets of Athens and all over Greece has been sold to bad Greek characters – weapons, ammunition, cars, radios and uniforms; many soldiers who have sold all have gone off either to the Orthodox church or to the Catholic church to marry Greek girls, regardless of morality, so as to be able to hide better from the Germans.

Fortunately, the remnants of our honour have been saved by some soldiers and officers who with Colonel Bartocinni have stuck with the German armed forces to make a nucleus for new Italian units to join.

From the Acropolis, from all our headquarters and from the Embassy our flag, which since May 1941 has waved in the blue air of Greece, has been torn down; roads and lanes are full of the ashes of our documents, while along

the streets of the capital we see long columns of our comrades marching as
prisoners under German escort towards concentration camps before the silent
and horrified eyes of Greek crowds, who cannot understand how such a
powerful army could dissolve into nothing within the short space of forty-
eight hours.

Thus in a few days, amid misery and blood, our military occupation of
Greece which lasted twenty-seven months has ended; what a wretched reward
for the heroism shown by our soldiers during the hard campign of 1940–41.

The diplomat also reported that, because of friendships between German
and Italian officers, the German headquarters had overcome the revul-
sion aroused by Italian treason and allowed some Italian artillery units to
remain with the German army in Greece; he enclosed a greeting from one
battery to the Duce. He added that all these troops wanted to join
Mussolini's new army, but were not allowed to do so by the Germans.[31]

The Germans took Vecchiarelli to Germany by air as they deported his
troops. By the first week in October there were only about 40,000 Italian
soldiers left in mainland Greece, plus those who had gone over to the
partisans and a number who lived in abject poverty in the towns, particularly in Athens. None of them had any means of support, so that more
and more surrendered to the Germans, although they knew they would
be sent to internment camps. Those who remained lived in hope of help
from Italy. This hope was vain, and they had to trust to Greek hospitality
which, with memories of Mussolini's invasion of Greece still fresh, was
forthcoming only in small measure; the plight of these dispersed Italian
soldiers was pitiful. They could get only menial work.

The Pinerolo Division was stationed around Larissa, Volo, Trikkala
and Kastoria. Here there were few German forces on 8 September, but
large bands of Greek partisans who were receiving substantial supplies by
air from the British in the Middle East. The Divisional Commander,
General Infante, refused to obey Vecchiarelli's order to lay down his arms
and on 18 September, after a battle with the Germans, contacted a British
Liaison Officer with the partisans, Colonel Hill. The partisans consisted
of both the Communist ELAS and the more right-wing EDES. Infante
signed an agreement with Hill and the commanders of EDES and ELAS
that his division would fight alongside the partisans; the British offered
to pay the Italian soldiers and to provide them with money for supplies,
while the Greek partisans agreed that the Pinerolo should control their
own sector of the part of Greece on the east coast which had been liberated
by the partisans.

Unfortunately EDES, who were sympathetic to the Italians, and ELAS
began to fight each other, and by false promises ELAS persuaded some
Italian units to hand over their arms.

On 14 October ELAS ordered that all the Pinerolo Division was to be disarmed, despite frenzied protests from the British Liaison Officers and General Infante. After some fighting the Pinerolo were disarmed, and Infante taken hostage. The Pinerolo soldiers were sent to three concentration camps run by ELAS, where they suffered terrible hardships and starvation; several thousands died.

With the help of the Italian navy a number of Italian units in Yugoslavia were repatriated by sea to Bari or Brindisi after holding off German attacks. Tito's partisans made a dash into the parts of Dalmatia where there were few German troops and forced the Italians to hand over a large part of their arms; a considerable number of Italian soldiers with Communist sympathies joined the Titoites. In Cattaro, Croat Ustase troops murdered many Italian soldiers and civilians.

At Cattaro in Dalmatia, General Butta was in command of the Emilia Division. He successfully defended the port against an inferior number of Germans; the Italian Government in Brindisi sent destroyers so that he was able to bring several thousand of his division home to Bari on the 23rd. He reported that the rest of his division had gone into the mountains to fight with Mihailović's Četniks against the Germans. This was incorrect. The Fascist consul who remained at Cattaro reported that when Butta sailed away, he abandoned great quantities of stores of every sort which were immediately looted by the Croats, and that several thousand soldiers of his division were left behind in such distress that many joined the Germans. Several Italian officers at Cattaro were shot without trial by the Germans, and at Spalato two Italian generals were shot after capture. Many Italian soldiers on the run were shot by Croats in Dalmatia, and Italian civilians were also murdered.

General Rocca, commander of a coastal defence brigade based on the island of Curzola near Ragusa and the neighbouring islands, succeeded in bringing back to Allied-occupied Italy on three Italian ships the bulk of his garrison and elements of other divisions – a total of 5,500 men. This was the most successful evacuation operation.[32]

At the end of September, Port Edda in Albania was beseiged by a mixed force of Germans and collaborating Albanians. General Chiminello, commander of the Perugia Division, was successfully withdrawing to the port, where ships were being sent by the War Office in Brindisi to evacuate his troops, now reduced to 6,500. On 22 September, Italian naval ships arrived and embarked around 2,000; the next day three more ships arrived. One was sunk but the other two embarked 2,000 more and took them back to Italy. On 26 September, when nearby Corfu had been lost, the point of embarkation was changed from Port Edda to Port Palermo. *En route* to Port Palermo, Chiminello's force was surrounded by Germans and their Albanian collaborators on the hillside of Borsch. After severe fighting, Chiminello surrendered. The Germans took the Italians to Port Edda, where on 5 October there was a mass execution of Italian officers and NCOs. They were machine-gunned or beheaded in front of their own men, and the bodies then sprayed with petrol and burnt on the ground. Barbarously, the Germans put the head of Chiminello on a bayonet and displayed it to his horrified soldiers. The German officers responsible later claimed they were acting in accordance with Hitler's order of 10 September that all Italian officers who fought against the Germans were to be treated as *francs-tireurs* and shot immediately after capture. Chiminello's stout resistance at Borsch, which resulted in heavy German casualties, had angered the local German commanders who, far away from any central control, decided on the massacre on their own initiative.[33]

On the day of the Italian armistice there were around 130,000 Italian soldiers in Albania, including 12,000 Albanians. A good number were repatriated, but by the autumn of 1944, following deportations by the Germans and other heavy casualties, their numbers were estimated at only 8,000, of whom 2,000 fighting with the partisans were in not bad condition. Apart from those who had been seized by the Germans in North Albania and used as labour gangs, the remainder were trying to live with the Albanian peasants and were in a very bad state. Most had no shoes or boots, malaria and other diseases were rife, and there were no doctors.

The only succour to the Italian soldiers came from the monks in the few monasteries in Albania. As the Germans withdrew, British troops landed at Port Edda in October 1944 with a view to capturing Corfu. The Apostolic delegate in Albania implored the British military to repatriate as many Italians as possible in view of their desperate condition, and British ships disembarking soldiers took back as many Italians as there was room for.[34]

On 9 September, near Spalato, General Becuzzi made an agreement with the Tito partisans and their British Liaison Officer Captain Butler whereby the Yugoslavs should safeguard the embarkation of all his troops who did not want to join the partisans, and 740 Italian soldiers embarked at Trau on four motor torpedo boats; one was sunk, but the others reached Pescara in German-occupied Italy on 18 September. There the officers found themselves in trouble with the Fascists for having resisted the Germans and co-operated with the partisans. On 23 September, again with the help of the Titoites, General Becuzzi kept the Germans at bay and embarked most of his men, almost 3,000, on Italian destroyers which took them safely to Bari and the protection of the British.[35]

A different story is that of the Venezia Division, commanded by the courageous General Oxilia and stationed at Berane and Friole, further inland in Yugoslavia in an area where there were no Germans; most of the country was controlled by Mihailović's Royalist Četniks. Anticipating an armistice with the Allies, Oxilia was on friendly terms with the Četniks in his area. The Venezia Division controlled the area of Montenegro leading south into Albania and east to the Sandzak, on the road into Serbia. Oxilia was immediately visited by Colonel Bailey, one of the British Liaison Officers with Mihailović, when the armistice was declared. Oxilia stated that he was ready to put his division at the disposal of the Allies at once, in accordance with the orders received from the Royal Government, but he had gained the impression from the BBC in London that Britain was backing Tito, whose troops were fighting against Mihailović's in this zone. Bailey persuaded Oxilia that this was not so, and that the Venezia Division should co-operate with Mihailović. Oxilia agreed, and the Yugoslav Royalists took over the civil administration of the city of Berane and the surrounding country.

Tito at once attacked Berane. Oxilia did his best to persuade the Titoites not to fight against Mihailović, pointing out that if they collaborated they had a great opportunity to make a thrust to the sea, brushing the German troops to one side. The Titoites refused, telling Oxilia he must keep out of internal Yugoslav politics. With the help of a British Liaison Officer, Major Hunter, the Titoites tried to persuade Oxilia that they alone had the support of the British; the BBC was now describing Mihailović's Četniks as 'enemies', which further impressed Oxilia.

The truth was that Mihailović was as useful an ally to Britain as Tito, but some British officers in the SOE office in Cairo failed to decode all the signals from the BLOs with Mihailović, which would have given firm evidence that Mihailović's troops were fighting hard against the Germans, and that Tito was using British equipment sent in by air to attack Mihailović.

After his initial support for Mihailović, Oxilia decided to change sides and throw in his lot with Tito, and SOE in Cairo sent orders to the BLOs with Mihailović that the Venezia Division must co-operate with Tito. Considerable quantities of Italian arms were seized by Tito from the Venezia depots, but the Division remained intact as a fighting force.

There was a certain 'musical chairs' element in the area at this time: because 10 Group of the Blackshirts (Palmieri), who should have been under Oxilia's orders, went over to the Germans and in conjunction with them attacked Mihailović in Friboj. For this they were publicly thanked by the German General Ötken when they returned to Italy in December 1943.[36]

Churchill had sent a personal friend, the Conservative MP Brigadier Fitzroy Maclean, to head the British mission to Tito. The Četnik Commander, Colonel Lasić, tried to persuade Oxilia to join in a counter-attack on the Titoites; Bailey urged Oxilia to do so. However, messages came from Maclean to Oxilia demanding the opposite course; Oxilia concluded that Bailey and Maclean were playing a double game, and after a conference with Tito's staff on 9 October decided to throw in his lot with Tito, even though the inhabitants of Berane were definitely pro-Mihailović, and Mihailović had 6,000 troops within the city. Oxilia pleaded in vain with the English BLOs to cobble up some agreement with Tito and Mihailović so that together they 'could fight the common enemy, the Germans'.

Although there were Communists among the ranks of the Venezia, Tito feared that if the Venezia operated under the orders of the Italian Government in Brindisi in his area, they would not co-operate fully, or endorse Communist propaganda among Italian soldiers and Yugoslav civilians. Accordingly, he persuaded Maclean that the Venezia would be more use if they were disbanded as a Division and became a 'Garibaldi' (Communist) brigade within Tito's Yugoslav army; Maclean agreed. Oxilia had now been joined by General Vivalda, Commander of the Taurinense Division, and about 1,200 of his troops. They were summoned to a conference with a Titoite colonel, who they soon realized was a bitter enemy of Italy; the colonel told them that the two divisions must be disbanded and made into one unit, to be called 'Italian Partisan Garibaldi Division', while all guns and vehicles were to be handed over to the Yugoslavs. Although the combined total of the Taurinense and the Venezia was 14,000, Tito's colonel said that only 4,000 were to be fighting troops; the remainder were to be disarmed and become labourers for the partisans. Oxilia had very different instructions from Brindisi and he refused, pending orders from his War Office. Maclean, as Churchill's friend, had influence with the British High Command, and the British 8th Army insisted that Oxilia should conform to the Yugoslav requests.

This was the height of folly, but the Italian War Office were in too weak a position to obstruct the British request. Marshal Messe, who had replaced Ambrosio, signalled to Oxilia that he must agree. However, the Venezia still considered themselves part of the Royal Italian Army, and Oxilia only agreed to the proposed arrangement in the light of implicit instructions from the War Office in Brindisi, who were passing on British orders.

At the end of December Churchill, misled by false reports from Communists within the SOE office in Cairo, had decided to withdraw all support from Mihailović and back Tito one hundred per cent. This encouraged Tito to make even more insulting demands on Oxilia. On 10 January Oxilia was ordered by the Yugoslavs not to communicate with the Italian War Office in future; and no longer to use the names 'Venezia' and 'Taurinense', only 'Garibaldi' (the title given all Italian Communist guerrilla fighters), since his troops were now part of the Communist Yugoslav army. The same day, Oxilia was ordered to set up committees of commissars to indoctrinate his troops with Communism; one of the commissars was an Italian deserter. At the request of the British, the Italian War Office agreed to the new status of the two divisions.[37]

Oxilia's troops suffered greatly at the hands of the Titoites. Officers and men were shot on the flimsiest of excuses, including General Isasca, second-in-command of the Division, and sixteen other officers, among them one chaplain.

Almost 12,000 men from the Venezia Division passed to the Garibaldi, with about 2,000 from other formations. They suffered heavy losses while attached to Tito. Only 6,000 remained to be repatriated to Italy in March 1945, although a further number were alive in Yugoslavia. When they reached Bari there was a parade and a public reception. Communists offered them bouquets of red roses; one corporal threw his bouquet to the ground, denouncing Communism and saying that if his son became one, he would shoot him. When the Italian Communists came to honour the 'glorious partisans' at Manfredoni, near Bari, the soldiers of the Venezia punched them and there were injuries. Their experiences with the Tito partisans had been so brutal that the iron had entered the soul of these Italian soldiers. General Browning, responsible to the 8th Army for the Italian Combat Groups, wanted to use these repatriated troops as reinforcements for the Friuli and Cremona Groups (see Chapter 10); these were being infiltrated by Communists, and Browning felt that, with their anti-Communist bias, Oxilia's troops would be a 'steadying influence'.[38] General Browning wrote that they had 'a tumultuous welcome', and were good fighting soldiers who had suffered much in Yugoslavia. Oxilia had reported on 19 February 1945 that 6,000 of his Garibaldi Division were ready in Dubrovnik to be repatriated. Casati, Minister of War in Rome, wrote a personal letter to Tito asking for them to be returned. Tito agreed.

After the Leros surrender Wilson wrote to Churchill, 'Leros . . . was a near thing . . . of the four fine battalions which acquitted themselves in the finest style of British infantry, I fear we shall not see many again.'

During the Leros fighting Churchill had worked himself up into a frenzy, writing that Leros was 'the most important thing happening in the Middle East' in a letter imploring Eisenhower to send help. He drafted, but did not send, a detailed letter to Roosevelt complaining bitterly of Eisenhower's luke-warmness over the Aegean, and stressing the need for a unified command in the Mediterranean. All the Americans would promise was that the capture of Rhodes might be undertaken after Rome had fallen. Churchill drafted (but again did not send) to Eisenhower after Leros had fallen: 'I hope you have not thrown away your crown.'[39]

However, although Hitler was successful in crushing the British effort to establish themselves in the Dodecanese Islands after the Italian surrender, his victory turned out to be an Achilles' heel. On 2 December 1943 the British Chiefs of Staff forecast that the Germans would not be able to 'supply' the Dodecanese; this proved correct. German signals giving details about the movement of their shipping between the Adriatic and the Greek islands were intercepted at Bletchley, resulting in unsustainable German shipping losses. Hitler withdrew many ships from the Black Sea to replace them but most of these in turn were sunk.

In November 1944 Hitler was forced to transfer ships from the Aegean to the Crimea, but they were sent back from the Black Sea in January 1945 when he evacuated the Crimea. The number of sinkings soon began to escalate. The British were able to send seven small aircraft carriers, which had been used for the invasion of southern France in August 1944.

Hitler believed, erroneously, that the British had six or seven assault-trained divisions ready in the Middle East to attack Crete or Rhodes, or even the Greek mainland. After Rome fell in June 1944, Hitler in desperation brought back to Greece bomber squadrons which he had withdrawn to Italy because of the Anzio landings near Rome in January 1944. Until June 1944 he was still bent on reinforcing the Aegean. Then the last U-boat in the Mediterranean was sunk, and British bombers also sank two of his largest merchant ships and three of their escorts off Crete. Commandos and the Special Boat Squadron made life hell for the German garrisons on the islands by kidnapping German officers (including one general on Crete), blowing up radio stations, cutting the land cables and damaging ships in harbour. At Simi the Commandos attached limpet bombs to two German destroyers in the harbour, damaging them so severely that they had to be towed back to the Piraeus for repairs.

In August Hitler began to withdraw from Greece but decided to leave garrisons in the Aegean islands, although he could no longer risk sending convoys there. Senselessly, he determined to continue to defend the islands, and gave orders that the garrisons were to consider themselves 'fortresses who must hold out to the last round, so as to prevent Allied troops being used elsewhere'.

On Samos, vulnerable because of its proximity to Turkey, the Germans had left a purely Fascist Italian garrison; the 1,600 Fascists showed little loyalty to Mussolini, and surrendered to fifty Greek guerrillas and a handful of British in October 1944.[40]

Salonika was evacuated, and occupied by the British on 30 October; 62,000 German soldiers remained on the islands but could not now be reinforced or supplied, and were subjected to heavy bombing. On Crete there were nearly 14,000 Germans, and 5,000 on both Rhodes and Leros. On Cos there were 1,000, and several hundred on Milos. Corfu, where only German stragglers were left, surrendered on 12 October.

General Wilson decided not to assault Rhodes, Cos or Leros because with Russian and Anglo-American armies on German soil there was now no point in opening up the Dardanelles route to Russia, and the casualties involved could not be justified. However, an unopposed landing on Crete was accomplished, the German garrison driven back into the hills and Greek rule reinstated.

Harold Macmillan, the British Resident Minister in the Mediterranean, paid a formal visit to Crete in December 1944. At that time there were still 10,000 German soldiers in the mountains, without any communication with their bases on the continent. Macmillan described them as being 'in voluntary imprisonment'. The same was true of the German garrisons in the other islands still holding out.[41]

Not until Hitler was dead and Jodl had signed a formal surrender on 7 May 1945 did the German garrisons on Rhodes, Cos and Leros give in. Hitler's Aegean adventure, which had cost so many Italian lives, ultimately served only to tie up German troops uselessly.

CHAPTER 9

Italians and British POWs

HISTORICALLY, BRITAIN AND Italy are bound by strong traditional ties of friendship. These were created by British help to Italy in the Napoleonic period and reinforced during the Risorgimento when Italophile volunteers from England helped Garibaldi in his romantic victories. Again, in the First World War, Britain and Italy were allies against the Austrians.

With the introduction of Fascist government under Mussolini in 1922, these ties loosened, and the declaration of war on Abyssinia in 1935 by the king and Mussolini alienated much British public opinion. George Trevelyan, whose books on Garibaldi and the Risorgimento had made Italian history such a popular subject, declared he would never write about Italy again while Mussolini was in power. The historian A.J.P. Taylor vowed he would never set foot in Italy until Fascism was removed thereby spoiling his doctorate thesis on the Risorgimento (he worked solely on Austrian documents, and in his published book not a single Italian document is quoted).

Finally, the declaration of war on Britain in June 1940 and the 'stab in the back' to France brought Anglo-Italian friendship temporarily to a sad end. Nevertheless, the succour given by Italians of all classes to escaping British POWs after 8 September 1943 is evidence that a love of Britain was still alive in the hearts of most Italians.

Many of the POW camps in Italy had secret wireless sets which could receive messages sent out by MI9 (Military Intelligence) at the War Office, who were responsible for captured British personnel; in addition, coded letters were continually sent from the same department. On 7 June 1943, when plans to invade Italy were mooted, the War Office signalled to Allied Forces Headquarters in Algiers and General Headquarters Middle Eastern Forces in Cairo that they were sending to the camps in Italy 'orders that they were not to make mass break-outs but in event of invasion to try and send escapers to give our forces information . . . we cannot authorize [mass break-outs] owing to possible danger mass reprisals' (the reference of the order was DDM P/W 87190).[1]

160

Brigadier Richard Crockatt (later Major-General), one of the Deputy Directors of Military Intelligence in the War Office, was responsible for this atrocious order; it is impossible to find out from the archives whether he consulted with superiors before sending it. British commanding officers in the POW camps were also to blame, for passing on the orders: they knew the circumstances on the ground, and how real was the danger of German troops moving in. As a consequence of the order, about half the British POWs in Italy found themselves under German armed guard within 48 hours of the armistice, and were sent to POW camps in Germany.

On 8 September 1943 the announcement of the Italian armistice came as a complete surprise to the numerous British POW camps in Italy, who heard the news at 7.30 in the evening. The majority stayed put, their commanding officers following the order from the War Office. Eric Newby has written that many thousands of British POWs were transported 'en masse to Germany, thanks to their ridiculous senior British officers who had forbidden them to break out of the camp under pain of court martial'.

Colonel Mander, a senior British regular officer with an interpretership qualification in Italian, told his commanding officer, 'Under no circumstances will I spend another night in this camp', and with others made off while the going was good.[2]

Crockatt's order was disputed by the Middle East Defence Committee in Cairo, who cabled to the Foreign Office and War Office on 1 August, when an Italian armistice was anticipated: 'Instructions [to Italian POW camps] might include also inducement to assist escape of prisoners. Temporary dispersal of latter all over countryside would prevent wholesale deportations to Germany and create difficulties for Germans.'

Crockatt replied to Cairo: 'Mass break-outs from POW camps likely to fall into our hands in the course of a few days are not of use as likely to add only to administrative difficulties.' Perhaps memories of the misfortunes of large groups of British POWs following the surrender of Germany in 1918 were fresh in the minds of First World War survivors.

The Middle East Defence Committee's message was followed by a personal signal to Crockatt two days later from Lieutenant-Colonel Simonds, who was responsible for POW escapes and had gone to Sicily to organize them as soon as Allied troops landed on the mainland: 'Understand POWs advised by you against mass break-outs. Presume you will issue fresh instructions should London act on Mideast's suggestion [the signal from Cairo quoted above]. We have worked out outline scheme for use in the event of escape, and might be able to arrange evacuations from western coast Italy.'

A draft plan prepared by Simonds was sent to Crockatt at the War Office. It included the following suggestions:

Senior Officers and NCOs are to organize all prisoners into small groups; each group to be self-contained as to rations and where possible with maps and compasses ... All such groups are to make their way to the nearest point of the eastern coast of Italy, and to hide up to await evacuation ... Allied representatives are being landed at numerous points on the eastern coast of Italy ... Send runners up and down the coast in your immediate vicinity to see if any craft can be seen in other local beaches. Remain hidden and await developments.[3]

These instructions were practical and sensible; it is strange that Simonds did not point out that Switzerland was the easiest safe point for many camps but, on the other hand, prisoners arriving there would not be able to take any further part in the war.

Simonds and his tiny staff planned for pamphlets to be dropped on POW camps and shipping to be laid on at Palermo for the pick-ups on the Adriatic coast, and he made a request for a 'section' of paratroopers to be placed at his disposal. Crockatt in the War Office was asked to inform all POW camps with a receiving set of Simonds' plans.

Crockatt refused to have anything to do with these plans, and replied on 23 August that the POWs had been ordered not to make mass break-outs, and that 'the War Office considered opinion was that ... no plans can be co-ordinated with those of invading forces. Possibly certain camps will disobey our instructions and organize mass break-outs but we cannot authorize them owing danger possible mass reprisals.'

Simonds was grievously disappointed. He cabled to Algiers that the War Office had rejected his plan out of hand; he received permission for a party of one American officer and three British officers to be attached to the US 5th Army when they landed at Salerno on 8 September, with the aim of assisting escaping POWs. This was pitiably inadequate, and left Simonds unable to give much-needed help to the 80,000 Allied prisoners in northern Italy.

During the armistice negotiations, Churchill had insisted that the Italians must do everything possible to prevent American and British POWs falling into German hands. As has been seen, on 20 August, during Badoglio's forty-five days, the Italian Foreign Minister peremptorily refused a German request to hand over British prisoners to the Germans. This refusal followed his receipt of two strongly-worded demands from the British (on 31 July and 18 August, by way of Switzerland), stating that allowing the Germans to take them would have 'serious consequences', and that this applied to British POWs captured by the Germans and now in Italian hands, as well as to those captured by the Italians. Again through Switzerland, the Italian Government promised to comply before the armistice was signed.[4] Loyal at least on paper to their commitment, on 6 September the Italian War Office sent out the following order, intending it to reach the commandants of all POW camps (the differentiation between coloured and non-coloured POWs would not have met with Allied approval):

British POWs

Prevent them falling into German hands. In the event that it is not possible to defend efficiently all the camps, set at liberty all the white prisoners but keep the blacks in prison.

Facilitate their escape either to Switzerland or along the Adriatic coast to southern Italy. Labour units in civilian clothes may also be helped, provided they are away from the German line of retreat. At the opportune moment the freed prisoners should be given reserve rations and directions as to which route they should follow.

This order was sent out with good intentions, but it is improbable that it was received by the commandants of all 72 POW camps.[5]

The 'labour units' referred to were 25 camps for NCOs and other ranks, scattered mainly over northern Italy, where the POWs were engaged in manual work not connected with the war effort. To continue to hold the blacks rather than releasing them was technically a breach of the armistice terms, but the Italian War Office perhaps considered that it would be easier to feed and maintain these prisoners if they stayed put. Coloured POWs included a number from the Abyssinian War of 1935–6.

On 8 September, the day of the Salerno landings and far too late, there was a change of heart at the War Office in London. Crockatt cabled to Simonds that 'the whole question action POWs in event Italian collapse' was under consideration by the Chiefs of Staff, and also told him of the Italian War Office order (quoted above) that all POWs were to be released, given ten days' food supply, and instructed to make either for Switzerland or an Adriatic port, whichever was the easier route.

The single US officer sent to help with the escapes, Captain R.B. Lewis, USAAF, reported in October on his operations: 'The opportunity of rescuing really large numbers of prisoners in Italy had already been lost when the armistice was announced'; he expressed the opinion that if action had been taken in advance on Simonds' proposals (which he had read in July), the results would have been far happier. He found that in almost every camp in Italy the senior British or American officer had given orders that no prisoners should attempt to escape, threatening anyone attempting to do so with court martial. In an exaggeration, he added that the Italian guards were usually instructed to shoot prisoners trying to escape. He went on: 'Not until more than two months after 8 September were orders given for mass rescue of prisoners at large.'

He stated that at the end of September, parachutists to help the

POWs were dropped in four inland areas, and beach parties landed by sea along four corresponding coastal strips. Their task was to contact and round up all POWs and shepherd them to the beaches to wait there until naval craft arrived to evacuate them. Captain Lewis claimed that more than a thousand POWs were evacuated from beaches between Ancona and Pescara, and that another thousand could have been brought to safety if the naval part of the operation had been as efficient as the military.

Lewis considered that the apathy and timidity of the POWs and their low morale posed the greatest difficulty.

Hundreds of prisoners refused to make the slightest effort to return to our lines, and out of 1,500 contacted by the two British officers Captain McKee and Lieutenant Macgibbon Lewis and given maps, compasses and detailed instructions, only 100 came through. On one beach 300 prisoners were gathered but when shots were fired by an Italian farmer at a dog they ran away, and only 25 were taken off.

He noted a major disaster at Francavilla, where hundreds of POWs waiting on the beach were let down by the navy failing to keep the rendezvous.

An RAF report stated that at Camp 49 Reggio (in Emilia) 1,700 POWs (an inflated figure, see below) marched out and went into hiding, but at Camp 52 Chiavari and Camp 107 Tor Viscos the strongly Fascist Italian camp commandants managed to detain the prisoners until the Germans arrived. The RAF remarked on the 'lavish friendship' and 'help' given by civilians and Italian ex-soldiers, who handed out not only civilian clothes and food but also railway tickets and considerable sums of money. The MI9 comment on the RAF report was that 'the "lavish friendship" is an interesting contrast to the hostility shown by all Italians to escaped POWs prior to the armistice.'[6]

A good number of escaped POWs from the north, especially officers, reached Switzerland, helped by anti-Fascists and often bribing guards to let them through the frontier wire, which consisted of a ten-foot-high chain-link fence topped by barbed wire. They followed the same mountain paths as Austrian soldiers after the battle of Lodi in 1796. One escapee, arriving in Switzerland, went to a restaurant and was asked if he minded sharing a table with Italians; he found himself next to the commandant of his POW camp and his wife; they had beaten him to Switzerland by a short head.

For the first few weeks after 8 September it was not difficult for escapees to reach Switzerland from northern Italy. Although the Germans had started preparations to police the Italian–Swiss frontier a month before the armistice, by the end of October only a few hundred middle-aged retrained German policemen were ready to assist the unenthusiastic *carabinieri* and the Italian customs officers (*Guardie di Finanza*) along the lengthy and inaccessible Alpine frontier with Switzerland. It is estimated that during the twelve months after the armistice, barely ten per cent of British escapees attempting to cross the frontier were arrested. The *Guardie di Finanza* were by no means Fascist-inclined, and usually allowed Allied escapees to cross as long as the Germans' backs were turned. Some guards allowed soldiers in uniform to cross, but turned back officers and those in civilian clothes.

Immediately after the German occupation, the strong anti-Fascist organization in Milan (the Committee of National Liberation) formed the *Ufficio Assistenza Prigionieri di Guerra Alleati* (Allied Prisoners of War Assistance Service) and got off to a flying start before German frontier guards were operating. Ferrucio Parri, a leading anti-Fascist who after the war was to become Prime Minister of Italy, saw the opportunity; at his instigation Giuseppe Bacciagaluppi, Managing Director of the American Standard Electric Corporation factory in Milan, who was married to an Englishwoman, at once organized an escape route from central and northern Italy to the Swiss border. Bacciagaluppi himself organized the escape of 1,000 British POWs into Switzerland before he was captured on 3 April 1944.[7]

The escapees were given civilian clothing and a rendezvous with special guides at stations such as Padua. The guides gave the POWs tickets to Milan and then hid themselves in carriages at the front and back of the train so that if Fascist militia searched it they could warn the escapees to walk along the platform to carriages which had already been searched. At Milan station the escapees usually hid in empty trains, but sometimes in safe houses, until they could catch a local train to Dervio or Dorio and stations further north on the east bank of Lake Como from where they crossed the lake to Cremia. At the lakeside they exchanged the guides from Milan for local guides, often smugglers, who escorted the escapees up the Cavargna valley to within a few hundred yards of a Swiss frontier post near Bogno which could be approached from Italy or Switzerland only by a path, not a road. Here the former prisoners-of-war gave back as much of their civilian clothing as they could spare before they approached the frontier guards. Once over the frontier it was an easy walk to the village of Bogno at the head of the Swiss Val Colla. Once there they could relax and stroll (a few limping badly) down peaceful empty roads to the shore of Lake Lugano, enjoying the magnificent views of the wooded slopes around the lake in their autumn colours. When they reached the cheerful bustling town of Lugano friendly Swiss showed them the way to the British consulate and the comfort of a neutral country. Out of the 4,000 prisoners-of-war who escaped to Switzerland, probably over half took the Cavargna route to Lugano.[8]

The crossing from Macugnaga towards the west above Lake Maggiore was far more hazardous. From Gravellona just north of Lake Orta they had to bypass German patrols in the long narrow Val Anzasca in order to reach the tiny ski resort of Macugnaga. From here precipitous mountain paths led to the Swiss frontier at the top of the Saas valley. Fortunately, the pass was only lightly guarded, but some sections of the path were within range of German machine-gun fire during daylight hours. It meant climbing up to 9,000 feet, and the crossing took nine hours. On this route escapers often met Jewish refugees who had bribed smugglers to bring them to Switzerland; one escapee met a guide carrying an elderly Jewish lady in a basket. The crossing from Macugnaga to the Saas valley lies in the shadow of Monte Rosa, described by Tennyson:

> How faintly flushed, how phantom fair
> Was Monte Rosa hanging there.
> A thousand shadowy pencill'd valleys
> And snowy dells in the golden air.

Once Allied prisoners-of-war arrived in Switzerland they were looked after by the British military attaché at the Legation in Berne, Major Cartwright. The Swiss Government would not allow even generals to be flown out, and as the Germans occupied all the land frontiers, they could go no further; they were kept under surveillance by the Swiss. Once the American armies who landed in the south of France in August 1944 had liberated the Franco-Swiss border, escaped POWs in Switzerland were allowed to go by train across France to the UK.[9]

The Italian War Office orders appear to have been obeyed in the Aquila province, where the Italian commandant 'opened the gates and released all prisoners' at PG 145 and its satellites (work camps); at Aquila camp PG 102 and its three work camps, nearly 1,200 were 'dispersed' into the hills by the guards. General Klopper, the South African who was in charge of Tobruk when it fell, was in the Villa Orsini five miles from the main camp, with other senior officers. They had received the London War Office order to stay put, but decided it was not operative in view of the armistice. They left immediately, and fifteen out of the eighteen had reached safety by Christmas. However, in this case the Italian commandant was not fully co-operative.[10]

As has been seen, the only large camp where the Italian order was obeyed and the whole camp departed in good order was near Reggio Fontanello, PG 49. The Senior British Officer, Lieutenant-Colonel de Burgh, enjoyed a good relationship with the Italian commandant and the whole 600, mostly junior officers, marched out and were given hospitality by the Italians in the neighbourhood. The majority of the 600 reached either their own forces or Switzerland. They have recorded the amazing generosity of their Italian hosts.

A branch of MI9 had been set up by the War Office to help British POWs in Italy to reach safety; although on 9 September they had no one on the ground; in succeeding weeks officers were clandestinely sent in to arrange routes to safety. They recruited Italian parachute officers and Alpini to set up staging-posts, with the help of co-operative local Italians; their reports are full of glowing praise of the help they received. Three large boat-loads of escapees were taken off from the Marche region, in December 1943 and March 1944. In addition, in April 1944 more than a hundred were taken off from the mouth of the River Tenna. As MI9 reported, 'there is no recorded incident that even under torture any Italian soldier revealed the work on which he was engaged with our organization. Almost without exception the Italian officers proved first-class and were key men in our mission.'[11]

Not all prisoners-of-war tried to escape to Switzerland or to the Allied lines. Some found living with sympathetic Italian families so enjoyable that they preferred to stay put rather than take the risk of being shot on the frontier. At a ceremony of thanks in July 1946 to Italians who had helped prisoners-of-war, another South African general said, 'The bond between my country and your country has been strengthened by the marriage of a good number of our troops to those women in Italy who so gallantly helped them.' More than two thousand prisoners-of-war were missing when the war ended; a proportion were living happily with Italian families and did not want to return to their homeland.

Escape to the advancing Allied troops in the south was not as easy as to Switzerland. The 8th Army had landed at Taranto on 9 September unopposed, and a week later the road from Bari to Salerno was open. Several officer prisoners-of-war travelled by train during the night of 8/9 September and reached stations in towns already occupied by the 8th Army on the Adriatic coast. With proper organization, many hundreds more could have taken the same route to safety. Many trains continued to function after 9 September, albeit with difficulty in the prevailing confusion. However, once the front line became continuous, all trains from the north terminated in the German zone.

Some officers took the train to Naples and remained in hiding until the town was liberated on October 1. Another party boarded a southbound train at Bologna on 14 September, reached Castel di Sangro after three days on the train, and then walked to the 8th Army lines; others took the train down the Adriatic coast to Termoli and had no difficulty in reaching already liberated Bari by 17 September, on foot. When Rome fell and the US 5th Army and the British 8th Army surged northwards through Florence to the Gothic Line, a great number of POWs who had been hiding with Italian families were rescued.[12]

The grand total of prisoners-of-war recovered reached 6,500 through the Allied lines, with 4,000 crossing the Swiss border. By the end of 1944, with the front stabilized again on the Gothic Line, official estimates were that 5,000 were at large in the northern regions. Fewer than a thousand, mainly shot-down air crews, were added to these totals during the last seven months of the war.[13]

Innumerable books of memoirs published after the war pay tribute to the way in which the Italian population helped the many thousands of British and American escaped POWs loose in northern Italy, often risking their lives by hiding them in their houses, since anyone harbouring an escaped POW was threatened with the death penalty by the Germans and Fascists. Other escaped POWs joined up with the partisans in the hills and fought with them until the end of the war.

Iris Origo has described the typical behaviour of one family of Tuscan peasants in her moving diary *War in Val d'Orcia*:

27 February, 1944. A peasant from a remote farm on Monte Amiata, Fonte Lippi, came to see me, bringing with him a letter from three of our POWs, who (after having lived for four months hidden in this man's farm) set off in January to try to rejoin their own troops. There were four of them, but when they got near to Cassino one of them was captured, and the other three have now returned, worn-out and ragged, to the same farm. Their note says: 'We realize that this man has robbed himself and his family to keep us', and begs me to help him in any way that I can. The peasant's story is remarkable. He took in these four Englishmen at the beginning of October, when they were obliged to leave here, and fed and housed them – disregarding the danger as well as the expense – for over three months. Then the Fascist militia of Radicofani (having been warned by a spy) came to search his house and threatened to shoot him for harbouring enemy aliens. They came in the middle of the night and turned the house upside down, but *della brava gente* (some good folk) had given the warning two hours before, and the prisoners had escaped into the woods in time – returning again to the farm the next day. 'We just couldn't turn them out,' said their host. 'They had become a part of the family – and when at last they left, my old woman and the children cried.' But meanwhile they had eaten up all the family's flour – everyone was going short – and at last, in January, they had set off – only to return again a fortnight ago ... The Englishmen have tried to join up with one of the bands on Monte Amiata, but their leader has told them to stay where they were for the present, as he too is short of food ... Finally, in despair, the peasant has come to us. He has also provided the Englishmen with clothes, at his own expense, and all he is asking for it is some wheat so that his family will not go hungry, and, if possible, some boots for his guests. We are providing the wheat (two quintals) – which will be taken down to the valley at night in the cart of one of our farmers who can be trusted – and there transferred to this man's ox-cart. Boots are as unprocurable as the crown jewels, but I have sent Antonio's last pair of shoes, some socks, cigarettes, books and playing-cards (for the men do not now dare to stir out of the house) and some money.

... Much has been said in these times (and not least by the Italians themselves) about Italian cowardice and Italian treachery. But here is a man (and there are hundreds of others like him) who has run the risk of being shot, who has shared his family's food to the last crumb, and who has lodged, clothed and protected four strangers for over three months – and who now proposes continuing to do so, while perfectly aware of all the risks that he is running. What is this, if not courage and loyalty?[14]

Iris Origo, daughter of an American father and an Anglo-Irish mother, was married to a wealthy Italian landowner, and records considerable additional evidence of the way in which escaped prisoners were helped by Italians of all grades of society; countless other tributes have been paid by British and American soldiers and airmen 'on the run'.

Through clandestine contacts with Italian civilians the British were able to organize escape routes to the Adriatic several months after the armistice, and on several occasions sent in tank landing-craft to pick up groups of POWs who had made rendezvous thanks to the help of dedicated Italians. This would have not been possible without the remarkable friendship and loyalty of nearly all Italians living in the Marche.

There is, however, the other side of the coin. Fascist sympathizers among the Italians betrayed escaped POWs to the Germans or the Black-shirts. All allegations of war crimes against the British in Italy were followed up by the British Army after the end of the war. The archives disclose that four Italians were executed for killing British POWs, and a handful convicted of maltreatment.

A considerable number of British escapees gathered in Rome while it was still occupied by the Germans. Major Derry and an Irish priest, Monsignor O'Flaherty, set up an organization through which all the POWs were billeted in safe houses; only a few were denounced to the Germans by Fascists. Some British officers found comfortable quarters with rich aristocratic anti-Fascist Italian families. Friendly Italians oblig-ingly cashed cheques, as did John May, valet to the British Minister at the Vatican. As a result, rash British officers could be seen lunching at Ranieri's (the famous restaurant frequented by the British on the Grand Tour in the early nineteenth century), to the certain knowledge of Weizsäcker, the German Minister to the Holy See. Several Allied soldiers drunk in the streets were picked up by police. In the end, Derry had 2,591

British and 800 other nationalities on his books, and was paying out two million lire a month. Not all these were in Rome, and eventually Derry had to try to discourage ex-prisoners from coming to Rome. There were 896 South Africans, 429 Greeks, 185 Americans and 425 Russians nominally in receipt of funds. Some ex-prisoners in Padua were given a large loan by friendly Italian industrialists, and this relieved the strain on the Vatican Legation's financial resources.[15]

When he was settled in Rome after walking out of his POW camp, Colonel Mander risked being shot out of hand as a spy: he operated a low-power transmitter in a safe house, and sent British Headquarters in nearby Anzio details of the German units he could recognize in Rome.

The following rules were drawn up by one regular officer on the run and distributed as widely as possible:

> When living in the plains, observe the following rules:
> 1 Never remain static; one night and day in a house is ample.
> 2 Don't let children see you, or, if they do, pretend to be a German if in uniform or an uncle if in mufti.
> 3 If the Partisans say there are 1000 Germans coming up the road, you are all right, but if they are laughing and happy and not worried, beware! They become easily over-confident.
> 4 Trust no one; there are spies everywhere.
> 5 The poorer the house, the safer it is: rich houses are invariably Fascist.
> 6 Women working in the fields are usually safe.
> 7 If a farmer sees you hiding in his fields, he will pass by where you are and pretend not to have seen you. Later he will come back and, if he is sympathetic, will ask if you are hungry and produce food. If he doesn't produce food, go away quickly.
> 8 Any farm with young men walking about is safe; they are deserters either from the Army or from Germany and in as bad a spot as yourself.
> 9 Cycle about with a pistol in your pocket and, if challenged, ride up to the sentry and shoot first. A pistol is the best weapon for a cyclist.
> 10 Once you have stayed at a house and eaten there, you are safe; they will not tell the Germans as their house would be burnt down for having kept you the one night.[16]

The Germans put up placards offering the Italians a choice between death for helping Allied prisoners or a reward of 1,800 lire (£20) for denouncing them (at present-day values, 1,800 lire would be around £750). Through leaflets distributed clandestinely, the Badoglio Government offered 5,000 lire to any Italian who gave hospitality to British or Americans.

Not surprisingly, unpleasant and tragic incidents had occurred during the long incarceration of British POWs in Italy prior to the armistice of

September 1943. Mussolini's propaganda was violently anti-British and under Fascism brutal elements of the Italian population had come to the fore.

General Bellomo was an anti-Fascist general in Mussolini's army: on 9 September 1943, immediately after the armistice, when the Germans attacked the Italian troops in Bari, Bellomo led a successful counter-attack and freed the port of Bari from the Germans. His colleagues and superiors in the area had been supine, and Bellomo's courage showed up the poor behaviour of the other Italian generals.

However, Bellomo had committed a war crime in 1942 by shooting at and killing one British officer and wounding another, on the pretence that they were trying to escape from a POW camp near Bari. At a hastily constituted field court martial in July 1945, soon after the war had ended, Bellomo was sentenced to death. The court martial was unsatisfactory. Bellomo was given an inexperienced officer to defend him, and the evidence was skimpy. Field Marshal Alexander confirmed the death sentence, and within weeks Bellomo was executed; this caused a furore in the Italian press, and Cyril Ray of the *Daily Express* and other British journalists also expressed grave concern. It was widely believed in Italy that Badoglio and other Italian generals did not intervene to save Bellomo because they did not want to emphasize how much better he had behaved than the majority of them when the Germans attacked.

In 1990 a BBC TV 'Timewatch' programme stated that 'the British had shot the only anti-Fascist Italian general (Bellomo)'. This was untrue – there were plenty of anti-Fascist generals. However, it would have been correct to say that the only Italian general executed by the British for a war crime was an anti-Fascist. It was unfortunate that Field Marshal Alexander did not show Bellomo the same mercy he later showed Kesselring.

Doubts about Bellomo's guilt were silenced in February 1946 when Captain Sommavilla, the commandant of the POW camp, was accused before another British court martial in Milan. More time had been allowed to collect evidence, and both the prosecution and the defence were better conducted. The Sommavilla trial made it clear that Bellomo had indeed perpetrated a horrible war crime. Two British officers, Captains Cooke and Payne, had tried to escape from the Bari POW camp; within hours they were recaptured. When General Bellomo heard of their attempt to escape he became hysterical with rage. He ordered the two to be brought out from the punishment cell with their hands tied. To the horror of Sommavilla and the other Italian soldiers Bellomo, his revolver in his hand, shouted and gesticulated at the prisoners, ordering the guards to push them to the point in the wire through which they had escaped that morning, in a pretence that they were escaping again. Bellomo fired five shots from his revolver at the prisoners, while ordering the guards to shoot at them with their rifles. The guards fired in the air. Both British officers fell to the ground; Payne was dead, and Cooke seriously wounded. Sommavilla saw Bellomo taking aim. Bellomo doctored Sommavilla's official report, and threatened him with punishment if he did not agree to the alterations. According to Sommavilla and other witnesses, a subsequent Italian Court of Enquiry was rigged. General Jengo, the Italian Inspector of POW camps, gave devastating evidence against Bellomo at Sommavilla's court martial. The court martial found Sommavilla 'not guilty', which is *a fortiori* proof that Bellomo was.

Still, in view of Bellomo's impeccable conduct on 9 September and the Italian furore over the case, it was a grave political mistake on Alexander's part to allow the execution to go ahead. It should also be borne in mind that, at the time, Italy had no death penalty. The Bellomo case remains an emotive issue in Italy to this day.[17]

A few other Italians were also executed for war crimes by the British, according to the archives of the Judge Advocate General. These included the Blackshirt officers Lieutenant Magnati and Lieutenant Rinaldi, who at Messola on the Po near Ferrara tortured and killed a British flight sergeant, Arthur Banks. Banks had crash-landed his plane near Rovigo and in December 1944 was trying to cross the Po to reach the Allied lines. Magnati and others behaved bestially, burning his belly and genitals with hot irons, and committing further indescribable obscenities. Banks was thrown half-dead into the Po; when he crawled out, Magnati shot him in the back of the head. Others involved, including one female, were sentenced to terms of imprisonment varying from five to twenty years.[*][18]

In April 1944 two brothers, Pietro and Luigi Musetti, both Blackshirt corporals, killed three British prisoners-of-war on the run in a farm house at Tavigliano near Vercelli. After they had been wounded by machine-gun fire they were beaten up, bayoneted and then shot with revolvers. Pietro was condemned to death; Field Marshal Harding confirmed the death sentence. Luigi was sentenced to twelve years in prison. According to a British officer, Eric Hamblin, who escaped unhurt from the house, they had been betrayed to the Fascists by a woman called Crote. She and another Italian involved called Quattrini were later shot by the partisans after a drum-head trial. Hamblin testified that he himself had 'taken responsibility for the shooting of Crote'. This is evidence of the

---

[*]The files on the Magnati trial and five other courts martial of Italians have been 'lost' in the Ministry of Defence, although they are catalogued in the PRO. It is perhaps as well that the Magnati documents are not available, because of their obscenity, but their actions are recorded in the trial of his accomplices.

bitter hostility between Fascist supporters and the partisans in northern Italy.[19]

In three other cases, Italian officers accused of murdering escaped British POWs were acquitted. Several Italians were accused of minor offences. Two officers of the Special Boat Squadron, Captains J. Verney and Imbert Terry, were captured in Sardinia in July 1943 and *en route* to the POW camp at Chieti they escaped on the island of Maddalena. When they were recaptured a Captain Firinu of the *caribinieri*, blind with rage, beat them and kicked them in the genitals and then shut them up for the night in a room with no lavatory accommodation. This happened in August 1943, after the fall of Mussolini and when sensible Italians were anticipating an armistice with Britain. Senior Italian naval officers were so shocked by Firinu's behaviour that they removed the British officers from his charge and apologized. At Udine prisoner-of-war camp Colonel Nuncio Nicita, a strong Fascist from Sicily, was found guilty of hitting and threatening with a revolver prisoners who had been recaptured after escaping. He was sentenced to four months' imprisonment.[20]

Every alleged instance of war crimes by Italians against the British was carefully investigated by British Field Security Police during and after the war. No doubt there are other instances of British escaped prisoners being killed by Italians where no trace has been left. However, considering the brutal record of Fascism, it is remarkable how few instances there are of Italian war crimes, compared with the thousands of German war crimes against British POWs recorded in the archives of the British Judge Advocate General.

Corporal Soddini was sentenced to death for shooting and killing Australian Corporal Simons during an altercation at a game of cricket at the Udine POW camp on 20 May 1943. Simons had been drinking, and it was alleged in defence that he threatened the Italian with a beer bottle. Both the Prime Minister, De Gasperi, and the Vatican made pleas for mercy, and the sentence was commuted to life imprisonment.[21]

Colonel Turco, the Italian commandant of the POW camp at Padulane near Bergamo, was sentenced to death for shooting while in a rage a Cypriot soldier who refused to work when there was doubt as to whether repairing an airfield was a permitted occupation for POWs under the Geneva Convention. According to a statement from the Judge Advocate General's department after the verdict, 'there was no apparent mitigating factor', but General Harding reduced the sentence to seven years' imprisonment. This was in 1947, when the climate over the death penalty was quite different from that in 1945 when Bellomo was executed. Colonel Turco had been awarded a British DSO in the First World War, receiving the award from the Duke of Connaught.[22]

A bizarre case was that of Colonel Bacci; in a camp near Ascoli Piceno he had refused to allow an emergency operation for appendicitis on a prisoner, who died as a result. The defence were able to prove the absence of adequate lighting, surgical instruments and drugs for the operation, and the Colonel was acquitted.[23]

In the immediate aftermath of Mussolini's return and the re-creation of a Fascist State, some Fascist officials behaved badly towards escaped British POWs at large in northern Italy. Pietro Cosmin,* a vicious Fascist, was reinstated by the Salò Government as prefect of the province of Verona. In November 1943 he ordered the execution without trial of a British officer, Lieutenant Clive Lyon William, together with the sixteen-year-old son of the house where he had been sheltering near Verona. An execution squad was ordered to arrest Lyon William and the son of Signora della Riva, the owner of the house. They were taken away in a car; the della Riva boy was shot dead in a cave, and Lyon William in the road. After the war one member of the execution squad was tried by a British court martial and sentenced to death after an unsatisfactory trial which aroused considerable publicity in the local press. The sentence was commuted to imprisonment. Two other members of the execution squad were charged and acquitted. Cosmin had already been sentenced by an Italian court to sixteen years' imprisonment, and was not brought before a British Court.

As it became increasingly clear that Germany was losing the war, and as the Allied armies approached the Lombardy plain, atrocities by bloody-minded Fascists against Allied POWs decreased.[24]

Throughout its existence from 1922 onwards, however, the Fascist regime was riddled with hideous cruelties and injustices. They arose because officials were responsible to the Party rather than to an elected body, and the Fascist hierarchy tended to overlook excesses committed by faithful and influential Party members.

Monsters like Cosmin were even freer to work their will during the 600 days of the Salò Government because the apparatus of Fascism was in disarray and the Germans overruled Mussolini's puppet regime. Mussolini himself issued the inhumane order that all partisans captured carrying arms were to be shot out of hand. However, he was strongly opposed to reprisals against civilians who helped the partisans, and to the burning of villages and houses in revenge for the killing of Nazi or Fascist soldiers. Italian soldiers of the Black Brigades and the SS, some brought up in a tradition of Fascist brutality, co-operated only too willingly

---

*In virtue of his office, Cosmin presided at the Verona Conference of Fascists; he also stage-managed the show trial of Ciano and the other members of the Grand Council who were condemned to death. He was responsible for having the death penalties confirmed in a bogus effort at legality, and for bungling their execution.

with the Germans in barbarous reprisals. Cases of Fascist brutality brought to light in the post-war trials are grim reading, and there must have been many others about which evidence is scanty or non-existent.

A well-known case of German brutality towards Italians who helped escapees was the murder of the brothers Rodolfo and Casperino Fiadino. They were shot at Carpacotta above the Sangro on 4 November 1943 by German troops for helping hundreds of Allied prisoners-of-war to cross the Sangro to the safety of the 8th Army lines. A third brother escaped from the hands of the executioners at the last moment. A plaque was put on the spot where the brothers died by the Association of British Escaped Prisoners-of-war (Monte San Martino Trust). A great number of similar killings occured, many of which are unrecorded.[25]

CHAPTER 10

The Royal Army and the Allies

AS SOON AS the armistice was signed by Eisenhower and Castellano at Cassibile on 4 September 1943, the Italian War Office prepared Memorandum OP 44, instructing Italian Army Corps and Division Commanders to face the Germans once the Axis was ruptured. When Badoglio and Ambrosio fled from Rome on the night of 8/9 September, they omitted to activate the Memorandum. Thus the only instructions the commanders had were those contained in Badoglio's broadcast on 8 September: 'Italian troops will resist all attacks from whatever quarter they come.' As a result, as has been seen, Italian commanders did not know whether or not to fight the Germans. When they telephoned to the War Office in Rome on the evening of 8 September they were told, 'If the Germans are leaving the country, let them. Try not to provoke conflicts.'

On the mainland of Italy during the evening of 8 September, the Memorandum OP 44 plan for fighting the Germans was known only to a small clique at the War Office; the Memorandum stayed at the Corps Headquarters in sealed envelopes, with strict instructions that it was not to be opened until orders came from Ambrosio. The War Office and Admiralty had not even countermanded their standing orders to resist an Allied invasion: at least one submarine approached the Allied invasion fleet at Salerno and was prevented from attacking only at the last moment.

On the rest of the mainland of Italy, the unprepared Italian army had no chance against the Germans. After celebrating the hoped-for end of the war with manifestations of joy on the night of 8 September, as has been seen, masses of soldiers took the Badoglio broadcast as their signal to desert and go home by bus, train, bicycle, tram or on foot and put on plain clothes.

German plans to put the Italian army out of action were thorough; they issued this order:

> Ask the Italians to give up their arms, telling them that the war is over for Italian soldiers and they are to go back to civilian life.

Occupy the telephone exchanges. All communication between towns must be forbidden.

Put into safe places all the arms and weapons. Proceed according to instructions already imparted.

The instructions 'already imparted' were to use force 'without mercy' if there was resistance.

Part of the Italian army acceded to the courteous German request to give up their arms, and were allowed to leave their barracks and go home. Those who resisted were made prisoners and immediately deported in cattle trucks to Germany to be used as forced labour. The Germans were furious over their 'betrayal' and, wherever the Italians refused to disarm or attempted counter-attacks, fought with ferocity and barbarity. Goebbels' propaganda was: 'The Italians have abandoned us in our moment of crisis . . . their treachery has turned all our plans upside down . . . If we could use the divisions now needed in Italy for the Russian front, we could throw the Bolsheviks back.' This enraged the German soldiers in Italy, arousing contempt and hatred amongst them for Italian soldiers.[1]

The Italian army in France collapsed immediately. At Nice, a French journalist described the rows of Italian prisoners on the Promenade des Anglais as 'pitiable, with two or three German soldiers in charge of hundreds of Italians in tattered uniforms'. They were shouted at and abused by the supporters of de Gaulle. Turin was surrendered to the Germans by a Fascist general; Asti, Mondovi, Alba, Bra and Tortona, where there were strong Italian units, succumbed without real resistance. In Lombardy and Emilia, Pavia, Piacenza, Parma, Reggio, Cremona, Brescia, Bergamo and the other garrisons surrendered; only at Milan did the politicians succeed in making Italian soldiers fight the Germans, but not for long. At Como and Varese the Italians were too strong for the Germans, but when General Ruggiero, in charge of this area, could get no orders from Rome, he came to an agreement with the Germans and sent most of his soldiers home. In the Alto Adige, especially at Bolzano and Verona, there was temporary resistance. A strong garrison at Bologna faced by tanks and armoured cars did not fight. The 5th Army units were stationed in Tuscany and around Chiusi Tarquinia and Viterbo; they made some effort to defend the Futa Pass and there was fighting at Pisa, but it soon ceased.[2]

In the south the 7th Army under General Arisio found themselves scattered, and powerless to put up proper resistance against the German divisions bound for the Salerno front. Even so, isolated pockets held out for 48 hours, notably at Trani and Matera. Only at Bari did the Italians defeat the Germans. When the Germans tried to sabotage the port installations,

General Bellomo enthused his troops, fought back and forced the Germans to surrender. The greater part of the Mantua and Legnano Divisions succeeded in making contact with the Canadians advancing towards Brindisi from the Straits of Messina; they remained intact and were able to provide a nucleus for a new Royalist Italian Army. Torsiello gives the whole sad story, and details of the Italian losses in the few situations where they fought.[3]

It must be remembered that not many senior Italian officers were anti-German. Years of Fascism and anti-British propaganda after the start of the Abyssinian War had had considerable influence. Memories of the fight against the Austrians during the Risorgimento and the First World War were becoming dim, and the battles in North Africa against the British and Americans had forged bonds of comradeship and friendship between the German and Italian armies. As Tamaro writes, 'No one should believe that in September 1943 all Italians hated the Germans. This hatred was markedly absent in much of the Italian army.'

However, it is true to say that by May 1945 the shocking behaviour of the Germans since September 1943 had engendered wholesale hatred. Benedetto Croce, the well-known and popular Liberal politician and world-famous philosopher, immediately after the armistice said in a broadcast that 'the pact of steel was contrary to all Italian national tradition'. This was untrue. Croce himself, in a book published in 1914, had expressed his 'deep admiration for the political and ethnic qualities of Germany'. It is undeniable that, in the south of Italy, anti-Austrian feeling resulting from the Risorgimento and the First World War barely existed.[4]

Fortunately for the king and the Badoglio Government, the situation was favourable for them in the islands of Corsica and Sardinia. Here, Italian troops outnumbered the Germans, and in contrast to the Aegean, Allied help was close at hand.

In Sardinia General Basso commanded four Italian divisions – Calabria, Bari, Sabauda and Nembo; in Corsica General Magli two divisions – Friuli and Cremona – plus a mountain infantry regiment and a battalion of Bersaglieri. The Germans had in Sardinia 90th Motorized Division commanded by General Lungerhausen. In Corsica they had only one armoured division, the crack Reichsführer SS under General Senger, especially well-equipped and secretly trained to fight the Italians. In Sardinia there were 180,000 Italians against 25,000 Germans; in Corsica, 80,000 Italians plus unlimited but almost unarmed local French partisans against 15,000 Germans.

If the Italian army in Corsica and Sardinia had received orders from the War Office to go into action promptly, the Germans must inevitably have surrendered, although fighting would have been heavy. Instead, they largely escaped to the mainland, to the intense disadvantage of the Allied Italian campaign.

In Corsica an Italian staff officer, Colonel Massa, heard the news of the armistice on Radio London on 8 September while General Magli and General Senger were having dinner together. The meal ended less warmly than it had begun. Magli told Senger that in accordance with Badoglio's broadcast the Italians would not resist Anglo-American landings, but knowing nothing of Memorandum 44 he said the Germans were free to make arrangements to leave the island.

At 2 a.m. on 9 September a despatch was received at the War Office from General Basso's Headquarters in Sardinia: '90 German Division seeks permission to leave island peacefully'. In violation of the armistice terms Ambrosio cabled his agreement a few hours before he abandoned Rome. Basso later spent two years in prison and was court-martialled. He should not have been blamed, because the Germans had not attacked him, and Badoglio's broadcast had said nothing about attacking the Germans gratuitously.

Basso gave the Germans eight days to leave using the route towards the ports of La Maddalena and St Teresa on the north of the island, where there was a short sea-crossing to Corsica.

Basso soon found himself in an impossible situation. Immediately the Germans seized Maddalena and captured the Italian coastal batteries, after harsh fighting and severe casualties. They made the Italian Admiral Bruno Brivónesi a POW, destroyed Italian aeroplanes on aerodromes around Maddalena, and attacked Italian troops near Oristano.

But worst of all for Basso, the Nembo Division was strongly Fascist. They were a parachute formation containing highly-trained, athletic volunteers from the Young Fascist movement. Most of the Nembo Division wanted to remain allies of the Germans and to leave Sardinia with them. The Nembo Chief of Staff, Colonel Alberto Bechi Luserna, argued violently that the Nembo Division must stay loyal to the king, and was shot by his own soldiers. A few other stray elements of coastal defence around Maddalena led by a Fascist colonel also sided with the Germans.

Using Siebel ferries, lighters and other landing craft salvaged from the Sicilian operations, the Germans evacuated the whole of 90 Panzer, plus service units and stores and most of the Nembo Division, to the nearby ports on the south coast of Corsica, Bonifacio and Porto Vecchio. Basso's troops let them go.

Magli, in Corsica, was in a dilemma. He had not been informed that the Italian War Office had authorized the movement of the German troops stationed in Sardinia across Corsica to the mainland.

Immediately Senger left his dinner-table Magli told the French authorities that they were to resume their civil authority and that the police were to keep order. Then at midnight he heard that the Germans had attempted to capture the inner port of Bastia, killing 25 Italian troops who so far had received no orders to fight the Germans.

Immediately Magli reacted correctly. He ordered General Cotronei, General Officer Commanding Friuli Division, Admiral Gonzaga, Commander Marine Defence, and General Stivale, Commander Port Defences, to counter-attack. Supported by the guns of the Friuli Division the French drove the Germans out of the port; they retreated to positions on the coast around Biguglia.

After the battle Senger went to Magli's Headquarters and expressed sorrow about the Bastia fighting. Magli then agreed that the Germans could use the east coast of Corsica for embarkation, and emphasized that he would not tolerate any further acts of hostility. Senger linked up with Lungerhausen, whose 90th Division had quickly been ferried across from Maddalena, and occupied Bonifacio, Porto Vecchio and the airfield of Ghianaccia. But on 11 September fighting between Italians and Germans broke out again both at Bastia and with the Bersaglieri at Casamoza on the route south from Bastia.

The divisional artillery of Friuli supported the Bersaglieri, and the strong point at Casamoza remained in Italian hands until heavy tanks arriving from Sardinia via Bonifacio reinforced the Germans. The Italian artillery commander reported that his 75/18s could not penetrate the armour of the Panzers and after a battle lasting 36 hours General Cotronei, at 7 p.m. on 13 September, ordered his troops to withdraw: the division was redeployed in the hills towards the south-west of the island, where they linked up with French partisans who were receiving drops of arms and rations from the Allies in North Africa. With the arrival of German armour, Magli could no longer defend the port of Bastia.

The highest Italian military award for valour was posthumously awarded to Captain Bruno Conti for his part in the battle of Casamoza: two silver medals and two bronze medals were awarded to other gunners. Captain Conti's citation runs: 'Commanding a battery at a strong point he was mortally wounded in a surprise German attack and was conscious until the end, ignoring his pain. For three hours he calmly gave fire orders to the guns. In the end, refusing any help, he stayed alone with the guns, with one soldier, ordering the others to escape so as not to fall prisoner.'

On the night of 11 September the head of the Corsica partisans, Colonel Paul Colonna d'Istria, suddenly appeared at General Magli's Headquarters, and at the same time came news that the French 4th Moroccan Division would land at Ajaccio on 14 September. An Anglo-American liaison officer soon arrived, and plans were made for the Friuli and Cremona Divisions to lie low outside the German zones, ready to help the French in an all-out assault on the Germans on 19 September.

On 11 September, Magli finally received orders from the Italian War Office in Brindisi to fight the Germans – which he had already been doing for 60 hours. The signal '5V' had been prepared for Magli and Basso on 8 September but never transmitted; it read: 'Implement Memorandum 44 and drive out all German forces in Sardinia and Corsica. On no account allow German Division 90 to pass from one island to the other. Signed Roatta.' If only this order had been sent on the 8th, General Basso must have won in Sardinia. Basso did not receive 5V until 12 September at 9 p.m. Basso replied on 13 September to War Office Brindisi: 'German armour being evacuated from Maddalena to Corsica. I cannot attack before 16th. Nembo Division not to be trusted.'

Thus, in Sardinia the Italian army did nothing to help the Allies. The armistice said the treatment given to the Italian nation would depend on how they co-operated in the war effort. Magli in Corsica felt it was up to him to prove the Italians could fight with honour.

On 14 September the French 4th Moroccan Division under General Henri Martin began to arrive at Ajaccio, transported in two Italian cruisers and one French submarine. They disembarked without opposition. First they deployed in the area Montegupio–Caso Balomi and built up supplies, ready to attack on 29 September. The Italians' biggest contribution was to be artillery support from the Friuli Division.

The Friuli Division artillery commanded by Colonel Brunelli was put under the orders of General Louchet, Infantry Divisional Commander of the 4th Moroccan Division. They had one battery of 100/17, four batteries of 75/18, two batteries of 20 mm, and one battery of mountain artillery. The mountain battery was detached to support the 1st Regiment Moroccan Tirailleurs. Thus, without any declaration of war and without any conditions in the armistice for the Italians to co-operate with the Allies, an *ad hoc* arrangement was come to in the field with the French, and it had important and favourable political connotations for the Italians.

Meanwhile, on 13 September Hitler had ordered the Germans to withdraw from Corsica to the mainland, and Senger's one idea was to embark his troops at Bastia or to airlift them from the nearby aerodromes.

After bitter fighting at Teghime the French infantry attacked Bastia, and the Italian guns pounded the roads on which the Germans were retreating, besides giving support to the French infantry as they attacked the German defensive positions. On 3 October the Friuli guns from positions at Prucinasca, Cardeto and Teghime battered the moles of the port of Bastia, inflicting heavy casualties on the Germans who were performing a Dunkirk-style evacuation.

At 5 a.m. on 4 October the last Germans had embarked. The rear guards surrendered. Twenty-one thousand German troops were evacuated, plus most of the Nembo Division. Forty-five German sea transports were lost from Allied air attacks, as were many aircraft flying a shuttle service from the Bastia airports.[5]

The French infantry commander, General Louchet, wrote to Colonel Brunelli commanding the Friuli artillery (35 Regiment): 'You have been a precious collaborator, and your men have shown both valour and technical expertise. I cannot thank you enough for the efficient support your batteries have given me during our attacks on Bastia. You gave me help without stinting, and I thoroughly appreciate what it has been worth.'

The 35 Artillery Regiment at least had changed sides with a vengeance, and proved to the Allies what a worthwhile contribution the Italians could make to the war effort against Germany.

The regimental history of the 35 Artillery Regiment states that in the fighting in Corsica their soldiers had written on 'a blank page with their blood a history of an episode which proves both the bravery and the courage of the Italian nation' and 'continued the Garibaldian tradition of the Risorgimento'. Certainly their behaviour was a welcome contrast to the collapse of most of the Italian Army, and their 28 dead and 85 wounded and their Gold Medal and numerous silver and bronze medals gained in Corsica are striking evidence of their zeal.

Soon after the Corsican fighting the Friuli Division was moved out of French territory to Sardinia. Here they had to kick their heels for a while without further opportunity to display the 'Garibaldian qualities' so proudly referred to later in the regimental history.

Their mountain artillery regiment had 600 mules, desperately needed by the Allies in their advance up mountainous Italy. So 700 artillerymen and 600 mules were transferred to the mainland to act as pack transport for the British 46 and 56 Divisions who were fighting with the US 5th Army on the west coast of Italy. Here they were invaluable and performed an excellent job.

Then in March they were transferred to the Cassino front, and owing to a mistake in staff work their British Liaison Officers were withdrawn and they were left without interpreters. In a mist they were sent down the dreaded Inferno track to the Cairo flats, overlooked by the German observation posts at Monte Cassino. There they bivouacked in olive groves. Next morning was fine and clear and the Germans shelled them for three hours, causing a few casualties to men but many to the tethered mules. All histories of the Battle of Monte Cassino refer to the ghastly smell of dead mules and the clouds of blue-bottles on the Cairo flats.[6]

Many regular Italian officers in the zone of south Italy occupied by the Allies were disgusted by the cowardice of the king and Badoglio in deserting Rome, and of the commander of the Italian Motorized Corps there during the moment of crisis; they were equally horrified at the news of the barbarities inflicted upon the Italian army by the Germans in northern Italy and in the Aegean. From them and from the former democratic politicians came a strong move for an independent force to fight against the Germans alongside the British and Americans, independently of the remnants of the Royal Italian Army and without allegiance to the king or the Badoglio Government.

A well known anti-Fascist, Captain Zaniboni, in the first week of October produced to Senator Croce in Sorrento a plan to form a Volunteer Irregular Legion to fight against the Germans. Zaniboni suggested that the Legion should be under US command and treated as an ally, and should owe no allegiance to the king or the Badoglio Government. Instead, it would have a 'Republican' affiliation, and like the Garibaldi Legion in the wars of liberation in 1859 and 1866 it would contain individuals from every political party. Croce persuaded Zaniboni that this would be unlikely to appeal to the Allies. Three days later Joyce Lussu, the wife of the prominent Sardinian politician and sister of the historian Max Salvadori, approached Croce with a similar proposition. She had crossed the front line from Rome. Croce persuaded her that any Italian fighting against the Germans must recognize Badoglio's as the constitutional government, and not take a stance against the monarchy.

With a leading anti-Fascist, General Pavone, Croce concocted a more acceptable plan, by which an Italian independent armed group of volunteers, not anti-Government, would fight alongside the Allies. William J. Donovan, Director of the American Office of Strategic Services (OSS), had come to Naples from Berne; he supported the plan, writing warmly to General Mark Clark, commanding the US 5th Army, to recommend that General Pavone should be allowed to recruit this force, and that instructors from SOE and OSS should be attached to them for training purposes. The plan was also supported by the British SOE, but the Foreign Office and Churchill disliked the anti-monarchical attitude of the volunteers, and their opposition to being enrolled in the regular Italian army. The historian Max Salvadori succeeded in getting the support of the Allied Control Commission. About five hundred volunteers were actually enrolled.

Two colleagues of Croce went to see Badoglio in Brindisi on 4 October; they suggested the volunteers should be known as the National Front of Liberation. Badoglio cold-shouldered the scheme, stating that if the volunteer soldiers were captured by the Germans, they would be shot as *francs-tireurs*. He told them that while he was eager to send regular Italian troops into the line, any proposals for an additional irregular volunteer force must come from the Allies.[7]

Badoglio did, however, assent to recruitment, and a long-winded manifesto was pasted on house-walls in Naples. This asked Italians to enrol in 'Gruppi Italiani Combattenti' to fight alongside the Allied armies in the spirit of the Risorgimento and with the ideals of Mazzini. Unfortunately for Croce's aspirations, at the insistence of the Foreign Office, General Alexander vetoed arming any Italians who were not in the Royal Army. Montgomery when consulted was also averse to the scheme, declaring that he would not accept irregular Italian soldiers within the 8th Army because it would become 'a dog's breakfast'. Nor did General Pavone choose his recruiting officers wisely. Field security in Naples discovered that an accountant, A. Thomas, who was recruiting for the Combat Groups under Colonel Guidi, was extremely left-wing and was putting out anti-Badoglio and anti-monarchist propaganda. He was immediately ordered to cease 'functioning'.[8]

Many anti-Fascists gravely resented the Allied refusal of an irregular volunteer force, and even today this question arouses controversy in Italy. However, after Montgomery had left to command the cross-Channel invasion a volunteer force, F Recce Squadron, was created within the 8th Army from officers and other ranks who for political reasons did not want to fight with the Badoglio army.

F Recce was unique. It was raised in December 1943 with the assistance of the Italian War Office, and put under XIII British Corps. Supplied with British transport, arms and uniform, it was almost indistinguishable from a British unit. All the personnel were enrolled as Italian soldiers and paid from Italian funds so they could not be regarded as *francs-tireurs* by the Germans if captured. F Squadron was always treated with suspicion and 'even latent hostility' by the Italian General Staff. Although only 120 strong it was composed mainly of former Italian parachutists, and within XIII Corps it enjoyed a fine reputation for courage. Another irregular formation was the Brigata Maiella, formed in the Abruzzi from partisan units in the summer of 1944. These partisans, mostly very young, were not openly hostile to the Italian Government, but preferred to fight separately; they operated under 8th Army orders until the end of the war. The existence of F Squadron and the Maiella Brigade never came officially to the notice of the British Foreign Office, but they fulfilled to some degree the frustrated aspirations of Croce and the anti-Fascists in Naples in the autumn of 1943.[9]

As soon as Italy changed sides in September 1943, a mass of applications to join the Italian fighting forces came through the British and American consulates in neutral countries – especially from the Argentine. An article in the *Nación*, the leading Argentine newspaper, pointed out that in the 1914–18 war over 40,000 Argentine nationals of Italian descent had volunteered to fight with the Italian army, whereas only one volunteer had gone from Argentina to fight on Mussolini's side. Britain and America made no attempt to keep a register of volunteers from overseas, and were not interested in recruiting them.[10]

The armistice of 8 September had specified that Italy could expect better treatment after the war if she was able to give substantial armed help to the Allies against the Germans. There were considerable numbers of Italian troops in the zone occupied by the Allies, although they were short of equipment and supplies. Badoglio and the king were anxious that they should fight the Germans, knowing that they could pick officers and men determined to revenge themselves on the Germans.

In November Badoglio persuaded Eisenhower to allow an Italian Division to go into the line. Italy had by now declared war on Germany and been accepted as a co-belligerent. In Sicily and the south of Italy there were enough lorries, weapons and ammunition in the depots to equip a motorized brigade with four infantry battalions and field and anti-tank guns. Called the 1st Italian Motorized Brigade (6,000 strong), they went into the line with the Americans on 7 December. The Americans were trying desperately to capture Monte Sammucro, south-west of Venafro and south-east of Cassino, so as to open up Route 6 to Rome, but their attack had ground to a halt. The Italians were asked to try, and they agreed to attack Monte Lungo from the south-west on the night of 8 December.

Several Italian infantrymen were so anxious to announce to their former allies that they were about to take their revenge for having been deserted in Africa and Russia that they crawled forward during the night yelling taunts and threats at the 15 Panzer Grenadiers holding Monte Lungo: this removed any element of surprise.

The Italians attacked with great valour and occupied the height, but before they could dig in on the rocky ground they were pushed off by a German counter-attack. Not much was gained and the Italians suffered nasty casualties, but it proved to the Allies that the Italians meant business and could be taken seriously as a fighting ally.

On 16 December a second Italian attack in the afternoon cleared the slopes of Monte Maggiore and this was a great help to the Americans in advancing to Venafro.

A vigorous effort was made to collect as many vehicles, ammunition, guns and weapons as possible from all the Italian depots in Sicily and southern Italy, and at the end of March 1944 an enlarged Italian motorized group commanded by General Utile went into the line in an important sector of the Adriatic front to the west of Ortogna. As Rome fell the Italians advanced through Chieti, Teramo and Macerata to Urbino and up to the Gothic Line. Fighting was not severe, but the Italians did well, and if they had not been available another British or American Division would have been required to hold this part of the line.

By mid-July it was clear to the Allied Command that if the Italians were to play any further part in driving the Germans out of their country they would have to be given Allied war *matériel* because their armament factories were in German-occupied Milan and Turin, and there were insufficient supplies of ammunition, guns or vehicles in occupied Italy.

Accordingly, at General Alexander's suggestion Churchill agreed to equip them from Allied sources. Immediately Roosevelt complained, and ordered that no US equipment of any sort was to be issued to the Italian Army. Churchill decided the British would go it alone, and Alexander was authorized to equip four Italian Divisions (or combat groups) entirely from British sources. These were the Friuli, Cremona, Legnano and Folgore.[11] If all went well, these four were to be followed by the Mantua and Piceno Divisions, who had not fought against the Germans in September but had remained homogeneous in the south of Italy. The first division to be equipped was the Friuli; they had distinguished themselves in Corsica, and it was intended that they should be the first to go into the line, as a reward for their success there.

The new Divisions, known as Combat Groups (*Gruppi di Combattimento*), consisted of 12,000 men formed into two infantry brigades, four batteries of 25-pounders, one anti-tank battery with 17-pounders, and one anti-aircraft battery with 40 mm guns, together with engineers and supporting arms, but no tanks.

On 15 August the Friuli Division started training at Benevento near Naples with British equipment. They changed their grey-green uniforms for battle-dress with Italian collar flashes, but not one shirt or tommygun – not even a cartridge, or a tin of bully beef – could be drawn from US dumps. Older married officers and NCOs were weeded out and replaced by the pick of those available in the liberated parts of Italy, which now extended to Florence and Pisa. Volunteers were plentiful. These were mainly young men who were anti-Fascist, and some lorry-loads arrived carrying Communist banners and singing the 'Red Flag'. But few were true Communists. All they wanted was to liberate their country from the Germans, and they were pro-Russian because they knew Russia was fighting the Germans. Once they were told firmly they were in the king's army the majority became nominal if not enthusiastic monarchists. Most of these young volunteers became high-quality soldiers, and contributed largely to the success of the Italian combat groups.

In training and equipping this new Royalist army with the most modern British weapons, the British encountered the same difficulties as the Germans had with Mussolini's four divisions for his new Republican army. With Roosevelt opposed to the creation of this force, the British had to supply not only all the new equipment and weapons, but also all the instructors. British Liaison Units were appointed to supervise the staff work, and training teams to give individual instruction. The problem was summed up in an 8th Army report: 'We are trying in a matter of weeks to train, convert and raise to British standards Italian formations of an army which has always been weak on officers and discipline.'[12] In November 1944 General Browning, in charge of the training of the Italians, commented: 'The rank-and-file are of first-rate quality. Give me two years with British officers and NCOs ... and we'd have an army as good as any in Europe.'[13] The British repeatedly commented on the low quality of the Italian officers; Napoleon, who used Italian troops in a similar way, also commented that Italian soldiers were only as good as their officers, but that with good officers they were top quality.

The training teams consisted of young officers being rested from infantry battalions which had suffered heavy casualties; they quickly established excellent relations with the Friuli. The liaison units consisted of surplus staff officers, and did not operate so happily.

Colonel Southby of the Rifle Brigade, who had been removed from the command of an infantry battalion during the Battle of Cassino, was strongly anti-Italian – as was his father, Sir Alexander Southby, a well-known extreme right-wing Conservative MP. Fed with information by his son, Sir Alexander put down questions and made derogatory remarks about the Italians in the House of Commons. A typical example was: 'Does the Right Honourable Gentleman [the Foreign Secretary] consider that Italy ought to enjoy the advantages which usually accrue to the wrong-doer who turns King's evidence?'[14] Colonel Southby had found as his interpreter the Principe Eugenio Ruspoli, of an aristocratic Roman family. Ruspoli was bilingual, having been at Eton and married an Englishwoman, the daughter of Henry Labouchère, founder of *Truth*, the famous debunking weekly magazine, which Principessa Ruspoli had inherited in 1910.* He had known – and disliked – the elder Southby at School, and in the Officers' Mess of the British Liaison Unit now read with distaste his remarks in the Commons. Eventually Colonel Southby and his interpreter were no longer on speaking terms; the author had to interpret for Southby at important battle conferences when the Friuli were in the line.

Unfortunately, between September 1943 and the July 1944 decision to make them a combat unit again, the Friuli had been badly plundered of their best men for transport companies, road-building and engineer

---

*Principessa Ruspoli died in Rome in December 1944. In the line Ruspoli, now sole owner of *Truth*, consulted the author about policy for the magazine.

units. Although the Granatieri Battalions were intact, the other infantry battalions were only collections of individuals, not units banded together by years of service. There was a shocking shortage of experienced drivers, the best having been taken off for other work, so road discipline was appalling, and the vehicles suffered from a plethora of minor accidents and bad maintenance. Colonel Southby, having failed as a battalion commander, was determined not to be let down by the Friuli when they went into battle. He delivered complaint after complaint to his superiors about the standard of the drivers and the lack of 'sound basic military knowledge' on the part of the officers. In addition, he described the divisional staff work as 'appalling', and succeeded in getting the elderly but conscientious commander, General Pedrotti,* sacked; fortunately, he was replaced by a veteran of Caporetto and a fine soldier, General Scattini.

Colonel Southby, however, got on little better with General Scattini than he had with General Pedrotti. Senior officers visiting the Friuli did not share Southby's pessimism; the artillery were described as well trained, their anti-tank battery putting up a fine performance at the British School of Artillery at Battipaglia. In a report on their artillery practice, one brigadier compared the Friuli to a pre-war TA division.

Southby sowed seeds of doubt about the Friuli's fitness to go into the line; in reports to General Harding, Alexander's second-in-command, two 8th Army brigadiers in charge of training described Southby as 'rattled', but because of Southby's adverse reports the Cremona (who had also distinguished themselves in Corsica) were put into the line first. The Cremona infantry had not been cannibalized to the same extent as the Friuli, and as a formation were better integrated.

Eventually a large Friuli training exercise was held in Chianti country 'to judge their fitness for war'. The Friuli acquitted themselves well, and on 8 January 1945 General Harding, who had taken a 'special interest', wrote that he had decided the Friuli could go into the line. The next day Colonel Southby, unaware of the General's decision, wrote to 15th Army Group (Field Marshal Alexander's headquarters at Caserta):

> Senior Italian officers are convinced they need no training and encourage their troops in their 'It will be all right in action' attitude. . . . The BLU are exceedingly anxious as to what will happen when this Group, by our standards very much less than half trained, and never having spent more than one night in the open, meets real shell-fire under really adverse weather conditions, and is required to stick it for days and nights on end. I feel that the lack of morale and discipline of the Group should be given even more weight than its lack of training when any decision is being taken as to its employment.

---

*Pedrotti had a good rapport with his men. He gave the author dinner the night before he was sacked; he had no idea of his impending fate, but was full of what he could do for his Division.

But he was too late, and fortunately his pessimism was soon proved unjustified.

General Berardi, the Italian War Office Chief-of-Staff, attended the exercises in Chianti in December 1944. General Scattini told him that the way in which Colonel Southby and his staff 'gave orders' had aroused resentment, and that he wanted the Friuli to go into the line without the liaison unit or the British training team. Berardi passed this on to 8th Army; the request was refused, and the training and liaison officers accompanied the Friuli into the line, just as the German 'minders' did with the Monte Rosa and Italia Divisions on the other side. Much to Berardi's annoyance, and to the dismay of the Italian Divisional Commanders, 8th Army ruled that all orders from Corps to Friuli and Cremona were to be passed through the liaison units, not sent direct to the Italian generals.[15]

On 6 March 1945, after four weeks in a not-so-quiet sector of the line, 8th Army reported to the Italian Government: 'Friuli has carried out the task required of it and yielded no ground, having casualties of two officers and fifteen soldiers killed, and two officers and fifty-four soldiers wounded.' Their morale was described as 'good'.[16]

On 4 February 1945 the Friuli Division had relieved the Polish Kresowa Division in the line between Riolo dei Bagni and Faenza on the River Senio front, with their Divisional Headquarters at Brisighella. Great was the amazement of the British 78th Division as the Italians poured along the road through their gun positions with new bren carriers, lorries, quads and 25-pounders. The 78th Division had the same old quads and 25-pounders which they had fought with in the western desert, and there was considerable jealousy about the former enemy having priority for new equipment. At first Friuli came under General Anders' Polish Corps. Soon came the dire news of Yalta. Great tracts of Poland were to be handed over irrevocably to Communist Russia, regardless of the Treaty of Riga, the heroic sufferings of the Polish Army which under Pilsudski had rolled the Communists back out of central Europe in 1920, and Chamberlain's promise in March 1939. The next day many Polish staff officers refused to speak to the British Liaison Officers, and would only communicate direct with the Italians. It was embarrassing.

For the first fortnight the front was quiet. The second night in the line, the Italian infantry triumphantly sent back two German POWs to Divisional HQ. They turned out to be Polish conscripts to the German army who had deserted, expecting to find the Kresowa Division in front of them. To the Italians' surprise, their German-speaking intelligence officers could not communicate with them – but there was no shortage of Polish interpreters.

Soon the Germans identified the Friuli Division, and the senior officers had to endure a barrage of abuse from the Fascist radio station in Milan and threats of reprisals on any families found in Republican Italy. A particular target was Colonel Achille de Biase, commanding the regimental artillery. He was well known as a devoted supporter of the Savoy monarchy, and an energetic and dedicated artillery commander. But although his wife was in her Milan flat as usual, neither the Fascists nor Gestapo made any move against her.

At Hitler's suggestion, Mussolini agreed to send units of the Republican Fascist Army into the line against the Friuli Division, and we had the horrible spectacle of two Italian armies fighting each other. The author saw one Republican sergeant POW sticking to his guns during interrogation at Friuli Divisional Headquarters and refusing to listen to arguments against Mussolini. He was as convinced a Fascist and German supporter as most of the Friuli Division were anti-Fascist and pro-Ally. However, he informed the Friuli that his battalion, the Barbarigo of Decima Mas Flotilla (600 strong), was only allowed to go into action 'sub-alloted', by companies, to German paratroopers. This showed the Germans had less trust than the Allies in Italian troops.

Irritated by the activity of the Friuli infantry, Kesselring decided to give them a bloody nose, and he put the Hermann Goering SS infantry into the line against them. These were still all Nazis, and fanatical fighting troops with a hatred of the Italians. On 14 March an SS fighting patrol captured Height 92 and took 30 Italian POWs. This was a bitter pill.

The Italian War Office immediately sent to Brisighella a company of parachutists who were being kept in reserve for commando-type operations. By now some of the Divisional Artillery of the British 1st Armoured Division, which could not be reformed after their heavy casualties in the Gothic Line, had been deployed to support the Friuli infantry. So in addition to their own artillery, Friuli had 51 Medium Regiment RA and 1st and 2nd RHA, with self-propelled guns which could occupy positions close to the enemy. They were approaching the strength of a normal British Division. General Scattini decided on the risky but courageous plan of throwing the German Goering detachment out of Height 92 by a daylight attack. At dawn on 18 March every gun of 35 Regiment and the supporting British batteries was concentrated on Height 92. Then at midday, under cover of smoke, Italian parachutists surrounded Height 92. Crucified by the intense fire, many Germans surrendered, and the writer can still remember the thrill of watching from an observation post the Italians disarming the SS and throwing their belts to the ground in the approved fashion. One 25-pounder gun played for two hours on the remaining German position, and X Corps reported that one 'sniping' gun of 35 Regiment fired at the strong point for more than an hour, scoring many direct hits. Finally, at 3 p.m., the last SS surrendered. Immediately the gunfire was transferred to the River Senio, where the Germans had built four little bridges with the obvious intention of trying to overrun nearly all the Friuli forward positions. Soon after, the Goering SS were withdrawn.

On 10 April the Friuli Divison took part in the final Italian offensive, designed to drive the Germans back to the Po.[17]

The Friuli's part in this operation was known as 'Playmate'. It was a 'cover', and X Corps had no plans to drive the Friuli attack through. Unfortunately, although General Scattini was not informed that his attack was a 'cover', the liaison unit was. Italian officers discovered this from papers the British officers left lying on their desks at Divisional Headquarters; it caused considerable offence, since the Italians were being asked to risk quite high casualties. The Friuli attack was designed to prevent the Germans moving reinforcements to counter the genuine drive by the New Zealanders and the Poles, lower down the River Senio.

78th Division had by now been moved to the north, and on their right flank Friuli had the glamorous but inexperienced and newly-recruited Israeli Brigade – young Jews of mixed nationalities, strengthened by a few Jewish British regular officers.

The Germans were deceived. An enormous barrage was laid down by the Friuli artillery and their British supports, and at dawn on 10 April the Friuli infantry advanced. Some strong points were taken, but the Germans replied with a counter-attack in strength, supported by considerable artillery fire despite their well-known shortage of ammunition. Helped again by their abundant guns, the Friuli line held, but casualties were severe. Their attack had served its purpose. The Germans had not withdrawn troops to face the other sector attacks which were intended to be driven through.

The Polish Kresowa and 3rd Carpathian Divisions were astride Route 9 leading to Bologna, on the right of the Israelis, and the New Zealanders were to the right of the Poles. A massive bombing attack on 10 April by USAAF Fortresses on the German positions beyond the Senio was only a partial success. Too many bombs fell on the Polish lines, causing casualties, and the New Zealanders did not escape scot free. Already the Poles' morale was low, following the division of their country at Yalta. Immediately he got the news of Yalta, Anders had told Alexander that he wanted a date fixed for his Poles to be withdrawn permanently from the line. Only by using all his powers of tact and persuasion could Alexander persuade Anders to hold the line: Alexander had no other troops of any description to replace the Polish Divisions.

The Poles secured no bridgehead over the Senio, but advanced using the New Zealanders' bridges. Towards Argenta to the north and on Lake

Commachio all had gone well, and soon 78th Division and the Italian Combat Group Cremona were streaming ahead into the Argenta Gap. To the south-west in the high mountains, 5th US Army was putting pressure on the Germans but making little headway.

Still Kesselring had no reserves, and as he could not check the British advance towards Argenta he had to retire down Route 9. Soon the Poles and New Zealanders were on the line of the Gaiana Canal, and Imola and Castel San Pietro had fallen. Friuli attacked again and again to the south of Route 9, winkling out German strong points and making an important contribution to the general advance.

On 20 April the walls of Bologna were visible to the Italians. Now there was no stopping them, and hard on the heels of the retreating Germans Friuli patrols penetrated Bologna in the early hours of 21 April. Immediately the partisans emerged from hiding and shot the Fascist mayor in the main piazza. The Poles obligingly mended the bridges but showed no inclination to advance fast, and at 7 a.m. Friuli vehicles and infantry alone were in the centre of Bologna.

Then occurred scenes of enthusiasm which must have been reminiscent of the days of the Risorgimento. The people of Bologna were sick of the Germans and ready to give a warm welcome to the British or American army. At first they did not realize that the battle-weary troops in British vehicles and battle-dress were Italians. But as soon as they did the shout went up 'Sono i nostri' (they are ours). Young people hurled themselves on the jeeps, kissing and hugging their liberators.

At 8 a.m. a Fascist Bologna journalist telephoned Mussolini, who was in Milan at the Police Headquarters: 'The Allies have arrived and the people of Bologna are showering them with garlands of flowers.' Mussolini cried out: 'It cannot be true. Bologna is the most Fascist of all Italian cities.' This news from Bologna helped Mussolini to decide his star had set for ever, but of course the journalist had been in such a hurry that he had not discovered the Allied troops were Italian, not British or American.[18]

The War Diary of X Corps states that 'Friuli were beaten by a short head into Bologna by 2 Polcorps, who entered the city at 0600 hours to meet 2 US Corps in the centre of the city a little later ...' This is incorrect; the Poles stopped at the River Savena, east of the city, and the Americans did not arrive until mid afternoon. The Friuli alone occupied the city in the early morning. The author accompanied the leading elements, and found all German resistance had ceased.[19]

During their training period the Cremona Division met personality problems similar to those encountered by both the Friuli, and Mussolini's divisions in Germany. In an 'Order of the Day' issued when they went into the line in January 1945, General Primieri wrote that 'regrettable incidents, recriminations and petulant queries have not been lacking'. There were several interpreters, mainly Maltese, in addition to the British officers of 51 British Liaison Unit and a large training team. In 1967 Colonel Alberto Bongiovanni, who commanded the 2nd Battalion of 22 Regiment within the Cremona, published his memoirs. In them he has described the head of the liaison unit, Lieutenant Colonel Webb Carter, as 'sour and awkward', as were most of his subordinate officers, although a few were 'charming' and 'always ready to accede to any request'. Bongiovanni was also scathing about the Maltese interpreters' lack of love for Italy. His *bête noire* was Major A. D. Woods, MC, an infantry instructor, whom he described as 'unpleasant, rude and difficult at all times'. The Italian army had a strong tradition of good manners, and the behaviour of some of the British officers attached to the Cremona fell well below Italian standards of courtesy. Bongiovanni was particularly irritated by Woods's habit of wearing his cap, not only inside tents but also when there was a ceiling over his head. In retaliation, Bongiovanni kept his Alpini hat with its long feather in his hand, and whenever Woods appeared indoors, immediately put it on. Bongiovanni describes how he became purple with rage one cold morning when Woods, while he and Bongiovanni were talking, gave in to a call of nature but insisted on continuing the conversation at the same time.[20]

Although Webb Carter's favourable report on the state of training of the infantry had decided the 8th Army to send Cremona into the line before Friuli, there had not been sufficient time to train the artillery regiment in the use of British guns and equipment. Accordingly, they went into the line without their artillery and were supported by three British Field Regiments, under Brigadier Starling. The decision to send Cremona into the line gave considerable satisfaction to the Italian Government, anxious to record military successes to help to secure a revision of the Armistice terms.

On 12 January 1945 Cremona relieved the 11th Canadian Brigade under V Corps, north-west of Ravenna in the marshes adjoining Lake Comacchio. They were in trenches and dug-outs reminiscent of the First World War, and very close to the German positions. At first things did not go well; on their second night the Germans took an important strong point which the Italians were unable to recapture, and Italians also came off second-best in encounters between patrols. On 21 January Webb Carter asked the Canadians to take over part of the Cremona sector, as too many outposts were being lost. With the help of British tanks and aeroplanes and through the joint efforts of Cremona and the Canadians, the line was restored. The tanks of the North Irish Horse were put at the disposal of the Cremona, and as reinforcements of enthusiastic volunteers arrived, the performance of the Cremona improved out of all expectation. As Major Woods reported, 'They are showing more aptitude for war' – although one attack by Bongiovanni's battalion failed abjectly because they arrived at the start line 'late'. The Germans used loud-speakers and sent over propaganda leaflets to tempt the Italians to desert, but this was ineffective.

General Zanussi, who had taken part in the armistice negotiations and had become friendly in September 1943 with Harold Macmillan and General Alexander, became second-in-command to Primieri. Confident, thanks to his connections in high places, and very courageous and ener-getic, he was a tower of strength.

Zanussi took over command of a sector of the line manned by the Cremona infantry. Determined to wipe out the bad impression made during Cremona's first weeks in the line, on 2 March he organized an attack with massive British artillery support. The Italians gained their objectives and took 149 POWs. It was, in the words of V Corps, 'a brilliant success', mainly thanks 'to the bravery of Captain Georgi'. War correspondents flocked to the Cremona headquarters and General Keightley, the Corps Commander, congratulated Primieri on his success.

V Corps reported to 8th Army that Zanussi had complete control of the situation, and on 10 April Cremona made a brilliant attack as part of the 8th Army's final main offensive. They quickly took 400 POWs and built bridges across the River Senio so that all their guns could cross. V Corps said Cremona had contributed 'much' to the success of their attack towards Argenta.

A partisan brigade, 28 Garibaldi, had come under Zanussi's control, and they also fought with efficiency and courage. Helped by British tanks, Cremona swept up the Adriatic coast along Route 16. They reached Chioggia and then, when the Germans withdrew, Mestre; with Venice evacuated by the enemy, they had the privilege of hoisting the Italian flag over the *serenissima* city on 30 April.

On 14 May Primieri went on leave and Zanussi assumed temporary command. Contact with the Garibaldi had been bad for discipline generally, and they also carried out summary executions of partisan anti-Communists as they advanced. On 16 May, Crown Prince Umberto came to congratulate the Division and inspected 1st Battalion 21 Regiment. He was barracked, although the artillery regiment behaved well. Furious, Zanussi sacked several officers, and there was a wholesale demobilization of undisciplined elements.

Field Marshal (he had been promoted in August 1944) Alexander expressed 'extreme dissatisfaction' at the bad behaviour of the infantry regiments during Umberto's visit. By 8 June there was a 'sit-in' because of the sackings, and a number of arrests were made. At that time there was a widespread feeling in certain quarters that the regular army was merely a device to keep the Italian monarchy in power.

A proposal was made to incorporate the Garibaldi battalion *en masse* in the Cremona, to make good their numbers; it was found, however, that this would only make the situation worse, and the British had to insist that the Garibaldi hand in all their automatic weapons. Reports were made to V Corps of slackness and lack of discipline. When it was found that Cremona were too undisciplined to be sent to look after prison camps in the Udine area, Zanussi in disgust asked to be relieved.[21]

On 24 September 1944 General Utile, commanding the Italian *Corpo di Liberazione*, issued his final 'Order of the Day', imparting the news that his Corps was to be broken up and reformed into two new Divisions or Combat Groups, the Folgore and the Legnano, which were to be given British weapons and trained in their use. The troops of the CIL, who now had many months of valuable battle experience, would have been more suitable material than either the Friuli or the Cremona from which to form the first two Combat Groups, but they had been in the line since March without rest and had suffered considerable casualties; furthermore, the training of the other two divisions had already begun before the CIL could be withdrawn from the Gothic Line. With their battle-experienced officers and troops, the Folgore and the Legnano created a much better impression on their liaison units and training teams than either the Friuli or the Cremona; fewer difficulties and tensions cropped up in the period of training.

In the first days of April 1945 both the Folgore and the Legnano went into the line, in the mountains overlooking the Lombardy plain. The Folgore was put under XIII Corps, now commanded by General Harding; the Legnano with the US 5th Army under the American II Corps. In the final attack which began on 10 April, both groups acquitted themselves well. General Harding told the author that the Folgore was far above the 'average' for an Italian division. Late on 21 April both groups arrived in the outskirts of Bologna on the south side and linked up with the Friuli.

The Mantua and the Piceno Groups had completed their training and were ready for action in May 1945, but were too late to fight before the Germans surrendered in Italy on 4 May.[22]

The existence of six well-armed Combat Groups was a source of great strength to the Rome Government in the weeks following the end of hostilities. As will be seen, there were disorders everywhere, and it was extremely difficult to impose law and order.

The Friuli were sent into the Trento, north of Verona. Here there was grave trouble with Austrian sections of the population, who wanted independence for the region; they had enlisted many pro-Fascists in their ranks; and in addition, partisans were taking private revenge on their enemies. Around Bolzano the Friuli found there was enmity towards both them and the Allied troops. They found hidden dumps of illegal arms and made numerous arrests. The situation was complicated by the presence of ex-German soldiers in hiding; many German-speaking residents of the area had become Nazi soldiers, and at this time quietly went home in plain clothes. Tito supporters enlisted their help and hid caches of arms. Tito's agents, in collusion with Italian Communists, were trying to bolshevize the area. The separatist movement in the Alto Adige grew strong, and when the Allies returned some of this part of Italy to the rule of the Rome Government on 1 January 1946, the presence of the Friuli Division was invaluable.

The Cremona were sent to Alessandria after the end of fighting. Here there was so much fear of the former partisans that some house-owners begged the Cremona officers to allow soldiers to sleep in their houses rather than in barracks. As the area had previously been policed, first by Brazilian soldiers with the US Army and then by a US 'Negro' battalion, the Cremona were a welcome change. They found many strong anti-monarchists in the area, who tended to regard the Cremona as a symbol of monarchism. From there the Cremona were moved to Lake Como and up into the Domodossola area, where they acted as frontier guards co-operating with the *carabinieri*. Disciplinary problems, which did not occur in the other Italian Combat Groups, still haunted them, and in July there was a short-lived mutiny at Intra. The unit involved was immediately demobilized, and those mainly responsible were imprisoned and charged. However, the Cremona were able to quell a riot in Turin prison after the prisoners had seized control of the gaol.[23]

Churchill's decision to equip Italian Divisions with British war *matériel* was a happy one for Italy. Not only did it help Italy to rehabilitate herself with the free nations as the Combat Groups proved their loyalty and valour in combat, but once peace came the existence of this modern and effective army was a boost to the precarious authority of the Rome Government. The officers of the Combat Groups were regular officers, nearly all monarchist and conservative. Communist ex-partisans would not enrol in a Royal Army, and over the months of training and fighting the NCOs and other ranks had forged strong links with their officers. Within Italy, Communists were trying to cause disorder; powerful separatist movements existed in north-west Italy, the Alto Adige and Sicily, and Tito's propaganda and other activities on the Yugoslav border were another menace. The British were generous in supplying their latest weapons and ammunition. Without these Combat Groups the Rome Government would have been immeasurably weaker when the British and Americans handed back complete power in January 1946, and would have found it extremely difficult to keep order.

The Rome Government continually emphasized to the generals and troops that a good performance against the Germans by the *Corpo di Liberazione* and the Combat Groups in the field would result in more generous terms for Italy in the Peace Treaty following the war; Eisenhower had stipulated this when he and Badoglio met at Malta in October 1943. The Italian navy, which had escaped from the Germans, co-operated loyally with the Allies in the Mediterranean and gave satisfaction. The pilots of the Italian air force who had escaped from German-occupied Italy with their planes also fought courageously, and once trained on Spitfires became even more efficient. The air force was deployed over Greece and Yugoslavia, and great care was taken that no Royalist pilots should be involved in action against Mussolini's Fascist air force.

Unfortunately, Italian hopes of an acceptable Peace Treaty came to nothing. Her efforts on behalf of the Allies were not given the weight which the Italian Government thought they deserved. After Mussolini's fall, Churchill told the House of Commons that Italy's colonies would not be restored (28 July 1943), and after her surrender that her Empire 'had been lost, irretrievably lost' (21 September).

While Badoglio was in power, Churchill had been in favour of helping his Government to retain popular support as far as possible, although when Harold Macmillan, the Resident Minister, suggested in May 1944 that a Peace Treaty should be drafted lest Italy be drawn 'willy nilly into the arms of Russia', Churchill ruled that this must 'await the capture of Rome'.[24]

When the Allies entered Rome on 4 June 1944, the pre-war Democratic parties refused to support Badoglio and appointed a broad coalition government under Bonomi which was strongly anti-monarchist. This made Churchill angry. He wanted the king and Badoglio to govern at least until the end of the war, and was strongly in favour of the monarchy. Churchill's view was that Italy was a conquered country and had no right to form 'whatever Government she pleased'. He told Roosevelt it was disastrous that Badoglio had been replaced by a group of 'aged and hungry politicians', and wrote to Stalin, 'We have lost the only competent man with whom we could deal.' This was far from the view of the Allied representatives dealing personally with Badoglio, one of whom had recorded that 'He only ticks before lunch'. Churchill complained that the dismissal of Badoglio had resulted from the bungling of 'that old woman, Mason-Macfarlane' (Head of the Allied Control Commission). However, Roosevelt told Churchill that 'The Bonomi Cabinet must be recognized without delay.' Churchill dismissed

Mason-Macfarlane, but had to accept – with bad grace – the Bonomi Government.*[25]

With an anti-monarchist Italian Government in office in Rome, Churchill set his face against giving Italy favourable treatment in a Peace Treaty, minuting on 16 June, 'There will be no special favours for the new Italian Government. They have got to work their passage', and later, 'The peace terms should wait until the general peace settlement . . . The present Government has absolutely no representative authority. They hold office only as a result of their own intrigues. They will certainly have none of their colonies back and will have to bear very serious losses in the North Eastern Adriatic.'[26]

It was sad for Italy that Churchill should have taken this turn against her in the summer of 1944 and refused even to consider a 'soft' Peace Treaty to reward her efforts in fighting the Germans; and it was also surprising, in view of his enthusiasm in 1941 for favourable peace terms for an anti-Fascist Government should Mussolini be toppled. After Wavell's army advanced from Egypt into Cyrenaica and captured Tobruk on 21 January 1941, taking over 200,000 Italian POWs, the Foreign Office reported sinking morale, powerful anti-Fascist opposition, and a desire in the Italian people to get out of the war. Churchill leapt at the promising news and decided on four measures to try to encourage these tendencies:

1 raising a free anti-Fascist army from the 200,000 POWs;
2 establishment of Cyrenaica as a free Italian colony, 'to be petted and made prosperous';
3 bribes to Italian naval officers to induce them to bring their ships to Alexandria and surrender them [the archives give indisputable evidence of anti-Fascist admirals negotiating through Stockholm];
4 a search for an Italian de Gaulle to lead the anti-Fascists outside Italy.

These efforts were embarked on in deadly seriousness. They are little known. Neither Churchill nor Eden referred to them in their autobiographies, and the official historians have also ignored them.

Sir Leonard Woolley, the distinguished archaeologist, then serving in Cairo, threw a damper on the Cyrenaica scheme when he reported that it would lose Britain 'all sympathy from Arabs everywhere'. When the Treasury was asked how an anti-Fascist colony in Cyrenaica might be financed, their response was cold. An effort to find a de Gaulle-type figure among the Italians captured by Wavell was unrewarding. General Bergonzoli ('Electric Whiskers') was hailed as a promising candidate, until

---

*Mason-Macfarlane gained his revenge when he stood as a Labour candidate in the 1945 General Election and defeated Brendan Bracken, Churchill's crony.

it was discovered that he was a 'mountebank'. It was only with reluctance in 1941 that Churchill give up his idea of a Free Italian Army, and Cyrenaica as a 'petted and prosperous' Italian colony.[27]

Churchill went to Italy on 11 August 1944. His attitude towards a Peace Treaty with an anti-Fascist government was now diametrically opposed to his 1941 stance. The elimination of Badoglio had the effect on him of a red rag on a bull. His attitude was softened by the enthusiastic reception given to him by the people of Italy, and in an interview Bonomi made a favourable impression. But in October 1944 Anthony Eden, the Foreign Secretary, confirmed in the Commons that the Government's decision that the 'Italian Empire is irretrievably lost will be strictly adhered to'.

At the Yalta Summit Conference in March 1945 between Churchill, Stalin and Roosevelt, an Italian Peace Treaty was touched upon only in general terms. Roosevelt was in favour of generosity, and the American President left a letter with Churchill which spoke of 'the dangers for us both of Italy's present condition of semi-servitude', and suggested that 'some constructive steps should be taken to move away from the present anomalous situation of onerous and obsolete surrender terms, which are no longer pertinent to the situation today'. Roosevelt was prepared to honour the pledge Eisenhower had given Badoglio at Malta, to the effect that the greater the help given the Allies by the Italians, the more generous would be the peace terms.

Unfortunately, Roosevelt died on 12 April 1945; Churchill's only response to his suggestion had been, 'We cannot ignore our public opinion'. The British Foreign Office tried for a harsher treaty than Washington wanted, and on 26 April 1945 circulated a document proposing that Italy should cede temporarily to the Governments of the UK, the USA, France and the USSR the whole of Venezia Giulia, Zara and the Dalmatian Islands, Pantellaria and the Pelagean Islands, the Dodecanese and all Italian possessions in Africa. The only benevolence they showed to Italy was the suggestion that Italy might retain Tripoli, and that the South Tyrol should remain Italian.

By now Britain had appointed an Ambassador in Rome, Sir Noel Charles, and Count Carandini was acknowledged as the Italian representative in London. Charles and Macmillan, supported by Field Marshal Alexander, pleaded for softer treatment, and in particular for Italy to be allowed to retain Tripoli and some form of trusteeship over Eritrea, and also for her to be allowed to retain as much of her fleet as possible.[28]

With the US and Britain at variance over the terms of a Peace Treaty, no progress was made prior to the Potsdam Summit Conference in July 1945. By the Treaty of Rapallo in 1920, Italy had acquired from Austria Trieste and its hinterland and the whole of the Istrian Peninsula; Eden was in favour of Italy retaining the province of Bolzano, but ceding the former Austrian territory in Istria to a four-power commission. This commission would eventually decide upon the frontier between Italy and Yugoslavia, and Trieste would be either given international status, or included in Italy; 'Italy might well be awarded rights of administration over Tripolitania.' This was the British brief, to be discussed at Potsdam with the Americans and Russians. At Potsdam, President Truman wanted Italy to be admitted immediately to the United Nations, and was ready to surrender all the rights claimed by the Allies under the Armistice. This would have meant Italy retaining much of her former Empire. Churchill would not consent, and Stalin was even more strongly opposed, being 'entirely unsympathetic towards Italy and quite disinterested over Italy's fate', according to the British Foreign Office.[29]

Russia insisted that the Peace Treaty with Italy must be delayed until those with Bulgaria, Hungary and Romania were ready. So it was not until 10 February 1947 that the Peace Treaty was signed (Stalin had demanded, to the consternation of the British but in vain, a Soviet share in the trusteeship of Tripoli). The problem of the Yugoslav frontier was dealt with by the creation in theory of the Free Territory of Trieste, under the United Nations, on the 1919 Danzig model. Owing to Tito's intransigence this 'Territory' never came into being, and although the Yugoslavs did withdraw from the town of Trieste, they refused to withdraw from Istria.

Despite American sympathy for Italy, the terms of the Peace Treaty were humiliating. Italy had to renounce 'all right and title' to her territorial possessions in Africa, and was only given one small sop by being awarded a ten-year trusteeship over Somalia, an amalgamation of Italian and British Somaliland. Had Churchill given in to the pressure from Macmillan and Alexander for an immediate Treaty in 1944, Italy would have fared far better. Roosevelt would have been magnanimous, and Stalin was at that time in no position to object, because Italian military help was vital for the Allies.

Italy was allowed to retain Pantellaria and the Pelagean islands and, because a compromise agreement about autonomy had been reached between Italy and Austria over both the Trento and Bolzano provinces, the Sud Tyrol also remained Italian.

As much resented as the loss of their colonies were the Treaty provisions concerning the Italian fleet. Its size was to be limited, and a substantial number of ships surrendered to France, the USSR, Greece and Yugoslavia. In London Carandini told the British Foreign Office that they would 'scuttle' rather than surrender the ships and Admiral Cunningham, still Naval Commander in the Mediterranean, warned that 'any show of or threat of force is likely merely to create a reaction amongst the Italians conducive to scuttling and to depress them so as to abolish all chance of their co-operation'.

It was only with difficulty that the Italian Government was able to persuade the Navy to give up the ships; the reception of the Peace Treaty in Italy was universally hostile. Only those who knew Italy then can appreciate how unpopular the British and Americans became overnight, when the terms were published; Italians felt that their contribution to the joint fight to liberate Italy from the Germans had been ignored and their sacrifice had been in vain.

As a result, few memoirs were written by Italians who fought with the Allied armies after September 1943, and the anti-Fascist admirals who had considered delivering the fleet to the British in 1941 became even more reticent. On the other hand, as has already been noted, accounts of the exploits of the partisans against the Germans were publicized in one book after another, and the impression given both in Italy and abroad was that the achievements of the regular army, navy and air force between September 1943 and the end of the war were trivial in comparison with the partisan efforts. The evidence produced in this book points to the contrary.

Fortunately, less than two years after the signature of the Peace Treaty, Italy was elected a member of NATO. This was as anomalous as her position as a co-belligerent between 19 September 1943 and May 1945. The Peace Treaty humiliatingly recorded Mussolini's act of aggression in June 1940 in its Preamble, and Italy was forced to accede to an undertaking to prevent the resurgence of Fascism. Italian newspapers expressed their whole-hearted disgust with the Preamble, as did the politicians. Fortunately, any moral stigma was removed when in May 1951 ten of the twenty-one signatories to the Treaty recorded that the Preamble had been replaced by the 'spirit of the UN Charter', and that the clauses re Fascism were now superfluous. As that eminent historian of Italy, Christopher Seton Watson, has written, 'Rarely in history can a Peace Treaty have been so short-lived.'[30]

CHAPTER 11

Partisans, SOE and OSS

DURING ITS 45 days of rule in Rome the Badoglio Government forbade any resurgence of activity by political parties who had been in hiding since their suppression by Mussolini in 1922. The five parties spontaneously formed a united front, and demanded that the king should include in the Government politicians from all the parties, and seek an immediate peace with the Allies. Despite the government ban a congress was held at Florence on the day before the armistice, and the day afterwards they met again in Milan; there, they unsuccessfully urged the military commander in the city, General Ruggiero, to include civilians in the fighting against the Germans (recalling the glorious five days of Milan in 1848, when the citizens rose and threw out the Austrians). When the Germans took Milan, the politicians formed themselves into the Committee of Liberation (CLN), which operated clandestinely on an ever-increasing scale until the end of the war; their first acts were to aid escaping Allied POWs and deserters from the Italian army.

The CLN argued that the king, by fleeing from Rome, had *de facto* abdicated; when on 10 October he broadcast from Brindisi in the deep south that his Government had declared war on Germany, they said it sounded 'like a voice from the tomb'.

Sporadic resistance to the Nazis began in German-occupied Italy almost immediately. In the mountain valleys and towns, armed groups were formed from Italian soldiers on the run (who feared deportation as forced labour to Germany) and Allied escaped POWs.

From the start the Badoglio regime feared an armed overthrow of its authority, either during or immediately after the end of fighting in Italy. Churchill and the British Foreign Office shared this view, but the Americans and the British High Command in the Mediterranean ignored it. As was shown in the last chapter, the British and the Badoglio Government killed at birth a plan by Benedetto Croce and General William Donovan of the OSS for the formation of an Italian volunteer corps under General Pavone, independent of the Italian War Office. The Allies were also cold at first towards the guerrilla movement of partisans who put up sporadic resistance to the Germans behind the front line in northern and central Italy, mainly in the mountain valleys.

The partisan movement began in Piedmont when, immediately after the fiasco on 9 September, units of the disbanded 4th Italian Army began to attack German lines of communication. In Rome and the surrounding countryside, Communists and disbanded soldiers formed groups ready to attack the Germans as soon as the Allies advanced on Rome. Royalist officers hiding in Rome after its surrender to the Germans were active, and made contact with the Italian War Office in Brindisi, but they became discouraged by the inability of the Anglo-American troops to make faster progress northwards.

Although the Allied Military Command disliked irregulars and were mistrustful of the early partisans, they became impressed by the success of the partisans in helping British POWs to escape to Switzerland, and by the wealth of intelligence about German troop movements which found its way to the British Secret Service at the Legation in Berne, and to the OSS office there. However, the Allies wanted the partisan activities to be confined to sabotage, facilitating the escape of POWs, and gathering intelligence about the Germans.

The aims of the Italian underground were far more political. In Milan, an organization was set up with the intention of controlling a large irregular army engaged in full-scale warfare against the Germans. They wanted to emulate Mihailović and Tito in Yugoslavia, and capture and hold large areas in mountainous country. Unfortunately, it soon became clear that if they captured territories they would try to set up governments which would challenge the Badoglio Government in the south. The British Foreign Office was already aware of the deleterious effect Tito's like policy was having on the Royal Yugoslav government-in-exile, and were adamant that this should not be repeated in Italy. The Prime Minister felt the same. Some of the most active partisans were Communist bands; within weeks of the armistice, a Communist Garibaldi band was active in the frontier area in north-east Italy, and co-operating with Tito's partisans on the Yugoslav frontier.

A deadly rivalry arose between partisans loyal to the Action Party (*Partito d'Azione*, a coalition of democratic politicians) and to the Communists. By November 1943 the Communists had set up an effective headquarters in Milan, with Luigi Longo in command and Pietro Secchia as Chief Political Commissar. They were both veterans of the Spanish Civil War, having fought on the Republican side. In the autumn of 1943 two non-Communist partisan leaders, Ferruccio Parri (a post-war Prime Minister) and Alfredo Pizzoni, a Milanese banker, arrived in Berne. Parri was a socialist, and Pizzoni's right-wing views made him acceptable to the British.[1]

On 3 November 1943 Parri and Pizzoni held a meeting in Lugano (Switzerland) with John McCaffery, head of the SOE bureau in Berne. McCaffery was amazed by the hostility of the two Italians to the Badoglio Government in the south; they were particularly outraged by Badoglio's action in sending General Basso to Campagna to purge anti-monarchical officers from the small army there, and pointed out that this gave the impression that the regular army was nothing more than a protective guard for the monarchy. The meeting was friendly, and the Italians were promised money and arms. Glowing reports of the partisans came from the numerous British and American POWs guided by them to the Swiss border.

Negotiations between all the underground political parties led to the formation in Milan of the Committee of National Liberation of Northern Italy (CLNAI) in January 1944. But they were too left-wing for the British Government. Their first Order of the Day contained the following:

> There will be no place tomorrow among us for a reactionary regime, however masked, nor for a limp democracy . . . it will be strong and effective democracy . . . the Government workers, small farmers, artisans, all the Trades Unions and other organizations of workers will share power.

A nation-wide CLN was now at work, with liaison between the underground former politicians in German-occupied Italy and the politicians in the south who were outside the Badoglio Government. The CLN was strongly anti-monarchist, and all the king's and Badoglio's hopes of controlling resistance to the Germans soon vanished. In effect, Italy had three governments – the legitimate government under Badoglio; Mussolini's Republic; and the CLN. The alleged socialism of Mussolini's Salò Government held no real attraction for organized labour in Nazi-occupied Italy. During the winter, war production in northern Italy was slowed down by political strikes, on the pretext that black marketeering and inflation were damaging the standard of living of trades unionists, and by sporadic sabotage on the part of the Communists. On 1 March 1944 a general strike broke out in northern Italy. It was initiated by the Communists but supported by all the political parties; it spread rapidly through the large centres of production and damaged production of war *matériel*. It was the only successful general strike in Nazi-occupied Europe during the war.

In Berne, the Italian military attaché General Bianchi co-operated enthusiastically with McCaffery and Allen Dulles (brother of John Foster Dulles), the head of OSS, who had not met Parri and Pizzoni in Lugano. When Dulles heard McCaffery's account of his talks, he agreed there should be co-operation between OSS and SOE in sending arms and liaison officers to the partisans. However, McCaffery had difficulty in fulfilling his own promises. He had reported to the Foreign Office on the quarrels between the Communists and the non-Communists within the CLN and their contrasting political and military objectives. The War Office in London had no taste for irregulars, and the Foreign Office, very conscious of their difficulties with Communist freedom fighters in Greece and Yugoslavia, did not want to incur the same problem in Italy. Parri and Pizzoni had stated frankly that the CLN wanted to hold large areas in inaccessible parts, and to be treated as the official government of German-occupied Italy, independent of the king and his government. This report from McCaffery made the Foreign Office suspicious of the partisan movement, and the files express the lukewarm attitude of the British Government; in consequence, only limited supplies were sent to the partisans in the winter of 1943/4, and only a handful of SOE British liaison officers.[2]

A well-informed article published in one of the Berne newspapers on 20 December 1943 stated:

Today it can be stated that all Italian partisans are under a single powerful and well-organized leadership. Since 1 November all activities have been directed by the National Committee of Liberation. The Committee is recruited from the ranks of the united front of the five anti-Fascist parties, each of which has one representative. The five delegates are responsible to one supreme leader [Parri] who, without belonging to the Army, possesses great military knowledge. Several weeks elapsed before the parties agreed on a leader.

The situation was especially difficult, as the Communists organized the first partisan groups in the beginning, in the mountain regions north of Lecco. This resulted in clashes and it soon appeared as if the partisan groups intended to fight each other rather than the enemy. The CLN succeeded in intervening and after much argument was able to place the Communists under the command of a Supreme Commander.

This article was read with interest by the Foreign Office in London; by over-emphasizing the control exercised by the CLNAI over the Garibaldi Brigades, it helped to give the British confidence in the CLNAI.[3]

Not until 23 December 1943 did the first 'drop' of war *matériel* from an Allied aeroplane take place, six weeks after the McCaffery–Parri talks in Lugano, and then it consisted only of equipment for thirty men. The CLN complained that the SOE and OSS were defaulting on their promises to send arms and supplies to the partisans, and that the Allies only wanted sporadic acts of sabotage, not a widespread resistance. However, an urgent appeal from the CLNAI to Berne for fifty million lire (£250,000) on 27 November had been met.

A much-publicized speech by Churchill in the House of Commons on 22 February 1944, in which he ran down the CLN and praised Badoglio, was a setback for the partisan movement. This speech came only a week before the successful general strike on 1 March 1944, when the Allies refused a further subsidy to make up the strikers' wages. On 21 March Parri wrote to McCaffery that they were claiming official recognition for the CLN from the Allies, and proposed to change from guerrilla activity to 'proper war' (*grossa guerra*). Pizzoni went to Berne to discuss this with McCaffery and Dulles; the Allied representatives were evasive, having no specific instructions from their governments. Meanwhile the Americans made heavy and destructive bombing raids on Treviso, Bologna and Padua, causing heavy civilian casualities and providing Mussolini and the Germans with useful propaganda. The CLN complained bitterly about this in Berne.

Given Churchill's hostile stance, CLN complaints about the Badoglio Government were unproductive in getting more military backing for the partisans from the British. However, everything changed when the Italian Communist leader Palmiro Togliatti returned to southern Italy from Moscow in March 1944. More sensible than the CLN politicians in Milan, Togliatti decided that the plight of his country was such that he ought to sink his ideological differences and join Badoglio's Government until the Germans had been flung out of Italy.

Once Togliatti had joined the Badoglio Government, the CLN decided to accept its authority and Badoglio was also able to bring in politicians from the other political parties. This produced a better climate with the Allies and there was a dramatic increase in Allied air drops to the Italian partisans in the summer of 1944, and more SOE and OSS officers and other ranks joined them.[4]

However, these liaison officers, in communication with the Allied troops by wireless-telegraphy, sent worrying reports of the behaviour of Communist commissars with the Garibaldi units and, as will be seen, of the murder of political opponents by some Communist leaders (see Staff Sergeant Isenberg's report, pages 222–3). There were conflicting views at Allied military headquarters in Italy about the value of the partisans. The following report, written in lucid Staff College style and emanating from Alexander's headquarters (15 Army Group) in May 1944, gave a balanced account of their performance and potential:

Partisan Movement in Italy

There are three Allied armies in Italy. The Fifth and Eighth in front of the enemy need no introduction but the Partisans fighting in the enemy rear have been the subject of so much tainted enemy propaganda and much extravagant and ill-informed scribbling from this side of the line that it is not surprising to discover how little of the truth is known about them by most people . . . they look to General Alexander as C-in-C for orders . . .

The winter of 1943/44 was hard for partisans, and the numbers dwindled for a while. But when the warmer weather coincided with the large-scale call-up of Italians for military service or labour in Germany, masses of evaders sought out the nearest partisan band and joined up. Since then the movement has grown steadily . . .

The Communists are at present without doubt the strongest political influence in the movement, followed by the Action Party, the Socialist and the Christian Democrats, and the Liberals. . . The only thing which all parties have in common is the desire to see the Allies beat the Germans in Italy. They are an astonishing mixture; Italians who may be elderly lawyers, ex-army men, youths in search of adventure; Russians, Poles, Slavs, Alsatians who have deserted from the Germans; American airmen, British, Indian, Canadian, New Zealand and French officers and men who have escaped from Italian prison camps; and in the north-east, tough Slovenes. . . Other bands are good militarily but also obsessed with political aims – Moscatelli, a strong Communist Division SW of Lake Maggiore, is an example. . . Bands exist of every degree, down to gangs of thugs who don a partisan cloak of respectability to conceal the nakedness of their brigandage, and bands who bury their arms in their back gardens and only dig them up and festoon themselves in comic opera uniforms when the first Allied troops arrive. . .

Assistance to the Italian partisans has paid a good dividend. The toll of bridges blown, locomotives derailed, odd Germans eliminated, small groups of transport destroyed or captured, small garrisons liquidated, factories demolished, mounts week by week, and the German nerves are so strained, their unenviable administrative situation taxed so much further, that large bodies of German and Italian Republican troops are constantly tied down in an effort to curtail Partisan activity. Occasionally pitched battles have been fought, with losses to the enemy comparable with those they might suffer in a full-scale Allied attack.

The CLN
A word on the Comitato Liberazione Nazionale. The one at Milan, called the CLNAI, is the 'GHQ' of the Partisan army. Under it Regional CLNs hold sway over various zone commands. Bands operate under the Zone Command. Owing to lack of rapid communications this hierarchy has little military control, but has to be content with broad policy directives. But – it should be noted that not every band acknowledges the supremacy of the CLN; a few remain sturdily independent.

What have the Allies done?
When the Partisan movement emerged as a fighting force, the Allies began to supply them with arms and equipment, principally by air. Begun at the end of 1943, this supply was stepped up throughout the spring and

summer of '44, during which time many hundreds of tons of stores reached the bands.

In addition to the stores, the Allies have sent considerable numbers of Italians and American and British officers and men, all with wireless sets, to the leading Partisan bands. These men organize and train, act as military advisers, pass intelligence and assess stores requirements. Often, indeed, they become leaders in all but name.

All the mountains in the quadrilateral Genoa to the Po to Bologna and down to the front, and the mountains SE of Turin to the sea and SW, west and NW to the French frontier, are firmly in Partisan hands, the Germans only controlling the main roads and railways – and even these are subject to constant sabotage. In all, 100,000 armed Partisans is a conservative estimate, and if arms could be delivered in unlimited quantities that number could be trebled.

If ever anyone is heard saying 'Those Partisans are just an infernal nuisance' or 'What do the Partisans do, anyway, beneath all this swagger?' he might be asked 'Have you thought just what it would be like if we had them to cope with instead of the enemy?' Large areas over which we could never motor except in protected convoy; in which no small body of men would dare to camp alone; a constant unnerving trickle of men who just disappear from the unit; all roads liable to be mined; bridges blown; supply and troop trains derailed from coast to coast; the necessity of strong guards on every installation; the exhausting business of combing hills far in the rear for an enemy whose earth is never stopped and of whom nothing may be seen or heard but a sniper's bullet now and then.[5]

This reveals that enthusiasm for the partisans at Alexander's Headquarters was much stronger than in the Foreign Office.

Support for the partisans was also stimulated by a further report (12 June 1944) by two senior British officers, Brigadier J. B. Coombe and Brigadier E. Todhunter, who had crossed the line by sea after escaping at the time of the armistice from 12 POW Camp, close to Seghatina in the Apennines. After months in northern Italy in contact with the partisans, they reported that their activities 'could be exploited with excellent results', but that the bands must be under direct Allied control, and that 'any suggestion that they should work under the control of the Badoglio Government or the King will produce no results at all'. They asked for British officers to be sent to the partisans, preferably of the rank of Major or Lieutenant-Colonel, with Italian instructors, and wireless sets, arms and explosives. They pointed out that in their experience, communications with Caserta had involved sending a messenger to Milan by train, thence on foot across the frontier to Switzerland and thence by wireless to London and from London to Caserta, which meant it took a month to get an answer.

The partisan unit who gave hospitality to the brigadiers was 8 Garibaldi

Brigade, located near Faenza. Corps Commanders General Neame, General O'Connor and Air Marshal Boyle had also been helped by this brigade after their escape from a POW camp. They had given 8th Army glowing reports of this unit and especially of its commander, Libero (a *nom de plume*), resulting in 8 Garibaldi receiving priority in air drops. The brigadiers stated that Libero had turned out to be a 'bad hat', was sacked by the CLN and then disappeared with two million lire of CLN money. However, 8 Garibaldi continued to operate under 'Mauro' and 'Pietro', and were liberated when Faenza fell in the autumn of 1944. After that, they did good work from the British lines.[6]

Kim Isolani was a British diplomat in charge of the Vice-Consulate at Bologna in 1946. He has informed the author that he knew Libero well after the war; with his Communist and partisan contacts, he was helpful in reporting on political developments during an unstable period in which there were regular political killings, and certain Communist partisans were still hiding in the hills for fear of prosecution. Libero's real name was Gollinelli, and he was a prosperous cattle dealer. Isolani states that Libero certainly did not 'disappear', and he does not think him dishonest; he disbelieves these allegations, and thinks the brigadiers may have been gullible enough to be taken in by anti-Communist smears.[7]

Coombe and Todhunter pointed out that Signor Nanni, head of the Committee of Partisans at Santa Sofia with whom they had been communicating, would have no dealings with the Badoglio Government. They wrote:

> It very soon appeared that there was more enthusiasm in words than in deeds, and finally when the Badoglio Government declared war on Germany, Nanni stated that he was no longer prepared to undertake any rebel activity. His reason was that he and his supporters were all Republicans and were not prepared to take any action which would tend to show that they were ready to support the King or Badoglio in any circumstances. This is typical of the attitude of mind of a large proportion of the Italian upper-class, who are quite prepared to lose sight of the main issue of defeating the Germans in order to obtain some small political advantage in the post-war struggle.

They also recorded that, from their experience of the German and Fascist efforts to suppress the partisans in the Romagna up until the spring of 1944, 'no Fascist unit without German support will ever be persuaded to make a serious attack upon the partisan forces in Italy, and that if the Germans want to take any action they will have to do it themselves.' There is an element of truth in this: the eagerness of Mussolini's troops to fight the partisans has been overemphasized by some Italian historians since the war.

Major Jim Davis, who fought with the partisans in the Parma area, reported: 'No garrisoning is done by Brigata Nera [the Black Brigades] because the Fascists are so frightened of the partisans that they cannot be trusted to hold out against them alone.'[8]

With the Government and Foreign Office in London hostile to the anti-monarchist parties who were known to be dominant in the partisan movement, McCaffery found it more difficult than Dulles to honour his promises to Parri. The British policy was only to give real help to the Resistance if they were sure British Liaison Officers were on the ground, and the Communists were not in control. The Americans were more open-handed. Massive requests not only for arms but also for money came to McCaffery in Berne, and in London Count Enrico Marone (head of Cinzano) raised 100 million lire (around £1 million). This, together with considerable sums from the Foreign Office, was sent to carefully vetted partisan units.[9]

It was unfortunate that the OSS recruited Italian speakers from the Mafia in the US, and from such organizations as Murder Inc. and the Philadelphia murder gang. An OSS major, William V. Holohan – not an Italian-speaker – was parachuted down near Lake Orta to act as a link between OSS in Berne and the CLN in Milan, carrying with him large sums of money in gold and notes. His OSS companions, Italian-speaking fellow-Americans, poisoned him; his body was dropped in Lake Orta with the help of so-called partisans, probably local Mafia. After the war, Major Holohan's brother insisted on an enquiry into his death; his body was recovered, and traces of poison were found. An OSS lieutenant and his sergeant were found guilty of the murder but, as so often with the Mafia, were never traced. This is the only recorded case of Italian involvement in the murder of an Allied liaison officer for his money; which says much for the Italian people, since all officers carried comparatively large sums and heads of mission many thousands of pounds in lire.[10]*

The hostility to the Badoglio Government of Communists and left-wingers within the CLN weakened even more when at the end of April 1944 Russia agreed with Badoglio for the exchange of diplomatic representatives. Eden was angry and ordered Sir Noel Charles to complain to Badoglio that in accepting a Russian diplomat he had presented the Allies with a *fait accompli*. Charles told Badoglio his move had aroused a suspicion that he was 'playing one Government off against another'. Churchill was displeased with Eden's action and minuted to Eden on reading Charles's telegram:

---

*However, Italian citizens affiliated to Tito's partisans murdered OSS in the Friuli, see pp. 253–4.

Was it not natural when so many were trying to boot out Badoglio and many more were all ready to let him go, that he should have 'clutched a helping hand?' One may be vexed at the Russians for their lack of etiquette, as I often am in many connections; but to beat up Badoglio for grasping at the only chance which would have enabled him to remain in his most difficult position, much to our advantage, is I think rather hard.

Another Foreign Office comment was that the king and Badoglio would 'have a new lease of life', since the exchange of representatives coincided with the arrival of Togliatti and the inclusion within the Government of representatives of all six political parties.[11]

Co-operation between the Royalist army and the partisans became closer and more efficient although the gulf between the Communist Garibaldi and the non-political Green Flames units was as wide as ever. Regular Italian officers trained in parachuting by the OSS and SOE were dropped to non-Communist partisan units with wireless sets, clothing and arms. They were well received.

On 27 April, at its first meeting, Badoglio's new all-party Cabinet announced that it was seeking not only a strengthened armed force, but also the contribution of all possible help to the Italian patriots fighting against the Germans. This gave the partisan movement an official boost and was in great contrast to the original Badoglio-orientated hostility to the creation of any armed movement independent of the Royalist Army. In a widely reported press statement, Kesselring had said on 9 April, 'Bands are melting away like the snow'. This contradicted reports in the neutral Swiss press that Mussolini's call-up to the Fascist army plus the deportation of workers and technicians to Germany had produced a large increase in the ranks of the partisans. Other Swiss papers reported clashes in German-occupied Italy between considerable numbers of armed partisans and German and Fascist forces, especially in the mountains around Lake Como near the Swiss frontier, near Biella, and in the Waldensian valleys of Piedmont.[12]

In May 1944 British and American help to the partisans was greatly increased. Encouraged by the arrival of more SOE and OSS officers and NCOs, who exhorted the partisans to carry out acts of sabotage, considerable damage was being done to the German lines of communication. After the war Kesselring stated that in June 1944 the partisans had become a serious menace. A strong partisan unit under a British officer, Captain Macintosh, gave well-organized and substantial help to the British in the capture of Florence in July.

Unknown to the Germans, they laid a telephone cable across the Ponte Vecchio (which Kesselring spared) so that the partisans could observe British artillery fire and report German movements. Even before Florence and Rome were taken, Alexander had issued his first official statement acknowledging the achievements of the partisans. He said that in May six of the twenty-five German divisions in Italy had to be diverted to northern parts to fight Italian patriots or Yugoslav partisans on the borders of Venezia Giulia.[13]

Many of the partisans who had helped in the fall of Florence wanted to continue to fight on the Allied side. To their disappointment they could find no role. When the Allied forces liberated areas they disarmed the partisans and tried to send them home or put them into civilian jobs. In July 1944 the new Bonomi Cabinet, unhappy at the treatment of partisans who had been overrun by the Allied advance, asked the Allies to incorporate partisan units in the Italian Army. The request was turned down because the Italian generals in close touch with the British and American High Command advised that they did not want to risk the Royal Army being subverted by left-wing elements into becoming a political and anti-monarchical force. The CLN also urged their incorporation, but the Allies ruled firmly that partisans could only apply to enrol in the Italian Army as 'individuals', not as 'units'. (F Recce and Maiella were, as has been seen, exceptions.) Voluntary enlistment was a failure. Most partisans, being Republicans, did not want to swear an oath of allegiance to the king, and disliked the idea of serving under regular career officers who, they felt, were tainted by Fascism. By 31 October 1944 only 807 ex-partisans had been enrolled in the Italian Army.[14]

On 19 June 1944 a military Headquarters was set up in Milan by the CLN and their fighters were titled the Corps of Volunteers for Liberty. Alexander called on the Resistance to extend their operations, and told the CLN that they would help the non-political partisan units (Green Flames) but not the Garibaldi brigades. Within the CVL, however, the Communists frequently stole supplies from drops intended for the Green Flames.

The Allies decided to send a senior Italian general whom they could trust to the CLNAI in Milan. They chose the conservative and strongly anti-Fascist Raffaele Cadorna who, as has been seen, had distinguished himself during the defence of Rome in September the previous year. Despite being in his mid-fifties he trained as a parachutist and dropped into the Val Cavallina (sustaining only minor injuries) with a young Italian-speaking British officer, Major Churchill, and a W/T operator.

Cadorna's remit was vague. Before leaving for north Italy, he and Major Churchill were interviewed by General Harding at Caserta, but no firm orders were given, either by the Allies, or by the Rome Government, who had been informed of his mission but had not bothered to try to get in touch with him. As a result, Cadorna 'was left with an open mind as to the scope of his work and the difficulties which he would meet'. He interpreted his brief as being to confirm to the CLNAI that the Allies would give the widest possible help for military action by the partisans, while stressing that it would be suspended if operations were hampered by political differences. Major Churchill, who stayed with Cadorna until 2 December, soon incensed the Resistance leaders by insisting that Cadorna should be in sole military charge, bypassing the CLN. The CLN sent a message to the Government in Rome stressing that they would not agree. Alexander was not able to see Cadorna at Caserta, but he sent him a warm letter of good wishes (which Cadorna proudly published in his memoirs). This letter gave no instructions whatsoever.

In Milan, Cadorna was at once welcomed by all the CLNAI as the military adviser they wanted. Major Churchill's view was that 'the arrival of Cadorna contributed little', because all operations were controlled by either the Communists or the Action Party, although many units would not take orders from anyone.

Major Churchill reported that not only were clashes between Communists and the other partisans rife, but there was discord between the American OSS and the British SOE. Cadorna found that one American officer parachuted in immediately accused the British officer in charge of the formation to which they were both attached of 'supporting Conservative and reactionary elements while the Americans intended to support the left wing'.

The effective heads of CLNAI were Parri of the *Partito d'Azione* and Luigi Longo of the Communists; they made the decisions and passed them on to the representatives of the other three parties only 'if and when they were able to meet'.

At their first meeting with the CLNAI, Major Churchill insisted that General Cadorna must be nominated as Military Commander by both the Allies and the Rome Government; Cadorna did not want to force the issue. In September the Liberals proposed Cadorna as Commander, but this was categorically rejected by Longo, on behalf of the Communists, as being 'unnecessary', and soon after this meeting the CLNAI was forced to go to ground.

When another meeting became possible in October, Longo demanded equal powers with Cadorna and the right to counter-sign all documents. Parri was not prepared to play second fiddle, and suggested that himself, Cadorna and Longo should all three have equal powers. The other three parties objected. Finally, after London sent a representative to talk to CLNAI spokesmen and McCaffery in Switzerland in November 1944, the CLNAI offered Cadorna the post of Commander with a general staff 'consisting of an amazing family of twin seconds-in-command and vice-chiefs'.

Cadorna told the CLNAI he would accept the post if senior Italian officers with clean political records were given positions in the regional partisan commands analagous to his own, and if the supply sorties were co-ordinated through him and not through the highest American or British officers within individual formations.[15]

Major Churchill reported to General Harding that he was most impressed by the units (already referred to) in the Biella area known as the Green Flames, under Eduardo Sogno, who was looked on by the Communists as 'an Allied tool and a reactionary'. He was right-wing and a daredevil partisan. He became a close friend of McCaffery, making several trips to Berne; he spoke almost perfect English and the Communists claimed he was a British agent. His soldiers were mostly young Alpini, strongly anti-Fascist; their operations were hampered by feuds with Communist Garibaldi units, who were also considered effective fighters against the Germans by Major Churchill. He did, however, criticize the Garibaldi strongly for seizing arms from the Green Flames. Major Churchill thought the population of north Italy was strongly pro-Ally, but said that popularity was being eroded fast by senseless RAF and USAAF raids on town centres and civilian factories, described by the Fascists, 'not without truth', as 'terror raids'; suburban tram passengers and solitary motorists had been killed. The most effective Fascist poster was circulated after an RAF raid which killed 250 children, and consisted of the photograph of four dead children with the slogan 'Long Live our Liberators'.[16]

In July 1944 the CLNAI and the CVL in Milan made a plan to seize a large area around Domodossola between Lake Maggiore and the Swiss frontier, expelling the Germans and Fascists and declaring it a Free Republic unconnected with the legitimate Italian Government in Rome. The intended Free Republic contained 82,000 inhabitants, covered 1,600 square kilometres, and had the frontier railway town of Domodossola as its main centre. They also had plans to free all the Valle d'Aosta and Val Comonica. The intended free zone consisted of a triangle with the base a line between Cannobio on Lake Maggiore and Domodossola at the head of the Simplon Pass, with the northern tip at the roadless Nufenen Pass leading into the Swiss Ticino.

The Resistance had been much encouraged by what had happened in August at Omegna, a substantial town on the north shore of Lake Orta on the road from Arona to Gravellona, 36 kilometres south of Domodossola. Because of the partisan strength and their success in skirmishes in July, the Germans had agreed to a neutral zone around Omegna and Crusinallo and halfway down Lake Orta; both sides agreed that neither armed partisans nor Fascist troops nor German troops would enter the town. The Germans guaranteed that there would be no reprisals against the partisans or their families and that the citizens of Omegna would be allowed to conduct their business unhampered, while the large public hospital of Omegna would look after wounded or sick from both sides. Order would be kept by the *carabinieri*, who would be allowed to carry arms and would wear a white armband inscribed 'Città di Omegna Zona Neutra' with the crest of the town. When Mussolini heard of this truce, he was angry.

The Italian state railway reported to Mussolini's Minister of Transport at Salò that on 26 August the partisans had cut the railway line from Domodossola to Ascona in Switzerland and from Domodossola to Novara, and that the partisans were now operating parts of the railway line, using state employees and rolling stock. Mussolini knew he was about to lose, at least temporarily, another piece of his decayed empire.[17]

As early as November 1943, partisan groups had liberated certain parts of the area near Domodossola, but after three days of fighting the Germans eliminated the partisans, inflicting many casualties. There was fighting at Megolo on 13 February 1944, when 500 Communist partisans under Filippo Beltrami were routed by the Germans. The partisans re-formed and sabotaged the railway and the power lines, causing shut-downs in important factories in Milan and Novara. Encouraged by this success, the partisans gradually achieved control of an area between Domodossola and Ascona. At the end of May the Germans used 16,000 troops in a massive offensive (*rastrellamento*), taking reprisals against civilians and killing 200 partisans, including 43 prisoners who were brutally shot.

By August 1944 the non-Communist partisan division Piave was in the Valle Cannobina and the Beltrami on Val d'Ossola, while the Valtoce partisans were between Gravellona and Ornavasso, and two Garibaldi divisions were in the Valsesia. With substantial drops of arms parachuted in by the Allies, partisan confidence was at a high level.

The idea of a Free Domodossola Republic was ill-received by the British and Americans. John McCaffery and Major John Birkbeck of SOE in Berne were given instructions to do their utmost to 'scotch' the plans. Their standing instructions from London were to use the partisans for sabotage and guerrilla attacks on the Germans and to discourage all political activity. In addition, on military grounds, they knew the proclamation of a Republic would provoke a German attack in strength. However, in McCaffery's words, the partisans had been 'bitten by the bug' of proclaiming an independent area. Both McCaffery and Allen Dulles warned that such a political action would have a 'negative reaction' upon the whole Italian resistance. Eventually McCaffery and Dulles realized there was no way of stopping the movement; half-heartedly they promised funds and supplies, and sent a liaison officer, Lieutenant George Patterson, a Canadian who had been fighting with the partisans for almost a year. McCaffery recorded that eventually he agreed to support the plan, but only in order 'not to undermine the morale of the Partisans'. The Foreign Office in London registered disapproval.[18]

Initial strikes against the Germans took place on 23 August when Baceno in Valle Antigore fell to the partisans after three days' fighting, and by 1 September all the territory north of Domodossola was under partisan control; Val d'Ossola and Valtoce soon fell as well. The town of Domodossola was surrounded by 3,000 partisans, and the German troops within were outnumbered.

Sensing a crushing defeat, the Germans sued for an armistice using a priest, Dom Luigi Pellanda, as an emissary. An armistice was signed on 9 September and the Germans and Fascists pulled their forces out of the area. On 10 September Domodossola town centre was thronged by an enthusiastic crowd, and a manifesto was read out proclaiming the Free Republic of Domodossola. A provisional Council was created to run the area, and all Fascist mayors and officials were removed from their posts. While the establishment of this 'Free Republic' was an insult to the monarchy and the Government in Rome, it was also a sharp set-back to Mussolini's Republican Government.

Professor Tibaldi, who was a close friend of McCaffery, was borne on a special train from Berne to Domodossola to assume the Presidency, and Gigino Battisti was put in charge of food and supplies. He succeeded in overcoming initial supply difficulties.

The Italian military attaché in Berne, General Bianchi, who had remained loyal to the Badoglio Government, managed to send down a number of volunteer regular officers (*Ufficiali di carriera*) who at the time of the armistice had crossed the Swiss frontier and been put in internment.

General Cadorna and Colonel Palumbo arrived, and tried to get the Communist and non-Communist commanders to co-ordinate plans for defence. They had little success, and military organization was chaotic. Cadorna declared that a unified command was vital and offered to take command himself. The Communists would not agree.[19]

Food ran short; McCaffery and Dulles provided funds to buy food from Switzerland, but food-rationing at a low level had to be introduced, although the position improved when a team from the Swiss–Italian Red Cross arrived.

Money was a problem, but the provisional Council made an agreement with the Banca Popolare of Novara to issue coupons in place of money; these coupons were to be redeemed eventually by the State, and after the Liberation of Italy in 1945 the bank was refunded. Postage stamps were overprinted 'CLN – Ossola Libera – 10.9.44'.

Two hundred schools were reopened for the autumn term, and the Fascist curriculum was replaced by a more enlightened one. News-sheets were produced by most of the political parties, and there were plans to open a radio station with a high-powered transmitter which would counter the propaganda from Mussolini's Salò Radio.

With an open frontier and two railway lines to Switzerland, the Domodossola Republic regime was well placed geographically. Domodossola is the Italian frontier town on the main Geneva–Milan line through the Simplon tunnel; it is also the junction for a branch line running through Italy to Locarno, passing the Swiss frontier at Ascona. The Swiss Government obligingly recognized the Republic, and much help came from the Swiss Red Cross. SOE and OSS were in direct contact through Ascona on the Swiss frontier; several Allied officers went in to help the partisans, and supplies were also parachuted in to them.

Inside the Republic, the Communist Garibaldi brigades almost refused co-operation with the other partisan bands. The Foreign Office disliked the situation, and sent instructions to McCaffery to take a firm line with the CLN over their declared independence from the Rome Government. On 27 September McCaffery wrote to Parri a sharp letter revealing the British attitude to the CLN effort in Domodossola:

> You must not pretend to be in charge of military operations, like Alexander and Eisenhower . . . Some time ago I said the greatest contribution you could make was continuous, widespread sabotage. I have only supported you at Domodossola because I recognize the moral value of it for Italy. The partisans have fought well but they want to be one of the Allied armies. Who has asked you to do so? Not us.[20]

Enrico Vezzalini, the Fascist prefect of the province of Novara, sent Mussolini this account of the partisans' triumph, saying they had used the 'free' city of Omegna as a springboard:

> Domodossola was occupied by bandits yesterday morning, 10 September.
>
> On Friday rebels strong in numbers and arms began to attack the few strong points in Val d'Ossola and Val Vigenzo.
>
> Blackshirts and frontier guards fought until Saturday morning and in the evening their survivors withdrew to Domodossola. The city, although surrounded and isolated, contained enough troops in my view to hold out at least for several days.
>
> The German commander instead decided to make a pact with the bandits, and his men were allowed to keep their arms if they left. It seems he came to this decision because he was frightened of the vast numbers of the attackers, but they amounted to only 3,000 men with some field guns.
>
> As I have repeatedly signalled, the bandits had been reinforced towards the

end of August by a first contingent from Switzerland of around 400 with many machine-guns and 20 mm field guns. This contingent had occupied Cannobio–Cannero–Oggébio [on the west bank of Lake Maggiore close to the Swiss frontier] and made secure the route for the entry of another 600 from beyond the frontier.

From Switzerland fresh units (around 1,000, according to unconfirmed reports) seized the block-houses and customs bay of Cannobio, Malesco and Sta Maria Maggiore and headed for Domodossola. At the same time bands operating north of Lake Orta took possession of the whole of Val d'Ossola. The Communist band commanded by Franz from the Val di Vedro completed the siege.

The worst feature was the intervention of the parish priests of Domodossola and Masera who, pretending to want to avoid bloodshed, persuaded our men not to fight, apart from the frontier guards who fought like lions and only retreated when they heard the others had gone.

Negotiations were carried on by the German town commandant and two Italian officers of the GNR. In Domodossola not one shot was fired.

Another message from Vezzalini informed Mussolini that Gravellona Toce had fallen late on the 14th, but that German and Fascist troops still occupied positions on the high ground dominating the entry into the Val d'Ossola.

Mussolini preserved in his papers an article published in the Swiss paper *Corriere del Ticino* on 13 September; they had interviewed a staff officer of the partisans:

On Sunday morning the situation in Domodossola was very tense. The local garrison consisted of 500 Germans and Fascists, mostly SS. This force was completely surrounded by the patriots, and it seemed certain that the city would become a battle-field. To avoid this danger the church authorities in Domodossola assumed the role of mediators. At twelve noon on Sunday agreement was reached in consequence of which the German troops were allowed to leave the city and go south to rejoin the rest of their troops. On the same day as the Germans left the partisans entered. Then the agreement was nearly broken because a bomb left by the Germans exploded, causing damage and wounding several people.

The partisans occupy the railway line Domodossola–Milan as far as Pallanza, Fondo, Toce, and the whole line of the Centovalle on which trains run regularly [to Locarno]. Between Brigue, Switzerland and Domodossola, the Simplon tunnel, there are two trains daily but reserved for the railway workers; one train runs each day between Domodossola and Paguzzo. There is no fighting on the front line. The partisans expect soon to attack towards Stresa and Novara, and also to link up with other partisan units on the French/Italian frontier in Piedmont.

Domodossola is calm and the people have received their liberation enthusiastically. The food situation is rather critical. The general impression is that the partisans dominate the military situation and that it will be difficult for the Wehrmacht to launch a counter-attack.

Vezzalini reported to Mussolini that the two Garibaldi divisions under Moscatelli who had occupied Domodossola were mostly Communists, although interspersed with more moderate 'idealists'; Superti's band was monarchist, and Didio's 'clerical', while all Massara's came from Switzerland (and were thus presumably monarchists, having been assembled by Royalist officers). According to Vezzalini, 'the Communist Moscatelli' dominated the situation and banks and industrial companies helped with money from fear of the consequences if they refused; he also alleged that the Church was giving a large subsidy (300,000 lire per month) to the partisans, and that the priests' insidious anti-Fascist propaganda had been responsible for lowering the morale of the Fascist troops. Less plausible was his remark that the priests' actions were in the hope of regaining 'temporal power'; this was the type of comment Mussolini enjoyed. Vezzalini also complained bitterly about the Swiss, who had sent a Government representative and much food to the Free area.

At this stage Mussolini was deeply concerned about the strength of the partisans. In September he wrote to Rahn, after reading all the accounts of partisan activity:

1   The 'bands' have become 'brigades' and 'divisions', properly organized and led by generals who are regular army officers supported by well-trained staff officers.
2   They have excellent arms; each unit has all they need.
3   In many places local German commanders have made pacts for a *modus vivendi* with the partisans which are real and binding agreements ... these have increased the strength and prestige of the partisans.
4   The partisan organization in Italy has a total of 100,000 men split up into sixty brigades; this constitutes an ever-increasing danger against which we are not acting with the necessary efficiency for many reasons – the chief being the split of the headquarters and responsibility for dealing with them between Italians and Germans.

I beg of you, dear Ambassador, to give ten minutes of your precious time to consider this.[21]

Rahn, as usual, ignored this *démarche* from Mussolini.

Under SS General Tensfeld, a combined force of Germans and Blackshirts was assembled to attack Domodossola. On 13 October the attack was launched. The partisans fought courageously but were at a grave disadvantage, resulting from the disorganization implicit in having no unified command headquarters. By 15 October the partisans were forced to scatter after suffering heavy casualties. A considerable number succeeded in reforming in an area near Lake Orta which remained in partisan hands, while the bulk escaped by train over the Swiss border at Ascona. Cadorna reported that the defeat was due to 'lack of proper discipline and proper command'.

This view is confirmed by Vezzalini's report to Mussolini, which stated (probably correctly) that the attacking forces of Germans and Blackshirts under SS General Tensfeld amounted to only 3,000, whereas the partisans had 6,000, and that the advance was handicapped both by lack of surprise and by adverse weather conditions, which made attacks on strong points in the mountains difficult.[22]

Three special trains took hundreds of partisans and civilians from Domodossola to Ascona in Switzerland, fleeing from the advancing Germans and Fascists. Many from the hills were in a 'bad state', as they had been unprepared for flight, although the Swiss papers noted also that some of the 'better class' from Domodossola itself were elegantly dressed, while the partisan soldiers in their berets and battle jackets were still 'cocky and even insolent'. They declared that they would have gone on fighting if they had not run out of ammunition. The Swiss Government sent all refugees to Basle, where they were sorted out and 'disinfected' in a large empty show-ground pavilion before being sent to camps in central Switzerland. Vezzalini reported that although three-quarters of the population had fled to Switzerland by train, most of them were returning as it became known that he was carrying out no reprisals. He admitted that German and Fascist soldiers had at first done much looting of empty houses, but claimed that this had ended after the arrest and punishment of both Fascists and Germans. He declared that residents who failed to return home by 31 October would be denominated 'political absentees', their possessions sequestrated and their houses let to political refugees, or to the families of wounded or dead soldiers. Mussolini was much annoyed by his report that the Germans had confiscated all the money left in the banks by Professor/President Tibaldi's Giunta or Council, and seized two ingots of gold; they had also requisitioned all the motor vehicles in the area, making food distribution almost impossible. With pride, Vezzalini informed the Duce that by 26 October all the frontier posts on the Swiss border were again in Fascist hands.[23]

The CLN complained bitterly that the Allies had not given all-out help to the Domodossola Republic; McCaffery claimed that they did all they could. At that time the RAF and USAAF were occupied in flying supplies from Italy to the Polish patriots besieged in Warsaw, and the airborne operation at Arnhem tied up large numbers of aircraft which might otherwise have been used to bring help to Domodossola.

Only if an Allied airborne brigade had been sent to Domodossola could the Republicans have held out, and to send an airborne force would have been impractical because of the difficulty of supplying them at such a distance from the Allied lines. With the Germans solid on the Gothic Line, the only supply route was over the Little St Bernard Pass from Chambéry in France, through terrain ideally suited for defence. The partisans were much disappointed at not being able to establish a link with other partisan units in the Valle d'Aosta on the French frontier but, as Cadorna pointed out, the French were in no mood to co-operate with Italian partisans, and those crossing the frontier in the Mont Blanc region were usually arrested and sent to concentration camps. The memory of the Italian 'stab in the back' of 1940 was too recent for the French.[24]

The establishment of the Republic of Domodossola was spectacular and courageous. It lasted for 34 days, and it was the only substantial part of Hitler's occupied Europe to achieve independence, and obtain recognition from Switzerland. Dissension between the Communists and the other parties revealed the inherent weaknesses of the CLN; not only did it contribute to their military defeat, but it gave an extremely bad impression to the Allies. McCaffery was an Irishman who had spent several years in a Rome seminary and then taught in an Italian university; he was a shrewd observer who understood everything about the Italian political divides, and his reports to the Foreign Office about Domodossola increased the British Government's fear that all-out aid to the partisans might lead to chaos and civil war when the Germans abandoned Italy.

A prototype of the Domodossola Republic had already been tried in the Montefiorino region in June 1944. In November 1943 partisan bands had initially occupied an area near Sassuolo; reinforced by other bands, they set up a *Commando Unico* in March 1944, overcame the German garrison at Cerradolo and occupied Fasano. By June, helped by British and American liaison officers and supplies dropped by air, they held an area with 50,000 inhabitants in the provinces of Modena and Emilia, south of Parma and east of La Spezia and not far behind the front line when the Allies occupied Florence. From here the Resistance had the potential to make damaging raids and interrupt the important road to the German front line around Massa, Pontromoli and Aula. A Republic was proclaimed on 18 June 1944 and a Democratic Council elected by the communities governed in conjunction with the partisan command.

The Allies considered that Montefiorino was close enough to the front line to merit direct support with troops. Accordingly, when the main offensive against the Gothic Line was in preparation in July, a plan was made to drop one battalion of parachutists from the Nembo Division (which had fought so well with General Utile's *Corpo di Liberazione* on the Adriatic earlier in the summer) to join the partisans of the *Commando Unico*. An advance party of two British liaison officers with W/T operators was dropped in the second half of July. The main party, including more British and Americans, was ready to go when the Germans unexpectedly embarked on a strong *rastrellamento* on 29 July; the partisan units melted away six weeks after the proclamation of the Republic, and the airborne operation had to be cancelled at the last moment.

The plan had been to drop the Nembo battalion near La Spezia in the Val di Taro at full moon, after emplaning from Brindisi in 42 aircraft at dusk on 11 August. That morning W/T messages from the chief British Liaison Officer, Major Johnston, reported that only 5,000 lightly armed partisans were under heavy attack by 12,000 Germans. The Allies had hoped to prevent the Germans withdrawing on the roads running north from Pistoia and Lucca if their main attack was successful. In the event the Allied attack on the Gothic line ground to a halt.[25]

The partisans in the Montefiorino area were commanded by Communists with the code names of Davide and Armando. Armando was Mario Ricci, who after the war became a well-known Communist senator. Davide was Oswaldo Poppi. Both had fought on the Communist side during the Spanish Civil War. The OSS liaison officer, Staff Sergeant Isenberg, was scathing about Armando:

The Modena Division under the command of Armando is thoroughly Communist. Each unit commander is flanked by a Communist commissar. Armando is credited with various cruelties and behaved dictatorially, especially in the period when the division occupied Montefiorino. Several persons – civilians, unit commanders, Italian army officers – who were officially reported killed in action instead have been eliminated by orders of Armando himself or by one of his more extremist commanders at his suggestion. Armando was able to eliminate personalities who had influence on the partisans because of their gallantry but had cast aspersions on his own character.

Men came from all over the countryside, as many as 8,000 partisans attracted by the easy life, the rich food and the authority they had over the civilian population. The population was unduly taxed and suffered much from the domination. Armando acted as dictator and governed over the zone by means of two general commissars, Ercole and Davide, who robbed and extorted from the population without pity. The only fight directed personally by Armando was the battle of Montefiorino, provoked and imposed by the Germans; few partisans have ever seen him in action. The battle of Montefiorino was a disaster for the partisans, caused mostly by Armando's incompetence and by the incompetence of the men surrounding him, each much more interested in saving their own lives and personal belongings than in the fight. Armando, after he had given the order for dispersion, fled on his horse, followed by five horses loaded with his personal property.

Armando fills in his lack of military knowledge with shrewdness and common sense. Politically he is a convinced Communist dominated by the idea of community . . . The partisan division salute, lifted right arm with a clenched fist, was changed to a military salute by order of Armando when the division crossed the line . . . the partisans of the Modena division, as far as it is possible to judge, are brave and deserve confidence. The shame is that these partisans are under the control of about 50 persons who have power of life and death and abuse this power out of ambition or private interests. By eliminating this noxious influence these partisans, well led, could still be of great help to the common cause.

Sergeant Isenberg continued that in the American counter-attack, the majority of the partisans who had remained with the American troops 'elicited praise'. According to him, there remained 573 of the Modena under arms to fight with the Americans around Barga.[26]

British SOE reports were equally deprecatory. One described Davide as a 'complete Communist Redhead all through. A soap-box orator but no military leader. He is hated by civilians but popular with the Red element of partisans. Unfortunately, no one available to replace him.' Another report on the Modena Division stated that 'Self-appointed Communist committees sit in judgement and pass death sentences on certain men for "betraying the Communist cause" or for "not being a true Communist" . . . One very good leader by name of Faccio was got rid of in this way, another leader by name of Tulio being detailed to put the sentence into effect'; a third reads: ' "Davide" – a Communist – tried to bring politics to the fore as much as possible to the complete exclusion of any military matters. There was definite danger of the whole division turning "red". Most commissars run like rabbits when there are any Germans in the vicinity.'

A shocking account was sent to SOE Headquarters in Monopoli of how enemy animal transport was being sabotaged: No. 8 shot was dropped into the ear of a horse or mule, which 'will drive him mad in 24 hours and he will die in 48 hours. German veterinary officers failed to find the cause of death even after several post mortems. A hundred and ten mules and horses were destroyed in this way.' Such extremely un-British behaviour sounds to the author like a tall story related by an Italian partisan to an over-credulous British officer.[27]

Major E. H. Wilcockson, a British Liaison Officer with Davide, has said in conversation with the author that both he and Armando were out-and-out Communists, only interested in politics and no good at fighting. In the end Davide proved such a bad military organizer that Wilcockson had to get rid of him by cutting off all his supplies. Wilcockson feels strongly that the partisans should have been confined more to producing information about enemy movements, and that their attacks on Germans produced very nasty reprisals on Italian civilians. He said that in each village there was at least one Fascist informer who, when German troops were carrying out revenge raids, revealed which houses had received the British mission, whereupon the Germans destroyed those houses. In his view, the Mongols (Chinese-looking Russians) in the German army were the most brutal, and it was safer to attack the Fascist troops.

Wilcockson has told the author that he and his colleagues had strict instructions to pay for all hospitality received, and wore money-belts when they were parachuted in. Unfortunately, much of the money was in 10,000-lire notes (Italian money, not military government currency) and as the peasants with their subsistence economy used little money, it was hard to get change.

Wilcockson was given £3,000 in Italian notes (all confiscated from the Italian banks in Tripoli after its capture), and says that this money was extremely useful in persuading Italians to feed the British. He spent eight months behind the lines, and thinks that as it became clear the Germans would be forced out of Italy, Italian civilians keen to keep a foot in both camps were more willing to lodge and feed escaped POWs. In his area Wilcockson found several escaped British POWs who would not cross the lines because they preferred living with Italian families to taking orders from officers.

British Liaison Officers were inadequately informed of the Italian political situation. Major Wilcockson relates that he was at Monopoli, not knowing whether he would go in to Yugoslavia or northern Italy as an arms and explosives expert. Eventually he was given 48 hours' notice to go to Italy, and no adequate political briefing. He had no interpreter, but was told optimistically he would be able to find English-speakers in the villages.

In his view, the British Liaison Officers should have looked on themselves as collectors of intelligence about the enemy, helped US airmen who parachuted from damaged planes, and trained the partisans in the use of weapons for the final assault on the Germans as the Allies advanced – not acted as organizers of indiscriminate attacks. He advised SOE headquarters not to send arms to the Modena Division under Armando because they were being sent on to Communists in Bologna who hoped to obtain control of the city when it was liberated.[28]

British Liaison Officers with the partisans in the area north of the line near Florence had witnessed the horrendous San Terenzo massacre in the marshes north of Florence (page 317); anxious to demonstrate their horror to the partisans, they concocted a plan to murder or capture General Max Simon, the Waffen SS general responsible. Major Barton, MC, a Commando with a fine record of landings behind the line on the Adriatic, was put in charge of 'Operation Cisco Red' to kill or capture Simon.

Barton left Brindisi in a Liberator on the night of 3 November and made a successful drop near the headquarters of Major Wilcockson, in charge of the Silentia mission with the partisan Modena division of Davide and Armando. He spent the night with Wilcockson at a comfortable house in Gova. Barton searched unsuccessfully between Reggio, Emilia and Modena for Simon; finally in Ferrara, with the help of the partisans, he interviewed German deserters and Russians and Poles among the partisans in all the villages. Although everyone knew where Kesselring was, he could get no information about Simon's headquarters.

Interestingly, Barton stayed in the house of a Fascist captain of militia who was 'a good Fascist' by day, and an even better partisan by night. He commanded a considerable area and was friendly with many useful Germans; ran trucks from Verona to the Brodeno area – one way he carried arms for the partisans, and the other way, goods for the Germans. He told Barton that Simon was probably in the Verona–Brescia area north of the Po. This decided Barton to abort his plan, and he crossed the line on foot from Gova to Catigliano, a 47-hour crossing.

Barton stated that twice a stick of Allied bombs fell within 200 yards of where he was sleeping, and both times there was no military target for miles, or a main road. Christmas Day he passed with a man whose wife and child had been killed by an Allied bomb. He called the Allied bombing 'wanton jettisoning', and stated that the civilian population was 'terribly frightened of the Allied air force'.

Major Wilcockson described Barton to the author as 'a mystery man' with a secret mission, who was 'never a proper member of SOE'; he doubts that 'Barton' was his correct name. Wilcockson came to the opinion that the partisans were afraid of the Germans, but very willing to fight the Republican Army; he estimated that 65 or 70 per cent of partisans were avoiding service in the Republican Army and were 'not very interested in fighting to liberate Italy'. These conclusions, contained in a written report sent on to the Foreign Office, must have damaged the case for sending more help to the partisans. Additionally, the monthly report from No. 1 Special Force at Monopoli in January 1945 warned that reports they had received from northern Italy 'left no doubt that those who control Communist bands are preparing to seize power by force when the Germans are expelled by the Allies', and that manifestos issued by the Communist party 'are becoming more and more violent to the people ... throughout the text can be seen a reflection of antipathy towards the efforts of the Allies in Italy'.[29]

They recommended that the Allies should no longer deliver arms which would be eventually 'used against us', and that the partisans should be instructed to concentrate on sabotage, for which explosives would be sent, together with clothing, food and protective arms only. As will be seen, this warning was seized on by the Foreign Office in London.

In September 1944 a Free Republic was established in the Friuli area north-west of Udine, in the mountains on each side of the Tagliamento Valley and extending up to the Austrian frontier west of Villach. It was known as the Republic of Carnia. Communists and other political parties uneasily shared power, and nominally accepted the authority of the CLNAI in Milan. There were continuous clashes between the Communist Garibaldi units and the others. The non-Communist Osoppo Brigade was well organized, but military plans to defend the zone could not be agreed with the Garibaldi. The great majority of the civilians were hostile to the Garibaldi soldiers because of the presence nearby of Tito's Yugoslav partisans, who proclaimed openly that they would make Carnia and the whole Friuli area part of Yugoslavia after the war.

The Carnia Republic was recognized by both the CLNAI and the Rome Government. It covered 2,580 square kilometres, with a population of 90,000; but it was short-lived.

The Germans took the announcement of the Republic as a challenge, and immediately prepared a large force to wipe it out. On 3 October, Germans and Cossacks crossed the Tagliamento River and attacked. The Cossacks under General Domanoff had sixteen regiments and were supported by a German SS Brigade (*Kartsjäger*). By the end of the month, the partisan forces had evaporated in disarray, and the Republic was dissolved.[30] Sir Thomas Macpherson, an Oxford Rugby blue and brilliant Classics scholar, who headed one of the SOE missions in the zone, described the Republic as 'fatuous' to the author; his assessment was correct.

CHAPTER 12

Divided Views on the Partisans

IN THE SUMMER of 1944 British and American liaison officers with the partisans told them with confidence that the Allies would break through the Gothic Line in north Tuscany in September and spread out into the Lombardy plain towards Milan, Turin and the Veneto. The partisans were agog with expectation that the time had come to revenge themselves on the Germans and Fascists. Alas, their hopes were dashed. The offensive against the Gothic Line failed.

The Americans had insisted on removing five of their Divisions from Italy for a landing in southern France ('Dragoon'), much against the wishes of Winston Churchill and Field Marshal Alexander. The 'Dragoon' landings in July 1944 were completely successful, and the Americans quickly liberated the Franco-Italian frontier and the French–Swiss border as far north as Basle. However, as the French frontier was set in impassable mountains, this was little help to the Italian campaign.

The initial attacks on the Gothic Line went well, and when American troops got within a few miles of the town, it appeared Bologna would fall. Kesselring wanted to leave Italy and withdraw to the Alps; he sent his plan for a retreat and subsequent holding action in the Alps to Hitler for approval. Hitler toyed with the idea, but on 6 October ruled firmly that the Lombardy plain must be defended, regardless. Hitler's strategy paid off: although the Brenner was covered in debris from bombs, the Allied offensive was petering out; and the last effort to capture Bologna failed at the end of November 1944, whereupon all plans for further Allied advances into the Lombardy plain were postponed until the spring.[1]

When Field Marshal Alexander realized his autumn offensive against the German Gothic Line in northern Italy had failed, he issued a proclamation that the partisans should stand down for the winter – that is, go on the defensive instead of initiating operations against the Germans. They were advised to go home and conserve their ammunition. Field Marshal Harding (Chief of Staff to Alexander) has told the author that he and Alexander took this decision solely on military grounds, without consulting SOE or OSS experts on the partisan movement or the Italians,

227

because they knew it would be at least five months before the Allies attacked the Gothic Line again, and they feared the partisans would suffer too many casualties during the long interim period. The CLNAI official response was that 'they would intensify the fight and not weaken their resistance'. They were angered by the proclamation; they claimed it was issued because the Allies considered the partisans too left-wing and difficult to control; and, with more reason, they considered that it made the Allied plans clear to the Germans, who would now withdraw troops from the line to attack the partisans – this must sap their morale. Although Italian historians impute all sorts of political reasons for the *Proclama Alexander*, Harding assured the author that there were no political considerations in their minds; they thought solely of the interests of the partisans.

Harding remembered other meetings and consultations with General Cadorna, but he could not remember discussing the Proclamation either with him, or with SOE in Berne or at Monopoli. His view was that 'the military advance had run out of steam by November 1944; the US 5th Army could make no progress in the mountains and the 8th Army were only making limited attacks to improve their position.' According to Harding:

> Alex and I thought if the partisans went on with their operations they would suffer so many casualties that they would not be able to play the part we wanted in the final offensive. We felt that once the main battle front became quiet, the Germans and the Republican Army would have plenty of troops to attack the partisans. We did not consider in detail the psychological effects of the declaration. We had little, if any, contact with SOE in Berne over their role in aiding the partisans.[2]

Paradoxically, only ten days before the Alexander Proclamation Churchill in London had urged increased air drops to what he termed 'the Italian Maquis', and Lord Selborne, the Minister in charge of SOE operations, minuted that he was 'disturbed at the meagre allotment of air lift for supplies to Italian Maquis', and 'gave vent' to alarm at the absolute priority which 'General Wilson had given to supplies for the Yugoslavian partisans'. Selborne told Churchill the Yugoslavs had received 10,000 tons, but northern Italy only 550 tons of supplies. Churchill drew the Chiefs of Staffs' attention to Selborne's minutes for their meeting on 31 October.[3]

He still favoured an ambitious landing by the 8th Army in Istria, where the Italian partisans could have given considerable assistance; but this was dependent on breaking the Gothic Line. Thus, when the 8th Army attack finally ground to a halt in the first week of

November, Churchill's enthusiasm for the Italian Resistance disappeared, and during the winter of 1944/5 they had low priority compared with Yugoslavia.

When Major Oliver Churchill left General Cadorna at the beginning of December 1944 to return to Caserta, he reported both verbally and in writing the difficulties Cadorna was having with the CLNAI, and how the Communists were playing a dominating role. One of Cadorna's problems was that he had no radio sets to communicate with leaders of the partisans, whereas the Communists had an efficient wireless network; a plane carrying wireless equipment for Cadorna had unfortunately crashed into the mountains.[4]

The Allies invited Parri and the Communist Gian Carlo Pajetta (substituting for Luigi Longo) to Caserta, because they felt that a military agreement with CLNAI might strengthen the position of the democratic parties and curb Communist domination of the Resistance. Cordial conversations were held in which the overall Commander in the Mediterranean, General Sir Henry Maitland ('Jumbo') Wilson, took part. This resulted in a bipartite military agreement being signed on 7 December. A tripartite draft agreement had originally been prepared, in which the participants would have been the Allies, the CLNAI and the Italian Government; unfortunately, before the final draft was ready the Bonomi Government had a typical Italian crisis. This meant only a bipartite agreement, between the Allies and the CLNAI, was possible.

The agreement committed the CLNAI to recognize the Rome Government and to hand over all their 'powers' to the Allied Military Government (AMG, or AMGOT) as soon as north Italy was cleared of Germans, and to promise to disband the partisan units and surrender their arms once fighting was over. The CLNAI were promised a large monthly subsidy of 160 million lire (about £1½ million at the rate of exchange operating in German-occupied Italy), to be distributed by the Allied Military Command but paid by the Italian Government as part of their contribution to the war effort. As distribution of the subsidy was to be at Alexander's discretion, Cadorna had more power within the CLNAI because he could pay out as he chose.[5]

As soon as Bonomi had formed a new government, he came to a formal political agreement with the CLNAI representatives on 26 December which stipulated that:

1 The Italian Government recognized CLNAI as the organ of antiFascist parties in territory occupied by the enemy.

2 The Italian Government delegated CLNAI to represent it in the struggle that patriots had undertaken against Fascists and Germans in parts of Italy not yet liberated.

3   The CLNAI agreed to act as the delegate of the Italian Government recognized by the Allied governments as the only legitimate Government in such parts of Italy as had been or would later on be returned to the Italian Government by the AMG.

The conclusion of these agreements produced 'howls of anguish' from the Foreign Office, who claimed they were faced with a *fait accompli* because 'not only had we not seen the draft of the 26 December agreement, but the text reveals almost complete disregard for our views and wishes which we have already expressed'.

The Foreign Office objected that the third paragraph did not amount to recognition of the Italian Government, and that it should have been stipulated that the Chairman of the CLNAI must be acceptable to the Italian Government. They also complained of the omission of any clause under which the Government could denounce either this agreement or the military agreement.[6]

Orme Sargent had an interview with Major Hedley Vincent, an expert on the Italian partisans who was back in London after a tour of duty with the Osoppo Green Flames in the Friuli. Vincent reported adversely, both on the lack of CLNAI control and on the fierce feuds between the Garibaldi and the other battalions. This had a strong influence on Sargent, who related his 'misgivings' about the agreements to the Foreign Secretary on 12 January 1945, stating that the Foreign Office was surprised that the agreements of 7 December and 26 December both failed to take their views and wishes into account. He objected strongly because there were no safeguards for denouncing the agreement if the CLNAI abused the powers being given to them and attempted to set themselves up in opposition as an alternative government to the one in Rome. He insisted that the British Government must reserve the right to denounce the agreement 'if the circumstances we envisage should arise'. He went on that there was a real danger that

> so useful and powerful a machine will be captured by the Communists. The picture in northern Italy is reminiscent in the strongest degree of Greece, and we may be helping to build up not only a rival to the Italian Government in Rome but also a rival to the Italian army now fighting on the Allied front, thus creating the essential elements for a civil war in which British troops would inevitably be involved.

He also lamented that Scoccimarro, the Italian Minister for Occupied Territory, was a Communist.

Eden minuted that he thoroughly agreed with Sargent, and sent a copy of Sargent's report to the Prime Minister, saying 'There is much in this story which reminds me of Greece. We must watch it closely.' By now, with the Istrian landings irrevocably cancelled, Churchill had little interest in the 'Italian Maquis' and went off at a tangent, replying,

> Can't we get the Americans to take charge? It will be very wise to hand it [*sic*] over. What interests have we there that would suffer? I will certainly put it across to the President.

Eden wrote on this minute, '. . . would not the Americans just let the Italians take charge?'

Both Sir Noel Charles, the British representative in Rome, and Harold Macmillan rallied to the defence of the agreement. Macmillan wrote that he 'much preferred two bipartite agreements to tripartite agreements, and that the denunciation clause was far more adequately provided for by financial control which remains in our hands. He who pays the piper calls the tune.'

The War Office comment was that the Foreign Office had been perturbed and ruffled by their fear of violent separatist movements, engendered in them by their experience in Greece; and by their annoyance at having what they considered a *fait accompli* being put over on them.

Eden decided that the Prime Minister, having lost interest in the Italian Resistance, was in no mood to expostulate, so he ordered Sir Alexander Cadogan, his Permanent Under Secretary, to try to enlist the help of the Chiefs of Staff. Cadogan's memorandum to them emphasized Eden's view that the clause about recognizing the Rome Government as the Government of all Italy was not strong enough; that the situation was reminiscent of Greece, and that General Wilson and the Rome Government should be asked to denounce both agreements if the CLNAI, on the strength of the powers now conferred upon it, attempted to set itself up in opposition to the Italian Government in Rome.

The Chiefs of Staff thought that any type of denunciation clause, as urged by the Foreign Office, would suggest that the partisans did not have the confidence of the Allies, and 'engender mistrust', and that, although there was no denunciation clause, either the Allied Commander or the Italian Government could denounce the agreement at any time. They also entirely agreed with the observation by Harold Macmillan that 'he who pays the piper calls the tune', and refused to put pressure on Wilson or the Americans to revise the agreements.

This was a storm in a teacup, brought on by Eden's hostility to Italy, and also by his extreme jealousy of Macmillan, who as Resident Minister in the Mediterranean frequently took decisions about foreign policy, with the backing of the Prime Minister, without consulting Eden. Both agreements were sensible. It was vital to curb Communist dominance of the partisans, as otherwise there was grave danger of civil war and a chaotic situation when the Germans withdrew. Wilson, Macmillan, Charles and Alexander, like the Bonomi Government, were on the spot and understood the situation in German-occupied Italy. Eden and the Foreign Office had little understanding of what was happening there.[7]

Allied Forces Headquarters at Caserta, commanded by Wilson, was an integrated headquarters (joint British and US). American consent would have had to be obtained to revise the agreements, and it would have been a much-resented snub to both Wilson and the Italian Government. It was, however, typical of Eden's insistence on trying to keep control over what was being decided with regard to Italy. In the event, the distribution of funds was 40 per cent to the Communist partisans and 60 per cent to the others.[8]

Because of their reservations about the value and role of the partisans, and their fear of another 'Greek situation', the Foreign Office insisted on a change of attitude by AFHQ, who established a new policy towards the partisans, discouraging uncontrolled 'armed expansion', and putting emphasis on sabotage and 'anti-scorch'. They were concerned because attacks on German army installations were always followed by reprisals against the civilian population, and this watered down the population's enthusiasm for the partisans.

A new directive laid down that in north-east Italy as much food, clothing, medical supplies and other non-warlike stores as could be sent would be provided, while 'only the minimum quantity of arms would be provided, as may be considered essential for individual acts of sabotage'.

> In north-east Italy only such warlike stores as are considered essential will be issued. Non-warlike stores are to be sent in as in the case of north-west Italy. It is laid down that the overriding consideration in this area is that Special Operations must be so controlled as not to aggravate the Italo/Yugoslav frontier problem, even if this may involve forfeiting a military advantage.[9]

The Yugoslav menace to north-east Italy had been appreciated by the British, if not by the Americans. By now, as will be seen in Chapter 12, the presence of great numbers of Cossack and Caucasian troops in the Friuli area was making partisan activity impossible east of the Isonzo, and the few partisans left in the field retired to the high mountains. SOE laid down that 'peak' partisan activity would be needed in mid-April, and that Italy should have priority over Yugoslavia. SOE noted that 'the CLNAI cannot be relied on with any certainty as an instrument of central control', and estimated that their airlift to the partisans in the twelve weeks from February until 15 April would be 1,230 tons, with 360 tons to the Apennines, 420 to the north-west, 390 to the north-east and 60 to the Po valley.[10]

The SOE had no idea how much the OSS would send but Colonel Beevor, SOE Chief of Staff at Monopoli, estimated it would be at least as much as the British since the Americans had more aeroplanes available for dropping supplies. Alexander's headquarters was now known as Allied Armies in Italy (AAI). Their advanced base at Siena was theoretically an 'integrated headquarters', but the Americans frequently acted on their own without consulting the British. Throughout the winter of 1944/5 the officer in charge of OSS operations, the US Colonel Riepe, sent massive amounts of arms to Communist and other partisan bands, indiscriminately. By the time of the final attack in the April of 1945, there were at least thirty SOE and OSS missions operating with the partisans behind the lines, and they were well equipped with weapons despite the British decision to go slow over sending arms.[11]

Parri and Pajetta returned to Milan, where they communicated the contents of the agreements to Cadorna and the CLNAI. Unfortunately, the Communists would not agree to Cadorna being Commander-in-Chief of the Resistance, as the Allies wanted. Soon Parri was arrested by the Germans, and this was followed by a string of further arrests, thanks to a traitor in the ranks – one Caruano, who after the liberation was immediately tried and executed. Cadorna lost eight of his officers, and the dashing Sogno was captured trying to rescue Parri.

In January 1945 the Allies had been disturbed by reports from liaison officers in north-east Italy that, following a speech by Tito claiming incorporation in Yugoslavia of an area of north-east Italy including Trieste and Gorizia up to the valley of the Isonzo, the Garibaldi formations in that zone had passed to the command of IX Yugoslav Corps, to which the Soviets had attached a mission; the Osoppo battalions remained under CLNAI.

The Garibaldi formations had not only become operationally dependent on the Yugoslavs; they had appointed political commissars who spent a great deal of time with the Russian mission at IX Corps and who, according to reports by British Liaison Officers, had succeeded by anti-British propaganda in seducing the allegiance of the Garibaldi 'whose rank and file, although professing Communism, had no real predisposition towards Slovene aims of annexing this part of Italy'. The Allied generals in Italy concluded that Tito wanted to extend his hold over as large an area of north-east Italy as he could, by military force and Communist propaganda, so that he could create a *prima facie* case for annexing as much territory as possible to Yugoslavia after the war was over. This had strong Russian support. It had also become clear that the Yugoslavs would oppose the setting up of Allied Military Government in that area after hostilities, although the UK, USA and USSR had agreed that all frontier rectifications must await the post-war Peace Conference.

Accordingly, the Allies sent a pointed request to the CLNAI to explain why they had allowed the Garibaldi formations in north-east Italy to pass under Yugoslav command. There was a flaming row at the meeting of the CLNAI when Cadorna produced this message from the Allies. Longo argued fiercely that the switch-over was in the best interests of the Italian Resistance. Cadorna became angry, and his pride was wounded by the insolence of the Communists.[12] He wrote to the CLNAI Secretary, saying that if he was not appointed GOC, he would resign. The letter was received on 6 January, but no reply was given until 21 February. Further stormy meetings achieved nothing. 'I will not be led by the nose like an ox,' Cadorna said, and again threatened to resign.

Eventually, at the end of February, a formula was designed with the help of the Partito d'Azione whereby Cadorna would be GOC, with two seconds-in-command and three political advisers. Agreement was reached in principle, but Cadorna was summoned to Berne to discuss plans for the final liberation of the north before he could exercise his new powers.[13]

Cadorna stayed with McCaffery in Berne. He saw Dulles as well, and reported that through Cardinal Fossati of Turin he had received feelers from General Leyers, the German Military Commander of Milan, for a pact under which the partisans would promise not to attack the retreating Germans as they left Italy, in return for which the Germans would promise not to sabotage industrial installations.

McCaffery opposed any dealings with the Germans, reiterating his government's insistence on unconditional surrender, but, according to Cadorna, Dulles was 'less rigid'. From Berne Cadorna went to Lyons where he met Colonel Roseberry, the head of the SOE office in London. Cadorna discussed with him the maltreatment of Italian partisans who, when they crossed the mountain frontier into France, were arrested and sent to concentration camps by the French. Roseberry promised to intervene on behalf of the Italians.

Cadorna went back from Lyons to Berne, where to his extreme delight he met Parri. The Germans had released him as proof of their sincerity in the negotiations for a pact for the safe exit of German troops from Italy in return for no sabotage (see Chapter 15). Cadorna was anxious to get back to Milan as soon as possible, but on 27 March orders came that he must go south with Parri to meet senior Allied officers to discuss the disarming of the partisans after victory.

In discussions at Siena, Colonel Riepe proposed a preposterous plan of placing all partisans in camps for three weeks after the German surrender, then sending them home without arms, but with a lump sum of money. Cadorna and Parri said this was ridiculous, and it was dropped. However, on behalf of the CLNAI, Cadorna promised that the partisans would be demobilized and hand in their arms as soon as the fighting was over. Not until 18 April did Cadorna return to Milan, much frustrated by not having been there to organize the final insurrection. But with the help of Max Salvadori, he was at last able to exercise his real function with the partisans.* He found the Piedmont command of the CLNAI had issued an order that after the Germans left, all senior Fascist officials and all members of the Fascist armed forces were to be summarily executed. Cadorna, backed by Longo, declared this order outrageous, as it would have resulted in the deaths of thousands, some guilty of only minor offences, and at once countermanded it. In his absence his aides had accomplished 'miracles' in reorganizing and strengthening not only the old Green Flame units, but many new units; now the Communists were outnumbered around Milan and Turin by the others.[14]

In September 1944, and mainly in order to ensure that soldiers of the Italian Royal Army taken prisoner by the Germans would be reciprocally treated, the Bonomi Government had agreed with the Allies that all Italian neo-Fascist troops in uniform should be treated as POWs, in accordance with the Geneva Convention. On 6 March 1945, Allied Forces Headquarters issued an order to this effect. The order stated that POW status would be accorded members of the Republican Army, Navy and Air Force, the Black Brigades, and the Guardia Nazionale Repubblicana, either in uniform or wearing some distinctive emblem; it would also be extended to unarmed men in civilian clothes who could prove they had been members of the armed forces of the Republic. It was further agreed that those charged with war crimes should be held in civilian gaols, and that Fascists charged with atrocities should be dealt with under Italian law.

It was a sensible decision to accord POW status to all Fascist forces; long columns of men gave up their arms to the partisans and the advancing Allied troops, and the deadly spectre of further civil war between Fascist soldiers and partisans did not materialize.[15]

Cadorna tried to ensure that the partisans also gave up their arms, and that the Communists allowed AMG to function in the newly liberated areas. Slowly the partisans became disarmed. Cadorna tried to constitute

---

*Salvadori was an outstanding hero of the Resistance. He was of mixed British-Italian parentage, and was given a commission in the British army.

a police force from the partisan ranks to help the *carabinieri* keep order, but even though several thousand extra *carabinieri* had come from southern Italy, they were impotent in face of the tens of thousands of anti-Fascists who ran riot. Partisan ranks had been greatly swelled by last-minute patriots who took up arms as the Fascists and Germans departed.

To everyone's relief, the last agonies of the Italian campaign were brief. The Allied final offensive began on the night of 9 April. Bologna was entered on 21 April, and by 1 May AMG had already been established in Genoa, Milan, Turin and Venice. Mussolini was captured on 27 April, and executed the next day. On 29 April the German armies in Italy signed an unconditional surrender in Caserta.

Executions by anti-Fascists began on a wide scale, and on more than one occasion bands of so-called partisans burst into prisons and massacred the Fascist occupants. The partisans set up *ad hoc* tribunals to try Fascists, and great numbers were summarily executed; some estimates are as high as 30,000, and may be correct.[16]

Robbery, blackmail and assassination were rife during the first few weeks of the liberation of the north. Fortunately they slowed down with the arrival of Anglo-American troops and the extra *carabinieri*, and the development of effective co-operation between AMGOT and the CLNAI.

As AMGOT officials arrived in northern Italy they found the threat that the CLNAI might set itself up as a revolutionary government had disappeared. In nearly every town the partisans had taken control several days before the Allied troops arrived, and the CLNAI had dismissed the chief Fascist officials, replacing them with their own choice as heads of the various departments. Relations between AMG and the CLNAI were smoothed by the confirmation of nearly all CLNAI choices in their office. Nor did AMG make any effort to enforce the detailed control which had been thought necessary in southern Italy when it was a war zone.[17]

The great fear of the Allies and the Italian Government was that, on Hitler's orders, the Germans would pursue a 'scorched-earth' policy as they left Italy, blowing up ports, water and electric plants and industrial installations. Plans were made by the partisans, with Allied collaboration, to stop this; but they would have been ineffectual had the German generals obeyed Hitler's orders. Explosives had already been placed in vital ports and industrial centres in accordance with these orders, and the partisans would have been quite unable to stop the Germans setting them off. Fortunately, the German generals realized in time that Hitler and Nazism were doomed, and Generals Wolff and Vietinghoff cancelled the orders for demolition.

In 1946 General Vietinghoff, who took over from Kesselring as commander of the German troops in Italy on 15 March 1945, stated in an affidavit to his war crimes interrogators that Hitler had ordered

'large scale demolitions' in northern Italy with the intention of crippling the ports of Genoa, Spezia and Trieste as well as all the heavy industries, the large dams and waterworks, the long distance electric supply, etc. ... I ordered that, in the case of a retreat, only those demolitions were to be carried out which were an absolute military necessity, and forbade all demolition beyond these narrow limits. To be sure that this prohibition was fully complied with, I ordered the withdrawal of demolition troops to the Brenner sector.

It is a pious delusion if the Italian patriots maintain that they prevented the demolitions ... they would never have been able to hinder systematic measures if I had ordered them as prearranged. The troops constantly guarding all important objectives consisted of high-class technicians who would have done the job before the first patriot could have been on the spot.

I can justifiably claim to have proved myself a true friend of the Italian people during the whole period of the Italian campaign.[18]

Few will accept Vietinghoff as 'a true friend of Italy', but the widespread claims by partisans that they saved the ports of Genoa, Trieste and La Spezia and other industrial installations at the last moment by their anti-scorch activities are not plausible. * By refusing to carry out the demolitions ordered by Hitler, the German generals in Italy did something to improve their black record.[19]

As the German front began to crumble on 17 April, Vietinghoff sent a letter to Graziani threatening the destruction and 'paralysing' of the key industrial 'implantations' during a German retreat unless the Italian people, and especially the partisans, refrained from interfering with the retreating Germans. Vietinghoff asked Graziani to entreat church leaders to put pressure on the partisans not to attack his soldiers. Although the demolitions did not occur, no 'true friend of Italy' would have resorted to such blackmail.[20]

General Meinhold, the commander of the German garrison in Genoa, had at least 7,000 fighting troops under his command. On 23 April he received orders to retire into Lombardy, and thereupon asked the Archbishop of Genoa to try to make a pact with the partisans whereby he would be allowed to retreat unmolested. On hearing that the Germans were about to retire, the partisans spontaneously attacked and were so

---

*For example, the SOE report on the liberation of Genoa stated: 'The anti scorch programme had been realized almost in its entirety, a result that was far beyond the wildest expectations of any of us.'

numerous and well-organized that they got the better of the fighting against the scattered German units; on 25 April, Meinhold suddenly and unexpectedly surrendered. American troops did not arrive until 48 hours later. By then, Popular Tribunals had already been at work, imposing summary executions on Fascists and collaborators. When AMG officials arrived they suppressed these courts and set up the Special Assize Courts provided for in emergency legislation by the Rome Government as elsewhere; the Special Tribunals simply went underground and for several more weeks administered secret judgement with on-the-spot executions, burying the bodies by night. The number executed in Genoa and the nearby Ligurian towns amounted to 1,500.[21]

The liberation of Turin began with a series of general strikes on 18 April. The Fascists and Germans lost control as the workers entrenched themselves in the factories, and partisans from the hills entered the city. Zero hour for an official insurrection was 1 p.m. on the 27th, and there was fighting. General Schlemmer, who had two armoured divisions under his command, threatened to bombard the city; thanks to the intervention of Cardinal Fossati he did not do so, and the Germans moved eastwards, severely harrassed by the partisans. When the Americans entered Turin on 30 April German snipers were still about, although the CLNAI was running the city, with public order well preserved and all services functioning.

In Turin and right through Piedmont, as around Genoa, the *ad hoc* Tribunals took revenge on Fascists, and a great number were executed. There was not, however, a single recorded case of looting. General Trabucchi, commander of the Piedmont partisans, excused these drumhead courts on the grounds that only by displaying 'great initial severity' through semi-judicial processes could he prevent a real massacre. Once AMG set up the Special Courts in June, the People's Courts went underground, as elsewhere. Trabucchi, who should be a reliable witness, has estimated that 2,000 were executed in Turin in the purging process.[22]

American troops entered Milan on 30 April. There they found that Cadorna had the military situation under control, and all public services were working as the Germans had not carried out any demolitions. There had been some street fighting between Fascist and German soldiers and the partisans, but the enemy had apparently lost all stomach for fighting, demoralized by the execution of Mussolini. Although the German commander had surrendered, there were still more than a thousand German soldiers in the city when AMG officials arrived, including 150 who had barricaded themselves in the main Post Office building; AMG officials worked quite happily in the same building for several days.

There was no public disorder in Milan after its liberation; about 60,000 anti-Fascists and partisans were armed. The drumhead tribunals set to work, with executions on a considerable scale. It is estimated that the number of victims was about 2,000 during the first few days.

There were many unofficial executions or revenge murders as well. The following report from Sir Noel Charles to the Foreign Office, dated 23 May, gives a good idea of the chaotic conditions, and also of how long it took before AMG could establish their Special Assize Courts:

As a result of recent measures number of assassinations in Milan at night are going down. Last night there were 4 as against a figure of 44 on the night of May 17/18. In the provinces shootings seem to be going on sporadically, varying from place to place according to degree of control exercised by local partisan leaders. In Lombardia special Assize Courts will be formally established tomorrow and should be functioning in Milan by the end of the week and elsewhere by the beginning of June. These courts are not popular with Communists, who prefer military Tribunals and may try to obstruct the satisfactory operation. Another great difficulty is that though prisons are full there is almost no evidence in majority of cases and people are unable or unwilling to come forward with it. Semi-legal extraordinary military Tribunals are functioning in Milan and Como and have imposed and carried out several death sentences. Procedure and organization of these courts are most unsatisfactory and it is hoped that once Assize Courts are functioning they can be put an end to altogether. CLNAI are still issuing orders which in some cases cut across those of AMG, and I understand that Colonel Poletti is seeing Morandi, Chairman of CLNAI,* this afternoon and telling him that this has got to stop and that after May 28th no order, decree or appointment made by CLNAI will have any force unless confirmed by AMG. In this connexion, I have suggested that text of agreement [the December 26 Agreement] between SACMED and CLNAI, containing undertaking that latter will hand over administrative powers, might usefully be published.†23

In Venice the partisans rose during the night of 26 April, and after desultory fighting the Fascists surrendered, including the commander of a Black Brigade, and the Venice CLN took control on the 28th.

---

*Poletti was head of the US section of AMG; Morandi, a lawyer, was the Socialist representative on CLNAI; despite objections from Christian Democrats he had been elected to replace the banker Pizzoni immediately after Pizzoni returned from the south in April.

†It is significant that as late as 12 May the CLNAI claimed that all correspondence between Rome and the prefects should pass through their hands. They objected also to obeying laws passed by the Rome Government, which were promulgated by sending truck-loads of the *Official Gazette* to the north.

The commander of the German garrison refused to surrender at first and threatened to bombard the ancient city from the Lido and mainland; this was despite strong advice given by the German Ambassador Rahn, shortly before he fled from Salò, to spare the city from destruction and to avoid all combat within it. A British Liaison Officer with the partisans persuaded the two sides to make an agreement by which the Germans could withdraw unmolested provided they abstained from destruction. The Cremona Division arrived at Mestre on 30 April (see Chapter 10) with some of the 8 Garibaldi Battalion, and the Royal flag was hoisted over Venice. Political differences between the monarchists and the others were temporarily forgotten in the joy of celebrating the liberation.[24]

In the autumn of 1942 Hitler's armies overran the Ukraine and the Cossack regions of the Don, Kubak and Terek in their advance on Stalingrad; on 10 November Hitler proclaimed a limited independence for the Cossacks. Collective farms were broken up, and the land restored to small farmers.

One Cossack Division changed sides without fighting and with their equipment in good order; 800,000 Russians were enrolled in the German army. The greater part were absorbed into German units as extra manpower, but on 31 March 1944 Hitler approved the creation of a Cossack Army to operate under their own generals, and a headquarters was set up in Berlin under General Krasnoff. Meanwhile, the Nazis promised the Cossacks that if the circumstances of war did not allow them to return to their former lands, the Führer would allocate them 'lands and everything necessary for their livelihood in Western Europe'. This was well received by the Cossack commanders, since after Germany's defeat at Stalingrad it had appeared that they had lost their native land for ever, with the Bolsheviks resuming possession of it permanently. The Cossacks formally thanked Hitler for recognizing that the Cossack people were faithful and honourable allies of Germany, and for offering them a chance to live their national life outside the dominion of the Moscow Communists, who were taking horrible reprisals against those Cossacks left in their homeland, accused of having co-operated with the Germans.

Hitler decided to use the Cossack Army to subdue the partisans in Carnia, and offered a large area in that part of Italy to the Cossacks as a 'new homeland'. The Cossacks and the Germans came to an agreement which promised a harsh future for the Italian population of this area. It stipulated that 'Any inhabitants of the Italian villages who are considered politically unreliable will be ejected from their houses, which can then be used by the Cossacks'.

It was an enormous task to transport the Cossack army and its civilian tail to Italy. Convoys began to arrive along the railway from Villach to Tarvisio on 20 July 1944, and the station of Carnia was the main staging point. Fifty trains came between 20 July and 10 August.

It was in no way a mechanized army. Transport was drawn by horses, mules, bullocks and camels. As the long trains of cattle wagons were unloaded there was a pungent stench of animal dung, and the air was full of neighing and the braying of camels and donkeys.

Carnia railway station is in a tiny village where the River Tagliamento meets the Aupa and the valley opens out. It became a railway junction in the days of Hapsburg rule, when a branch line had been built to Tolmezzo and up to the small towns higher up in the Val Degano. As a result, unlike most of the stations on the single line from Austria with its innumerable bends and tunnels, there was an adequate unloading ramp.

Around Carnia station there was a wide, flat area where the exhausted Cossacks could bivouac for the night with their animals after they had unloaded. Their first sight of Italy was depressing; the valley is enclosed by steep, inhospitable mountains which give no indication of fertile land. But as the Cossacks moved slowly south they soon came into soft green little foothills covered with grapes, fruit and high crops of maize. Unlike the rest of Italy the soil in Carnia in August is never a parched brown, thanks to the thunder-storms which sweep down all summer from the Friuli mountains.

These green hills were as manna to the eyes of these agricultural people from the Russian steppes; a few miles further south they became even happier as they reached the vast fertile plain of Udine, with its irrigation sweeping down to the sea at Trieste. For many it recalled the rich black soil of the Ukraine. After their tribulations it seemed an Eldorado, and they thought they had arrived in their promised land. Their leaders told them this was the territory which Himmler had promised to them if they swore allegiance to Hitler and shed their blood in the Nazi cause.

General Vlassov, head of the anti-Communist White Russians, had signed an agreement with Himmler in which the Germans promised the White Russians 'an independent State' after the war. Himmler would give no indication where the new territory was to be. Hitler had no intention of allowing the White Russians to take over this attractive area, which had been Austrian territory until 1866 and 1918; he had already decided that Friuli should be part of Austria in a new, greater Reich. Yet the Nazis deluded the Russians into believing they were entering their new homeland by christening it 'Kossackenland.' But the sophisticated White Russian generals must have known in their hearts that this was a delusion, and that they had been sent into Italy only to subdue the partisans and block the entry of Tito's Yugoslav army into north-east

Italy. If Hitler ever redeemed his promise of a new homeland, it would probably be carved out of one of the defeated countries occupied by the Germans.

Unknown to the Russians, partisans lurked in the deep forests covering the mountain slopes. There were over 20,000 armed men in the first wave of Cossacks and Caucasians (plus their families), and against this influx of troops on the German side the partisans who tried to defend the Free Republic of Carnia had no chance.

Once they and the Germans had disposed of the partisans and their short-lived Republic, the Cossacks, now joined by a large contingent of Caucasian troops (whose homeland had not been overrun, but who were violently anti-Moscow), proceeded to organize themselves and make plans for a permanent 'new anti-Communist Russia' in Italian territory.[25]

Mussolini must have been horrified by a letter from the Archbishop of Udine, Giuseppe Nogara, written on 3 October and describing the behaviour of the Cossacks. After recounting massacres by the Germans at Denchia and San Pietro Natisone, and the total destruction in May 1944 of Forni di Sotto, with 1,500 inhabitants, and the destruction of Esemon, di Quinis and Subito, the Archbishop went on:

> Last week most of Faedis, Masarolis, Nimis, Sedilia and Torlano, together with other townships, have been almost totally destroyed. On Sunday, 1 October, Attimis was burnt; on Monday the inhabitants of Trasaghis and Bordano were all marched out; the same fate overtook Carnia, which is now completely deprived of food and which contains around 60,000 inhabitants.
>
> There are thousands and thousands of people forced out of their homes without shelter or rations of any sort; the majority had to leave with the clothes they had on their backs at the moment of forced eviction. There are hundreds of young men and women, mature men and women brutally arrested and inhumanely treated, thrown into prison and left whole days without food; there are thousands and thousands of women, old men and sick thrown on to the roads, their suffering unheeded.
>
> What is their crime? The truth according to the accusers is that they favoured the partisans. But who is not a partisan when he is up against force? Machine-guns or rifles or their soldiers, grenades . . .? Everyone knows that these citizens were unarmed and defenceless . . . They should have denounced the partisans, they add; but who would not try to save himself when faced with violence? But it should be noted that the bulk of the partisans were not inhabitants of those places, but came from afar. Is it right that because of a few the great mass should be punished? Because of a few supposed guilty, thousands and thousands of innocent people suffer. I want to be straightforward and tell the whole truth.
>
> Germans have never been welcome here; they dislike us because we are

Italian and want to be independent; in addition, there is the lively memory of what happened in the years of Austrian occupation between 1917 and 1918. The treatment meted out today intensifies the dislike.

Duce – I appeal to the noble sentiments which inspire you. I beg you in the name of God that you demand just measures against those who have perpetrated these crimes.

Germany proclaims herself the protector and moving force of Christian civilization; what is happening here proves this false. You cannot imagine the hatred of you that has been aroused, and this can explode at any moment into a terrible vendetta.

I hope I am not appealing in vain to your kind heart. My feelings are justified and they ought to arouse in you some pity and kindness. If you want a victim to blame for all this . . . take me, throw me in prison, send me into exile; I am in your hands. But leave my flock in peace.[26]

Another report, sent to Mussolini by the prefect of Trieste, confirmed the Archbishop's worst fears:

The need for widespread reprisals against the partisan movement in the Friuli in no way justifies the importation of a very high number of Cossacks who have come with their wives and children, having been guaranteed land and houses by the Germans. The way in which long convoys of carts and horses transporting men armed with weapons of every type, clothed in strange and varied uniforms, have been directed to predetermined areas in the valley of La Tirre and Tagliamento reveals the detailed intentions of colonization which have surprised even the local commanders of the SS.

This odd manoeuvre followed the decision of the German command to take strong action against the Free State of Carnia. Attima and Faedis have been sacked; in Trasaghis, Bard and Avasina the people have been forced out of their houses with only a few hours' notice. The Cossacks appeared on 9 October, divided into two columns – one of combatants, who instead of fighting made violent assaults on unarmed people that disgusted both the Germans and the Italians (girls and women ravished or killed, houses robbed, destroyed and burnt); the second column, the non-fighting one, consisting of both women and men, have taken possession of houses, evidently intending to stay permanently.

They allege the Friulians are going to leave to make room for them. They say that they have orders to go into Istria and colonize it, and when they go they will have left here misery, feuds and hatred against themselves and against the man [Hitler] who has sent them. It is terrible to think that Friuli will be governed by these illiterate savages, and for the population it is a punishment which transcends every shame.[27]

Any doubt in Mussolini's mind about the truth of those two reports must have been dispelled by a report sent by Professor Alberto Ciannoni to Angelo Tarchi, Minister of Economics at Garda, about Cossack behaviour:

The most serious part of the Cossack invasion is in the Friuli foothills. They have arrived with carts, women and children, entering houses, ejecting the occupants and eating food without payment. At Nimis every day they requisition horses, kill beef cattle and seize maize and hay. In twelve days they did more damage than a cavalry army. I have seen all these things personally.

Many Friulians have been shot dead with the excuse they were partisans; but really killed by Russian soldiers while they were drunk and buried in the fields. Women are also raped. It is clear from the way in which they are killed that they were not active partisans.

The Germans do not seem to have any authority over these rough creatures; the Cossacks do not recognize orders, documents, etc. issued by the Germans, and not even orders from Cossack headquarters to which they do not belong. As well as the soldiers, Russian civilians have been quartered on all the families around. They behave like gypsies, partly criminally and partly like beggars. With soldiers and civilians there are 30,000 and this figure might double. The Russian civilians say they have been given promises of land to farm and houses ready for them; having arrived here and seen the magnificent countryside they believe it is their promised land.

It is clear that the Cossacks in the zone of Val del Torre as far as Forni and Veltri in one direction and Trasaghis, Bordano and Osoppo in another are determined to live there permanently, replacing the Friulians; there are around 16,000 armed Cossack soldiers which reveals its importance. Republican Fascists in Friuli are impotent to stop the daily killings, which reach around 200.

My detailed observations in Carnia show that after the reprisals and attack on the partisans by the Fascist and German troops, 16,000 Cossacks have invaded Carnia and have sacked the following places: Amaro, Cavazzo, Carnico, Chiasis, Intimante, Versamis, Villasantina, Canova Casanova, Terno, Impulso, Ilogio, Forncase, Zulio, Sessa, Cadunea, Cearonia, Sarta, Piano d'Arta, Paluzza, Troppe, Cloulia, Tianu, and Sutrio.

The Cossacks once arrived in these places with their families, in addition to widespread robbery have committed acts of murder, violence and destruction; there have been over sixty cases of rape including teenage girls and women in an advanced state of pregnancy. In addition to removing furniture and household linen the Cossacks have taken away large stores of every type of food – meat, grain, potatoes, fruit and wine that were the winter reserves of the populations. Not only have the cattle, sheep, goats and pigs been taken, but blacksmith and carpenters' buildings and shops of the Co-operative of Carnia, and the chemists' shops have been completely despoiled. The total losses amount to 2,000,000,000 lire, and at Tolmezzo and Arta in the lower valley of the But 148 cattle, 866 sheep and 137 pigs have been removed.

A great burden on the population are the innumerable horses of the Russians; in Carnia there are 6,000 and they are eating all the hay which is essential for the well-being of the farmers of Carnia. To escape from the Russians many families have taken refuge in neighbouring villages, where-upon the Russians install themselves in their houses and share out their land; it seems the German authorities have been ordered to promise them houses and land.

Tarchi forwarded the professor's letter to Mazzolini, Mussolini's foreign Minister, who replied that he had passed it on to Rahn, the German Ambassador, taking care not to disclose Professor Ciannoni's name. Mussolini did not complain to Hitler in writing about the Cossack invasion and their misdeeds, but in talks he raised the matter strongly with Rahn. He got no satisfaction.

In a minute to the Duce dated 17 January 1945, Mazzolini noted that in reply to his complaint about the Cossacks, Rahn told him that he had summoned a senior SS officer from Trieste to Garda. This officer had told Rahn that it was 'out of the question' to replace the Cossacks with German troops, but that 'their behaviour now was perfect', and relations between them and the Italian population were cordial; the troubles complained about by Mussolini had all occurred in the first days of their occupation, but they had now opened schools, and they annoyed no one. Rahn asked Mazzolini to let him know of any incident reported to him or the Duce.[28]

Moved by reports of the plight of the Friulians, Mussolini sent large quantities of household linen, stockings, shirts, men's suits and other supplies, which were distributed by civil servants.

Today in the part of Friuli occupied by the Russians in 1944 and 1945, the older people who remember them mostly say they were *brava gente* (decent people) with *buona anima* (kind hearts), unless they were provoked or drunk. Many of them are remembered as being so primitive and uneducated that even a bicycle was a novelty to them. They were a mixed lot, mostly from the Steppes of the Don, but included many Caucasians and Moslems from other parts of Russia where the Stalin regime was hated. The officers were well educated and included many *émigré* White Russians from the Czar's army and their sons, who had been living in Paris, Budapest and other cities, subsequently overrun by Hitler, where *émigrés* had flocked after the defeat of Denikin's armies in 1918.

Once the fighting against the partisans defending the Republic of Carnia was over and the Russians found they were not surrounded by a Communist population, a *modus vivendi* was established, although the Friulians hated the prospect of the Russians taking over their farms.

When Cossack soldiers were billeted in houses they behaved well and were usually affectionate, calling their landladies 'Mamma'. Today, survivors of this wartime Russian army hold reunions with the Friulians. Although, as with all armies, there were sporadic incidents of bad behaviour, the two communities settled down to a peaceful winter. They were both harassed by the Communist Garibaldi partisans, who were disliked by the inhabitants because their attacks resulted in reprisals by both the Germans and the Russians. A great difficulty for the Russians was that the Germans made no effort to supply the large quantities of hay and corn needed for their livestock, and they had to live off the country.

The Ataman General Krasnoff arrived in November (an Ataman is the head of one of the numerous ethnic communities of the Cossacks). Discipline improved; all schools were open and frequent concerts were given by both communities. Krasnoff knew that farming opportunities for such a large Russian community were limited, and he made plans to use all the skilled workers in new light industries, but their occupation proved too short for anything to materialize. Attempts were made to revive forgotten Friuli nationalist folklore, and on Christmas Day at Tolmezzo there was an enormous Christmas tree in the piazza, and scenes of fraternization and warmth.[29]

The Russians issued great numbers of leaflets, obviously compiled with the aid of the Germans, advocating the principles of Hitler's New Order and the importance of defending Europe against Communism.

ITALIANS,
Does anyone tell you that we have come here to fight against the Italian people, and against your church, to conquer your territory? ANYONE WHO SAYS SO IS NOT SPEAKING THE TRUTH: IT IS A LIE.

They are capitalists who have no interest in the well-being of ordinary people, but only in their own wealth; either they lie to you in their own interests or they are the agents of Jewish Communists who want to deceive you with their lying propaganda as they have deceived 200 million Russians.

ITALIANS,
Our hearts are full of deep sympathy for you. Your soldiers together with German soldiers liberated us from indescribable torments and insupportable terror, and gave us back the NAME OF CHRIST, THE CHURCH AND FAITH, AND THE RIGHT TO WORK IN FREEDOM.

Cossacks and their children have always looked after the graves of all the best and most courageous Italians who fell on our soil fighting against the enemy of the human race, Bolshevism. We hailed your soldiers as our liberators and our priests pray for them.

We fight against Jewish Communism, Bolshevism, that has cost Russia thirty million innocent lives, that destroyed the church, that ordered the shooting or the deportation to Siberia of believers in Christianity. We would rather die than be slaves of Jewish Bolshevism.

ITALIANS,
Think! Listen to us who talk to you from bitter experience because we have paid for our blind faith with millions of lives. Come with us; let us fight together for the national liberty of all the peoples and for a NEW ORDER in Europe based on justice and Christian religion.

The Free Republic of Carnia was soon wiped out not because of this propaganda but through the overwhelming military superiority of the Germans and Russians. As one BLO with the Ossopo Brigade put it: 'The partisan forces, suffering significant losses, were forced to retreat higher into the mountains, with a six-man British mission following as well as they could, to the protection of Tito's IX Yugoslav Corps.' On 2 October Major Tom Rowarth reported that all the valleys were occupied and the partisans disorganized, but he continued to operate in disguise, sending back radio messages which enabled the RAF to bomb the Villach–Tarvisio railway effectively.[30]

After the September defeat, relations between the Osoppo and the Garibaldi worsened, with frequent quarrels. The Garibaldi made no secret that they supported Tito in his claim to attach Venezia Giulia to Yugoslavia after the war. Tito's IX Yugoslav Corps had its base in Chiapovano Valley, north-east of Gorizia. From there they had tried to push west and extend their grip on the territory east of the Isonzo Valley. As Gorizia had a predominantly Slav population this infiltration was not much resented, but trouble started when Tito's guerrillas moved west. Here, although much of the population was of Slav origin, they had lived amicably with their Italian neighbours since 1866 under Italian rule. Tito's guerrillas behaved badly, in marked contrast to the Italian partisans.

On 22 November there was a meeting between the leaders of the Garibaldi Brigade and the Osoppo, arising from a dispute over a cartload of provisions, bought from the farmers by the commissariat of the Osoppo and then seized by the Garibaldi. Vanni, the political commissar of the Garibaldi, told the Osoppo leader Bella during a four-hour meeting that all partisans in north-east Italy must place themselves 'by the side of the patriotic units of Tito', and that the Italian Communist Party had decided that all those who did not intend to support adhesion to the new Yugoslavia were enemies of the Italian State.

He declared that Garibaldi partisans would never permit the installation in Italy of a democratic regime to suit Britain, and affirmed that all the territories of Venezia Giulia were legitimate Slovene territories over which the IX Yugoslav Corps already had full rights of jurisdiction; he further demanded that the Osoppo should renounce their allegiance to the CLNAI and join the IX Yugoslav Corps. He said that the Garibaldi would ignore Alexander's directive to cut down their activities for the winter, told the Osoppo not to recruit any longer, and warned them not to carry out the slightest anti-Tito propaganda.

Bella objected that he would not take orders from IX Yugoslav Corps but would only operate under the orders of the Italian War Office and the local committee of the CLNAI. He refused point-blank to carry on propaganda in favour of annexation of territory part of which had been Italian since 1866 and the rest since 1919, and insisted on the right to recruit as he wished.

Major Rowarth's report of this meeting was sent to the Foreign Office by SOE in Monopoli, and contributed to their lukewarm attitude over sending further military supplies to the partisans, especially in north-east Italy.[31]

Posters and leaflets issued by the Garibaldi and Tito's agents made Tito's intentions clear. Particularly pernicious were two leaflets widely distributed by the Communists in Trieste and in Milan and Venezia Giulia which gave the completely false impression that the CLNAI had made an agreement with Tito under which Trieste, Fiume, Gorizia and Pola would become part of Yugoslavia when the war was over:

ITALIAN COMRADES,
We the Slovene Communists salute you on the occasion of an agreement between us and the Committee of National Liberation of Northern Italy. Under this agreement the CLN recognizes the existence of a free Slovene State, and decides that at the moment the Nazi Fascist oppressor is chased out, the city and territories of Trieste, Gorizia, Fiume and Pola will revert to their natural Slovene position; this is of historical importance.

By renouncing the Slovene proper rights over the territories of Venice and Udine they have shown the wish for peace and good will.

After twenty years or more of slavery our martyred cities are restored. It is a fine act of justice and understanding that only the anti-Fascist parties can accomplish.

At the same moment as Fascist imperialism and oppression are thrown aside, beside a free Italy will emerge a free Slovenia, who will pardon neighbouring countries the faults of the past and begin a march together towards the fraternity of all the free countries of the world.

ITALIAN COMRADES,
The Slav cities of Trieste, Gorizia and Fiume and Pola are solemnly recognized and guaranteed for the future. All our rage against you is cancelled.

We send you a fraternal salute and say at last you are more than comrades; you are brothers.

Death to Fascism. Freedom for the People. Free Slovenia. Free Italy.

Communism for ever. Signed: World Union of the Soviet Socialist Republics.

Another, falsely claimed to have been issued by the CLNAI, was circulated in Milan:

MILAN CITIZENS:
The Committee of the CLNAI is happy to give you the noble message that the delegates of Communist Slovene Serbia have reached an agreement of historic importance between our two peoples.

No honest citizen who is truly Italian can fail to rejoice on learning that at last justice is being done to the Slovene people so oppressed and cruelly treated by hated Fascism. Trieste, Gorizia, Pola and Fiume, the 'martyred Slovene cities', will be at last restored to the Slav nation, our new sister.

In vain a clique of Imperialists, reactionaries, aristocrats and war mongers want to create the myth of the Italian nature of those lands and involve the Italian people in a bloody war of extermination and conquest.

Only the megalomaniac and stupid Fascist imperialism can extol such conquests and draw the Italian people again into new dangerous adventure to realize 'their natural ambition', which in fact would produce the slavery of innocent peoples.

The anti-Fascist parties linked in the CLN, conscious of the need for reconstruction, once their freedom is regained, want as their first international act since their existence to conclude an agreement with the Liberation Front of the Slovenes. It is a fine act of justice which will show to the world how true Italians – those who are not corrupted by Fascism know how to do their duty spontaneously without awaiting the imposition of an armistice by the Allies or a future peace settlement.
Signed: Committee of National Liberation of North Italy.[32]

This and similar propaganda in favour of Venezia Giulia being handed over to Communist Yugoslavia aroused apprehension among the population. The prefect of Trieste wrote to Mussolini of rumours circulating that the German troops would be replaced by Pavelić's Croat army, who had terrified the Italian population in Zagreb, Pola and Fiume, but said that when Borghese's Decima Mas arrived as a garrison, the population became 'happier'. The prefect of Trieste was so concerned about the menace from Tito that he wrote again to Mussolini, urging negotiations with the partisans to make a combined front against the Yugoslavs, on the grounds that they would combine with the Decima Mas to defend the area if the Germans withdrew. No encouragement for this plan was given by Salò.[33]

Borghese was ready to change sides when his Decima Mas was posted to Venezia Giulia from Liguria in December 1944. He sent emissaries to

Admiral de Courten (Naval Minister in the Rome Government) and to Field Marshal Messe (the overall commander) suggesting negotiations, and Major Rowarth became involved in talks, which lasted from December to early March 1945. Some elements of the Decima Mas remained near Trieste until the end of the war and were viewed with suspicion by the Germans, who had persuaded Graziani to transfer part of the Division back to Liguria in February.

Lieutenant Piave, an Italian member of the British mission 'Bergenfield' to the Osoppo, had been captured by the Decima Mas on 14 December 1944; they freed him in order that negotiations might be opened for the Decima Mas to change sides. Major Rowarth was invited to be present at a meeting between Verdi, the Osoppo chief of staff, and the Decima Mas. For an unknown reason, he declined to go. However, he was able to send the following report of what occurred to Monopoli. The Decima Mas representatives stated that:

> The formation was not pro-German or Fascist, but believed in a strong National State and fought only for that end.
>
> Further activity against patriotic Italian partisans would not be carried out but an effort would be made by the leaders of X [Decima] Flotilla M.A.S. to unite the patriots and help them against German destruction of Italian property and the safeguarding of Italian territory. All efforts would be made to destroy the totalitarian attempts at Government of Italy by Communist forces, be they Italian or Slovene.
>
> Arms, officers and troops would be put under command of any patriot force wishing to avail themselves. No attempt would made by X Flotilla M.A.S to control in any way material and men so accepted.
>
> All officers of X Flotilla M.A.S would accept trial by an International court after the Armistice.
>
> As many towns as possible will be handed over intact to the Allies when the Germans leave and the important power stations of NOVE (G.1884) and FADALTO (B.7223) will be handed over intact.

Major Rowarth reported further that the Decima Mas had proposed to send two representatives with himself and Verdi to Allied Forces Headquarters to discuss possibilities for united action, and that on his advice, no action of conciliation between Osoppo troops and the Decima Mas was brought about, but the subject was put to Allied Forces Headquarters for consideration.

Further signals sent by Rowarth show that the negotiations made progress, and must have been authorized by Allied Forces Headquarters:

27 January 1945   Am in contact with Prince Borghese X [Decima] Mas, who seems ready to turn against the Germans. He is an Italian national hero of oldest Roman family . . . assures me he is not Fascist nor pro-German, but a patriot and will not send troops against patriot partisans. Although late in the game I think it possible to use his troops against German withdrawal on Tarvisio escape route. May be able to send him to Allied Command if you are interested.

6 February 1945   Borghese makes definite promise to Osoppo to supply arms to ex-partisans forced into his formation . . . Intermediary is Piave, whom I understand and trust. Borghese asks for direct talks with me since Osoppo will do nothing without my consent, and in any case he wants to make direct proposals to Allies. My advice is to open preliminary talks in Rome since we lose nothing.

10 February 1945   X Mas have already proposed joint anti-Slovene activity with Osoppo and prepared fortified line of resistance against Slovene probable attacks. Also are well disciplined.

Eventually Rowarth was ordered by AFHQ not to continue these promising negotiations, and on 6 March reported that he had advised 'Osoppo leaders to have no further contacts with Prince Borghese and his formation'.

At his post-war trial as a war criminal by an Italian court, Borghese stated in evidence that in early 1945 in Venezia Giulia, as there were no Italian troops opposed to them, only Serbs and Cossacks, he had tried to come to an agreement with the Osoppo partisans, who 'would not quite come round to his point of view, but he took care not to molest them'.

In April some Decima Mas officers reopened talks with the Osoppo, but by now the bulk of their units had been sent to the Lombardy plain, and the talks came to nothing. It was alleged after the war that Borghese's troops had been 'notoriously ferocious' in dealing with partisans.

At the same trial Ferrucio Parri, who in 1944 had been Chairman of the CLNAI in Milan, testified that he had known at the time of Borghese's approach to the Osoppo, and that it was all part of a 'double game' being played by Borghese. According to Parri, when Borghese sent a message through a POW to Marshal Messe, commander of the Royal Army in Rome, that he wanted to negotiate a surrender, AFHQ replied with a radio announcement that the reputation of the Decima Mas was so 'infamous' that they would not communicate with them. Parri also stated that AFHQ were prepared to negotiate with representatives of Graziani's army. As will be seen, this was incorrect; there is evidence that the Allies turned down out of hand suggestions of surrender by the Republican Army made through SOE in Berne in December 1944.[34]

With hindsight, it appears that the Allies may have thrown away a good chance of shortening the campaign in Italy. As has been noted, until the Malta Conference on 31 January 1945 Churchill, against Roosevelt's wishes, had been enthusiastic for an Allied landing in Istria. With Decima Mas co-operation, the chances of success must have been greatly increased. However, no report of the Decima Mas–Rowarth negotiations reached Churchill before the Istrian landing project had been irrevocably abandoned (see also pp. 228–9).

News of Borghese's activities was leaked to the Germans. Rahn told Mussolini that all German headquarters were 'buzzing' with rumours of Borghese's treachery. However, as the Italia and Monte Rosa stayed near Trieste until March 1945, a massive defection of the Republican Army might have been organized if the Allies had still been planning an Istrian landing. It is on the cards that Trieste and its magnificent port might have been taken in an almost unopposed landing, because Italian troops greatly outnumbered the Germans in the area, while the Russians could probably have been persuaded to change sides. Such are the 'ifs' of war.[35]

By the end of November 1944, after further Russian and German attacks, the Garibaldi partisans in the hills of Carnia had all dispersed or moved east of the Isonzo. There they passed completely under Yugoslav control, although they refused to admit this to the CLNAI. A few Osoppo partisans lay low in the high villages where Cossack and German patrols did not penetrate, but the majority went home.

The Garibaldi informed the British missions that they intended to ignore Alexander's October proclamation to go slow, and in evidence made a successful attack on a cement factory at Canalutto, and killed and wounded a few Cossacks at Faedis in another, pointless attack. To the horror of the civilians the Germans replied by burning houses and shooting civilians in Faedis. The British Liaison Officers tried to stop these attacks, asking the Garibaldi to concentrate instead on sabotaging the railway from Villach to Udine, and to make preparations for massive destruction of road and railway bridges when the enemy eventually tried to withdraw. Tito's government, however, gave orders that the railway was not to be destroyed.

A number of the Garibaldi objected to being under the Yugoslavs, and were disconcerted by the intense Communist propaganda which laid down that all Friuli must become Yugoslav and Communist after the war. They felt their leaders had betrayed them to the Slovenes. When a number deserted to the Osoppo, the Garibaldi leaders were furious, as were IX Yugoslav Corps, and the Garibaldi's relations with both the Osoppo and the British missions became openly hostile. British Liaison Officers who tried to counter the Communist propaganda found their lives threatened.

Major Rowarth reported that the villagers and the Osoppo partisans were extremely hospitable and helpful, but food and fear of Communism were the main factors in their lives, as well as 'a widespread antipathy to the Slovenes'. Rowarth thought that if the Osoppo commander approached the Cossacks it might be possible to arrange large-scale Cossack desertions if their safety were guaranteed, and in his view a non-aggression pact could have been agreed with local Cossacks. However, the Osoppo commander would not attempt this.

By the time Rowarth left the Friuli area to return to SOE Headquarters in Italy at the end of February, he found that the IX Yugoslav Corps looked on the Osoppo as 'their natural enemies', and had started a campaign of propaganda against them, coupled with forcible disarmament; they also vetoed any recruiting by the Osoppo in their zone. He felt the feud would worsen after his departure; the Yugoslavs had already arrested and disarmed a demolition squad he had sent to sabotage the railway. Rowarth stated that 'the avowed intention of the Yugoslavs was to destroy the Osoppo'; this was confirmed by Captain Gibb, a British Liaison Officer with IX Yugoslav Corps. But Rowarth felt that many of the Garibaldi would desert to the Osoppo at the first opportunity.

In February Rowarth was alarmed by a violent anti-British and anti-American campaign launched by the Garibaldi commanders. Major Fielding of his mission was threatened with imprisonment for arguing against Communism, and an attempt was made on the life of Captain Prior. Furthermore, the Garibaldi had stolen 450,000 lire from the British mission, and seized a cache of arms which had been dropped to the Osoppo in Natisone. Sir Thomas Macpherson, who succeeded Rowarth, told the author he was threatened with death.

From a well-known and much publicized Italian post-war trial it has been established that at Porzus on the Italian–Yugoslav frontier the Garibaldi disarmed and shot fourteen Osoppo partisans. The Communist leader Mario Toffanin (known as Giacca) was condemned to death, but as he had escaped to Yugoslavia the sentence could not be carried out and he is still alive.

The same Garibaldi partisans also killed the British Corporal Trend, who was Hungarian-born and Italian-speaking and under Macpherson, and all the members of the US 'Texas' and 'Mercury' missions. These OSS missions had been parachuted into the Carnia Republic, and after the Republic dissolved lost their wireless sets. When Macpherson met them they were wandering around aimlessly but later they joined the Garibaldi. Angry at the Communist propaganda the Americans tried to counter it, and got on bad terms with the partisan leaders. Macpherson confirmed to the author that both Trend and the Americans were carrying large sums of money so that it may be that, like Major Holohan, they were murdered as much for this as for their anti-Communist stance. After the war, Toffanin admitted he was present when the OSS were killed.

In their hostility to the British and American missions in the Friuli the Garibaldi were obeying orders from IX Yugoslav Corps that the Allied missions were to be bypassed or eliminated.[36]

CHAPTER 13

Frontier Problems

AT THE END OF April 1945 the 8th Army and Tito's IX Yugoslav Corps took part in a race to be first into Trieste as the German armies collapsed in Italy. Unfortunately, no agreement had been reached with Tito as to the Military Government of Istria after liberation. Field Marshal Alexander went to Belgrade, which had been captured by the Russians in October 1944, and told Tito firmly that when British troops occupied Austria, he [Alexander] would need to control Trieste and the whole of the territory west of the frontier between Yugoslavia and Italy, including the ports of Pola and Fiume, so as to supply his armies. Alexander explained that this would be without prejudice to the frontier to be agreed later by the Peace Conference; it was obvious that Yugoslavia would claim this territory, which had been taken from Austria by Italy after the First World War. Tito told Alexander he would agree to Allied Military Government over the whole of Istria (referred to as Venezia Giulia) provided he was allowed to retain his own 'civil administration', which he said was already operating in certain parts. Unfortunately, there was no firm written agreement between Alexander and Tito, while the USA insisted on Allied Military Government over the whole of Venezia Giulia, and would not consider negotiating a demarcation line between Tito and the Allies.

In Fiume, Hitler's order to blow up the port installations had been obeyed. Rainer, the Gauleiter of Venezia Giulia, fled from Trieste on 26 April, and left the German military authorities ready to go ahead with similar demolitions there. However, Dr Hinteregger and Dr Huber, of Rainer's civilian staff, decided they must do everything possible to prevent the same disaster in Trieste, and somehow avoid a rising by the partisans against the German garrison, which was still 7,000 strong. Dr Huber asked the Bishop of Trieste, Monsignor Santin, to act as an intermediary with the CLN. On 28 April Huber and Santin talked; he and the Bishop agreed that inside Trieste the Austrians, the Germans and the Italians had one common enemy – Tito. Santin asked Huber to keep a German garrison within the city until the Anglo-Americans arrived; if this could be done, he would try to get the CLN to agree to prevent the partisans attacking the German soldiers. Huber spoke to the German military commander, pointing out the terrible consequences of an uprising by the Triestinians following any blowing-up of the port, and persuaded him to disobey the orders from Berlin for the destruction of the harbour and other installations, provided that the partisans promised not to attack the German soldiers. The Bishop contacted the CLN leaders, who agreed to keep the city calm while the German garrison defended it against the Yugoslavs until the 8th Army should arrive.

As a result of this agreement, the port was saved; on 1 May the Yugoslavs were stopped by the Germans at Opicina, on the eastern outskirts of the city. Not a shot was fired by the Germans at the New Zealanders of the 8th Army as they arrived from the west on 2 May, and the German garrison surrendered to them. Unfortunately, despite a promise to the contrary, they were then handed over as POWs to the Yugoslavs; most were shot.

Some Yugoslav troops had bypassed the Germans and slipped into Trieste 48 hours before the 8th Army arrived. They took over the radio station soon after the Bishop had broadcast an appeal for calm, and suppressed the local daily newspaper, the *Piccolo*, using its presses to publish a propaganda sheet in favour of union with Yugoslavia and exalting the virtues of Communism. To his credit, Hinteregger had refused to obey an order to blow up the radio station after the Bishop's broadcast, although it was in the hands of the SS.

The entry in XIII Corps War Diary for 1 May reads:

Today saw the final dash across north of Italy and the link-up with Tito's forces. The New Zealanders went at lightning speed from the Tagliamento, crossed the Isonzo and met Tito's men just east of the town [Trieste]. 6th Armoured Division cleared Vittorio Veneto and moved towards Belluno.

The New Zealanders allowed Tito's troops to enter the town and immediately reported that 'the situation was unclear', because 'the Yugoslavs have set up an administration and regard it as their commitment'; this contravened the orders to the New Zealanders to instal Allied Military Government and open up the port. Only the personal intervention of the Divisional Commander, General Freyberg, prevented the shooting of one hundred Triestine citizens immediately arrested as hostages by the Yugoslavs.*

A few days later Alexander ordered the 91 US Division into the Gorizia area and sent one battalion into Trieste itself 'to show the flag' and make

---

*As soon as they reached the city centre the New Zealanders traded their tinned rations for fresh food.

it clear that the Trieste occupation was a combined Anglo-American affair. Tito refused to permit AMG to operate in Trieste and the area he occupied, but allowed Alexander to use the port of Trieste. Trieste was thus occupied by both Yugoslavs and New Zealanders, who faced each other coldly but without major incidents.

Trieste and parts of Venezia Giulia now became subject to 'double occupation and administration' by British and Yugoslav troops – a situation which was disastrous for the Italians. Clashes between the troops were avoided but the Yugoslavs behaved far worse than the Germans had, especially in Trieste itself. Forty days of Yugoslav oppression began for Trieste.[1]

General Freyberg, commanding the Allied troops in Trieste, had a reputation as a battle general, but neither a taste for nor an interest in politics. As the Titoites committed one atrocity after another in Trieste he remained supine, to the horror of the citizens. In theory the Yugoslavs occupied the town and the New Zealanders the dock area. However, in Trieste the docks lie in the centre of the town, with the Town Hall only two hundred yards from the port. General Freyberg made his headquarters in the Lloyd Triestino building in the main square, and New Zealanders and Yugoslavs were billeted jointly in the town.

On 3 May the Titoites took over the Municipio (Town Hall) and refused to recognize that the CLN should have any say in the administration of the town. The next evening all the walls of Trieste were covered with large posters declaring that Trieste was now part of Yugoslavia. The Yugoslavs were effectively in charge of the city, issuing orders to the local government officials, with no obstacles being placed in their way by Freyberg. On 5 May there were riots expressing opposition to the Yugoslav rule, and a number of people were killed and wounded.

General Freyberg failed to take a firm line even when on 9 May Tito's General Keuder announced from the balcony of the Town Hall that Trieste was annexed to Yugoslavia. The people of Trieste were perplexed by the 'incomprehensible inactivity of the Allies'.

At the end of May the Yugoslavs set up *ad hoc* People's Tribunals to try men and women accused on flimsy grounds of being pro-Fascist; several hundred were found guilty and either put to death or sent to concentration camps in Yugoslavia.

Civilians who assisted the British by giving information about the harbour installations were arrested by the Yugoslavs, who also made an attempt to tow away the largest floating crane to Fiume but were prevented by the Royal Navy. The New Zealanders were horrified by the wholesale arrests of Italians by Tito's troops; they saw 150 being marched off in one batch on 9 May, and on 22 May reported many arrests, 'mostly professors'.

C. R. Harris, the official British historian, fails to describe adequately the failure of General Freyberg and General Harding to try to curb Yugoslav excesses within Trieste. Harris even quotes a misleading comment by an observer from Macmillan's staff attached to XIII Corps, who claimed there was 'no reign of terror'. However, Harris does admit that acts of violence against members of the Italian administration were widespread, and 'by no means confined to notorious Fascists'. He also agrees that the Yugoslavs removed, 'wholesale', property belonging to Italian inhabitants, and deported without trial persons accused of 'Fascist crimes'.

The closure of the *Piccolo*, the take-over of the radio station, and the declaration that Trieste was annexed to Yugoslavia, made a mockery of 'double administration'; it was the duty of General Freyberg to resist any encroachments on Italian liberties, and he should not have allowed the illegal People's Courts to condemn Trieste citizens to death or deportation.

Field Marshal Alexander was well aware of the atrocities being committed within Trieste by the Titoites. He reported on 6 May:

All Italians of any standing in Trieste except Yugoslav sympathizers are being arrested. Complete control of activities being taken over by Yugoslavs. Banks are being forced to hand over their securities today. All manpower between ages sixteen and sixty being conscripted; Italians for forced labour, sympathizers of military age being armed. Rifles actually being issued to batches of men. Requisition of grain and other supplies by Yugoslavs on a big scale is taking place west of River Isonzo. Priests believed arrested and many others threatened ... impossible to set up any form of AMG ... Yugoslav policy is to commandeer all large buildings and post sentries in Trieste; all seven barracks denied to us.

Churchill replied: 'Am much concerned about all this. Please let me know whether any lack of authority is hampering you.' Alexander replied that he was acting as if he had 'full powers', but this was misleading; Alexander was standing aside while Freyberg allowed the Yugoslavs to behave as they liked in Trieste, although it was supposed to be jointly occupied by British and Yugoslav forces.

Unfortunately, in a widely-circulated telegram which went to Washington as well as to London, Alexander expressed doubts about the morale of his troops if they were asked to fight the Yugoslavs: 'They have a profound admiration for Tito's partisans and a great sympathy with them ... We must be very careful before we ask them to turn away from the common enemy to fight an ally.'

Churchill was angered by this weakness on Alexander's part, replying that this telegram had done much harm: 'I have been much distressed by the paragraph [*re* morale] and wish that as far as British troops are concerned it had not been given such a wide circulation.' Later Churchill told Alexander, 'I was surprised that you did not welcome more ardently the all-powerful backing I have been gathering for you.'

Alexander was mistaken about his soldiers' unwillingness to fight the Yugoslavs: they disliked and despised them, and were furious about the brutalities they witnessed within Trieste.

Sir Noel Charles sent a telegram from Rome on 12 May revealing that Alexander was not taking a firm line, despite prodding from the Prime Minister:

> Italian press contains daily reports of violence on the part of Yugoslavs against Italian population of Trieste and Gorizia. Arrests, executions and mass deportations are apparently being carried out with the object of eliminating all Italian influence and resistance in anticipation of a plebiscite. . . Fact that this is being done almost under the noses of Allied troops inevitably saddles us with a certain responsibility.

Immediately Trieste was taken, Tito began to build up his forces in the area around Trieste, Monfalcone, Gorizia, Gemona and Cividale, and installed Yugoslav rule. Around Trieste and the other centres between 1 May and 12 June Tito's forces seized 4,768 Italian civilians; they disappeared without trace, almost all being shot at night. The Garibaldi brigade of Italian partisans had abandoned the CLN and made common cause with the Yugoslavs. As a result, some CLN delegates who came to parley with the Titoites were arrested and executed; bloody reprisals were taken by the Yugoslavs in the territory they occupied against anyone who opposed its annexation and incorporation in Yugoslavia.

Churchill became extremely angry at the news of Tito's occupation of Italian territory, and especially over reports of the atrocious Yugoslav behaviour within Trieste. His view was that 'it was not much use arguing with Tito', and he wanted to use force to eject the Yugoslavs. The Prime Minister signalled to Alexander that 'our line' with Tito should be that all would be settled at the Peace Conference, and meanwhile 'peace and goodwill should reign on all contacted fronts'. Alas, Tito's goodwill was non-existent.

Churchill's plans needed American military support; President Truman, who understood little of the issues involved, had told Churchill that he wanted to avoid using US troops in combat over the 'disputed politics' of the Balkans. However, he came to see the problem of the Yugoslavs in a different light, and on 12 May in a telegram to Churchill stated that 'the USA would not allow uncontrolled land-grabbing or tactics reminiscent of Hitler and Japan'. He urged that the Allies must insist on complete and exclusive control of Trieste and Pola, adding,

'I do not believe that Tito or Russia want to provoke a major clash while American armies are in Europe.' Churchill was delighted and told the War Cabinet he interpreted this as meaning British and American troops should move into all the former Italian territory, driving out the Yugoslav army if it did not withdraw first.

However, either Truman changed his mind or it was changed for him; on 14 May he told Churchill that unless Tito actually attacked, he could not 'involve the United States in another war', and at the same time he declined to make a 'standstill' order to stop American troops eaving Italy.

Churchill, deeply disappointed, made another entreaty to Truman, who replied that Alexander, with help from Eisenhower, should reinforce his troops to such an extent that the Yugoslavs would realize 'the firmness of our intentions and our preponderance of force'. Ominously for Churchill's plans, he added that he was 'was most anxious to avoid interference with the despatch of US troops [from Italy] to Japan'.

Stalin now suggested a 'demarcation line to be agreed between Tito and Alexander'. Churchill wanted nothing to do with a compromise, and told Truman we should refuse to negotiate; on 2 June Churchill said that a military operation would be 'sharp and short', and expressed the hope that Truman would act in the spirit of his 'robust' message of 12 May. Truman refused, having decided to concentrate US military might on Japan, and to ignore the Balkans.

Churchill had to eat humble pie; he rescinded his order for the 8th Army to occupy all Venezia Giulia up to Pola, and authorized Alexander to negotiate a demarcation line. This was soon agreed; it left Istria in Yugoslav hands, the boundary within a few miles of the centre of Trieste. It was known as the Morgan line. To the surprise and delight of the citizens of Trieste, the hated Yugoslav troops began to move east out of their city on 12 June. Alexander's agreement with the Yugoslavs laid down that all persons deported by the Yugoslavs should be freed and all property confiscated should be returned. These clauses were not honoured by Tito, but for Trieste the 40 days of purgatorial Communist rule were over. Allied Military Government began to operate immediately. The People's Courts were abruptly abolished and peace and calm returned. However, for a further nine years the threat of possible annexation by the Yugoslavs hung like a black cloud over Trieste.

In the post-war negotiations for a Peace Treaty with Italy, the British attitude was that, although the 1920 frontier was unfair to Yugoslavia, she would not support extreme Yugoslavian claims for former Italian territory, and would oppose a settlement which deprived Italy of Trieste and the predominantly Italian areas in Gorizia and at the mouth of the Isonzo. Britain suggested that Italy should cede to the four victorious powers all the area between the 1914 and 1920 frontiers; these powers would at a later date decide the frontier line, with the proviso that Trieste itself, if it did not become a Free Zone like pre-war Danzig, must be returned to Italy.

Finally, after years of frustrating negotiations, the British and American Governments decided in October 1954 to hand back Trieste to Italy, and the nightmare was over for Trieste citizens, even though the frontier finally agreed lay within the suburbs of the town.[2]

At the end of April 1945, about 20,000 of Mihailović's Royalist Army crossed Venezia Giulia, making towards Friuli with the objective of escaping from the Yugoslavs and the Russians and surrendering to the Anglo-Americans. They were under General Damjanović and had with them women and children. They had been joined by the Serbian Corps under Nedić, who had been collaborators with the Germans in Serbia, and by units of the Croatian army of Pavelić – also collaborators. A representative of Mihailović had reached agreement with the Croats at Zagreb for the Croat Ustase troops and those of Nedić to join forces with the Royalists to keep back the Communists while they crossed Slovenia and Croatia *en route* for the Allied lines. Tito's army attacked these columns, as did the partisans, and there was heavy fighting near Gorizia.

General Harding gave orders that no German POWs were to be evacuated to the Po Valley until the Četnik and Russian evacuation was complete. On 4 May 12,000 Četniks surrendered at San Vito; they were under General Damjanović, and 8th Army were asked to give permission for evacuation 'soonest, to avoid trouble'. Strict orders came from Alexander that no promises of being treated as POWs were to be given to either the Cossacks or the Četniks; instead, they were termed 'disarmed hostile troops'.[3]

On 7 May a further 1,500 Cossacks at Pontebba surrendered and an assembly area was set up at Palmanova, from where convoys of 8th Army lorries swept many thousands of Cossacks and Royalist Yugoslavs to Forli, out of the path of the Red Army and Tito's forces. Around 15,000 of Mihailović's Četniks and 20,000 Cossacks surrendered to XIII Corps. They escaped the dreadful fate of the Četniks and Cossacks who crossed the Plöcken Pass into Austria, because the Labour Government with Ernest Bevin as Foreign Secretary refused demands from Stalin and Tito in 1946 to repatriate them, and they were eventually liberated.[4]

The most bitter fighting in Venezia Giulia after the armistice of 1 May was between Tito's IX Yugoslav Corps and Mihailović's army. 'A rather difficult situation' was reported by 56 British Armoured Division when they reached Cormona, Cividale and Caporetto in Italian territory north of Trieste, because they contacted a large group of Četniks who 'although willing to surrender to British troops, will not give themselves up to Tito's'; clashes between them were common and fierce. General Harding, Commander of XIII Corps, gave special priority to the evacuation of the Mihailović troops in order to ease the tension with IX Yugoslav Corps, and more than a thousand a day were evacuated to the Forli area, where the football stadium was requisitioned for a camp. During the evacuation of the Četniks from the area of Cormona, Yugoslav advance guards approached the town but were persuaded by the British to halt for one hour to give time for their hostile fellow countrymen to be got out of the way.[5]

With the bulk of the German garrison of Trieste and Istria, Rainer, the German Gauleiter, attempted to cross Friuli and fall back into Austria over the Plöcken Pass; his column was joined by three divisions of Cossacks who had reluctantly decided to flee from the domain 'donated' to them by Hitler. Several large Četnik units joined the same column.

On 2 May, as the multinational column of horse, motor transport and marching men and civilians passed slowly through a steeply-banked defile, partisans sniped at them from the cover of trees and rocks, causing between 70 and 80 casualties. The Germans were furious because they had already received news that Vietinghoff had signed a cease-fire at Caserta earlier in the day. In reprisal, a horrible massacre of civilians was carried out by the Germans in the village of Avanzis; the partisans had fled into the safety of the mountains. Fifty-one defenceless civilians were killed in cold blood, including women and children, and 25 left wounded. The column attacked by the partisans at Avanzis consisted of Germans, Croats, Bosnians, Herzegovinians, Romanians, Hungarians, Ukranians, Finns and Italians under *ad hoc* command of the German Kartsjäger Brigade. Responsibility for this final massacre lies with SS Colonel Wagner of the Prince Eugene Division.[6]

There is no evidence that Rainer was responsible for the killings at Avanzis. When the column reached Austria, Rainer went into hiding. He was found by the British Military Police and kept in custody for several months. When the Anglo-Americans decided he was not guilty of any war crimes, he was extradited to Yugoslavia. After a mockery of a trial at Ljubljana, a Yugoslav court condemned him to death, and he was executed.

These attacks by partisans on enemy columns intent on leaving Italian soil were senseless. As with many attacks on German troops in other parts of Italy, they produced only bloody reprisals against law-abiding civilians. Doubts about the utility of this type of attack have contributed to the controversy over the merits of the partisans which is still hotly contested in Italy today. In Friuli the partisans were unpopular because the bulk of the inhabitants wanted to live in peace with the Russians. Unfortunately, the massacre at Avanzis was duplicated by a similar one at Ovaro in the But Valley. On 30 April, as Russian and Yugoslavian troops approached the Friuli, General Krasnoff in Tolmezzo decided on a panic retreat from Carnia over the Plöcken Pass to Lienz in Austria. He knew that if any of his troops were captured by Titoites, they would be handed over to Soviet Russia and face barbaric treatment, but he felt sure that if they reached Austria, which was being occupied by the British, they would be treated as prisoners-of-war under the Geneva Convention.

Some Garibaldi partisans who were not politically conscious had returned to their homes in Carnia, and at the end of April they formed a joint group with the Osoppo. On 30 April Count Burgos, a naval officer who was the leader of both the CLN and the Osoppo in the But Valley, decided to go down the valley towards Udine to contact Major Macpherson of the SOE mission, who had sent a message that he wanted to talk to Burgos about setting up civil government in the mountain valleys coveted by the Communists.

Without Burgos the CLN became irresponsible, and at a hastily-arranged meeting on 30 April a narrow majority of the CLN Committee at Tolmezzo voted, after much argument, for an attack on the retreating Cossacks in the But Valley. The BLO at Tolmezzo, having been out of contact with base for six weeks, had decided to move south to Udine.

The partisans planned to ambush the retreating Russians on 2 May in the pretty village of Ovaro, where the steep cliffs of the valley open out into rolling meadows and gentle, wooded slopes, and there are spectacular views of the white crags and peaks of the Alps. This area was heavily damaged by earthquakes in the 1950s, but to judge from the number of bullet-holes in the walls of houses which have survived, there was a fierce battle. In Ovaro itself on 2 May the Cossack General Diakonov was shot at close range by a partisan who probably mistook him for Krasnoff. The partisans also blew up part of a building in which Russian soldiers and families were sheltering. From early morning and from both sides of the valley, the partisans shot at the continuous columns of Cossacks passing through the village, and Russian casualities were heavy. Eventually the partisans ran out of ammunition and sidled off to hide in the dense woods.

Furious, the Cossacks decided on a Nazi-style revenge on the innocent inhabitants of Ovaro. In the words of one inhabitant, Major Nausikof, commander of the Cossack garrison in Ovaro, went mad. He shot the parish priest and the curate, threatened the doctor who was doing his best to tend the casualties on both sides, and shot out of hand 21 civilians, including women and children. Fortunately most of the inhabitants, angered by the ambush and frightened of its consequences, had fled to the hills.

The villagers of Ovaro were furious with both the Cossacks and the partisans. As the bodies of the victims were being buried in a mass funeral on 6 May, the villagers wrote on the walls of Ovaro that the killings were the result of an irresponsible partisan attack on the Cossacks. There were shouts of 'Death to Communist partisans', and insults were yelled at the few partisans present at the funeral.[7]

The village doctor, Dr Covassi, made a protest to the first British officer who arrived in Ovaro, and his written denunciation was passed to the United Nations War Crimes Commission. It stated that two priests had been killed, and 'besides these barbaric massacres' the Cossacks had threatened women, robbed them, and burnt down houses, including the Town Hall, while the citizens were forbidden to make any effort to put out the fires. Major Nausikof was named as the Russian officer responsible. No charges could be made against him by the War Crimes Commission because after crossing the Plöcken Pass to Austria he had been sent back to the Russians. This is the only recorded instance of an attempt to charge a White Russian with a war crime.

Both the ambush and the massacre were inexcusable. From dawn on 2 May the Germans had sent out radio signals from Bolzano to their troops, telling them to lay down their arms; these must have been picked up by the Cossack column, which had Germans with them, while the partisans must also have known that the war was over and the Russians were leaving Italy. The partisans wanted the prestige of enforcing the surrender of the Cossacks, but their emissaries had been cold-shouldered the day before, the Cossacks telling them they would only surrender to the British. The partisans at Ovaro numbered only 200, while there were literally thousands of Cossacks. Alas, this was typical of the behaviour of too many wild Italian partisans.[8]

British Liaison Officers Major Macpherson and Major Mosdell were with the partisans who occupied Treviso on 30 April before the 56 Division arrived; at Pordenone, in sharp contrast with what was happening further north, they helped to arrange a truce between the Germans and partisans 48 hours before the cease-fire. Had BLOs been with the partisans on the Austrian frontier, the useless attacks on the convoy making for the Plöcken Pass might have been avoided, and the massacres at Ovaro and Avanzis prevented.[9]

Some stiff-necked German commanders claimed in parleys with the BLOs that they were not bound by Vietinghoff's surrender on 1 May because they were part of the Balkan Army – not the Italian Army, which alone had surrendered. As a result, the retreating Germans attacked the partisans until 9 May, with useless loss of life on both sides.

On 7 May 1945 at 10.40 p.m. the whole German army surrendered to the Allies, with active operations ceasing at 10 minutes past midnight on 8 May. Unfortunately, partisans fought isolated actions against pockets of Germans and Cossacks until 14 May, with further useless casualties.

After 9 June, Venezia Giulia east of Trieste fell under Yugoslav rule. It was Communist and totalitarian, with only the pretence of free elections. Local government was run by a series of committees nominated by the central government in Belgrade. No political criticism was permitted, and secret police had unlimited powers of arrest and execution without trial. In 1947 the Treaty of Paris assigned the area to Yugoslavia permanently; Tito allowed no Italian families to live in this territory. Istrian Italian communities today are only commemorated by Associations in Rome, Milan and other large Italian towns.

A horrible postscript to the wartime horrors on Italy's eastern frontiers is that in spite of promises made at the moment of surrender, the British decided to send back to Tito about 30,000 Yugoslav troops and civilians who had surrendered to the British at Klagenfurt in Austria. This occurred in June, after Tito's troops had withdrawn from Austria. On arrival in Tito's hands they were machine-gunned and thrown into mass graves; this event received extensive publicity in 1990 during the Aldington/Tolstoy libel case. The Cossacks and Caucasians who had surrendered as prisoners-of-war to the British at Lienz in Austria were similarly betrayed; the greater number of them were forcibly repatriated to Russia, where most suffered the same fate as the Yugoslavs. Fortunately, the sections of the Royalist Yugoslav army in camps in Italy eventually went overseas and resettled happily, particularly in Australia.

While the Yugoslavs tried to annex Italian territory on the north-east frontier, France began a similar move in the north-west. De Gaulle ordered the French army to cross the frontier into Italy as the German armies crumbled, and sent agents to organize a propaganda campaign to persuade Italians in the zone to express a preference for annexation by France.

During 1944, Italian partisans who were forced by the Germans to cross the mountains into France were in contact with the Maquis. Often there was co-operation, but ill feeling was aroused when a number of Italian partisans seeking asylum were put into internment camps in central France.

Rumours of de Gaulle's plans of annexation reached the Bonomi government in Rome. On 9 February 1945 the Foreign Secretary, Alcide de Gasperi, informed Admiral Stone, Head of Allied Military Government in Italy, of a threat of a French coup as soon as the Germans should leave north-west Italy. In a letter to Stone, de Gasperi strongly deprecated the occupation of any part of Italy by French troops just as he was 'trying hard to re-establish cordial relations with France'. Stone told de Gasperi such fears were groundless, because the French army on the Italian frontier was under the direct command of General Eisenhower at Versailles, and could not move into Italy against the wishes of the Allies. Dissatisfied, de Gasperi asked Prime Minister Bonomi to raise the matter with Couve de Murville, the French Ambassador in Rome. De Murville was frank, and gave Bonomi the impression de Gaulle would stage a coup as soon as the Germans were out of the way. Accordingly, Bonomi wrote to Stone on 28 March:

> I have just had a chance meeting with the French Ambassador, Couve de Murville.
> He confirmed to me that there are two French divisions on the Italian frontier; one regular and one of partisans; there are no Moroccan troops.
> When I questioned him about their intended use he would not give me a precise reply; but from his attitude I have the impression it is definitely not excluded that they may descend upon Italy if the war made this opportune.
> Because of all this I ask you, dear Admiral, to be careful and to do everything you can not to disturb the good relations which we are trying to maintain between Italy and France.[10]

A few days before, General Infante, head of the Italian War Office, had written to Stone to say that his intelligence reports disclosed that the French had stationed on the Italian north-west frontier 27th Alpine Division commanded by General Mole and 1st Alpine Division, plus some Moroccan mountain troops, and that the French had recruited 15 pro-French extremist agitators from the Val di Susa who would be used to whip up disorders as soon as the Germans left.

Infanti said the French coup was being organized in Paris by Soustelle, a devoted Gaullist who had shared his exile in London, and was later to lead the right wing take-over in Algeria.

On 30 March Bonomi discussed the threat with Harold Macmillan, the British Minister Resident at Allied Forces Headquarters, Mediterranean, and Admiral Stone. Afterwards he told Stone that he proposed to release to the press the substance of his talk with de Murville. Stone pooh-poohed the threat and told the Prime Minister that if any story about the French intentions was quoted in the Italian newspapers he would deny it completely.

Still, Field Marshal Alexander, commander of the Allied armies in Italy, took the threat seriously and issued orders to the French troops not to cross the Italian frontier, and the Allies became even more suspicious when de Gaulle gave orders for the establishment of the 'Army detachment of Alps' under General Doyen along the Alps.[11]

In the Aosta corner of Italy there are important hydro-electric power stations vital to the Italian economy, an easy target for sabotage under the

Germans' scorched-earth policy. Accordingly, the Allies parachuted in OSS and SOE officers and officers of the Italian army to organize the partisans to prevent them being blown up.

On 7 April Major Morton of the SOE parachuted down to Sala Biellese, and three days later he was reinforced by Italian commandos. The Germans had placed charges on the hydro-electric works but their commanders in the area, Colonel Schmidt and Colonel Steiner, agreed with Morton on 22 April that if they and their 1,200 German soldiers were allowed to proceed unmolested to the Swiss frontier, they would guarantee not to carry out the demolitions which they had been ordered to execute; these included not only the power stations, but bridges and roads in the rocky mountain gorges which had also been mined. The Germans agreed to pull out of the Valle d'Aosta on 28 April.

On 28 April, following a CLN order for a general partisan rising, the city of Aosta was occupied quietly by the partisans; the German troops had left on the 26th, and Republican troops and the Fascist Black Brigade proceeded obediently to internment camps at Chatillon and St Vincent. Count d'Entrèves, a distinguished Italian scholar who later became a professor and Fellow at Oxford University, was appointed prefect of the Aosta province by the Turin CLN.

To Morton's horror, on the 29th French officers arrived and said they had orders to occupy Aosta with their troops, who had been delayed by deep snow on the Little St Bernard Pass. Information from Italian partisans confirmed that the French were on their way, bringing with them their own CLN consisting of Italians in favour of the region becoming part of France.

Morton warned the French officers that if their troops occupied the valley, the Italian partisans would fight them. That evening a French Colonel de Gelbert arrived at the Hotel Posta in Aosta. Morton told him that there was no need for French troops because all the Germans had withdrawn, but the French insisted on occupying the villages at the top of the pass from St Didier to Introd. Morton agreed to ask the partisans to quit that area.

On 2 May, the day of the agreed German cease-fire, news arrived at Aosta that there were still 5,000 Germans at Ivrea at the bottom of the valley. When the cease-fire came into operation they surrendered to the Americans. Nevertheless, the French commander insisted he must send units down the valley to Ponte Martino just west of Ivrea to deal with the 5,000 Germans, although Morton emphasized that 'there was no military reason for this'. Thus French troops blocked both ends of the Val d'Aosta.

At Aosta, Morton found a considerable number of French officers had arrived; they made no secret of the fact that many of them were political officers, and that de Gaulle intended to incorporate the Val d'Aosta into France. On 4 May news arrived in Aosta that American troops were coming up the valley. To the dismay of the French their jeeps, cars, tanks and trucks clattered through the streets with sirens screaming.

Meanwhile, the Princess of Piedmont had arrived on foot across the Swiss frontier on 30 April, carrying a rucksack. She stayed in Sarre Castle, an ancient royal residence of the Savoy family. She was popular locally, and attended the thanksgiving mass in Aosta Cathedral, where she was well received by the Italians, French and Americans.

Morton insisted that half the partisans should keep their arms, to help the American troops patrol the frontier; he reported that their behaviour and discipline were 'exemplary', and it continued to be so as more and more French troops infiltrated the valley. The partisans, who had rounded up the worst Fascists without shooting any, demanded from Morton that they should be allowed to set up People's Courts to try obvious war criminals. This was summarily vetoed by the US commander, Major Rooney. Morton's final report stated that the Americans were allowing the French to flood into the valley and carry out propaganda in favour of annexation by France:

> The French intended to occupy the valley right away. The fact that the partisans freed Aosta before they could get there forestalled this plan. They therefore decided to occupy the valley in stages. The placing of a company at Ponte San Martino (near Ivrea, closing the road up the valley) was the first stage. In this too they were forestalled by the arrival of the Americans. Now they will spread the gospel of annexation as hard as they can and if ordered to leave the valley they will demand an immediate plebiscite.

Morton's daily reports by radio rang alarm bells in Rome, and reports from other parts of the north-west frontier region were even more disturbing. By 25 May the French had nineteen battalions on Italian soil and were refusing to allow the AMGOT officials to operate.[12]

The French tried to persuade the local people to favour annexation by means of a liberal distribution of foodstuffs, including salt, then in very short supply, promises of no taxes for several years, and a pledge to build a tunnel through Mont Blanc. Ballot papers were distributed in all the French-occupied areas, attached to ration cards. As the former Fascist ration cards had been abolished, this gave the impression that anyone who did not sign the ballot paper would have no right to rations – which were distributed on a far more generous scale than in the area where AMGOT operated. Those who did not sign the ballot cards in favour of annexation had them marked, ominously, 'non-voting'.

French flags were substituted for Italian everywhere, and francs for lire at the rate of two lire for one franc. The banks took this calmly, only pointing out unavailingly that the exchange rate should have been 1½ francs for a lira. An official visit was made by the prefect of Nice to Briga, and its name was changed from Briga Marittima to Briga de Nice.

More serious than this crude propaganda, which converted few Italian citizens to the French cause, were the steps taken to drive out of the district anyone who had refused to sign the ballot papers.

Particularly alarming for the Italian government was the French seizure of all the important hydro-electric stations in the upper Roya valley. The French refused to allow Italian electricity officials or AMGOT officers access to these power stations. They cut the leads connecting them to the Italian grid, and linked them to the French electricity system to supply the Nice area, especially the town of Fontanel. This diverted power that was needed for the railways running from Ventimiglia to Genoa and Genoa to Turin.

With the French in militant mood, Allied Military Government officials had a very difficult time. An AMGOT officer arrived in Tenda on 31 May and started to put up his posters. These were torn down by French soldiers, and the French high command sent an order to expel all Italian local government officers appointed by the Allies, and warned AMGOT officials not to interfere with the French administration in the Briga Tenda area. In order to avoid clashes General Crittenberger, the regional AMGOT head, ordered all his subordinates to quit their offices in the town halls.

In Liguria French troops occupied most of the province of Imperia up to the river Nerva. This area contains 14 communes, including Ventimiglia, although here there were few French-speaking inhabitants or French nationals. The same ration card ploy was followed, and a French identity card was offered with the right to supplementary food rations – including tinned American food, which had been shipped to France especially for the French civilian population. For a few weeks the French were popular in Ventimiglia, which had been so heavily bombed that only 2,000 inhabitants were left in a state of great misery; they were especially delighted when the French immediately undertook a vigorous rehousing and building programme. Here there was considerable support for French propaganda for an autonomous French and Italian free zone – not incorporation with France.

The prefect of Vinadio complained to the Allied Control Commission on 22 May: 'What seemed at first a liberation has in the last few days become a merciless domination; schools are occupied, benches burnt, the hospitals occupied as barracks, and all linen and furniture destroyed. On top of this, there has been a lot of robbery by French soldiers.'

On 30 May, in response to an appeal from Alexander to allow AMGOT administration to be set up in the areas occupied by his troops, General Doyen replied: 'No written demand has been received by France to put an end to the state of war existing between France and Italy since May 1940. France cannot be bound by the 8 September 1943 armistice, to which she was not a signatory. France has had to protect her frontiers against the Fascist divisions . . . I have received orders from my Government to occupy and administer this territory and this is incompatible with the setting up of AMGOT. I am obliged therefore to oppose it.'

There was little bloodshed during this period. A French corporal was killed by partisans at Limone on 29 May; an Italian partisan called Landoni was arrested for hitting another French corporal and sentenced to five years' imprisonment for assaulting a French soldier.

At Introd an Italian partisan, Sergio Vevey, was shot and killed by French soldiers. The French had interrupted a secret Italian partisan meeting at Villa Nova Introd which was planning the seizure of a French hostage as a bargaining counter for the return of Landoni. Vevey was ordered to report to the French Headquarters to see the commander the next day. When he arrived the commander was out and he refused to stay. The French then shot and killed him, on the pretext that he was escaping from an arrest.

At 3 p.m. on 23 May, Italian partisans blew up the Albergo di Sole at Susa with a time-bomb. Here the French gendarmes had their Headquarters and living quarters. Three French were killed and nine wounded. Their Italian cook was also killed. A crowd gathered quickly and shots were fired in the air. French patrols then saturated the town. A road block was set up at Bussolero, and the French assumed complete command of the town, refusing admission to Italian investigators and US AMGOT officers. The few US troops in the town were confined to barracks and a curfew was imposed.

By the middle of June the position had become so serious for the Allies that President Truman wrote personally to de Gaulle, informing him that all supplies, except possibly rations, would be cut off from the French army in France if General Doyen did not promise to withdraw his troops to the French frontier. This threat forced de Gaulle to eat humble pie. The French General Carpentier was ordered by the Paris government to make an agreement with the Americans. It was ratified on 11 June, and worked smoothly. All French troops were to be withdrawn behind the 1939 frontier according to the following schedule: French troops from Val d'Aosta by 28 June; from Susa, Oulx, Cesena by 1 July; from Tenda, Ventimiglia and the Italian Riviera by 10 July.

The Americans, British, French and Italians were all anxious that as little news as possible should leak out about this attempted French annexation of part of Italy. No official announcement of the French withdrawal was ever issued, although it leaked into the American and British press. At first the Italian Government wanted to make press statements, but was dissuaded after approaches in Rome by the British and US ambassadors. On 21 June AMGOT sent regional commissioners into Piedmont and Liguria, with strict instructions to hush up the whole incident. An ignoble chapter of French military history was closed.[13]

CHAPTER 14

The Axis bites the Dust

AS HE CAME to the end of a full year as leader of the Salò Republic, Mussolini's spirits were sinking to a new low. Despite his vigorous protests, the Germans were removing much important industrial machinery; particularly disastrous for Italy's economy was the dismantling of the Innocenti works at Milan. Mussolini was appalled by Hitler's bad faith over the 600,000 interned soldiers in Germany, about whose shocking living conditions he received one report after another, and whose well-being had not been improved following his visit to Hitler on 20 July, although the Führer had promised that they would be set free and work under good conditions.

The disbandment of the Republican Air Force was a great shock to the Duce. A number of officers and ground personnel had reported for duty again after the débâcle of 8 September 1943, and the few pilots loyal to Mussolini had been gallant in combat against Allied planes. Early in the morning of 23 August 1944, Colonel Dietrich of the Luftwaffe called on the Under Secretary for Air, Manlio Molfese, and told him that at that moment, in a co-ordinated action, the Luftwaffe was taking possession of all the airfields, stores and barracks of the Republican Air Force. Mussolini's air force was to be disbanded, its personnel given the option of enrolling voluntarily in a new Italian Air Legion which would be subordinate to, and an integral part of, the German army; any officers or men who did not want to enrol would be posted to anti-aircraft units. Dietrich told Molfese this action was being taken with the agreement of Mussolini. This was untrue; Mussolini knew nothing about it. Molfese picked up the telephone and got through to the Duce. Mussolini was livid with rage. He immediately got in contact with Hitler, who a few days later promised to suspend the operation.

At the Republican aerodromes chaos ensued. Most of the men, finding themselves surrounded and threatened by armed German troops, remembered 8 September 1943, and ran away. Only a few pilots volunteered for the new Legion, in the belief that Mussolini had endorsed the operation.

Molfese wrote to the Duce that the Germans had committed 'an act of real sabotage' which showed that they did not want Republican pilots to fly; he said that if it was due to German hostility towards him personally, he was ready to resign.

For once Mussolini received some satisfaction from the Führer. The move to suspend the Republican Air Force had been initiated by von Richthofen, in charge of the Luftwaffe in Italy. The Republican Air Force had at first been led by Carlo Botto, whom von Richthofen admired. Mussolini lost faith in Botto after a heavy daylight air raid on Turin in which much damage was inflicted on factories: Republican planes did not take off to intervene. Mussolini wrote to Botto:

> You put up no defence against the attack – not a gun-shot nor an aeroplane. Nine fighter planes on the Turin aerodrome did not take off. Our pilots were out of action in the hotels. This inaction must stop, or we shall never be able to overcome the passive demoralization of the Italian people.

Shortly afterwards Mussolini sacked Botto and replaced him with General Tessari. Von Richthofen took this as a personal insult, because of his friendship with Botto, and seized on the inefficiency of Tessari as an excuse to dismantle Mussolini's air force. To Mussolini's delight, Hitler replaced von Richthofen with General Oswald von Pohl, who behaved reasonably well to the Italians in the difficult circumstances.

After the round-up on the aerodromes on 23 August the Republican Air Force could not operate any longer. A few weeks later the best pilots were sent to Germany, where they were trained to fly Messerschmitts; they returned to Italy around Christmas. Although Rahn had assured the Duce that the Messerschmitts would carry the Italian flag, he said that for safety reasons they must also show a swastika. Their numbers were small, but the pilots flying German aeroplanes from Italian airfields in 1945 had a high morale, in spite of the Allies' command of the skies; the Luftwaffe in Italy scarcely existed. Their miniscule force was inspired by the charisma and courage of Major Visconti, who was killed by partisans shortly before the end of the war.[1]

In September 1944 Mussolini knew a few days of despair when it seemed that the Allies must break through the Gothic Line, overrun the Lombardy plain and capture the northern industrial centres. In a panic he suggested taking his Government to a 'last redoubt' in the mountains north of Lake Garda. He asked Rahn to submit the following considerations to Hitler urgently:

a. His government must stay on Italian soil.

b. It must be as close to the invaded parts of Italy as possible.

c. With shortages of petrol and motor transport, it was advisable not to go too far away.

d. Carnia or Cividale in the Friuli [which had been suggested by Wolff and Rahn] were too remote, and it would take too long to clear them of partisans.

e. The only area which met his requirements was the Sarca Valley, Arco and its surrounds – a small town in the Trento, a few miles north of Lake Garda.

He wanted to use boats for transport on Lake Garda for the Civil Service, and to move units of both Graziani's army and the Black Brigades to its defence; in a telegram direct to Hitler, Mussolini asked for an immediate affirmative.[2] But once the front was stabilized with Bologna still in Axis hands, and with the news of Alexander's order to the partisans to stand down promising respite, Mussolini lost interest in a 'redoubt' of last resort. He only took up the plan again within a few days of his end, when he chose Sondrio in the Valtellina.

Mussolini was seriously concerned when he heard rumours from Milan that the Germans had shot 63 Italians at the concentration camp of Fossoli in retaliation for a mythical attack by partisans on German soldiers. He was furious when the news was confirmed in Switzerland on 17 August in the Lugano newspapers. The victims were mostly members of the Italian Socialist Party. Widows in mourning and relations suspecting their husbands or fathers had been shot made pilgrimage to Fossoli and sent letters of protest to the Duce.[3]

Anfuso, the Italian Ambassador in Berlin, on whom the Duce relied greatly, was also pessimistic in the extreme. He wrote to Mussolini on 20 September 1944 that the Germans had no chance of winning the war unless they were able to drop an atomic bomb on England, and he was very doubtful if such bombs really existed, because widespread German hope of the atom bomb was just the optimism of a people worn out by five years of war who were clutching at a straw. He went on:

As the German military situation worsens, their distrust of us increases. The German newspapers go out of their way to emphasize our surrender last September and attribute to it the major responsibility for the situation in which they are now. Today they no longer say 'Italy of Badoglio', but just 'Italy', to describe who has betrayed them.

It is impossible ever again to have real Italo-German friendship on terms of equality ... The balance sheet of a year of the Socialist Republic, I must admit with bitterness, is that the Nazis have no intention of letting Italy be a major power again, after all their sacrifice of blood on Italian soil.

Here is a list of the main events which have damaged the Italian nation and also sabotaged Hitler's aims:
1   The difficulty of making Italian Government work while it is continually hampered by German authorities both military and civil.
2   The hiving-away of a large part of Italian territory (Pre-Alps, Veneto, Trentino, Alto Adige) to be administered by Austrians who are potentially

anti-German and openly anti-Fascist and often in contact with pro-Badoglio Italians.

3 Deliberate obstruction of all international activity by Italy, with the consequent destruction of our interests in the Balkans and the Mediterranean.

4 Destruction of all economic activity at home and abroad.

5 Progressive failure to recognize the ideals and potential of Italian Fascism, and constant repetition of the old adage which Winckelman stoutly denied – 'Italy is a nation that can do nothing seriously'.

6 Complete sabotage of the renaissance of the Italian army, so that today General Morera has to beg for the Italia Division to be sent back to Italy, although the men want nothing but to die for their country.

7 Senseless ill-treatment of our interned soldiers who after ten months were promised their freedom and incorporation into German Trade Unions, but who have not had any improvement in their living conditions.

8 Stiffening of the attitude of the German authorities against our large community of conscripted workers and soldiers inside Germany.[4]

Mussolini's feelings towards the Nazis and Hitler were identical with Anfuso's as he was forced by the German military and civil authorities in Italy to accept one humiliation after another.

On 10 October Mussolini received a seventeen-page report from the *Questore* of Milan, Bettini, a sensible Fascist civil servant whose word could be trusted, describing the barbaric behaviour of Pietro Koch's special Italian police unit, which was under German command. Bettini reported that because of complaints about ill-treatment, he and the commander of the Fascist Muti Legion had visited the Koch headquarters, where they found Italian civilian prisoners in a pitiable condition after being tortured, confined in tiny, dirty cells. He described the after-effects of the torture in horrible detail from a report by surgeons from the Medical Department of the University; they had been tortured to force them to confess to crimes against the Germans; nearly all were members of the Socialist Party, and Koch had given no notification to the Italian police of any of his arrests.

Koch and his officers had illegally used large sums of public money for their own purposes, and given bonuses to police who made arrests. They had also robbed many persons arrested by them. As a result of his investigation, Bettini had arrested Koch and some of his minions and taken away documents, money and valuables from their office. On 28 September, the day following Bettini's descent on Koch's headquarters, Captain Saveke, head of the German security police, protested against infractions of Koch's authority, saying that he worked in collaboration with the Germans, and insisted that Koch and his minions must be released from prison. Saveke expelled the Italian police from the Koch headquarters and put a German guard on it.

Bettini's 'conclusion' was that his 'investigation' had given irrefutable evidence of inhumane torture of prisoners, which Koch and his staff did not try to deny; that Koch and others kept their mistresses at the headquarters at the expense of the State; that they ill-treated the prisoners at night when drunk, and took large quantities of drugs and lived a notoriously dissolute life.

Bettini added that the arrest of Koch and the occupation of his headquarters by the normal police had made a most favourable impression on the ordinary Milanese, who had been amazed and worried by the high-handed illegal behaviour of the Koch force, and that there would be deep disillusion if the Germans allowed the Koch organization to function again.[5]

Mussolini had already been informed of the misdeeds of Koch by Cardinal Schuster and by his Minister of Justice, Pier Pisenti, who had received shocking reports from eminent lawyers in Milan. When Bettini's report arrived, Mussolini picked up the telephone and ordered Bettini to keep the leaders of the 'band' in prison. He was displeased that the Germans had operated a section of Italian police for their own purposes, without informing the civil authority in Milan of what they were doing.

Mussolini was even angrier when he heard on 1 November that the German police had removed some of Koch's agents from the Milan prison, San Vittore, and allowed them back into their headquarters at Villa Trieste. The Germans claimed that the Koch band was necessary for the security of their army, and succeeded in getting Bettini removed from his job. However, Pisenti, strongly backed by Mussolini, gave firm orders that Koch must stay in prison while the Public Prosecutor collected evidence so that charges could be brought against him in court as soon as possible.

On behalf of the SS, Kappler went to Salò to intercede with Pisenti for Koch's release. According to the memorandum sent by Pisenti to the Duce, the interview was stormy. Kappler extolled the good work Koch had done in Rome and Milan over the safety of the German army, and emphasized that anti-Fascists had issued a leaflet defaming Koch, which had been repeated on Radio London; he said to Pisenti, 'Surely the Italian Government does not intend to leave me with the impression that because of a scandal campaign organized by the enemy at home and abroad it is going to stop its police doing a job of the highest importance?'

Pisenti replied that the antecedents of the Koch band were no affair of the Ministry of Justice; there was prima-facie evidence that Koch and his accomplices had committed serious crimes by their cruelty in torturing Italian citizens under arrest. He went on, 'I am not going to be intimidated or prejudiced by public clamour; I am only going to see that justice is done, and that evidence from medical and legal sources is above suspicion.' Kappler excitedly declared, 'If you put Koch on trial, it will be a scandal.' Pisenti replied that it would be a worse scandal if Italian citizens who had committed serious crimes on Italian soil were not brought to justice. Kappler then said that the German Government and High Command were heavily involved for reasons of military security; Pisenti tried to end the interview, saying that he had taken the decision to prosecute, and given instructions to the Public Prosecutor. Kappler then shouted, 'Koch and his men are under our orders, and you cannot keep him in prison.' Pisenti's last words were that the steps taken against Koch were in accordance with Italian law.

Mussolini was delighted by Pisenti's firmness, and General Wolff, Kappler's SS superior, refused to intervene. As will be seen, he had already decided that Germany had lost the war, and was about to embark on peace negotiations with the Allies.[6]

Koch was kept in gaol. In the confusion after the liberation of Milan at the end of April he escaped, but was recaptured at Florence. He was tried before an Italian tribunal in Rome, condemned to death, and executed.

The Gauleiters of the Pre-Alps and the Veneto, Hofer and Rainer, were Austrians; Mussolini became increasingly concerned as Italian local government officials were dismissed and replaced by others of Austrian descent. He knew that this part of Italy, which had been Austrian until the Treaty of Versailles, would be annexed by Hitler if the war was won by Germany. Particularly ominous was the appointment by the Germans of Count Marino Pace as prefect of Gorizia. He replaced Cariolata, a Fascist of long standing and a 'faithful friend of Mussolini'. Reports reached Mussolini that Pace was anti-Italian and anti-Fascist, having supported Mussolini only until the *Anschluss* (the Union of Germany and Austria in 1938), from which time onwards he had conducted a 'clandestine campaign against both Fascism and the Italianity of the region'. In the Vipacco Valley on the Isonzo, Italian had been abolished in the schools and lessons in Slav and German substituted, while Pace insisted that anti-Fascists and Freemasons must be allowed to carry on their activities so as 'Not to create alarm'. Pace had also appointed 'an Austrian and a Slav' to be *podestà* of Gorizia. According to Mussolini's informant (a professional spy), Pace's conduct was much applauded by the Austrian aristocracy in the region, who were delighted by any snub to Fascism.

In December 1944 the German military commander in Udine, alarmed by the incidence of venereal disease among his troops, ordered the arrest of 26 known whores. Instead of arresting known prostitutes the Germans, under a Captain Schmitken, took into custody all young women who were in the streets between 6 p.m. and 11 p.m. Eighty women were arrested and taken on lorries to the barracks, and sent from there to the hospital for a medical examination. All were found to be free of VD, some to be virgins. In another incident, newspaper reports claimed that armed SS German soldiers had surrounded Bussolengo near Verona, and taken most of the male inhabitants away for forced labour.

Mussolini was so angered by these two examples that on 10 December he complained strongly to Rahn that the Germans were treating Italians as enemies, not as allies, and demanded that the German officers responsible be punished. As usual, Rahn refused to treat the complaint seriously.

Mussolini also complained fruitlessly to Rahn that at Trento (also formerly Austrian), Hofer had altered the laws about debt collection and marriages to conform with Austrian practice. 'All this', wrote Mussolini, 'has nothing to do with our conduct of the war in common.' Again Rahn ignored him.[7]

Although Hofer maintained in a talk with Mazzolini that nothing had changed in the legal situation in the Pre-Alp zone, reports flowed in to Salò that under German control the South Tyrolese were carrying out long-matured plans for the return of the region to Austria on lines laid down in 1919. Another report, on Bolzano and Trento, informed Mussolini that all Italian authority in Bolzano had been extinguished, and that the Italian Director of Education was 'a mere subordinate of the German High Commissioner [Hofer]'. A further report from the Pre-Alps stated that Italian officials were cut off from their Ministers at Salò, while many former German-speaking residents were returning to the zone.

A report on Tarvisio stated that there was 'a gradual transmission of all authority to German officials' with the 'obvious intention of incorporating the area in Germany or in a reconstituted Austria'.[8]

Anfuso raised Mussolini's complaints in a long talk with Ribbentrop. He received no satisfaction. Ribbentrop reiterated that Germany was administering the provinces in north-east Italy solely because of military necessity, and that once the war was over Hitler and Mussolini would deal with the question in the spirit of compromise and friendship which had always characterized their personal relations. Ribbentrop ignored a request from Anfuso for a declaration about Italian rights in that area; he then went off into a long digression, relating how in July 1943 he had sensed that Italy was about to abandon Germany, and had telephoned to Hitler 'there is danger everywhere', and how he was thus responsible for the despatch to Italy of the armoured divisions which had held the Anglo-Americans, first at Salerno, then at Cassino, and defended Rome until June 1944. This was typical of Ribbentrop's conceit, and the interview is further evidence that no one in the top Nazi hierarchy had any use for Mussolini at this stage.[9]

On 13 December Mussolini told Mazzolini he had decided to make an important speech in Milan on 16 December, its purpose to strengthen his position in Italy *vis-à-vis* the Germans at a moment when his authority was being more and more flouted by the occupying Germans. Some Italian historians state that Mussolini chose the date to coincide with Rundstedt's Ardennes offensive, which began at dawn on 16 December and was immediately successful, but there is no evidence to support the view that Mussolini was told in advance the date of this long-planned offensive.[10]

Mussolini's last speech in Milan, and his first there for seven years, was made in the Lyric Theatre which was packed with masses of would-be listeners overflowing into the street outside. Mussolini's rapport with Italians was as evident as ever; the speech was a resounding success, and engendered euphoria, but there is little in the written record to justify its magnificent reception. However, Mussolini was supremely confident, and gave the impression that he could lead Italy out of her slough of despond; he even made overtures to the CLNAI and promised Socialist reforms and nationalization of industry.

Bombastically he spoke of 'secret new weapons which would certainly win the war', and his final peroration asking for 'supreme sacrifice' was: 'We want to defend the Po valley tooth and nail; we want to remain Republican while waiting for the whole of Italy to be Republican ... and it is Milan which must give the men, the arms, the will and the signal of insurrection.' This was laughable, as it was well known that the number of fighting troops Mussolini could field was tiny, ill-armed and ineffective. 'Frenetic applause' greeted the end of his speech, and was repeated when he appeared before the crowds outside.

It was Mussolini's day. With Allied armies invading the south of Italy and Hitler's armies occupying the north, the ordinary Milanese citizen was desperate at having two conquerors on Italian soil. Although the full humiliating details of the Long Armistice (see Chapter 1) had not been made public, there was an awareness that the Anglo-Americans were behaving arrogantly in the south, and had allowed inflation to get out of hand. There was fear of the harsh penalties which the victorious Allies might impose on Italy after the war, while the horrors and barbarity of Nazi occupation were already upon them. Mussolini somehow made his audience feel that he was the only man who could extricate Italy unscathed from her dreadful plight.

The euphoria could not last. There was no substance behind Mussolini's words. He had pulled off a confidence trick. Strangely, there was no evidence of opposition from the Communists or partisans. Not a single hostile voice was raised in the large crowds. For the previous twenty years Mussolini had organized a squad of Fascists to lead the applause during all his speeches. It is certain that a strong squad of applauders was sent to the Lyric, and as soon as Mussolini began to speak outside they would have rushed to join the crowd. However, those present are convinced that the applause and enthusiasm were not orchestrated. They were too strong for that, and quite clearly spontaneous. Security was almost nonexistent as he walked into the excited crowds to shake hands. Such scenes indicate how great was the magnetism of Mussolini's personality for the Italian people. He had thrown off his chronic depression and become again for a few days the showman who had duped the Italian people for 22 years.

As he drove back to the Prefecture the crowds hailed him like a victor, thousands of enthusiastic Milanese pressing forward to greet and cheer him. Later in the day he met industrialists and trade unionists and explained to them his plans for nationalization. No record of these talks exists, and they are of no historical importance. No Italian with any sense of realism could take his last-moment advocacy of Socialism seriously.

The Lyric speech received world-wide publicity, and much space in the German papers. But Mussolini was angry to find, when he received the German press cuttings, that none of them referred to the part of his speech in which he had excused the Italian people from all blame for betraying Germany and Fascism at the time of his overthrow. He had said, 'One can proclaim that with regard to our ally Germany the Italian people committed no betrayal (*Si puo affermare che nei confronti dell'alleato germanico il popolo Italiano non ha tradito*).' He went on to extol the virtues of Socialism, even quoting from Mazzini's writings.[11]

The next day Mussolini inspected the Black Brigades in their barracks. As would be expected, they gave him an enthusiastic reception, but more surprising were the crowds who gathered in the streets outside. Mussolini stood up in an open car acknowledging the almost frenetic applause of the crowds as he drove away to visit a hospital.

On the third day (Monday), as he prepared to leave Milan, crowds surged around the Prefecture and then overflowed from the piazza into the adjoining streets. Only with difficulty could the police open a way for his car as the Duce stood up in it on his way to bless the colours of Young Fascists. On that Monday in Milan it would have been impossible to believe that these same Milanese, spontaneously applauding the Duce, would five months later be spitting on his corpse in Piazzale Loretto. Why was there no evidence of hatred of Mussolini and Fascism during his three days in Milan in December 1944? This is one of the mysteries of modern Italian history.[12]

Mussolini's elation over his three brilliant December days in Milan did not last long. In the early weeks of 1945 he sank again into depression and apathy. He wanted to move his government to Milan, and from there to push on with a programme of Socialism and nationalization of industry. The Germans thwarted him on both issues. Mussolini felt strongly that through the introduction of Socialism he would obtain the co-operation of the Italian Socialist Party, so influential in the CLNAI; he also deluded himself into believing that this would somehow rehabilitate him with the French Socialists and the British Labour Party.

With this end in view, Mussolini kept in close contact with Bombacci, who had been a firm friend since their youth, and who had drawn up the Verona Manifesto. With Communist and Socialist antecedents, Bombacci had long-established connections, not only with the Italian left but with French and British Socialists. Unrealistically, Mussolini put considerable faith in Bombacci's power to bring Italian Socialists and Communists into negotiations, even at this late stage. Nothing resulted.

As the Russian advance on Berlin became ever more ominous, Anfuso arranged for 400 families and minor officials there to return to Italy in a special train. Even Rahn lost his optimism, and after reading of the Yalta Conference on 13 February Mazzolini wrote up his diary in terms of extreme pessimism. Mussolini admitted to Mazzolini that the war was lost by Germany, and that Hitler's secret weapons, which were to turn defeat into victory, were probably an illusion.[13]

Mazzolini was taken ill and died on 23 February, a bitter blow because he was the most impressive figure in the ragtail Salò Government. Ponce de Leon Mellini, the Civil Service head of the Foreign Office, then acted in Mazzolini's place, although Mussolini officially appointed Anfuso as Under Secretary. (The Duce remained his own Foreign Secretary until the end.) Fortunately, Mellini was conscientious and trustworthy, and wrote an excellent record of Mussolini's twists and turns in his last days. The Duce told his German doctor he dreamt of creating new roads, and of tearing down the slum quarters and replacing them with fine new buildings. Mussolini said in this conversation that he wanted every house in Italy to have electricity, and had made ambitious plans to improve state education. He said he wanted to go down to history as the pioneer of modern technology, the arts and architecture. He also wanted a great expansion of Italian commercial aviation, for both passengers and goods.[14]

Out of this unreality he came down to earth with a bump when he heard that Tamburini and Apollonio had been arrested and sent to Dachau by the German SS. Both were old Fascist friends from Trieste whom he held in high esteem. Apollonio was an important police official on Mussolini's private staff; Tamburini had been prefect of Trieste in 1942/3 and was at the time of his arrest the Deputy Chief of Police at Salò.

Unknown to Mussolini, through the British SOE office in Berne the two men had treacherously begun negotiations for the surrender of

Graziani's army (these were the negotiations mentioned by Parri at the post-war trial of Borghese). Few details of this episode are known, but the following letter from General Harding at Alexander's headquarters to General Wilson's in Algiers is revealing:

SUBJECT: *Fascist Deserters.*   *SECRET.*

Adv Headquarters,
Allied Armies in Italy.
105/C (Ops) "B"

                                                                    5 Dec 44.

A.F.H.Q.
Information has been received by H.Q. No. 1 Special Force from their Swiss representative to the effect that 17,000 Italian Fascist troops from the SAN MARCO M.A.S. and M.U.T.I. in PIEDMONT and LOMBARDY wish to join the Patriots with their arms if we will indicate an area for them to concentrate. A condition for such action is that the C.L.N. will not be informed by us. It is pointed out that the troops in question are seeking favourable treatment from us.

It is considered at this H.Q. that as these Fascist troops have seen fit to take up arms against the Allies after the Armistice and have been engaged in action against the Italian Resistance Movement, they cannot now expect favourable treatment from us, nor can we expect the Italian Resistance Movement to look favourably on such condonation by us.

There appear to be, therefore, three courses open to these troops:
1. To desert and disperse to their homes.
2. To desert and come through our lines and surrender as Prisoners of War.
3. To desert and individually seek enrolment, if they can, in the Resistance Movement.

It is considered that the first course is most likely to succeed and that they should be encouraged to adopt it. Before replying your guidance is requested as the action taken may have political repercussions. H.Q. No. 1 Special Force can arrange a meeting by their Swiss representative with one TAMBORINI [*sic*], ex neo-Fascist police chief and ex prefect TRIESTE, who, it is understood, is willing to conduct negotiations.

(Signed) JOHN HARDING. Lt. Gen.[15]

The 'guidance' given by General Wilson vetoed further progress, although Tamburini was anxious to negotiate. Perhaps an opportunity was lost. For some reason, no information about this attempted treachery was passed on to the Foreign Office, although Macmillan, the British Resident Minister, was informed. If Churchill had learnt about it he might have become excited, since at this time he still hankered after a landing in Istria and the capture of the port of Trieste.

After a staff discussion in Algiers on 7 December, the following reply was sent to Alexander's Headquarters:

December 1944.

SUBJECT: *Fascist Deserters.*
TO: *Commander in Chief, A.A.I.*

1. Answering your 105/C (Ops) B of 5 December, subject as above, it is agreed that ITALIAN Fascist formations now professing disaffection from the enemy cause should be encouraged to desert and disperse to their homes.

2. In the unlikely event of ITALIAN Fascist units spontaneously deserting en bloc with their arms to patriot forces as a result of direct negotiations with the latter, this HQ can see no objection to such a course. Neither No. 1 Special Force nor OSS should, however, be a party to any negotiations to this end, and should advise that the course in para 1 above is the only alternative to unconditional surrender. The forces of Resistance can scarcely be expected to regard this tardy Fascist repentance with other than mistrust.

For the SUPREME ALLIED COMMANDER [General Wilson]:

Signed: J.A.H. GAMMELL,
Lieutenant General,
Chief of Staff.[16]

Mellini describes graphically Mussolini's rage at the deportation of Apollonio and Tamburini. However, the Germans did not tell the Duce about their treachery; whether Graziani was party to Tamburini's overtures to the British in Berne is unclear, but seems probable to the author.

The Duce instructed Mellini to make the strongest possible complaints to both Rahn and Wolff about these arrests, and also about the continued brutal behaviour of Kesselring's troops in Tuscany and Emilia. Both Germans protested to Mellini that they were doing everything they could to obtain the most tender treatment for Italians, but that the war zones were outside their jurisdiction. Mellini told the Germans that the Duce insisted on being given all the documents about Apollonio and Tamburini's crimes, and would then ensure that they were brought to justice under Italian law. The Germans refused to give any indication of why they had been deported, but rumours were circulated by the Germans that Tamburini had tried to send gold belonging to the Fascist Party to Switzerland. This silence maddened Mussolini.

Mellini told Wolff that the 'climate' between the German and Italian authorities could only be improved if Apollonio and Tamburini were released to Italian captivity, together with all the evidence against them, so that they could be brought before an Italian court martial. Wolff promised to authorize the Gestapo to produce the evidence to the Duce, and stated that these cases had nothing to do with the sacking of Buffarini Guidi; he had been Minister for Home Affairs and was summarily dismissed by Mussolini, much to the annoyance of the Germans, who found him co-operative. Wolff did not keep his promise about the Tamburini papers, and this made Mussolini even more vindictive against the Germans. When Mellini reported his interviews the Duce said: 'I have already made plain to the Führer the extent of the useless cruelty, violence and robbery. It is too late. I have drained the poisoned chalice to the dregs.'[17]

The truth was that Wolff and Rahn were themselves engaged in secret negotiations with the Allies in Berne behind Mussolini's back, through Cardinal Schuster in Milan, and did not want any probe to be made about Italians using the same channel. Wolff claimed after the war that he was prompted to communicate with the Allies through Cardinal Schuster by suggestions made to him by the Pope at a secret audience in the Vatican on 10 May 1944, shortly before the Germans left Rome. Then as proof of his sincerity Wolff, at the Pope's request, released from prison Professore Giuliano Vassalli, a suspected partisan, who after the war held high office in the Italian Government. Wolff declared to a church tribunal for the Beatification of Pius XII in March 1972 that he had the tacit consent of Hitler to discuss possible peace negotiations with the Allies through the Pope, but claimed he had told Pius XII that he feared Germany was drifting into chaos, and that he would be prepared to risk his life by making peace overtures even without Hitler's consent.

Immediately after the interview Wolff was ordered to return to Germany, and by the time he came back to Italy Rome had fallen, so that he was unable to reopen the discussions with the Vatican through Abbot Pfeiffer, as the Pope had suggested. Father Robert Graham, SJ, the Vatican historian, has told the author he is convinced the Wolff interview took place, but that no written account was made in the Vatican for the archives, in case they fell into German hands. In 1990 Vassalli stated his belief that Wolff's account of the interview is substantially true. Shortly after his capture in May 1945, Wolff told his British interrogators that he had visited the Vatican in May 1944, talked to the Pope, and secured the release from prison of a leading Rome lawyer.[18]

By October 1944 Wolff had convinced himself that Hitler had lost the war, that its continuation would only produce useless bloodshed on both sides, and that the longer it continued, the worse would be Germany's post-war condition; he approached Cardinal Schuster, who offered to act as a link between Wolff and the CLNAI and the Allies through Berne. Rahn co-operated with Wolff. A proposal was made for an agreement between Kesselring and the CLNAI that if the Germans promised not to destroy Italian industry the partisans would allow the German army to leave Italian soil unharmed. When Alexander's proclamation asking the partisans to stand down for the winter was issued, these negotiations collapsed.

Meanwhile Franco Marinotti, head of the giant Milan plastic manufacturers SNAI, took a message from Wolff to the British secret service in Berne that Himmler had authorized Wolff to treat for the surrender of all the German armies in Italy. Unfortunately, the Foreign Office sent abrupt orders that no negotiations with the German military authorities in Italy were to be carried on.

The Americans were more co-operative, attracted by the possibility of the surrender of twenty German divisions in Italy and the peaceful takeover of northern Italy. A go-between was found in Baron Parilli, who acted as an Anglo-American agent, with a radio link to Caserta. Starting his contacts in December, by February Parilli had persuaded Allen Dulles, in charge of OSS in Berne, of the importance of Wolff's approach. Dulles obtained the consent of Washington to a meeting with Wolff's emissaries in Switzerland. Himmler was informed by Wolff, and gave his consent without informing Hitler. On 28 February Wolff, Rahn and General Harster, the German police chief, met at Wolff's headquarters at Desenzano on Lake Garda. They chased a hare by discussing how the German forces in Italy might fight the Russians with the consent of the Allies, but finally came to the important decision that Wolff's adjutant, together with Eugen Dollmann who also worked for Himmler, could meet Dulles in Lugano in Switzerland on 3 March. The Americans demanded, as a test of the Germans' good faith, the immediate release of Ferrucio Parri, who had been arrested by the Gestapo. Parri was released; to the Germans' extreme embarrassment, this was leaked to the Swiss newspapers, which also carried reports of German emissaries meeting Americans in Switzerland. Wolff and his fellow-conspirators feared immediate arrest by Hitler, but Himmler persuaded the Führer it would be worthwhile to discover the attitude of the Allies to negotiations to end the war in the west so that Germany in combination with the Allies could continue to fight the Russians.

Alexander sent the British General Airey and a US General Lemnitzer to Switzerland to meet the Germans, and Kesselring authorised Wolff to start talks with the Allies. However, Hitler removed Kesselring from Italy to take over command of the armies in the west on March 9, and his successor Vietinghoff did not arrive for a fortnight. On 10 March news came through Berne that Wolff had told Lemnitzer and Airey in Lugano that he wanted to take north Italy out of the conflict. Wolff said that a military surrender would be difficult, and preferred a capitulation preceded by the statement that 'continued struggle is hopeless and merely causing needless bloodshed'. According to Wolff, Kesselring was not yet 'won over', and his 'adherence' was essential. However, Rahn was completely in agreement that fighting must be ended.

Alexander proposed to the Foreign Office that the German envoys should come to Berne with a signed authority to treat, and then Lemnitzer and Airey would tell the Germans they must go to Caserta for detailed military discussions.

Churchill agreed that negotiations should go ahead, but insisted that the Russians must be informed, and that there should be no further contact with Wolff until a Soviet reply was received. The Prime Minister told Alexander, 'If they are *bone fide*, the results will be invaluable. If they are fraudulent, we lose nothing.' The Germans had raised the question of surrendering generals being immune to prosecution as war criminals; no reply was given by the Allies.

Stalin immediately agreed, but wanted to send two Soviet generals to Berne to take part in the discussions. This was difficult, as Russia had no diplomatic relations with Switzerland, and the two countries were indeed on such bad terms that it would have been almost impossible for a Soviet general to cross the frontier. However, Stalin was told by the British Foreign Office that his generals would be 'welcome' at the talks. This irritated Churchill, who minuted that they would be merely observers, 'Welcome to what? They have nothing to do with a military surrender of the German army in Italy ... it is expressed so politely that there may be subsequent recriminations.' He was right.

Averell Harriman, the American Ambassador in Moscow, objected to Soviet generals taking part in the talks in Berne; he was backed by Roosevelt, and Stalin was told that his generals could not go to Berne, but could be present as observers at subsequent talks in Caserta. Harriman's argument was that Stalin would take his generals' presence in Berne as a sign of weakness, since he would not allow Allied officers to be present at similar negotiations in eastern Europe, and that the Soviet presence 'might jeopardize success'. Churchill scrawled on Harriman's telegram: 'These are tremendous arguments. I feel we were too complaisant, I especially. WSC.'

Clarke Kerr, the British Ambassador in Moscow, was told to emphasize that the talks in Berne were only a preliminary to sending the Germans to Caserta. This aroused Russian suspicions that the Allies might be trying for a separate peace. Molotov complained bitterly, and demanded that the negotiations should be broken off because they were being conducted 'behind the back of the Soviet Union, which is bearing the brunt of the war'. Churchill minuted: 'The Russians may have a legitimate fear of our doing a deal in the west to keep them well back in the east.'

On 3 April Stalin sent an extremely provocative telegram to Churchill and Roosevelt:

No doubt negotiations have taken place [Soviet spies in Switzerland had reported the contacts] on the basis of which Kesselring will open the front and permit Anglo-Americans to advance to the east, and the Anglo-Americans in return have promised to ease the German surrender terms. Otherwise why have you refused entry of the Soviet representative to Berne? . . . At the present moment the Germans have ceased the war with Britain and America.

Churchill told Roosevelt:

We must always be anxious lest the brutality of the Russians' messages do not foreshadow some deep change of policy . . . it is of the highest importance that a firm and blunt stand should be made, in order that the air may be cleared and they realize there is a point beyond which we will not tolerate insult.

This triggered off a firm reply to Stalin from Roosevelt on 5 April, in one of his last telegrams before his death; it expressed his astonishment, as there had been no negotiations in Berne, and said that 'Soviet representatives are welcome at any meeting to arrange surrender. I cannot avoid a feeling of bitter resentment towards your informers, whoever they are, for such a vile misinterpretation of my actions.'

Happily, this altercation did not prevent Mrs Churchill being well received in Moscow during her trip of goodwill which began on 1 April. On 7 April Stalin wrote to Churchill:

Neither I nor Molotov had any intention of blackening anyone . . . my messages are personal and strictly confidential. This makes it possible to speak one's mind clearly and frankly. If, however, you are going to regard every frank statement as an offence, it will make this type of communication very difficult. I can assure you that I had no intention of offending anyone.

Churchill told Roosevelt that he had a feeling 'this is about the best we are going to get out of them, and is certainly as near as they can get to an apology.' He was right.

Meanwhile, Wolff had left to see Kesselring at his new headquarters on the western front; Parilli sent a message that the Germans would like to make an arrangement whereby they would be permitted to withdraw over the Italian frontier after giving up their arms. He was told that this was out of the question, and that talks were to be only about sending German representatives to Caserta.

On Wolff's return to Italy he held a meeting with the German army commanders on 6 April at Fasano on Lake Garda; he told them he would hold each responsible for preventing destruction in his own area. Vietinghoff had meanwhile arrived in Italy to replace Kesselring as GOC. Parilli was sent back to Berne with a message for the Allies that Vietinghoff would agree to surrender if his army could depart from Italy with military honours at the end of the fighting; the major part of the army could then be used to keep order within Germany; Vietinghoff also said that he would be willing to sign an unconditional surrender 'if it could be put in a form consonant with his honour as a soldier', and asked for a draft instrument of surrender to be sent to Berne at once. The Germans were told that a draft would only be handed to them if they went to Caserta.

On reading this report, Cadogan minuted to Churchill that at this stage Vietinghoff obviously had no intention of surrendering his forces on terms acceptable to the Allies, and that it was dangerous to continue the talks. Roosevelt had died on 14 April, and Churchill's first message to the new President Truman was that talks should be broken off.[19]

Both Vietinghoff and Wolff believed that they still had bargaining power, being under the mistaken impression that the Allies would want to use the German army to contain the Russians in the east. Vietinghoff had appointed Schweinitz and Wenner as his representatives to go to Caserta, and they were in Berne, ready to go. However, the Allies firmly ruled on 20 April that there were to be no more negotiations.

Wolff had seen a 'very depressed' Kesselring in Germany and received a sympathetic hearing, but Kesselring was 'surrounded by untrustworthy people' and unable to speak frankly. However, he authorized Wolff to speak to Vietinghoff on his behalf. After seeing Kesselring, Wolff had to visit Hitler's headquarters. It is open to doubt how accurate his account of his talk with Hitler is. Wolff recorded, immediately after the cessation of hostilities, that he had seen Hitler, who for once was calm. Wolff claims that he told the Führer 'all' about his negotiations in Berne, and that he expected the German armies would be allowed to withdraw 'freely' with side weapons and light arms. According to Wolff, Hitler told him to carry on negotiations and keep the doors open, because 'they are the only doors open to us; we must fight it out to gain time. I shall join the party which approaches me first. It makes no difference which.' Wolff claims to have spoken about the senselessness of further resistance in Italy, but Hitler did not react.

The British interrogators who received Wolff's statement in the prisoner-of-war camp disbelieved his account of this talk with Hitler. The author's view is that if Wolff had told the truth about his talks in Switzerland, he would not have left Hitler's headquarters a free man, and that he must therefore have prevaricated, to give the impression that he was only sounding out the Allies on possible terms for peace negotiations with Hitler. He was lucky to have met Hitler during one of his calm periods.

Wolff knew that his life was in danger when he saw Hitler. He discovered that Himmler was opposed to him meeting the Allied representatives in Switzerland, even though Himmler himself was trying to negotiate with the Allies in Sweden; and that he had been denounced as a traitor by Walter Schellenberg, Himmler's trusted adviser.[20]

A bizarre interlude throws some light on Wolff's state of mind. Towards the end of February the Black Brigade reported to the SS that a British Captain Tucker had arrived from Switzerland, and had been captured. Tucker declared he had been sent with a secret message from Alexander to Graziani, which aroused suspicions of Graziani's loyalty in the minds of the Germans.

'Captain Tucker' was in fact Richard Mallaby, the bilingual British radio operator who had been an important link at the time of the armistice negotiations in September 1943. He had crossed the frontier near Lugano with some Italians to link up with the CLNAI in Milan on 15 February. Exhausted by walking across snow-covered mountains, and very hungry, they went into a restaurant at Lecco. The strain was too great for the Italian members of his party, who began to talk excitedly about Lugano and Switzerland. This aroused suspicions in Fascist sympathizers at nearby tables; they reported to the Black Brigade, who found on interrogation that each member of the party had more than one set of identity documents, plus packets of Swiss coffee and Swiss cigarettes. They were all arrested.

Once in a cell, Mallaby thought of his previous arrest and how he had been released to play an important role in the armistice talks, and of the comfortable treatment he had received then. Accordingly, he invented a cock-and-bull story that he was the bearer of 'a highly confidential message to Marshal Graziani from Alexander'. He asked to be taken to Graziani. The initial result was that Mallaby was taken to the Officers' Mess of the Black Brigade at Como, given dinner in the Mess, and 'very well treated'.

From Como Mallaby was taken to Milan, where an Italian general told him that everyone hoped 'his mission would be crowned with success'. The general took him to his private villa at Gardone where he dined with the family, and then on to Wolff's headquarters at Fasano.

Graziani was informed of Mallaby's arrival and that Wolff would interview him; the Italian commander was not asked to attend. The SS, deeply suspicious that Graziani might have sent a previous message to Alexander, and that Mallaby was bearing a response, kept him strictly to themselves.

On 26 February Mallaby had a two-hour interview with Wolff. Mallaby stated that his message was a personal one to Graziani from Alexander, to find out what arrangements were possible to ensure that Graziani's troops would help to preserve the industrial installations and public services from destruction by the Germans when they withdrew from Italy, and that the Republican army would not attack the Allies or the partisans as the Germans retreated.

Wolff told Mallaby that he had 'personally agreed with Cardinal Schuster that when the Germans withdrew they would not blow things up, but would merely immobilize industrial plants for not more than one year'. With regard to Graziani, Mallaby reported Wolff as saying that:

> ... he was a great personal friend and they had already agreed that when the Germans withdrew from N. Italy Marshal Graziani's men should withdraw too, shoulder to shoulder with their German comrades. There will thus be no question of Fascist troops remaining behind to preserve order.

Surprisingly, Wolff then gave Mallaby a half-hour lecture about the SS, explaining how it preserved the finest 'chivalrous ideals of mediaeval knighthood, and that the SS were now the only people in Germany who are in a position to see that any agreement made with the Allies is carried out'. He went on that anyone could see the Germans had lost the war, and that some sort of end would have to be put quite soon to the present conflict; as a personal friend of both Hitler and Kesselring, he could be useful. He asked that Mallaby should make the following offer to Alexander:

> If the Allies would desist from their present policy of supplying arms to Communist formations in North Italy, he would guarantee that the armed formations of other political groups in North Italy should be allowed to cross unmolested to South Italy.

Wolff was cordial. The Germans escorted Mallaby back to the frontier at Chiasso, but owing to a breakdown in the SOE arrangements with the Swiss he was interned until 9 April, and thus this important news about Wolff's intentions was not reported to Caserta. When Mussolini heard that Mallaby had been sent back to Switzerland without a word to him, he said, 'There is no hope of genuine and sincere collaboration with the Germans.' Graziani had no intention of allowing his troops to march over the Brenner Pass arm in arm with the Germans: he knew their only wish was to discard their uniforms and return home.

In the POW camp after the surrender, Wolff gave a very different account of his interview with Mallaby. According to Wolff, he told Mallaby that he was lucky not to have been shot as a spy, and asked him to give his word of honour he was an emissary from Alexander. 'He seemed a very decent boy, and I told him Graziani was a madman.'[21]

Even at this stage, Mussolini was dead against truces or parleys with the partisans. He had been very angry over the truce at Omegna on Lake Orta in September 1944, and was much put out when in January 1945 he received a report of the truce which had been made at Voghera (twenty miles from Pavia, south of the Po): in a neutral zone at Montesgalo near Sanguinana, the parish priest had organized a conference in the house of Conte Onecco between the partisans, the local German commanders and the commander of the Blackshirts, Captain Brusci. The initiative had been taken by the Germans because they wanted to secure the release of an interpreter, Engineer Troop, who was useful to them and had been taken prisoner by the partisans. Tuninetti, the prefect of the province, was not party to the talks, which produced a two-way traffic in food and household goods between the plain and the mountain. Eventually Troop was taken into the hills and shot because no partisan prisoners were released.

On receiving this report, Mussolini sent an order to all prefects that no talks were to be carried on with the partisans, and demanded an account of any that had occurred. The prefects all disclaimed any knowledge of truces, but without telling the Fascist authorities the Germans continued to negotiate with the partisans for the exchange of hostages and prisoners.[22]

As the Allies advanced into the Po Valley, Hitler ordered Jodl to instruct Vietinghoff that 'every foot of Italy must be defended'. As late as 21 April, Hitler ordered that 'positions must be defended with fanatical zeal, as this is the only means of breaking the Allied attack'. As Bologna had fallen at dawn on 21 April and the German troops, in disarray, were desperately trying to retreat across the Po by makeshift means because all the bridges were destroyed, these were the ravings of a lunatic. But Vietinghoff and Wolff obeyed, despite their overtures to the Allies.[23]

However, certain that the war was lost, not only in Italy but on both the western and eastern fronts, and strongly backed by General von Pohl, commander of the Luftwaffe, they were determined to put an end to unnecessary bloodshed. On 23 April, Wolff left Garda for Lucerne to meet the plenipotentiaries selected by Vietinghoff, Colonel Victor von Schweinitz and Major Max Wenner, who had been given written authority by Vietinghoff to sign an unconditional surrender of the German armies in Italy with Alexander at Caserta.

As soon as Wolff met Schweinitz and Wenner in Switzerland they tried to make an appointment to see Dulles, but he had just received a telegram from Washington, ordering him not to treat with any Germans. Wolff too received a telegram, from Himmler: 'The Italian front must be held intact; negotiations with the enemy, even of a local character, are forbidden.' Hitler was aware that his generals were considering abandoning him, and the peace negotiations Himmler himself had been pursuing in Sweden went far beyond the limits authorized by the Führer. It was an unpromising start.

However, at midnight on 24 April Wolff sent Dulles a copy of the original document of the authority to surrender signed by Vietinghoff. Dulles immediately got in touch with Caserta, reporting the arrival of the German delegation from Vietinghoff's headquarters and communicating the text of the authorization to sign a surrender. Alexander felt that such an overture must not be rejected, and asked London for instructions, emphasizing that the German envoys would have valid authority to sign a surrender document and that Vietinghoff, as the German commander in Italy, was capable of putting an armistice into immediate effect.

During the night of 25/26 April the British Prime Minister sent a personal message to Stalin explaining the situation and saying that he would give Alexander authority to accept the surrender of the 'considerable army on his front', but that all political issues were reserved for the three Governments – the USSR, USA and Britain. Churchill added, 'We have spent a lot of blood in Italy, and the capture of the German armies south of the Alps is a prize dear to the hearts of the British nation, with whom in this matter the United States have shared the costs and perils.' On 26 April Stalin sent his agreement; at last the way was clear for Wolff, after the long delay consequent on Stalin's obduracy. Churchill commented to Truman that 'the tone of Stalin's reply was greatly improved'.[24]

On 26 April Alexander was given permission to bring the German delegation to Caserta, but was told that no bargaining or negotiations could be carried on in Switzerland; if the German envoys refused to travel to Caserta, 'all contact with them must be discontinued'. Alexander was also ordered to inform the Soviet General Staff of this renewed approach, through the British military mission in Moscow, and to make it clear that it was a German initiative; he was also told to invite the Russians to nominate a representative to attend the negotiations in Caserta.

At Caserta, the Germans produced these formal authorities:

22 April 1945.

Lieutenant-Colonel von Schweinitz has been authorized by me to conduct negotiations within the frame of the instructions given by me and to make binding commitments on my behalf.

Signed: V. Vietinghoff.

25 April 1945.

I hereby authorize my chief adjutant SS Major Wenner to negotiate on my behalf and to make binding commitments on my behalf.

Signed: Wolff.

During the discussions, Schweinitz stated that he wanted assurances that all surrendering Germans would be treated as POWs and kept in Italy. He said that otherwise, bodies of men would refuse to surrender and take to the hills. General Morgan for the Allies replied that if they did so they would 'just be slaughtered'; Vietinghoff must surrender and then do his best to persuade his troops. Eventually this was agreed; tactfully and sensibly, Morgan added that he was sure it would not be British policy to keep German soldiers as POWs for a long period, and definitely not to send them far from Italy. He emphasized that this was a 'statement', not an 'agreement'.

The German delegates stated that they had authority from Graziani to include the Republican Army in the surrender; Graziani had given them this authority without consulting Mussolini.

At 2 p.m. on 29 April the surrender document was signed, with the cease-fire to operate from 2 p.m. on 2 May. However, the Germans said that it must be ratified by Vietinghoff, and there was no way of communicating with him by radio in Bolzano in code. It was vital that the surrender be kept secret, because if Hitler heard of it he would intervene at once. Schweinitz and Wenner had a long journey: they were flown to Lyons, and from there had to travel by car through Switzerland to Bolzano.[25]

News of the suspension of the negotiations in Switzerland on 25 April, after Vietinghoff had given his binding authority on 22 April, caused alarm at German headquarters in Bolzano. A heated wrangle broke out as Wolff, Vietinghoff and Hofer waited for the return of the delegates from Caserta. Hofer regretted losing his overlordship of the Pre-Alps, which he had enjoyed enormously, and on 30 April, without consulting the others, telephoned to warn Kesselring that Vietinghoff was about to surrender. This nearly wrecked the arrangement. Hitler had ordered Kesselring, as he had ordered Vietinghoff, to fight to the finish. Kesselring knew that if he became party to the defection of the German armies in

Italy, Hitler would probably have him arrested and executed. Such a fate had greeted another German general at Hitler's headquarters in Berlin a few days previously.

On 28 April Hitler had placed Kesselring in overall command of the Italian front as well as the western front. On receipt of Hofer's telephone call on 30 April, Kesselring gave orders for Vietinghoff's dismissal and replacement by General Schulz, who appeared at the Bolzano headquarters after a meeting with Hofer at noon on 30 April. An official investigation of the surrender negotiations was ordered, and Kesselring reported Wolff's treachery to Hitler.

Thus, when the delegates arrived back at Bolzano at midnight on 30 April, everything was in a state of flux. Fortunately, Wolff kept his head and remained firm. He arrested Schulz and his Chief of Staff, and cut telephone communications with Germany. Schulz, although under arrest, became reasonable in discussions, and finally he, Vietinghoff and Wolff agreed to put a 'fair case' to Kesselring for his decision. Last-minute efforts to reach Kesselring by telephone failed. Alexander demanded confirmation that the Caserta agreement would be honoured. Finally Schulz, Wolff, Pohl and Vietinghoff agreed to send out surrender orders to the units without authority from Kesselring.

At 11 p.m. the death of Hitler was announced on the radio. Even then, Kesselring refused to agree to the surrender, and sent teleprinter orders for the arrest of Vietinghoff and other officers. Wolff called out a special detachment of his SS with tanks to defend the headquarters. At 2 a.m. on 2 May, with the cease-fire due in twelve hours' time, Kesselring made contact with Wolff by telephone.

According to Wolff's account, Kesselring was 'removed from reality', and still believed that if the German armies in Italy capitulated they would be allowed to return to Germany to fight the Russians alongside Allied units. Wolff claimed to have told Kesselring that he would be the greatest war criminal of the lot if he refused to surrender to Alexander, and that any German general was a war criminal who went on fighting after Hitler's death had released them from their oath of loyalty to him.

By now the chief staff officers of the two German armies in Italy (Colonel Beelitz of 10th Army and Colonel Runkel of 14th Army) had arrived in Bolzano. They told Wolff their commanders would support any surrender terms because they did not even have enough ammunition to fight effectively against the partisans. And with Hitler dead, Schulz became strongly in favour of capitulation.

Wolff had sent a signal to Alexander, through a secret operator who had come from Switzerland with Wenner, that as Kesselring had deprived Vietinghoff of his command, Vietinghoff was not in a position to honour the signature of his representatives at Caserta; but that the commanders of the 10th and 14th Armies would give orders for surrender on their own responsibility, without Kesselring's authority and in spite of his opposition. This caused consternation in Caserta and London, and Alexander told the Foreign Office that he would only announce the surrender if his monitoring stations picked up wireless orders for surrender being passed to German units. Kesselring's refusal to agree to the surrender even after Hitler's death is inexplicable. He makes no reference to it in his memoirs.

Half an hour after Kesselring had put the telephone down, he rang Wolff again and said that he would agree to the surrender, but wanted 48 hours' delay before the public announcement. Alexander ignored this request; after his monitoring station picked up messages *en clair* in the late afternoon of 2 May from German commanders, ordering a cease-fire, he announced the surrender at 6.30 p.m. – four hours later than had been agreed at Caserta. Finally Italy's long agony was over.[26]

CHAPTER 15

Mussolini's end

IN EARLY MARCH, 1945, Mussolini decided to make an approach to the Allies. He sent his son Vittorio to see Cardinal Schuster in Milan to discuss the possibility of opening negotiations with the Allies. This was kept strictly secret from the Germans.

Vittorio met Schuster at the Cardinal's palace, and told him his father expected that Germany and the Fascist Italian Republic would soon change sides and 'move into the Anglo-American camp' in order to block the spread of Communism and the bolshevisation of all Europe; and that his father hoped for the help of the Vatican in contacting the Allies. Vittorio also said that an American officer had recently arrived with a message from General Mark Clark for Graziani, suggesting negotiations with the Republican Government. This, Vittorio said, had encouraged the Duce to turn to the Holy See for help. Schuster doubted the truth about the message to Graziani. Vittorio, who was stupid, must have accepted a muddled version of the arrival of Mallaby ('Captain Tucker').

The Cardinal said that if Mussolini put down his proposals in writing, he would send them to the Vatican for onward transmission to the Allies. Through the Papal Nuncio in Berne, Monsignor Bernardini, Schuster immediately sent a cable to the Vatican about this approach.

On 13 March Monsignor Tardini, assistant to Maglione, the Vatican Secretary of State, minuted to Pius XII in connection with Schuster's telegram:

1   It is absolutely astonishing (*sbalorditiva*) that Mussolini expects the Anglo-Americans to enter into an alliance with him and Hitler at a moment when they refuse any sort of negotiation.

2   In my view the Holy See should *not* try to act as a go-between because the response must be 'No' and then the Russians will seize on it as an excuse to fulminate even more fiercely against us.

3   The situation will become embarrassing if Mussolini does send written proposals because we can hardly refuse to pass them on, whereupon we should suffer the adverse consequences outlined in my point 2.

4   Taking everything into account, I feel we should reply with one of the following drafts:

a. It has recently been confirmed to us that the Allies will NOT depart from their formula of 'Unconditional Surrender'. Thus the Holy See, although in favour of a just peace, cannot act.

b. Your Eminence knows well the Holy See is working for a just peace. Recent authoritative information convinces us that the Allies will not depart from their 'Unconditional Surrender' formula.

NB We must not at any time give the impression that the Holy See is trying to divide the Anglo-Americans from the Russians.

The next morning Pius XII approved draft 4b, changing only one word in blue pencil, and a telegram was despatched to Schuster.[1]

Mussolini also sent Abbot Pancini, a close and trusted friend, to visit Bernardini in Berne and discuss the proposal for an alliance between Germany, Fascist Italy and the Allies. Pancini saw Bernardini on 9 March and gave him a pitiable account of conditions in north Italy, emphasizing the excesses of the Communist partisans and the Russian Mongol troops under German command. He said Mussolini knew that Himmler, but not Hitler, wanted to treat with the Allies, and gave details of a plan similar to the one disclosed by Vittorio Mussolini to Schuster, saying that Mussolini wanted Bernardini to pass this on the Vatican.

Pancini added that he had had several long and intimate conversations with the Duce since he came to Salò; Mussolini had become very unstable and subject to sudden changes of mind, often contradicting himself about important matters in the space of a few minutes; for example, in December he had told Pancini it was 'urgent' to talk to the Allies, in January he said such negotiations were 'three months too late', and a few weeks previously he had described them as 'premature'. Bernardini passed on to the Vatican Pancini's comments about the Duce's unreliability.

Bernardini wrote to the Vatican that it was his duty to warn the Pope that Schuster was 'far too optimistic' about the chance of success of Mussolini's new initiative, which was certain to be received badly by the local CLNAI. He also commented that there was no possibility of it 'being taken seriously'.

Tardini's telegram was too late to prevent Mussolini's unwelcome written plan arriving at the Vatican via Schuster and Bernardini. Schuster wrote that he was sending it purely out of 'charity', although he knew 'it was useless'.

The Duce suggested that when the German army left Italian soil, the Fascist Republican Government should install itself in another area, chosen in advance, from where it would put up strenuous resistance until the last man and cartridge. As an alternative to a last stand, the Duce proposed arriving at an agreement whereby the Republican troops would keep order, and the Allies would promise to prevent the partisans looting;

both the partisan and the Fascist forces would lay down their arms. He stipulated that all soldiers and civilians who had been serving the Fascist Republic should be exempt from prosecution, and in return promised he would dissolve the Republican Fascist Party.

After reading the document, Pius XII minuted to Tardini on the morning of 2 April that he should in strict secrecy ask D'Arcy Osborne for his opinion, although his Holiness also wrote that he was in no doubt that the Allies would refuse to relax their demand for unconditional surrender.[2] That evening Pius XII learned that the Russians had violently attacked Switzerland on Radio Moscow for being a party to peace negotiations, and as a result he decided that Osborne must not be approached. Schuster was informed that the Vatican believed there was no alternative to unconditional surrender.

The March 1944 Mussolini proposals belong to the dustbin of history, and are of interest only as betraying his state of mind as he realized that the total defeat of the Axis was close and inevitable, and as evidence of the Pope's extreme caution. Humiliated by receiving no response from his approach to Schuster in April, Mussolini seized again on a plan for a 'last redoubt', this time in the Sondrio area in the Valtellina, close to the Swiss and Austrian frontiers. He convinced himself that if he withdrew there with the rudiments of a government and surrounded himself with loyal Republican troops reinforced by strong German armour, he would be in a position to bargain with the Allies. He continued to delude himself into believing that once the war with Germany was over the Allies would want to move their armies urgently from Italy to block the Russian advance into central Europe.

Neither Wolff nor Graziani would entertain the plan for a redoubt in the Valtellina. Graziani knew about Wolff's efforts to surrender to the Allies, and had decided that he too would surrender his army, regardless of Mussolini. Pavolini, who commanded the Black Brigades, was enthusiastic for Valtellina, but pointed out to Mussolini that its success would depend on one hundred per cent German co-operation.

For four hours on 14 April Mussolini discussed the Valtellina plan with Wolff, Vietinghoff, Rahn and Graziani. The Germans were noncommital, but had privately repudiated it in advance since it contradicted their own plan to surrender to the Allies. Vietinghoff made difficulties about the amount of time needed to transfer enough German troops to the Sondrio area.

As the front in the Po valley began to crumble, Mussolini finally decided to defy the Germans, and moved himself and as much of his government as was practical to the Prefecture at Milan on 19 April. As he left Salò he was entirely in the dark about Vietinghoff and Wolff's efforts to surrender; he was convinced that if Milan fell he could slip back along Lake Como to Sondrio, protected by a strong screen of retreating German divisions. Although he had ordered Pavolini to transfer most of the Black Brigades to Sondrio, nothing was in fact being organized.

To keep his options open, Mussolini told Mellini to contact in Milan the Swiss representative accredited to Salò, Troendl, who courteously told Mellini that the Swiss Government would allow all the families of the leading Fascists to take asylum in Switzerland, and that, should Mussolini and his ministers appear at the Swiss frontier, they would be received, but put into internment. When Mellini related this to Mussolini, the Duce appeared relieved. Later the Swiss Government went back on Troendl's promise.

After seeing Troendl, Mellini returned to Salò, where on 23 April Rahn told him that secret negotiations were in progress at Caserta and about to be brought to a successful conclusion; this, according to Rahn, would prevent useless bloodshed in Italy and safeguard the Duce's person so that he would be able to play 'a useful role in the future in the fight against Bolshevism'. Rahn said he was waiting for just one more message, and then he would put something concrete before the Duce.[3]

From Salò Mellini had no way of contacting Mussolini, except by post office telephone on a public line. He dare not give the Duce such sensitive news when there was a danger of it being overheard. All Mellini told Mussolini by telephone was that Rahn would shortly come to Milan with 'very interesting news'. Had Mellini been able to inform him of the surrender negotiations, it would have made a great difference to the Duce's conduct and to his future. Although Rahn had seen Mussolini in Milan on 20 April, he had said nothing about Wolff's and Vietinghoff's approach to Alexander. Instead, he pressed Mussolini to leave Milan for the safety of the Bolzano area, where Vietinghoff's defeated troops were being concentrated as they retreated before the Allies.

In Milan, Mussolini tried to contact the CLNAI. At first he was unsuccessful. However, on 25 April Achille Marazza, the Christian Democrat leader, and General Cadorna agreed to meet Mussolini later in the day at Cardinal Schuster's palace, to discuss a peaceful take-over of Milan by the partisans. At 3.30 that afternoon, the Communists dissenting, the Committee of the CLNAI authorized Marazza and Cadorna to attend, provided the basis of any agreement was 'unconditional surrender'. As we have seen, the CLNAI had already come to an agreement in principle with Wolff at local level for the German troops to leave Milan without being attacked, so long as they committed no industrial sabotage. Wolff was expected to join the discussion with Mussolini at the Cardinal's palace, but was held up by the partisans.

The story that Wolff intended to come to Milan on 25 April to sign a surrender to the Allies of all the German army in Italy, though given by several Italian historians, is without foundation. The Allied governments had vetoed any negotiations other than those at Caserta. Wolff knew this, and was seeking only a local arrangement with the CLNAI for Milan – again, of course, behind Mussolini's back.

While they were waiting for the other delegates to arrive, Mussolini and Schuster chatted in the Cardinal's study. Mussolini told Schuster he proposed to dissolve the Republican Army and the Fascist militia and retire to the Valtellina with 3,000 men. When Schuster remarked that 3,000 men must be an exaggeration, Mussolini smiled and said, 'You may well be correct.'

Cadorna, Marazza and Lombardi were the CLNAI representatives, while Mussolini brought Barracu, Zerbino, Graziani and Bassi, the prefect of Milan. Mussolini stated that he was ready to talk, on the understanding that the CLNAI would guarantee his own safety and that of the other Fascist leaders and their families.

Cadorna reminded him that the Allies had offered to treat all soldiers of the Republic, whether conscripts or volunteers, as prisoners-of-war. One of the Fascists then said that they were all soldiers, by virtue of being members of the Fascist Party. However, Cadorna brought them up sharply by saying that POW treatment would not be extended to those accused of war crimes, and that all they could promise Mussolini was a fair trial; the terms were unconditional surrender within two hours; then, if the Fascist troops concentrated in the Milan–Lecco–Como triangle, they could lay down their arms and go home. Mussolini nodded and appeared to be about to agree.

Graziani said they could not sign an agreement without informing the Germans, because loyalty to an ally was a tradition of honour in the Italian army, and the main reason why they had continued to back the Germans. This was insulting to the CLNAI, insinuating as it did that breaching the German alliance in September 1943 had been dishonourable. Marazza said the CLNAI did not need lessons in honourable conduct. Cadorna pointed out that worries about honour relating to the Germans were irrelevant, because they were negotiating with the CLNAI without telling Mussolini.

This produced an explosion from Mussolini. Schuster went off to his study and came back with the papers relating to the negotiations between Wolff and the CLNAI in which he was the intermediary. Nothing had been signed, but he read out the draft clauses and said the Germans would sign that evening.

Furious, Mussolini yelled, 'Now I can say Germany has stabbed Italy in the back. The Germans have always treated us as slaves; I am going to telephone to their Vice Consul [also named Wolff] and tell him that as the Germans have been traitors I am now free to act as I like.' He threatened to broadcast the news of Wolff's treachery at once, but Schuster begged him to be patient. When Cadorna then said that surrender by the Germans was much more important than a Fascist surrender, Mussolini shouted, 'The German army is disintegrating.' Schuster reminded the meeting that it was vital to reach an agreement in order to save the population much suffering, and they must stay calm.

Graziani then became aggressive again, pointing out the number of atrocities the partisans had committed and producing documents about them. The CLNAI delegates said that a decision must be reached as the situation was critical and the crowds were getting out of hand. Bassi said the Milanese would stay calm if they were not provoked by the Resistance. Mussolini added, 'I have no illusions; once the first shot is fired ...', and threw up his hands in a gesture of resignation.

Both Cadorna and Lombardi now felt some pity for Mussolini; as had so many Italians over the years, they found his voice, mouth and eyes compulsive, and understood how he had so often mesmerized his political opponents into supporting him against their better judgement. Cadorna said he was moved by seeing 'an idol fall from his pedestal', and Lombardi whispered to him, 'Deep down I feel for him.'

The Cardinal pressed Mussolini to come to a decision. He replied that he needed an hour to talk to the German Vice Consul, and then he would reply. After Mussolini left, the German Vice Consul, Wolff, appeared, as did Sandro Pertini, the fiery leader of the Socialist Party, together with Communist members of the CLNAI. Pertini said either the Germans must surrender, or the partisans would attack them, and that Mussolini must be tried at once by a CLNAI court. Vice Consul Wolff, a polite diplomat, replied that he was not able to get in touch with his superior, General Wolff. According to Cadorna, the Communists did not want any pact, and the meeting ended when they heard that Mussolini had suddenly left Milan without sending a reply. The Duce had ordered an immediate departure for Como with his entourage, telling the German officer in charge of his escort, 'Your General Wolff has betrayed me'.

It was a fatal mistake. Apart from Mussolini's one outburst, the tone of the conference had been calm (perhaps because Pertini and the Communist members of the CLNAI arrived late); if Mussolini had agreed to surrender, he could have stayed safely in the palace until American troops arrived. And there would have been no bloodshed in Milan. As it was, there were considerable casualties on both sides. Probably he decided to leave because Bassi told him of the stormy intervention of the left-wing CLNAI members after he left the meeting, and of their threat of a summary trial. By dawn the following morning the partisans were in command of Milan, and issued their first radio broadcast.

As soon as he arrived at Como, Mussolini wrote to his wife Donna Rachele that she was to seek asylum with their younger children in Switzerland, and that the Swiss had agreed to receive her (in the event, she was turned back at the frontier). He added: 'Everything is over.'[4]

At Como Mussolini stayed in the Prefecture. He and his colleagues debated whether to go to Switzerland or the Valtellina. Mussolini was still under the impression that Pavolini had organized a strong force of Blackshirts at Sondrio, and that another column would shortly arrive from Milan. He was hopelessly wrong. The men of the Black Brigades were deserting fast and going home, as the Royal Army had after 8 September 1943.

Buffarini Guidi, who had been living in Como since his dismissal, turned up and urged Mussolini to escape to Switzerland. He made a probing sally to see if the road to the frontier was open. He was stopped by partisans, and returned to tell Mussolini that his only route of escape was up the lake to Sondrio. Then came news that Troendl had been instructed to retract his promise that Mussolini would be allowed to cross the frontier. The Duce was trapped.

In the early hours of 27 April the Duce and his party moved to Mennagio, after Pavolini arrived with only a single armoured car. Graziani refused to go with them, saying that his duty was to stay with his army. He went to Wolff's headquarters at Fasano, where he wrote out a formal authority for the German delegates at Caserta to surrender the Republican Army on the same terms as the Germans. He neither asked permission nor informed Mussolini of this.

A column of 200 Germans arrived at Mennagio, trying to reach Austria via the Stelvio Pass. Mussolini and his ministers, including Pavolini, attached themselves to the German column and proceeded up the west side of Lake Como. At Musso the convoy was stopped by partisans. After a long parley the Germans were told they could continue, as long as there were no Italians with them.

Mussolini put on a German helmet and greatcoat and hid in the last truck. His unmistakable features were recognized by a partisan, and he was taken to Dongo as a prisoner amid loud cries of 'We have got Mussolini'.

His companions were machine-gunned to death at the lakeside. They included Pavolini, Bombacci, Barracu, Zerbino, Petacci (the brother of Claretta, Mussolini's mistress), and Lacistri, whose only guilt was that he was Mussolini's personal pilot. The next morning, 28 April, Mussolini and Claretta Petacci were shot, on the orders of the CLNAI in Milan and strictly against the instructions issued by the Americans. Their bodies, together with those of fourteen other Fascists shot at Dongo, were taken to the Piazzale Loretto in Milan and hung upside-down from the roof of a garage. There the corpses were derided by the citizens of Milan, who only five months before had hailed Mussolini as a hero. He was 61.[5]

When captured, Mussolini was carrying documents which he hoped to use in his defence at his trial as a war criminal. They were stolen by the partisans, as was a large quantity of gold from a vehicle in the convoy. Probably these documents were laudatory letters from Winston Churchill and Austen Chamberlain, who prior to the Abyssinian War had admired Mussolini and emphasized how he aligned Italian foreign policy with Britain's. Both the gold and the letters have disappeared.

Graziani was more fortunate than Mussolini and the others. He telephoned to Cadorna that he would surrender. Cadorna and an American escort took him to Milan, where he was put in the San Vittore prison. He narrowly escaped assassination: as they arrived at the prison, a bomb was let off near his car, blinding one of the Americans. Graziani was unscathed, and afterwards expressed his deep thanks to the American escorting officer, Lieutenant Dadderio, for saving his life.[6]

Notes

Initials and numbers refer to classification in the Public Record Office, Kew. The Italian Documents reference numbers refer to their classification when in the Foreign Office Library. The important Italian Government official history of the military events of September and October 1943 was written by General Torsiello. I refer to it as 'Torsiello'.

CHAPTER 1: ITALY CHANGES SIDES

1. Lamb, *The Ghosts of Peace*, pp. 147–58.
2. Butcher, *My Years with Eisenhower*, p. 348.
3. Deakin, *The Brutal Friendship*, p. 495.
4. Italian Documents 103287.
5. FO 371/37331; Prem 4/100/8.
6. Lamb, op. cit., p. 195; Prem 3/476/9; Albert Garland and Howard Smith, *Sicily and the Surrender of Italy*, pp. 451–511, 522–53; Castellano, *La Guerra continua*, pp. 113–16; Castellano, *Roma Kaputt*, pp. 124–5.
7. Castellano, *Roma Kaputt*, pp. 124–5.
8. WO 214/1307.
9. Ibid.
10. Castellano, *Roma Kaputt*, pp. 108–9, 135, 186–7; Castellano, *La Guerra continua*, p. 135; Westphal in Richardson, *The Fatal Decision*, p. 169; Castellano, *Roma Kaputt*, pp. 108–17.
11. Zangrandi, *1943*, pp. 399–440; WO 204/7301.
12. Torsiello, *Le Operazioni delle unità Italiane, Settembre–Ottobre 1943*, pp. 49–52; Kesselring, *Memoirs*, pp. 175–9, 200–2.
13. Cadorna, *La Riscossa*, pp. 48–66; Paolo Monelli, *Roma 1943*, pp. 253–336. Monelli gives an authoritative account from Italian sources of the surrender negotiations, the fighting around Rome and other events described in this chapter.

CHAPTER 2: MUSSOLINI RETURNS

1. Italian Documents 007013–18.
2. Graziani Trial, Vol. II, p. 1166.
3. Deakin, op. cit., p. 355.
4. Ibid., p. 558.
5. FO 371/43905.
6. Deakin, op. cit., p. 567.
7. Graziani Trial, Vol. I, pp. 206–9.
8. Ibid., Vol. II, p. 1165.
9. Bocca, *La Repubblica di Mussolini*, p. 52.

10. Tamaro, *Due Anni di Storia*, Vol. II, pp. 205–9. The original draft in Mussolini's execrable handwriting is hardly readable.
11. Dolfin, *Con Mussolini Nella Tragedia*, p. 71.
12. Ibid., pp. 86–91.
13. Ibid., p. 53.
14. Ibid., p. 90.
15. Italian Documents 045420.
16. Ibid., 045434.
17. Deakin, op. cit, p. 588.

CHAPTER 3: ITALIAN JEWS UNDER THE NAZIS

1. Trabuco, *La Prigionia di Roma*, pp. 11–13.
2. Steinberg, *All or Nothing*, p. 106.
3. Ibid., pp. 117, 130, 131.
4. Ibid., p. 1.
5. Ibid., p. 56.
6. Ibid., pp. 47–84.
7. Ibid., pp. 76–113.
8. Stille, *Benevolence and Betrayal*, p. 74; Steinberg, op. cit., p. 10.
9. Stille, op. cit., pp. 88–9.
10. Meir Michaelis, *Mussolini and the Jews*, pp. 352–91.
11. From the trial of Kesselring and the joint trial of Mältzer and von Mackenson it is possible to reconstruct in detail the pogrom of October 1943 and the Ardeatine cave massacre. The full Kesselring trial is in WO 235/366–376; Mältzer and von Mackenson, WO 235/438–440.
12. Michaelis, op. cit., p. 365; WO 235/366.
13. *Actes et Documents du Saint Siège relatifs à la Seconde Guerre Mondiale*, Vol. IX, pp. 511, 530.
14. Ibid., pp. 505, 507.
15. Cab. 122/866; FO 371/37255.
16. *Actes et Documents*, Vol. IX, pp. 509–10.
17. Michaelis, op. cit., pp. 366–77.
18. Ibid., pp. 352–64; *Actes et Documents*, Vol. IX, pp. 505–6.
19. A. von Kessel, 'Der Papst und die Juden' in F. J. Raddatz (ed.), *Summa iniuria oder Dürfte der Papst Schweigen* (Hamburg 1963), pp. 167–71.
20. Georgio Gariboldi, *Pio XII, Hitler e Mussolini: Il Vatican Fra le Dittature*, pp. 206–7.
21. Gariboldi, op. cit., p. 217 *et seq.*, where he reproduces oral evidence given by General Wolff to the Tribunal for the Beatification of Pius XII. It should be noted that Wolff is unreliable as a witness. Wolff's statement as a POW, in FO 371/46787, also confirms that he saw the Pope.
22. Thomas Moloney, *Westminster, Whitehall and the Vatican Role of Cardinal Hinsley 1935–43*, pp. 230–7; Anthony Rhodes, *Vatican in the Age of the Dictators*, pp. 260–1.
23. Gariboldi, op. cit., pp. 147–55.
24. *Actes et Documents*, Vol. V, pp. 319–20, quoted in Gariboldi, op. cit., p. 162.
25. Michaelis, op. cit., p. 390.
26. Ibid., p. 351.
27. Pier Carnier, *Lo Sterminio Mancato*, p. 380.
28. Primo Levi, *If this is a Man*, pp. 22–5.
29. FO 371/439050.
30. Michaelis, op. cit., p. 351.
31. Bucca, op. cit., pp. 205–10.
32. Deakin, op. cit., pp. 620–1.
33. Italian Documents 088560–088564.

34. Stephen Roberts, *The House that Hitler Built*, p. 262; Bocca, op. cit., p. 208.
35. Michaelis, op. cit., p. 387.
36. R. Katz, *Black Sabbath*, p. 296.
37. De Felice, *Storia degli Ebrei sotto il Fascismo*, p. 522; Origo, *War in Val d'Orcia*, p. 117.
38. Michaelis, op. cit., pp. 405, 392.

CHAPTER 4: KESSELRING'S ATROCITIES

1. Katz, *Death in Rome*, p. 17.
2. WO 235/366.
3. Katz, op. cit., pp. 102–4; Gariboldi, op. cit. p. 270.
4. WO 235/366; WO 235/439.
5. Ibid.
6. Gariboldi, op. cit., pp. 205–45; WO 235/366.
7. Mellini, *Guerra Diplomatica a Salò*, pp. 2–22.
8. Gariboldi, op. cit., p. 247.
9. Katz, op. cit., p. 239.
10. WO 235/439.
11. WO 235/366; WO 235/439; Gariboldi, op. cit., pp. 236, 432.
12. WO 235/366; WO 204/11497.
13. FO 371/43876.
14. WO 235/375; Kesselring's order is Exhibit 16.
15. WO 204/11716.
16. WO 235/366.
17. WO 235/366: WO 235/584 (Simon's trial).
18. WO 204/11497; WO 235/584.
19. Montanelli, *L'Italia della Guerra Civile*, pp. 200–2; WO 235/589.
20. WO 235/585.
21. Bergonzini, *La Lotta Armata*, p. 355.
22. Montanelli, op. cit., pp. 248–63; Italian Documents 104830.
23. WO 204/11471; WO 235/366, Exhibit 11.
24. WO 235/366.
25. WO 204/11497.
26. WO 235/584.
27. Italian Documents 112494–8; Cione, *Storia della Repubblica Italiana*, pp. 242–3.
28. WO 235/375, General Kreseman's trial.
29. Ibid., Documents 44, 45, 46.
30. WO 235/290, General Tensfeld's trial.
31. Algardi, *Processo ai Fascisti*, p. 220; WO 235/584–588, General Simon's trial.
32. WO 235/92.
33. WO 235/128.
34. WO 204/11497.
35. WO 235/375 (Exhibit 59).
36. Prem 8/707; WO 235/438.
37. FO 1060/493.
38. Kesselring, *Memoirs*, pp. 174, 228, 230, 224, 301.
39. Letter to author from Sir Ian Fraser; WO 204/11496.

CHAPTER 5: VERONA, 1944

1. Deakin, op. cit., pp. 626–8.
2. Montanelli, op. cit., p. 119.
3. All the minutes are in the Italian Documents. See also Deakin, op. cit., pp. 629–32.
4. Dolfin, op. cit., p. 97.

5. Bocca, op. cit., pp. 115–16.

6. Pisenti, *Una Repubblica necessaria*, pp. 92–8.

7. Deakin, op. cit., p. 642. A detailed account of the Verona Trials can be found in Vicenzo Cersosimo, *Dall'istruttoria alla fucil'azione*; Montanelli, op. cit., p. 134.

8. Dolfin, op. cit., p. 197.

9. Pisenti, op. cit., pp. 96–8.

CHAPTER 6: MUSSOLINI'S NEW ARMY AND THE FATE OF 600,000

1. Deakin, op. cit., pp. 587–90; Graziani, *Processo*, Vol. 1, pp. 260–73.

2. Deakin, op. cit., p. 591.

3. Italian Documents 045767–045771; 045714; 045715; 045723–4.

4. Deakin, op. cit., pp. 593–4; Italian Documents 045757–045761; 045714.

5. Deakin, op. cit., pp. 596–606; Italian Documents 048296–048449.

6. Italian Documents 045804–045813.

7. Italian Documents 045794; 045925–45; Memoranda from Canevari.

8. Italian Documents 097361–097364; Bocca, op. cit., p. 105.

9. Italian Documents 044541–044556.

10. Italian Documents 045532, *et seq.*

11. Zangrandi, op. cit., pp. 730–3.

12. Dolfin, op. cit., pp. 282–4.

13. Italian Documents 044541–044556.

14. Italian Documents 045540–045650.

15. Italian Documents 045663.

16. Italian Documents 048130–048134; Lazzero, *Le SS Italiane*, pp. 115–16.

17. Italian Documents 045718–045732.

18. Deakin, op. cit., pp. 681–9.

19. Zachariae, *Mussolini si confessa*, pp. 110–20; Italian Documents 049851 – text of Duce's speech to San Marco Division.

20. Italian Documents 048150–4; Panza, *L'esercito di Salò*, p. 182.

21. Panza, op. cit., p. 194.

22. Italian Documents 048286–048289.

23. Italian Documents 048190.

24. Deakin, op. cit., pp. 706–14; Zacchariae, op. cit., pp. 123–31.

25. Deakin, op. cit., p. 722.

26. Italian Documents 00694–006965; Mellini, op. cit., pp. 37–8.

27. Italian Documents 006975.

28. Italian Documents 007043–007050; Mellini, op. cit., pp. 159–71.

29. *Actes et documents*, Vol. X, pp. 595–626.

30. Ibid., pp. 553 and 607; Mellini, op. cit., p. 60; Spampanato, *Contro Memoriale*, Vol. II, p. 320.

CHAPTER 7: THE NEW ARMY DISAPPOINTS

1. Deakin, op. cit., pp. 715–26; Mussolini's letter to Himmler, Italian Documents 048219–048220.

2. Dolfin, op. cit., p. 199, quoting from Mazzolini's unpublished diary.

3. Italian Documents 048243–048246.

4. Italian Documents 048248.

5. Italian Documents 048024.

6. Italian Documents 048017.

7. Graziani, *Processo*, Vol. I, p. 310.

8. Italian Documents 048120–048121.

9. Italian Documents 048101–048105.

10. Italian Documents 048261 *et seq.*

11. Italian Documents 048119–048120.
12. Italian Documents 048254.
13. Deakin, op. cit., p. 735.
14. Author's recollection.
15. Zachariae, op. cit., pp. 135–8.
16. Italian Documents 048058.
17. Italian Documents 048034–048039.
18. Italian Documents 048085–048089.
19. Italian Documents 048092–048099.
20. Liddell Hart, *Rommel Papers*, p. 371.
21. Graziani, *Ho difeso la Patria*, p. 455; Panza, op. cit., p. 186.
22. Italian Documents 048100 ('boiled in oil'); Panza, op. cit., pp. 188–96.
23. Panza, op. cit., pp. 200–9.
24. Zangrandi, op. cit., pp. 732–3.

CHAPTER 8: AEGEAN TRAGEDY AND ATROCITIES

1. Prem 3/3/3.
2. WO 204/106; Lamb, *Churchill as War Leader*, pp. 237–8.
3. Eduardo Scala, *La Riscossa*, p. 29; Zangrandi, op. cit., p. 481.
4. Zangrandi, op. cit., p. 535; Professor Vaccarini, Paper to Anglo-Italian Colloquium.
5. Torsiello, op. cit., pp. 465–99; Italian Documents 005526–005547; Trial of General Lanz, formerly in FO 680/141 in PRO, now in Imperial War Museum.
6. Giulio Lazzati, *Ali Nella Tragedia*, pp. 18–20; 29.
7. Author's recollection; Lazzati, op. cit., p. 29.
8. Torsiello, op. cit., p. 486; WO 204/1307.
9. R. Formato, *L'Eccidio Cefalonia*, pp. 25 *et seq*; Moscardelli, *Cefalonia*, pp. 58 *et seq*. G. Giraudi, *A Cefalonia e Corfu*.
10. Torsiello, op. cit., pp. 465–97.
11. Italian Documents 005525–005548.
12. FO 680/141; FO 680/142; Trials and Documents in Lanz case, now in Imperial War Museum; Giraudi, op. cit.
13. Torsiello, op. cit., pp. 501–24; WO 204/1307.
14. Torsiello, op. cit., p. 517; WO 204/106.
15. Torsiello, op. cit., pp. 510–24.
16. Prem 3/3/3.
17. Torsiello, op. cit., pp. 541–72; Report of General Kleeman's German interpreter, in archives of Commissione per lo Studio della Resistenza dei militari Italiani all' estero, Via Sforza, Rome; WO 201/2519.
18. Prem 3/3/3; Lamb, *Churchill as War Leader*, p. 241; Torsiello, op. cit., p. 540.
19. WO 201/2519: long, detailed report by Major Dolby on his mission.
20. WO 201/2399.
21. Prem 3/3/3; Lamb, op. cit., p. 243.
22. WO 201/2511; WO 201/1709; Lamb, op. cit., pp. 239–43; Torsiello, p. 544.
23. Prem 3/3/9; Prem 3/3/3.
24. WO 201/2399; Lamb, op. cit., p. 245.
25. Cab. 106/603: Report by General Tilney on fighting on Leros.
26. Espinosa, *Regno del Sud*, p. 287.
27. Prem 3/3/9.
28. Torsiello, op. cit., p. 577.
29. Italian Documents 049820; account of Monseigneur Mario Schierano, in archives of Commissione per lo Studio della Resistenza Italiana all'estero; Torsiello, op. cit., pp. 436; 456–9.
30. Torsiello, op. cit., pp. 445–50.

31. Italian Documents 046047–046056.
32. Torsiello, op. cit., pp. 403–22; Italian Documents 093198–093209.
33. Torsiello, op. cit., p. 381.
34. WO 204/106.
35. Torsiello, op. cit., pages 353–7.
36. Lamb, op. cit., p. 255; Italian Documents 048142.
37. Tamaro, op. cit., Vol. II, pp. 294–315; Michael Lees, *Rape of Serbia*, pp. 99–103; Lamb, op. cit., p. 255.
38. Tamaro, op. cit., Vol. II, p. 501; WO 204/1780.
39. Prem 3/3/3; Lamb, op. cit., pp. 240–7.
40. Hinsley, *Military Intelligence in World War Two*, Vol. III Part I, p. 133; WO 200/2806.
41. H. Macmillan, *War Diaries. The Mediterranean 1943–1945*, p. 664.

CHAPTER 9: THE ITALIANS AND BRITISH POWS

1. WO 208/3253. The reference number of the infamous 7 June signal is DDMI 87190. This stands for Deputy Director of Military Intelligence. There were three Deputy Directors, but Brigadier Crockatt was in charge of everything to do with captured British soldiers. Telegrams from the War Office do not normally include the name of the sender.
2. Letter from Colonel Mander to author.
3. WO 208/3253.
4. WO 208/3253; Italian Documents 102386.
5. Torsiello, op. cit., p. 64; FO 371/37273.
6. WO 208/3253; WO 208/3250.
7. Absalom, *A Strange Alliance*, pp. 37–63.
8. Ibid.; WO 208/4255
9. WO 208/4255; McCaffery Diary; Absalom, op. cit., p. 67.
10. WO 208/3374b; WO 208/2262; Absalom, op. cit., pp. 209–21.
11. WO 208/3250; Absalom, op. cit., p. 240.
12. WO 208/4916.
13. WO 208/3416; Absalom, op. cit., pp. 35–6.
14. Iris Origo, *War in Val d'Orcia*, pp. 145 *et seq*.
15. WO 208/3396.
16. Mander, *Mander's March on Rome*, page 114; WO 208/3396.
17. WO 235/19, Bellomo Trial; WO 235/80, Sommavilla Trial.
18. WO 235/1980; WO 235/252.
19. WO 235/324.
20. WO 235/245; WO 235/323.
21. WO 235/98.
22. WO 235/111.
23. WO 235/139.
24. WO 235/81.
25. Information from Keith Kilby, Chairman of San Martino Trust.

CHAPTER 10: THE ROYAL ARMY AND THE ALLIES

1. Tamaro, op. cit., Vol. I, pp. 500 *et seq*.; Torsiello, op. cit., pp. 143–90.
2. Ibid.
3. Torsiello, op. cit., pp. 143–266.
4. Croce, *Cultura Tedesca e politica Italiana*, p. 6; Tamaro, op. cit., Vol. I, p. 491.
5. Torsiello, op. cit., pp. 267–301; 589–634.
6. Privately published history of the '35 Reggimento Artigliera' by General de Biase; author's experience.
7. Croce, *Quando L'Italia era tagliata in due*, p. 146.

8. WO 204/6653; Kogan, *Italy and the Allies*, pp. 100–1.
9. WO 170/4260. X Corps War Diary has much evidence on the Maiella. The full story is in Carlo Bonciani, *'F' Squadron*.
10. FO 371/37364.
11. Lamb in *Diplomazia e storia della relazioni Internazionali*, pp. 468–70; Lamb in *War Monthly*, no. 69.
12. Ibid; WO 204/7586.
13. Kogan, op. cit., p. 73 (quoting from the Allied Commission *Weekly Bulletin*, 16 November 1944).
14. *The Times*, 13 October 1943; WO 170/7501.
15. Author's recollection; WO 170/4260.
16. WO 204/7586.
17. WO 170/4261; Lamb, op. cit.
18. Ibid.; WO 170/7501, War Diary of 50 BLU with Friuli Division.
19. WO 170/4261, War Diary X Corps.
20. Bongiovanni, *Guerra in Casa*, pp. 169–80; WO 170/7504, War Diary of 51 BLU with Cremona.
21. WO 170/4261; WO 170/7504.
22. WO 170/4286; WO 204/7588, XIII Corps War Diary; WO 170/7506, War Diary of 56 BLU with Mantua; conversation with Field Marshal Harding.
23. WO 170/7501; WO 170/7504; Bongiovanni, op. cit., pp. 244–9.
24. FO 371/43911; Christopher Seton Watson, 'Il trattato di pace Italiano, La prospettiva Inglese', *Italia Contemporanea*, Vol. 182, March 1991.
25. Lamb, *Ghosts of Peace*, pp. 213–14; FO 371/43857; FO 371/43814.
26. FO 371/43805.
27. Lamb, op. cit., pp. 146, *et seq.*; FO 371/29924; FO 371/29936.
28. FO 371/49759; FO 371/50779.
29. FO 371/50782.
30. Seton-Watson, op. cit.; FO 371/57080; FO 371/57082; FO 371/60703.

CHAPTER 11: PARTISANS, SOE AND OSS

1. Kogan, op. cit., pp. 100–4.
2. Kogan, op. cit., p. 103; Salvadori, *Resistenza ed Azione*, pp. 234–5; Battaglia, *Story of the Italian Resistance*, pp. 140–96; McCaffery, unpublished diary.
3. FO 371/43876.
4. McCaffery, op. cit.
5. WO 204/7283.
6. WO 204/9905; WO 106/3964.
7. Letter to author from Kim Isolani.
8. WO 106/3964; FO 371/43879.
9. McCaffery, op. cit.
10. L. Lewis, *Echoes of Resistance*, pp. 78–81, 110–12.
11. FO 371/43111.
12. FO 371/43876.
13. *The Times*, 13 May 1944.
14. Kogan, op. cit., p. 105.
15. Cadorna, op. cit., pp. 118–20.
16. FO 371/49797.
17. Italian Documents 112216, 112564.
18. McCaffery, op. cit.
19. Cadorna, op. cit., pp. 161–4.
20. McCaffery, op. cit.
21. Italian Documents 112583–112584; 50022.
22. Cadorna, op. cit., p. 164; Italian Documents 112586.

23. Italian Documents 112579–112594; 112561–112563.
24. Cadorna, op. cit., p. 165.
25. WO 204/7304.
26. WO 204/11415.
27. WO 204/7301.
28. Author's interview with Major Wilcockson, August 1992.
29. WO 204/7301.
30. FO 371/49796; Lewis, op. cit., pp. 70–1.

CHAPTER 12: DIVIDED VIEWS ON THE PARTISANS

1. Hinsley, op. cit., Vol. III, Part 2, pp. 313–14.
2. Author's interview with Field Marshal Harding, July 1985.
3. WO 106/3964.
4. FO 371/49797.
5. WO 106/3964.
6. FO 371/49796.
7. FO 371/49796.
8. Kogan, op. cit., p. 110.
9. FO 371/49788.
10. WO 204/1993.
11. Ibid; information supplied by C. M. Woods, SOE Adviser, Foreign Office.
12. FO 371/49798; Cadorna, op. cit., pp. 178–206.
13. Cadorna, op. cit., pp. 207–22.
14. Ibid., pp. 246–52.
15. Harris, *Allied Military Administration of Italy*, p. 302; WO 204/9934.
16. Ibid.
17. Harris, op. cit., pp. 302–16.
18. WO 311/359.
19. Documents supplied by Gervase Cowell, SOE Adviser, Foreign Office.
20. Italian Documents 032156.
21. Harris, op. cit., p. 302.
22. Ibid., p. 305.
23. WO 106/3965A.
24. Harris, op. cit., p. 307.
25. Carnier, *L'Armata Cosacca in Italia 1944–1945*, pp. 15–32.
26. Italian Documents 096593–096595.
27. Italian Documents 096402–096406.
28. Italian Documents 096407–096414.
29. Carnier, op. cit., pp. 56–60.
30. David Goodwin in *No. 1 Special Force*, Vol. II, p. 178; Lewis, op. cit., p. 77.
31. FO 371/49797.
32. Italian Documents 106568–106569.
33. Italian Documents 064236–064250.
34. WO 204/7301; FO 371/49799; Algardi, *op. cit.*, pp. 220–26.
35. Italian Documents 004646.
36. Transcript of Porzus Trial in archives of the Istituto regionale per la storia dei movimenti di liberazione nel Friuli Venezia Giulia, Villa Prima, Salita di Getta 38, Trieste; Carnier, *Lo Sterminio Mancato*, pp. 252–3; WO 204/7301; FO 371/49797.

CHAPTER 13: FRONTIER PROBLEMS

1. Carnier, *Lo Sterminio Mancato*, pp. 225–30; Harris, op. cit., pp. 328–49; WO 170/4286, War Diary of XIII Corps; the War Diary of 2 New Zealand Division has not survived; *Trieste e Venezia Giulia 1943–1954*, p. 140.
2. WO 170/4286; FO 371/48814; *Trieste e Venezia Giulia*, pp. 165–251; Harris, op. cit., p. 244;

Lamb, *Churchill as War Leader*, pp. 272–5; Valdevit, *La Questione Di Trieste*, pp. 94–109; 250–75.

3. WO 170/4286.
4. McLynn, *Fitzroy Maclean*, pp. 272–86.
5. WO 170/4286.
6. Carnier, op. cit., pp. 218–19.
7. WO 170/4285; Carnier, op. cit., pp. 170, *et seq.*, information from C. M. Woods, SOE Adviser, Foreign Office.
8. Carnier, op. cit., p. 201; WO 204/2190; information from Contessa Burgos and Signora Covassi.
9. Carnier, *L'Armata Cosacca in Italia 1944–45*, p. 171; FO 371/49797.
10. WO 204/9789.
11. Ibid.; Harris, op. cit., pp. 317–18.
12. FO 371/49803; Major Morton's Report.
13. Harris, op. cit., pp. 319–27.

CHAPTER 14: THE AXIS BITES THE DUST

1. Italian Documents 050009–050014; 061938–061949; 062059–062083; Bertoldi, *Salò*, pp. 85–6; Lazzati, *Ali nella Tragedia*, pp. 224–5. Lazzati shows the great courage displayed by Fascist pilots when the war was clearly lost by the Axis.
2. Italian Documents 096605–096661.
3. Italian Documents 050017–050018.
4. Italian Documents 112075, *et seq.*
5. Italian Documents 006968–006976.
6. Italian Documents 078640–078656; 061110–061167.
7. Pisenti, *op. cit.*, pp. 83–7.
8. Italian Documents 113052–113053; 050042–050045.
9. Italian Documents 00705–00712; Mellini, op. cit., pp. 52–3.
10. Mellini, op. cit., pp. 50–1; Deakin, p. 741.
11. Deakin, op. cit., pp. 742–4; Mellini, op. cit., p. 55; Zachariae, op. cit., pp. 190–2.
12. Zachariae, op. cit., pp. 190–7.
13. Mellini, op. cit., pp. 202–3.
14. Zachariae, op. cit., pp. 175–6.
15. WO 204/7283.
16. WO 204/1993; Cione, op. cit., p. 442.
17. Mellini, op. cit., pp. 94–104.
18. Gariboldi, op. cit., pp. 215, 251, 253; FO 371/46786.
19. Prem 3/198/2
20. FO 371/46785; FO 371/46786.
21. Mallaby File in SOE Archives in Foreign Office; Italian Documents 032154; FO 371/46785.
22. Italian Documents 112204–112208.
23. Hinsley, op. cit., p. 707.
24. FO 371/46784; FO 371/46785.
25. WO 32/11456.
26. FO 371/46785; FO 371/46786.

CHAPTER 15: MUSSOLINI'S END

1. Vatican *Actes*, Vol. II, pp. 703–4.
2. Ibid., pp. 708–9; 723.
3. Mellini, op. cit., pp. 148–50.
4. Cadorna, op. cit., pp. 250–3; Cione, op. cit., pp. 458–60; Spampanato, op. cit., Vol. III, pp. 102–11.
5. Spampanato, op. cit., Vol. III, pp. 125–69.
6. Cadorna, op. cit., p. 201.

Bibliography

Absalom, Roger, *A Strange Alliance* (Florence, 1991)

Aga-Rossi, Elena, *L'Italia Nella Sconfitta* (Naples, 1985)

Alfieri, Dino, *Dictators Face to Face* (1954)

Algardi, Zara, *Processi ai Fascisti* (Florence, 1958)

Anfuso, Filippo, *Roma Berlino Salò (1936-1945)* (Rome, 1950)

Augenti, G. P., Mastino Del Rio, G., Carnelutti, F., *Il Dramma Di Graziani* (Bologna, 1950)

Battaglia, R., *Story of the Italian Resistance* (1957)

Bergonzini, Luciano, *La Lotta Armata* (Bari, 1975)

Berti, Alberto di, *Viaggio Nel Pianeta Nazista* (Milan, 1989)

Bertoldi, Silvio, *Salò* (Rome, 1976)

Bocca, Giorgio, *La Repubblica di Mussolini* (Rome, 1977)

Boccazzi, Cino, *Missione Col Di Luna* (Milan, 1977)

Bonciani, Carlo, *'F' Squadron* (1947)

Bongiovanni, Alberto, *La Guerra in Casa, Settembre '43-Aprile '45* (Milan, 1967)

Butcher, Henry, *Three Years With Eisenhower* (1946)

Cadorna, Raffaele, *La Riscossa* (Milan, 1983)

Carnier, Pier, *Lo Sterminio Mancato* (Milan, 1988)

—— *L'Armata Cosacca in Italia 1944-45* (Milan, 1990)

Carter, Barbara Barclay, *Italy Speaks* (1947)

Castellano, Giuseppe, *Come Firmai L'Armistizio Di Cassibile* (Milan, 1945)

—— *Roma Kaputt* (Milan, 1963)

—— *La Guerra Continua* (Milan, 1967)

Cersosimo, Vincenzo, *Dall'istruttoria alla fucil'azioni* (Rome, 1949)

Chadwick, Owen, *Britain and the Vatican during the Second World War* (Cambridge, 1986)

Cione, Edmondo, *Storia della Repubblica Sociale Italiana* (Caserta, 1948)

Colummi, Cristiana, et al., *Storia di un esodo Istria 1945-1956* (Trieste, 1980)

Croce, Benedetto, *Cultura Tedesca e Politica Italiana* (Rome, 1914)

—— *Quando L'Italia Era Tagliata in Due* (Rome, 1948)

Deakin, F. W., *The Brutal Friendship - Mussolini, Hitler and the Fall of Italian Fascism* (1962)

De Biase, General A., *35 Reggimento Artigliera* (privately published)

De Felice, Renato, *Storia degli Ebrei sotto il Fascismo* (Turin, 1952)

De Luna, Giovanni, *Storia del Partito d'Azione 1942-1947* (Milan, 1982)

Derry, Sam, *The Rome Escape Line* (1960)

Dolfin, Giovanni, *Con Mussolini Nella Tragedia* (Milan, 1949)

Dollmann, Eugen, *The Interpreter* (1967)

Domenco, Roy Palmer, *Italian Fascists on Trial 1943-1948* (1991)

Dulles, Allen, *The Secret Surrender* (1967)

Ellwood, David W., *Italy 1943-1945* (Leicester, 1985)

Espinosa, Agostino, *Il Regno del Sud* (Rome, 1946)

Farran, Roy, *Winged Dagger* (1948)

Federazione Italiana Associazione, Partigiani, *Special Force*, Vols I and II (Bologna, 1990)

313

Formato, Romualdo, *L'Eccidio Cefalonia* (Milan, 1968)
Foot, M. R. D. and Langley, J. M., *MI 9* (1979)
Fusi, Valdo, *Fiori rossi al Martinetto* (Milan, 1968)
Gariboldi, Giorgio, *Pio XII, Hitler e Mussolini* (Milan, 1988)
Garland, Albert N. and Smith, Howard, *Sicily and the Surrender of Italy* (Washington D.C., 1965)
Garzia, Italo, *Pio XII e L'Italia* (Trento, 1988)
Giraudi, G., *A Cefalonia e Corfu* (Milan, 1982)
Goodwin, David, *No. 1 Special Force*, Vol. II (Bologna, 1987)
Graziani, Rudolfo, *Processo*, Vols. I–III (Rome, 1948–1950)
—— *Ho Difesa la Patria* (Rome, 1947)
Harris, C. R. S., *Allied Military Administration of Italy 1943–45* (1957)
Hinsley, H. *Military Intelligence in World War Two*, Vol. III, Parts 1 and 2 (1990)
Katz, Robert, *Death in Rome* (New York, 1967)
—— *Black Sabbath* (1969)
Kessel, A. von, *Der Papst und die Juden* (Hamburg, 1963)
Kesselring, Albert, *The Memoirs of Field Marshal Kesselring* (1954)
Kogan, Norman, *Italy and the Allies* (Cambridge USA, 1956)
Lamb, Richard, *The Ghosts of Peace* (Salisbury, 1987)
—— *Churchill as War Leader* (1991)
—— 'Cooperazione Militare fra l'Italia e gli alleate 1943–45', in *Diplomazia e storia della relazioni Internazionali – Studi in onore di Enrico Serra* (Eds Alessandro Migliazza & Enrico Decleva) (Milan, 1991)
—— 'Rome 1943' in *War Monthly*, No. 69, 1981
Lazzero, Ricciotti, *Le SS Italiane* (Milan, 1982)
—— *Le Brigate Nere* (Milan, 1983)
Lazzati, Giulio, *Ali Nella Tragedia* (Milan, 1970)
Lees, Michael, *The Rape of Serbia* (New York, 1990)
Lett, Gordon, *Rossano ('An Adventure of the Italian Resistance)* (1955)
Levi, Primo, *If This is a Man* (1987)
Lewis, Laurence, *Echoes of Resistance* (Tunbridge Wells, 1985)
Liddell Hart, B. M., *Rommel Papers* (1953)
McCaffery, John, *No Pipes or Drums* (unpublished Diary)
Mack Smith, Denis, *Mussolini's Roman Empire* (1976)
—— *Mussolini* (1981)
Macmillan, Harold, *War Diaries: The Mediterranean, 1943–1945* (1984)
Mander, d'A., *Mander's March on Rome* (Gloucester, 1987)
Mather, Carol, *Aftermath of War* (1992)
McLynn, Frank, *Fitzroy Maclean* (1992)
Mellini, Ponce de Leon, *Guerra Diplomatica a Salò* (Bologna, 1950)
Michaelis, Meir, *Mussolini and the Jews* (Oxford, 1978)
Moloney, Thomas, *Westminster, Whitehall and the Vatican Role of Cardinal Hinsley* (Tunbridge Wells, 1985)
Monelli, Paolo, *Roma 1943* (Milan, 1948)
Montanelli, Cervo, *L'Italia della Guerra Civile* (Milan, 1983)
Moscardelli, Giuseppe, *Cefalonia* (Rome, 1945)
Moss, Eric, *Solvitur Ambulando* (Saved by Walking) (Swanage, 1990)
Origo, Iris, *War in Val d'Orcia* (1984)
Pansa, Giampaolo, *Il Gladio e L'Alloro* (Milan, 1991)
Pavone, Claudio, *Una Guerra Civile* (Turin, 1991)
Pisenti, Piero, *Una Repubblica Necessaria* (Rome, 1977)
Reviglio, Antonio, *La Lunga Strada del Ritorno* (Milan, 1975)
Rhodes, Anthony, *The Vatican in the Age of the Dictators, 1922–1945* (1973)

Richardson, William (ed.), *The Fatal Decision* (with commentary by General Siegfrid Westphal) (London, 1965)

Roberts, Stephen, *The House that Hitler Built* (1937)

Salvadori, Max, *Resistenza ed Azione* (Bari, 1951)

Scala, Eduardo, *La Riscossa* (Rome, 1948)

Scalpelli, Adolfo, *San Sabbia*, Vols I & II (Milan, 1988)

Serra, Enrico, et al., *Italia e Francia dal 1919 al 1939* (Milan, 1981)

Seton Watson, Christopher, 'Il Trattato di pace Italiano', in *Italia Contemporanea* Vol. 182, March 1991 (Milan)

Spampanato, Bruno, *L'Italia Liberata* (Rome, 1951)

—— *Contro Memoriale* (Milan, 1952)

Steinberg, Jonathan, *All or Nothing – The Axis and the Holocaust, 1941–43* (1990)

Stille, Alexander, *Benevolence and Betrayal* (1992)

Tamaro, Attilio, *Due Anni di Storia 1943–1945*, Vols I–III (Rome, 1948, 1949)

Teatini, Giuseppe Corrado, *Diario Dall'Egeo* (Milan, 1990)

Toscano, Mario, *Dal 25 Iulio all'8 Settembre* (Florence, 1962)

Torsiello, Mario, *Le Operazioni Delle Unità Italiane Nel Settembre–Ottobre 1943* (official War History) (Rome, 1975)

Trabuco, *La Prigionia di Roma* (Rome, 1945)

Trieste e Venezia Giulia 1943–1954 (no editor's name) (Rome, 1960)

Trionfera, Renzo, *Valzer di Marescialli 8 Settembre '43* (Milan, 1979)

Vaccarini, Prof., Paper to Anglo-Italian Colloquium, Imperial War Museum, September 1991

Valdevit, Giampaolo, *La Questione Di Trieste, 1941–1954* (Milan, 1987)

Vatican, *Actes et Documents du Saint Siège Relatifs à la Seconde Guerre Mondiale*, Vols. 9–11 (Rome, 1975, 1980, 1981)

Wilhelm, Maria de Blasio, *The Other Italy* (1988)

Zachariae, Georg, *Mussolini Si Confessa* (Italy, 1948)

Zangrandi, Ruggero, *1943: 25 Iulio–8 Settembre* (Milan, 1964)

Zuccotti, Helen, *Italians and the Holocaust* (New York, 1987).

Appendix

A. Kesselring's Order, dated 20 June 1944

In my appeal to the Italians I announced that severe measures are to be taken against the partisans. This announcement must not represent an empty threat. It is the duty of all troops and police in my command to adopt the severest measures. Every act of violence committed by partisans must be punished immediately. Reports submitted must also give details of countermeasures taken. Whenever there is evidence of considerable numbers of partisan groups a proportion of the male population of the area will be arrested, and in the event of an act of violence these men will be shot. The population must be informed of this. Should troops etc. be fired at from any village the village will be burnt down. Perpetrators or ringleaders will be hanged in public. [Signed] Kesselring

[WO 204/11496]

B. Extract from Order by German 5 Corps, 1 S. No. 391, 9 August 1944

The public must be made to realise that any signs of partisan activities in their midst will have the most unpleasant consequences for them as well.

111. In areas where partisans are found in large numbers, or where acts of sabotage are of frequent occurrence and the criminals cannot be found, the following steps are to be taken:

(a) *Arrest of Hostages.* These are to be chosen on the recommendation of the Fascist Militia, the Secretary of the Fascist Party or the Prefect of the Province. The enemy of the country is the Communist. Prefects, Party Secretaries, and other Fascist Headquarters are instructed to prepare lists of all Communists in the area, so that these elements are always at their disposal. Hostages may be taken from the circles which produce these criminals, so that, should shooting be necessary, a blow is dealt at others of the same ideology. It is a mistake to concentrate on the so-called 'rich and upper classes'.

(b) If there is a recurrence of acts of violence, an appropriate number of the hostages will be shot. I reserve the right to order the shooting. This is to be brought to the notice of the population in advance, so that their responsibility in this matter is established and brought home to them.

(c) If crimes of outstanding violence are committed, especially against German soldiers, an appropriate number of the hostages will be hanged. In such cases the whole population of the place will be assembled to witness the execution. After the bodies have been left hanging for 12 hours, the public will be ordered to bury them without ceremony and without the assistance of any priest.

[WO 204/11496]

C. Massacre at Bardine San Terenzo, 17–27 August 1944

STATEMENT OF:

> Padre Lino DELLE PIANE,
> Convento dei P.P. Francescani di Soliera.

Who saith,

I am a Padre at the above convent.

On the 21 August 44, at the request of Major CONTRI of the LUNENSE Brigade of Partisans, I went to the village of BARDINE to officiate at the burial of a number of bodies.

As I approached the River BARDINE which runs immediately in front of the village, I saw on both sides of the road, a number of bodies. The majority of these were tied by the neck to fencing posts, others were tied in similar manner to poles which support the wires. All had been shot.

Further along the road I found the wreckage of a burned out German motor lorry. To the chassis of this I found four other bodies tied by the neck to such projections as the headlamps, radiator cap and door handles. They too had been shot.

I counted the corpses and there were fifty-three in all. I was present when various photographs were taken of them. I have since seen these and I definitely identify them as authentic reproductions of what I saw. [These revolting pictures were produced as evidence at Kesselring's trial and are in the PRO.] These men were not of BARDINE or SAN TERENZO. There is a strong belief that they had been brought by the SS from NOZZANO CASTELLO and were formerly inhabitants of PIETRASANTA.

I later saw in the locality of VALLA, one hundred and seven bodies of men, women and children. These were all persons of SAN TERENZO and all had been shot. Five were men, the remainder women and children.

Scattered around the vicinity of VALLA, I found a further ten bodies. These were men.

That day, one hundred and seventy persons were killed in the district of SAN TERENZO. Ten persons for every German killed.

In the vicinity of the German truck I found two notices written in Italian. These had been left by the Germans after the killing of the fifty-three hostages.

The signs read:

> 'This is the way all anti-Fascists
> and enemies of the Axis shall end.'

> 'This is the first revenge taken for
> the seventeen Germans killed at BARDINE.'

[WO 235/375]

D. Massacre at Bardine San Terenzo, 17–27 August 1944

AFFIDAVIT

I, John BAXENDALE, a former Serjeant in the Corps of Military Police, serving with 78 Section, Special Investigation Branch, Central Mediterranean Forces, with a permanent home address at 49 Leeds Road, Otley in the County of Yorkshire, make oath and say as follows:

1. On the 27th of August 1945, acting on instructions, I commenced investigations in the area of BARDINE SAN TERENZO, Italy. During my investigations I questioned a considerable number of Italian civilians and as a result of the statements made by 37 of these civilians, I discovered that between the 17th and the 27th August 1944, German troops killed 369 Italian civilians, mostly women and children, as reprisals for partisan activities.

2. In the above area, during August 1944, a considerable amount of partisan activity was directed against the German troops. The 16 SS Reichsführer Division was deployed to counteract this activity. On 17th August a party of SS troops returning from a requisitioning raid were attacked by partisans, and in the resulting action 17 Germans were killed and their vehicle destroyed by fire. On the same day in another area, close by, a Staff car was attacked and a Colonel of the German Army and a passenger killed.

3. As a result of these actions SS troops at once searched various villages in the vicinity, looted houses and killed 24 civilians. 53 men from a nearby SS detention centre were taken to the burnt-out German vehicle. Some were tied to the vehicle, and some to posts nearby, and were shot, 49 were killed. Their bodies were not removed. About the same time SS troops visited San Terenzo, rounded up civilians, chiefly old men and women and children, and took them to the village of VALLA and indiscriminately shot them. The reprisal lasted till 19th August and resulted in 175 persons killed, 104 of whom were women and children.

4. By 23 August it was apparent that arrangements were being made for a further, and more extensive reprisal. That evening a conference was held at the Officers' Club at CARRARA, and was attended by 23 SS Officers and a Colonel LUDOVICI of the 'MAI MORTE' Bn (Italian). The meeting was endorsed by an SS German Major. It was decided that a reprisal should take place in the area of the APUANIA ALPS, and should commence that night or early next morning. The Italian Colonel promised 100 Fascist soldiers to operate with the SS troops.

5. Early the next morning large numbers of SS and Italian troops entered a large number of villages and commenced an organised massacre and looted and burnt houses and farm buildings. The reprisal was continued for four days.

6. Between the 17th and 27th August 1944 altogether 369 persons, chiefly women and children, were massacred. Damage included 454 houses totally destroyed.

[WO 235/375]

E. Massacre at Cintolese, 23 August 1944

STATEMENT OF:

BARNI Elisa,	Female,
No. 41 Cintolese,	aged 55 years.
Commune of Monsummano,	
Pistoia.	

Who saith,

I am a widow living in CINTOLESE where I have lived all my life.
In June 1944, together with my son BARNI Dante aged 27 years, and his family I

evacuated from here and went to live in the marshes. Living in the same house were a number of other evacuees, whilst a short distance away lived my married daughter Iole and family.

Early on the morning of the 23rd August 1944, I heard several bursts of machine-gun fire coming from the marshes. A short time later Signora Neda CIOLI, and her father called to see us. Soon after their arrival a party of German soldiers appeared. They ordered us from the house and began to search it. After this all the other women and myself were told to go towards the CASTEL MARTINI while the men were taken away in another direction.

I remained in the vicinity of the castle the whole morning during which time the firing continued in the marshes. Several times I tried to go and see what was taking place there, but I was prevented by the German soldiers.

About 1900 hrs I managed to go in search of my daughter and her family. When I reached a point about 200 yards from the house where they had been living, I came across the dead bodies of BRINATI Iole, my married daughter, 29 years of age, who was wounded in the face. BRINATI Pietro, her husband aged 34 years. Their daughter Giovanna aged 8 years, who had a wound in the head. BRINATI Carlo, 41 years of age, the brother-in-law of my daughter. BRINATI Celia, 41 years of age, his wife, and Giovanni their 15 year old son. I remember seeing about five more bodies there, but I was so upset at this discovery that I cannot recall who they were.

I returned to the castle and stayed the night along with the other women. The following morning in consequence of what was said to me, about 1000 hrs I went to the cemetery near the castle. There I saw about 20 corpses of men, women and children. I walked around and recognised one as that of my son DANTE who was wounded in the head. All these people appeared to have been shot.

Neither my son nor any of my relatives were connected in any way with the Partisans and did no harm to the Germans whilst they were here. I cannot describe any of the Germans I saw that day and I do not know where they came from.

[WO 235/324]

F. Massacre at Cintolese, 23 August 1944

STATEMENT OF:

DON QUIRICONI Renato   Male
No. 2 Cintolese.   Aged 33 years.

Who saith,

I am the assistant priest of CINTOLESE, a position I have held for the past six years.

About 0900 hrs on the 23rd August 1944, I had just taken mass when I learned that three Italian civilians had been killed in the marshes. I wanted to go there but I understood that it was dangerous and so I remained at the church. About this time I could hear a lot of shooting coming from the direction of the marshes which continued throughout the morning.

Later that day I was informed of the deaths of some more civilians and the bodies had been taken to the cemetery at CINTOLESE. I went there where I saw the bodies of a number of people who were inhabitants of this district. They had bullet wounds in various parts of their bodies and appeared to be dead. I performed Benediction on these bodies whilst their relatives were bringing more victims. I understood that these people had been killed in the marshes by German soldiers.

About noon the following day, I was at the cemetery when some German soldiers brought more bodies in a truck. By this time graves had been prepared so I officiated at the burial service on the following:

8 Members of the ARINCI family
7 Members of the GIACOMELLI family
6 Members of the MALUCCHI family
5 Members of the ROMANI family
4 Members of the LEPORT family
3 Members of the TOGNOZZI family
3 Members of the SIMONI family
2 Members of the PARLANTI family
2 Members of the IOZZELLI family
5 Members of the BINI family
3 Members of the CRIACHI family
3 Members of the GRASSI family
3 Members of the MALUCCHI family
2 Members of the FIDI family
2 Members of the INNOCENTI family
2 Members of the OCCHIBELLI family

together with ROMITI Alciste, COIA Walter, MONTI Ferdinando, ZERBINI Dario, MALUCCHI Gino and DISPERATI Lino.

I continued this burial service on the following day, when the following bodies were interred: ROMANI Giuliana, LEPORI Angelo, PARLANTI Ada, LEPORI Cesare and GIANNINI Livio.

On the 28th August 1944, I officiated at the burial of FERRONI Angelo, and again on the 20th Oct. 1944, of MALUCCHI Maria, MALUCCHI Pierina and LEPORI Gino, these last three named had previously been buried in the cemetery at PESCIA. This I understood was because they had died of their wounds in the hospital there.

Owing to the fact that the following fourteen bodies were found near CASTEL MARTINI they were buried in that cemetery. They were six members of the SILVESTRI family, seven members of the NATALI family and BARNI Dante.

[WO 235/324]

G. Massacre at Tenerano, 24 August 1944

STATEMENT OF:

Priest Don Marino POLI,
Cecina.

Who saith,

I have carried out the duties of the village priest of TENERANO for the past twelve months.

On the 24th August 1944, about five hundred German and Fascist troops collected in TENERANO. At this time the LUNENSE Brigade of Partisans held the commanding heights about two kilometres from and overlooking the village. There was considerable exchange of fire between these partisans and the troops, until the soldiers withdrew from this area the following day.

The people of TENERANO fled on the arrival of the Germans in their village. Three men who returned later to their property, were shot. The village was systematically destroyed by fire, only a few houses remaining undamaged.

Prior to the destruction of the village the houses were looted. The cattle were rounded up and taken away by the troops when they left.

During the morning of the 13th September 1944, about fifty German soldiers returned to TENERANO. Most of the people by this time had returned to their houses and were surprised by the arrival of these troops. On the outskirts of the village, the Germans killed eleven people in front of their houses, three men, three women, and five children.

[WO 235/580]

H. Massacre at Compignano, 2 September 1944

We were refugees at Balbano, Cipriani's house, when on the 2nd of September at about 5 p.m. the SS soldiers broke in my house, ordering us to evacuate the house in an hour and go up the mountains toward Compignano. We begged them to let us remain because we did not know where to go, and besides that we had with us my 75 year old mother who was paralysed; but they didn't let us do this and strongly insisted, threatening us if we didn't leave. We decided, therefore, to go away and started to put together a few of the most necessary things we might need. Meanwhile, the criminals had noticed my two sons: Giotto, 24 years old, Claudio, 20 years old and 5 relatives who were living with me as refugees.

With the excuse of taking them to work, they took them away. Instead of putting them to work as they had assured us, they were assassinated, killed by machine-gun shots and then thrown in a nearby canal. The ground where they had been killed near the church of Compignano, was covered with lime in order to hide this criminal action.

In all, 13 people were assassinated, two of them were my sons, other five, relatives of mine and other six people from Massarosa; all this was referred to us and confirmed by a person who survived from the assassination, who now lives near the lake of Massacciuccoli (Pisa).

Miss Anna Luciano (Pisa) was the interpreter of this Compignano Hqs. She is the daughter of Andrea Luciano and sister of Antonio Luciano who live in Via La Tinta, Pisa. She was very nasty and malicious in her expression so that these people would be assassinated. The above mentioned spy and interpreter followed that Command up north on the 5th of Sept. 1944, date of their retreat.

Actions against the parents of this spy are very urgent, and as soon as possible she should be found and punished. If possible those German war criminals should also be killed as well as the Italian criminals who helped them in this murder; I ask this to revenge my two innocent sons.

The Father of the two murdered
Sons Giotto and Claudio

Bianchi Arturo
Via Alessandro della Spina, 5
Pisa

[WO 204/2190]

I. Kesselring's Order, 24 September 1944

[Because of complaints by Mussolini, Kesselring issued this order; the following documents show how it was ignored.]

1. Army HQ Staff 10 Army
2. Army HQ Staff 14 Army
3. Army in LIGURIA
4. C-in-C Opz Zone ALPENVORLAND
5. C-in-C Opz Zone ADRIATIC Coast
6. Gen Pierip of German Armed Forces ITALY
7. German Naval Command ITALY
8. Luftflotte 2
9. Supreme Head of SS and Police ITALY

Info: 10. Plenipotentiary of Greater German Reich with Italian Government Ambassador Dr RAHN.

With respect to the operations against Partisans and larger scale fighting against them incidents have occurred within the past few weeks which caused the greatest harm to dignity and discipline of the German Armed Forces which had nothing to do with the punitive measures.

Because operations against partisans should be conducted with all means available, innocent elements sometimes are made to suffer.

Major Operations instead of pacifying a district bring greater disquiet amongst the population and cause food shortages of gravest degree, which eventually fall as a burden upon the German Armed Forces; this is a clear sign that the action was wrongly carried out and can only be considered as a 'Robber's Raid'.

The Duce as well, has complained bitterly to the plenipotentiary of greater German Reich with the Italian Government, Ambassador Rahn, about the method of execution of various operations against partisans and punitive measures, which have lately been conducted against the local population and not against the partisans proper.

The result of these enterprises is that the confidence in the German Armed Forces has been gravely undermined, has gained us new enemies and assisted the enemy's propaganda.

The responsible leader of the individual operation against partisans must therefore issue before the commencement of operation clear orders relating to the general situation, as to the treatment of the population in the partisan infested district and specifically to the degree requisitioning is permissible and what punitive measures may be taken. Such punitive measures are not to be left to the discretion of subordinate Commanders. The principle must be that measures are only to be taken against the actual partisans, and not the innocent civilian population. I appeal herewith to the sense of responsibility of the individual leaders, who are responsible for the maintenance of the dignity and discipline of the German Armed Forces and Police. As heretofore the partisans are to be attacked with all possible means; in the case of unjustified attacks on the civilian population I shall relentlessly bring these responsible to account.

(signed) KESSELRING

[As translated for the Kesselring trial: WO 235/375]

J. Massacre at Marzabotto, 29 September 1944

[Evidence of one of the few survivors of the Marzabotto massacre]

> PIERINI Lidia, 18 years of age,
> daughter of Olindo (deceased), housewife,
> Resident at MURAZZE di MARZABOTTO
> (Prov. BOLOGNA)

From January 1944 I was living in CERPIANO. On the morning of the 29th September 1944, about 7.30 hrs, I saw that some houses below CERPIANO were on fire. I was afraid and went to CASAGLIA, which is a locality 3 km. South of S. MARTINO, where I arrived about 8 hrs. I took shelter in the church together with other people.

About 9 o'clock of the same day 6 or 7 Germans arrived and entered the church; I noticed that they were wearing a grey-green uniform, were armed and were wearing two white signs which I knew to be those of the SS. The Germans ordered us to leave the church and made us go to the cemetery of CASAGLIE which is about 150 m. from the church. We were about 50 in number composed of women and about 20 children. I can affirm that that morning no partisans were in the village and that I heard no shots.

The Germans made us line up in front of the chapel of the cemetery. Two persons only were questioned by a German who spoke fair Italian; these two persons were questioned in the church of CASAGLIE. As soon as we were lined up in the cemetery the Germans started firing at us with their rifles, I was hit in the right thigh and fell to the ground unconscious. A short while after I came to and saw the Germans leaving. I remained on the ground in the cemetery throughout the 29th September and on the morning of the 30th September I managed to return to CERPIANO. During my walk I hid in a wood where I remained until the evening of the same day. Then I went to an air raid shelter near CERPIANO where I found other civilians.

[WO 235/580]

K. The SS at Marzabotto, 29–30 September 1944

STATEMENT OF:

> Pte. LEGOLL Julien,
> Infantry Gun Platoon,
> 5 Company, 16th SS PG. Division Recce Unit

I am 20 years of age and am a student of Natural Sciences from ALSACE.

I was conscripted into the German Army on the 23rd May 1943, and attached to the 16th SS PG. Division Recce Unit, on about the 20th September 1944.

On the night 28/29th September 1944, No. 1 Company Recce Unit, together with Infantry Gun Platoon of 5 Company attached to which I belonged, were paraded in MONTORIO.

We were then addressed by the C.O. No. 1 Company – Obersturmführer SEGELBRECHT – and told that we were to go into action against partisans and that our orders were to retaliate by the indiscriminate shooting of all persons in the vicinity in the event of our meeting with any fire whilst on march. He added that these orders had been received from the C.O. of the Recce Unit – Sturmbahnführer REDER.

Ammunition was then distributed and we were then marched off at about 0600 hours, 29th September 1944. We came upon a group of three farmhouses, from the cellar of one of which a burst of tommy-gun shots was fired, without any casualties resulting. One of the farmhouses was about 50 to 70 yards away from the other two, which were close together and the shots came from the solitary farmhouse. No. 1 Company Recce attacked the other two farmhouses, meeting with no resistance and fetched out the inmates; about 30 civilians in all, two of whom were elderly men and the remainder women and children. These civilians were stood up in front of a wall and killed by a machine-gun fire by a private, whose name I cannot remember, on orders of Obersturmführer SEGELBRECHT. The bodies were left lying where they fell and the buildings were set on fire. I saw these civilians shot and it happened about 0800 hours. I was standing some 15 metres from Obersturmführer SEGELBRECHT when I heard him give the order, which was 'SHOOT THEM ALL AT ONCE'.

After about half-an-hour's march we saw three women and three or four children, fleeing from us. When they were first spotted the N.C.O. in charge of the Infantry Gun Platoon, Unterscharführer Wolf, gave the order to shoot them all. Two men, whose names I can't remember, went off in pursuit and I saw them shoot them from a distance of between 10 and 20 metres. Afterwards, one of these two men was detailed to make sure that they were dead, but they were all dead and the bodies were left lying where they fell.

About half-an-hour later we met two male civilians carrying firearms, whom we took to be partisans. These civilians were fired at and shot dead on the spot from a distance.

The two farmhouses, from which these two civilians had been seen to come, were then searched. Nothing was found and the houses were set on fire. Whilst burning, I heard five or six grenades go off.

About 0930 hours, we came upon a solitary farmhouse, outside of which I saw two women and three or four children. Without any orders, one man from No. 1 Company, whom I do not know, ran forward and placing his machine-gun on the ground, opened fire and shot them. The bodies were left there and the house was burnt. We descended into the valley and at about 1100 hours came upon a farmhouse with a small outhouse. In the house we found fifteen to twenty women and children and one male civilian and apprehended them. They were marched along with us for about fifteen minutes, when we met the O.C. No. 1 Company, Obersturmführer SEGELBRECHT and the O.C. 5 Company Obersturmführer SAALFANG, and the latter ordered us to take these people along for a few kilometres and then release them.

We then retraced our steps, climbed another hill and about 1500 hours came across a small party of four civilians (one old man about 70, one woman, one girl and a boy aged about 14 to 15 years). Two men from the Infantry Gun Platoon, one of whom was Sturmann PIELTNER, advanced and without orders given shot them at a distance of 50 to 60 metres by rifle fire. They were left lying where they fell. They were shot in front of a house. In the course of the march the Infantry Gun Platoon had fired about 15 to 20 farm buildings.

Between 0330 and 0400 hours on the 30th September 1944, No. 1 Company, together with Infantry Gun Platoon of 5 Company attached, marched off from MONTORIO. At about 0800 hours the Infantry Gun Platoon was detailed to go off and capture a place described as SAN MARTELLO. We reached this locality about 0900 hours, it consisted of a church and three farm buildings. Unterscharführer WOLF deployed the Platoon, consisting of 20 men around the village and small-arms fire was turned upon it for about ten minutes . . . As we drew near to one of the houses we heard the screams of a frightened woman. The N.C.O. in charge of No. 3 section Rottenführer Knappe approached a window of this house and without looking inside threw in a hand grenade. Four of us then entered the building and found a woman aged 50 to 60 dead. She had undoubtedly been killed by the grenade. I was among the party that found her. The whole village was then set on fire but the church would not burn. When setting these houses on fire furniture was piled together, hay or straw was placed underneath and fired. In the church an attempt was made to burn the seats of wood without success. Before the attempt to burn the church the platoon commander, Wolf, gave orders for the altar to be destroyed, and being a Catholic I left the church. I returned however in time to see that the altar had been wrecked, and attempts made to destroy the church by fire.

Our short rest was interrupted by the appearance of about 30 to 40 women and children escorted by three SS men whom I believe belonged to No. 2 or 3 Company of the Recce unit. They brought the party up to where we were sitting, and asked Röhler what was to be done with them. Röhler said 'They will be shot'. The three SS men then left. The women and children were then stood up against the wall of the farmhouse where the old woman had been killed. They made an attempt to get away but were collected again. Röhler then ordered Sturmann Pieltner to execute them with his machine-gun. I heard Pieltner mumble an objection, whereupon Röhler drew his revolver, under the threat of which I then saw Pieltner mow down the women and children with his machine-gun.

On our return to billets Segelbrecht addressed the company by platoons, and he told us the action had been very successful and that he had heard from Sturmbahnführer Reder (Major) that 800 partisans had been killed and that he (the Sturmbahnführer) congratulated the company on our work. Personally I am of the opinion that the majority of the partisans killed were women and children. In addition to the civilians I saw shot, I also saw single and groups of corpses from about one to ten in number laid out over our line of march during the two days.

[WO 235/375]

L. Massacre by Cossacks at Ovaro, 2 May 1944

[This is the only recorded case of the United Nations War Crimes Commission considering accusing a White Russian of a war crime. However, the officer cited had been deported to Russia.]

TRANSLATION NO. 747   OVARO, 3 May 1945
WAR CRIMES COMMISSION

On 2 May the *volontari della liberta* fighting against a contingent of Cossacks grouped in Ovaro, were compelled after several hours to retire due to the arrival of great number of Russian reinforcements. During the battle four Volontari della Liberta were killed, while others were more or less seriously wounded.

After the retreat and firing was stopped, Major Vausico, commander of the Cossack unit, headed Russian reinforcements and ordered them to take reprisals against the civil population.

Following this order, the troops scattered savagely in all the homes of Ovaro, killing barbarically all of the men they found in the houses. The greater part of the victims show horrible wounds in the head and is composed mostly of middle-aged and old men, among whom there are two priests and a lone sick old woman.

The following are the names of those killed: Priests – Don Pietro Cortula and Don Virgilio Pavoni, engineer Rinaldo Cioni and his father-in-law Attilio Rossi, the father of the chorister Iavoni Tullio Silvio; the carpenter Fedele Elio, aged 70, Mrs Mirai Giuditta, widow Marcuzzi, the laborers Gressani Vittorio, Celman Matteo, Agarinis Antonio, Gettardis Matteo, Agarinis Dante, Gonano Antonio, Collinassi Gino, Pietra Giovanni, Pavoni Giacomo, Rupil Rinaldo and Truscoli Antonio, Traveschi Gio Batta, both aged over 70.

The persons listed above represent the great part of the men who remained in town, as the others had succeeded in fleeing.

Besides these barbaric massacres, they threatened women, robbing them and after burning all the broken articles, including the Communal Ambulance. The citizens were forbidden to make any attempt to extinguish the fire.

It is to be added that the prisoners (1 Patriot and 3 or 4 Georgiani) were killed and the corpses of the georgiani, who were fighting with the Italian volunteers, were found barefoot and arranged in the shape of a star.

THE MEDICAL OFFICER
Covassi Luigi

[WO 204/2190]

M. Graziani and the Atrocities against the Partisans

In evidence at the Graziani trial Professor Parri said: 'I declare the Black Brigades to be guilty of terrible reprisals, and the Decima Mas carried out ferocious reprisals and were involved in most serious atrocities. All the other units taking part were dependent on the German and Fascist authorities including those of Marshal Graziani. In my opinion there were between 2,000 and 3,000 actions of reprisal. To carry out 2,000 or 3,000 operations much force is necessary, and the forces at the disposition of the Government of North Italy were not very great; evidently they used everything available to them except their main garrisons in the town.'

This was hotly disputed by Graziani and the session in which Parri made this accusation had to be suspended with the public shouting in favour and against Graziani; the President rang his bell ever louder but in vain and could not quell the tumult.

In reply Graziani stated he commanded only the Army of Liguria with the task of fighting the Allies, and [said]: 'The fight against the partisans was always the province of the German High Command; in the front line and for twenty kilometres behind it Marshal Kesselring was in charge; behind this and up to the Alpine passes General Wolff presided. Thus all the larger reprisal actions were ordered by General Wolff and carried out by his subordinates in the SS and specially by General Tensfeld; these included those in which Italian troops participated under orders issued directly by Mussolini.' Graziani disclaimed any responsibility for orders by Mussolini to support the Germans in action against the partisans.

At the same trial Parri alleged that the partisans were responsible for preventing the very large demolitions planned by the Germans. He produced no detailed evidence. During this session Graziani yelled to the President of the Court 'My mind is always completely clear even when I am mad with rage.'

[*Processo Graziani*, Vol. II, pp. 200–6, 218 and 233–58, 2 November 1948]

Index

328

5/03
26 aug
lost mt
17/02